Byzantine Churches
in Constantinople

Alexander Van Millingen

Byzantine Churches
in Constantinople

VARIORUM REPRINTS
London 1974

ISBN 0 902089 72 2

Published in Great Britain by
VARIORUM REPRINTS
21a Pembridge Mews London W11 3EQ

VARIORUM REPRINT B15

BYZANTINE CHURCHES
IN CONSTANTINOPLE

THEIR HISTORY AND ARCHITECTURE

BY

ALEXANDER VAN MILLINGEN, M.A., D.D.

PROFESSOR OF HISTORY, ROBERT COLLEGE, CONSTANTINOPLE
AUTHOR OF ' BYZANTINE CONSTANTINOPLE,' ' CONSTANTINOPLE '

ASSISTED BY

RAMSAY TRAQUAIR, A.R.I.B.A.

LECTURER ON ARCHITECTURE, COLLEGE OF ART, EDINBURGH

W. S. GEORGE, F.S.A., AND A. E. HENDERSON, F.S.A.

WITH MAPS, PLANS, AND ILLUSTRATIONS

MACMILLAN AND CO., LIMITED
ST. MARTIN'S STREET, LONDON
1912

PLATE I.

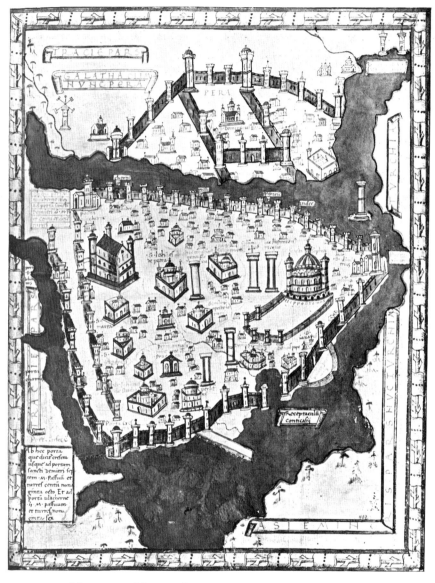

MEDIAEVAL MAP OF CONSTANTINOPLE BY BONDELMONTIUS.

Frontispiece.

NOTE ON THE MAP OF CONSTANTINOPLE

For the map forming the frontispiece and the following note I am greatly indebted to Mr. F. W. Hasluck, of the British School at Athens.

The map is taken from the unpublished *Insularium Henrici Martelli Germani* (*B.M. Add. MSS.* 15,760) f. 40.
A short note on the MS., which may be dated approximately 1490, is given in the *Annual of the British School at Athens*, xii. 199.
The map of Constantinople is a derivative of the Buondelmontius series, which dates from 1420, and forms the base of all known maps prior to the Conquest. Buondelmontius' map of Constantinople has been published from several MSS., varying considerably in legend and other details :[1] the best account of these publications is to be found in E. Oberhummer's *Konstantinopel unter Suleiman dem Grossen*, pp. 18 ff. The map in *B.M. Arundel*, 93, has since been published in *Annual B.S.A.* xii. pl. i.

In the present map the legends are as follows. Those marked with a dagger do not occur on hitherto published maps.
Reference is made below to the Paris MS. (best published by Oberhummer, *loc. cit.*), the Venetian (Mordtmann, *Esquisse*, p. 45, Sathas, Μνημεῖα, iii., frontispiece), and the Vatican (Mordtmann, *loc. cit.* p. 73).

TRACIE PARS—GALATHA OLIM NVNC PERA—Pera—S. Dominicus—Arcena —Introitus Euxini Maris.
ASIE MINORIS PARS NVNC TVRCHIA.—TVRCHIA.

TRACIE PARS—Porta Vlacherne—†Ab hec (*sic*) porta Vlacherne usque ad portam Sancti Demetri 6 M.P. et centum et decem turres—†Porta S. Iohannis[1] —Porta Chamici[2]—Porta Crescu—Porta Crescea—†Ab hec (*sic*) porta que dicitur Crescea usque ad portam Sancti Demetri septem M. passuum et turres centum nonaginta octo. Et ad portam Vlacherne 5 M. passuum et turres nonaginta sex —Receptaculum Conticasii[3]—Porta olim palacii Imperatoris—Porta S. Dimitri —Iudee[4]—Pistarie p.[5]—Messi p.—Cheone p.[6]—S. Andreas—S. Iohannes de Petra—Hic Constantinus genuflexus—†Ad S. Salvatorem—†Columna Co(n)s ? —Hic Iustinianus in equo[7]—Sancta Sophia—Hippodromus—S. Demetrius—S. Georgius—S. Lazarus—Domus Pape—Domus S. Constantini—Sanctorum Apostolorum—Porta antiquissima mire (*sic*) arte constructa[8]—S. Marta[9]—S. Andreas —S. Iohannes de Studio—Perleftos.   F. W. H.

[1] S. Romani?
[2] Porta Camidi, *Vat.*
[3] Receptaculum fustarum dein Condoscalli, *Par.*
[4] Porta Judea, *Par.*
[5] Porta Piscarii, *Par.*
[6] Porta Lacherne, *Par.*, delle Corne, *Vat.*, del Chinigo (*i.e.* Κυνηγίου) in the xvi. cent. Venetian maps.
[7] Theodosius in aequo eneo, *Ven.*   In hoc visus imp. Teod. equo sedens, *Vat.*
[8] Porta antiquissima pulcra, *Par.*
[9] St. Main (as ?) *Ven.* Sts. Marcus, *Vat.*

PREFACE

This volume is a sequel to the work I published, several years ago, under the title, *Byzantine Constantinople : the Walls of the City, and adjoining Historical Sites.* In that work the city was viewed, mainly, as the citadel of the Roman Empire in the East, and the bulwark of civilization for more than a thousand years. But the city of Constantine was not only a mighty fortress. It was, moreover, the centre of a great religious community, which elaborated dogmas, fostered forms of piety, and controlled an ecclesiastical administration that have left a profound impression upon the thought and life of mankind. New Rome was a Holy City. It was crowded with churches, hallowed, it was believed, by the remains of the apostles, prophets, saints, and martyrs of the Catholic Church ; shrines at which men gathered to worship, from near and far, as before the gates of heaven. These sanctuaries were, furthermore, constructed and beautified after a fashion which marks a distinct and important period in the history of art, and have much to interest the artist and the architect. We have, consequently, reasons enough to justify our study of the churches of Byzantine Constantinople.

Of the immense number of the churches which once

filled the city but a small remnant survives. Earthquakes, fires, pillage, neglect, not to speak of the facility with which a Byzantine structure could be shorn of its glory, have swept the vast majority off the face of the earth, leaving not a rack behind. In most cases even the sites on which they stood cannot be identified. The places which knew them know them no more. Scarcely a score of the old churches of the city are left to us, all with one exception converted into mosques and sadly altered. The visitor must, therefore, be prepared for disappointment. Age is not always a crown of glory ; nor does change of ownership and adaptation to different ideas and tastes necessarily conduce to improvement. We are not looking at flowers in their native clime or in full bloom, but at flowers in a herbarium so to speak, or left to wither and decay. As we look upon them we have need of imagination to see in faded colours the graceful forms and brilliant hues which charmed and delighted the eyes of men in other days.

In the preparation of this work I have availed myself of the aid afforded by previous students in the same field of research, and I have gratefully acknowledged my debt to them whenever there has been occasion to do so. At the same time this is a fresh study of the subject, and has been made with the hope of confirming what is true, correcting mistakes, and gathering additional information. Attention has been given to both the history and the architecture of these buildings. The materials for the former are, unfortunately, all too scanty. No continuous records of any of these churches exist. A few incidents scattered over wide tracts of time constitute all that can be known. Still, disconnected incidents though they be, they give us glimpses of the characteristic thoughts and feelings of a large mass of our humanity during a long period of history.

The student of the architecture of these churches likewise labours under serious disadvantages. Turkish colour-wash frequently conceals what is necessary for a complete survey ; while access to the higher parts of a building by means of scaffolding or ladders is often impossible under present circumstances. Hence the architect cannot always speak positively, and must leave many an interesting point in suspense.

Care has been taken to distinguish the original parts of a building from alterations made in Byzantine days or since the Turkish conquest ; while, by the prominence given to the variety of type which the churches present, the life and movement observable in Byzantine ecclesiastical art has been made clear, and the common idea that it was a stereotyped art has been proved to be without foundation.

Numerous references to the church of S. Sophia occur in the course of this volume, but the reader will not find that great monument of Byzantine architectural genius dealt with in the studies here offered. The obstacles in the way of a proper treatment of that subject proved insuperable, while the writings of Salzenberg, Lethaby, and Swainson, and especially the splendid and exhaustive monograph of my friend Mr. E. M. Antoniadi, seemed to make any attempt of mine in the same direction superfluous if not presumptuous. The omission will, however, secure one advantage : the churches actually studied will not be overshadowed by the grandeur of the 'Great Church,' but will stand clear before the view in all the light that beats upon them.

I recall gratefully my obligations to the Sultan's

Government and to the late Sir Nicholas O'Conor, British Ambassador at Constantinople, for permission to make a scientific examination of the churches of the city. To the present British Ambassador, Sir Gerard Lowther, best thanks are due for the facilities enjoyed in the study of the church of S. Irene.

I have been exceedingly fortunate in the architects who have given me the benefit of their professional knowledge and skill in the execution of my task, and I beg that their share in this work should be recognized and appreciated as fully as it deserves. To the generosity of the British School at Athens I am indebted for being able to secure the services of Mr. Ramsay Traquair, Associate of the Royal Institute of British Architects and Lecturer on Architecture at the College of Art in Edinburgh. Mr. Traquair spent three months in Constantinople for the express purpose of collecting the materials for the plans, illustrations, and notes he has contributed to this work. The chapter on Byzantine Architecture is entirely from his pen. He has also described the architectural features of most of the churches; but I have occasionally introduced information from other sources, or given my own personal observations.

I am likewise under deep obligation to Mr. A. E. Henderson, F.S.A., for the generous kindness with which he has allowed me to reproduce his masterly plans of the churches of SS. Sergius and Bacchus, S. Mary Panachrantos, and many of his photographs and drawings of other churches in the city. I am, moreover, indebted to the Byzantine Research and Publication Fund for courteous permission to present here some of the results of the splendid work done by Mr. W. S. George, F.S.A., under unique circumstances,

in the study of the church of S. Irene, and I thank Mr.
George personally for the cordial readiness with which he
consented to allow me even to anticipate his own monograph
on that very interesting fabric.   It is impossible to thank
Professor Baldwin Brown, of the University of Edinburgh,
enough, for his unfailing kindness whenever I consulted him
in connection with my work.   Nor do I forget how much I
owe to J. Meade Falkner, Esq., for kindly undertaking the
irksome task of revising the proofs of the book while going
through the press.

I cannot close without calling attention to the brighter
day which has dawned on the students of the antiquities of
Constantinople since constitutional government has been
introduced in the Ottoman Empire.   Permission to carry
on excavations in the city has been promised me.   The
archaeology of New Rome only waits for wealthy patrons to
enable it to reach a position similar to that occupied by
archaeological research in other centres of ancient and
mediaeval civilizations.   But the monuments of the olden
time are perishable.   Of the churches described by Paspates
in his *Byzantine Studies*, published in 1877, nine have either
entirely disappeared or lost more of their original features.
It was no part of wisdom to let the books of the cunning
Sibyl become rarer and knowledge poorer by neglecting to
secure all that was obtainable when she made her first or
even her second offer.

ALEXANDER VAN MILLINGEN.

ROBERT COLLEGE, CONSTANTINOPLE.

Πόλις ἐκκλησιῶν γαλουχέ, πίστεως ἀρχηγέ, ὀρθοδοξίας ποδηγέ.

NICETAS CHONIATES.

CONTENTS

CHAPTER I

CHAPTER II

CHAPTER III

CHAPTER IV

CHAPTER V

CHAPTER VI

CHAPTER VII

CHAPTER VIII

CHAPTER IX

CHAPTER X

CHAPTER XI

CHAPTER XII

CHAPTER XIII

CHAPTER XIV

CHAPTER XV

CHAPTER XVI

CHAPTER XVII

CHAPTER XVIII

CHAPTER XIX

CHAPTER XX

CHAPTER XXI

CHAPTER XXII

CHAPTER XXIII

CHAPTER XXIV

CHAPTER XXV

NOTE ON THE CHURCH OF S. THEKLA
(Chapter XIII.)

On page 209, note 3, I have said that if the mosque Aivas Effendi (more correctly Ivaz Effendi), which is situated behind the Tower of Isaac Angelus within the old area of the palace of Blachernae, could be proved to stand on the site of a church, the argument in favour of the identification of the Church of S. Thekla with Toklou Dedé Mesjedi would be weakened. Since this book went to the press, my learned friend Mr. X. A. Siderides has shown me a passage in the historical work of Mustapha Effendi of Salonica, published in 1865, where the mosque of Ivaz Effendi is described as a church converted into a mosque by a certain Ivaz Effendi who died in 1586, at the age of ninety. In that case we should have a Christian sanctuary whose position corresponded strictly with the position occupied by the Church of S. Thekla "in the palace of Blachernae," an indication not exactly accurate in regard to Toklou Dedé Mesjedi. In view of the late date of Mustapha Effendi's work, and the absence, so far as I can judge, of Byzantine features in the structure of the mosque, it is difficult to decide if the arguments in favour of the identification of the Church of S. Thekla with Toklou Dedé Mesjedi are entirely overthrown by the statement of Mustapha Effendi.

PLANS AND ILLUSTRATIONS

xvii

In this reprint the Plates have been grouped at the end of the volume , accordingly the pagination given below no longer applies.

PLATES

CHAPTER I

BYZANTINE ARCHITECTURE

I. Planning

At the beginning of the fifth century, which is a suitable point from which to date the rise of Byzantine architecture, three principal types of church plan prevailed in the Roman world :—

I. The Basilica : an oblong hall divided into nave and aisles, and roofed in wood, as in the Italian and Salonican examples, or with stone barrel-vaults, as in Asia Minor and Central Syria.

II. The Octagonal or Circular plan covered with a stone or brick dome, a type which may be subdivided according as (1) the dome rests upon the outer walls of the building, or (2) on columns or piers surrounded by an ambulatory.

The Pantheon and the so-called Temple of Minerva Medica at Rome are early examples of the first variety, the first circular, the second a decagon in plan. S. George at Salonica is a later circular example. An early instance of the second variety is found in S. Constanza at Rome, and a considerable number of similar churches occur in Asia Minor, dating from the time of Constantine the Great or a little later.

III. The Cross plan. Here we have a square central area covered by a dome, from which extend four vaulted arms constituting a cross. This type also assumes two distinct forms :

B

(1) Buildings in which the ground plan is cruciform, so that the cross shows externally at the ground level. Churches of this class are usually small, and were probably sepulchral chapels rather than churches for public worship. A good example is the tomb of Galla Placidia at Ravenna.

(2) In the second form of the Cross church the cross is enclosed within a square, and appears only above the roofs of the angle chambers. An example is seen in the late Roman tomb at Kusr en Nûeijîs in Eastern Palestine. In this instance the central square area is covered with a dome on continuous pendentives ; the four arms have barrel-vaults, and the angles of the cross are occupied by small chambers, which bring the ground-plan to the square. The building is assigned to the second century, and shows that true though continuous pendentives were known at an early date [1] (Fig. 8).

Another example is the Praetorium at Musmiyeh, in Syria,[2] which probably dates from between 160 and 169 A.D. At some later time it was altered to a church, and by a curious foreshadowing of the late Byzantine plan the walls of the internal cross have entirely disappeared from the ground-plan. The dome rests on four columns placed at the inner angles of the cross, and the vaulted cross arms rest on lintels spanning the space between the columns and the outer walls.

From these three types of building are derived the various schemes on which the churches of the Byzantine Empire were planned.

Of the basilican form the only example in Constantinople that retains its original plan is S. John the Baptist of the Studion (p. 56), erected c. 463 A.D.

The church of SS. Sergius and Bacchus (p. 70) and the baptistery of S. Sophia (p. 78) represent respectively the two varieties of the octagonal plan. In the former the dome rests on piers surrounded by an ambulatory ; in the latter

---

[1] *Eastern Palestine Memoirs*, p. 172. A similar dome is given by Choisy, *L'Art de bâtir chez les Byzantins*, Plate XV.

[2] De Vogüé, *Syrie centrale*, i. p. 45, Plate VII.

the dome rests upon the outer walls of the buildings. Both are foundations of Justinian the Great.

Of the Cross church plan showing the cross externally at the ground level no example survives in the city. But at least one church of that form was seen at Constantinople in the case of the church of the Holy Apostles. This was essentially a mausoleum, built originally by Constantine the Great and reconstructed by Justinian to contain the sarcophagi of the sovereigns and the patriarchs of New Rome.[1]

The church of S. Mark at Venice was built on the plan of the Holy Apostles. It is a cruciform church with aisles, but the galleries which might have been expected above them are omitted. The central dome rests on four piers, and four smaller domes cover the arms.

Professor Strzygowski gives examples of cross-planned cells in the catacombs of Palmyra,[2] and in many Eastern rock tombs.[3] Such cross plans are found also in the Roman catacombs. These subterranean chapels, of course, do not show the external treatment, yet there can be little doubt that the external cross plan was originally sepulchral, and owes its peculiar system of planning to that fact. On the other hand, it was adopted in such churches as S. Mark's at Venice and in the French examples of Périgord for aesthetic or traditional reasons.

In passing now to a consideration of the distinct forms developed from these pre-Byzantine types of church building, the classification adopted by Professor Strzygowski may be followed. In his *Kleinasien* he has brought forward a series of buildings which show the manner in which a dome was fitted to the oblong basilica, producing the domed basilica (*Küppelbasilica*), an evolution which he regards as Hellenistic and Eastern. In contrast to this, Strzygowski distinguishes the domed cross church (*Kreutzküppelkirche*), of which S. Theodosia in Constantinople (p. 170) is the typical example and which is a Western development. A

[1] Dürm, *Handbuch*, Part II. vol. iii. pp. 115, 149. A restored plan is given in Lethaby's *Mediaeval Art*, p. 47.

[2] *Orient oder Rom*, p. 19.   [3] *Kleinasien*, p. 152.

comparison of the two forms is of great importance for the study of certain Constantinople churches.

The domed basilica, as the name indicates, is a basilica with nave and aisles, in which a square bay in the centre of the nave is covered by a dome on pendentives. To north and south, within the arches supporting the dome, appear the nave and gallery arcades of the basilica ; and as the galleried basilica is a usual Eastern form galleries are usual in the domed basilica. As seen from the central area, therefore, the north and south dome arches are filled

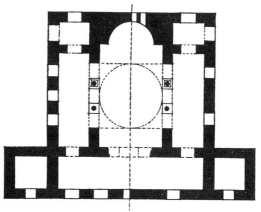

FIG. 1.—KASR IBN WARDAN (Strzygowski).

in with arcades in two stories, and the side aisles and galleries are covered with barrel vaults running parallel to the axis of the church. At the west end a gallery over the narthex may unite the two side galleries. At Kasr ibn Wardan, instanced by Strzygowski as a typical domed basilica,[1] there is such a western gallery (Fig. 1). According to Strzygowski the domed basilica is older than the fifth century.

The domed basilica remains always an oblong building, and whilst the two sides to north and south are symmetrical, the western end retains the basilican characteristics—it has no gallery or arcade communicating with the central area. The narthex communicates with the nave by doors, and if a

---

[1] *Kleinasien*, p. 121 *et seq.*

gallery is placed above it, both narthex and gallery are covered by barrel vaults.

In the domed cross church (*Kreutzküppelkirche*) the central dome rests on barrel vaults which extend to the outer walls of the building and form the arms of the cross, the eastern arm forming the bema. The lighting of the church is by windows in the gable walls which terminate the north, south, and west cross arms. The prothesis and diaconicon open off the side arms, and two small chambers in the western angles of the cross bring the plan externally to the usual rectangular form.

The domed cross church may have galleries, as in S. Theodosia (p. 170), or may be without them, as in SS. Peter and Mark (p. 193). Where galleries are present they are placed in the cross arms and are supported by arcades at the ground level. The vaults beneath the galleries are cross-groined. The domed cross church is a centrally planned church, in contrast to the domed basilica, which is oblong, and therefore we should expect that where galleries are used they will be formed in all three arms of the cross, as is the case in S. Theodosia.

There are a number of churches which vary from these types, but which can generally be placed in one class or the other by the consideration of two main characteristics : if the dome arches extend to the outer walls the building is a domed cross church ; if the galleries are screened off from the central area by arcades the building is a domed basilica.

The church at Derè Aghsy,[1] for instance, if we had only the plan to guide us, would appear to be a typical domed basilica (Fig. 2), but on examining the section we find that the north and south dome arches extend over the galleries to the outer walls and form cross arms (Fig. 3). The building is, in fact, a domed cross church with no gallery in the western arm. Above the narthex at the west end, and separated from the western cross arm, is a gallery of the type usual in the domed basilica, so that Derè Aghsy may be regarded as a domed cross church with features derived from the domed basilica. S. Sophia at Constantinople,

---

[1] Oskar Wulf, *Die Koimesiskirche in Nikaea*, p. 71.

the highest development of the domed basilica, has a very similar western gallery.

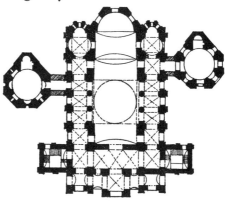

FIG. 2.—DERÉ AGHSY (Rott).

The church of S. Nicholas at Myra[1] (Fig. 4) has a gallery at the west end, but the cross arms do not appear to be carried over the galleries. The plan is oblong and the

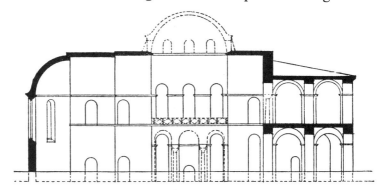

FIG. 3.—DERÉ AGHSY—SECTION (Rott)

cross-groined vault is not used. The church, therefore, takes its place as a domed basilica.

[1] H. Rott, *Kleinasiensche Denkmäler*, p. 329.

The church of the Koimesis at Nicaea[1] (Figs. 5 and 6) has no galleries to the sides. The aisles open into the central area by arcades, above which are triple windows over the aisle vaults. At the western end is a gallery above the narthex. The aisles are barrel-vaulted, and as the church is planned on an axis from east to west, and is not symmetrical on all three sides, it is regarded as a domed

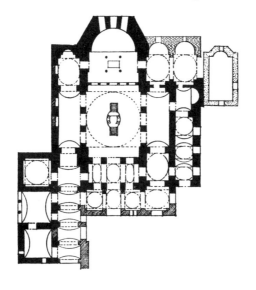

10 0 1 2 3 4 5 6 7 8 9 10 11 12 13 14 15 16 17 18 19 20 METERS

FIG. 4.—S. NICHOLAS, MYRA (Rott).

basilica. It is such a form as might be developed from a basilica without galleries.

In Constantinople there are three churches which seem to constitute a type apart, though resembling in many ways the types just considered. They are S. Andrew in Krisei, (p. 117), S. Mary Pammakaristos (p. 150), and S. Mary Panachrantos (p. 130). In these churches, as originally built, the central dome is carried on four arches which rise above a one-storied aisle or ambulatory, allowing of windows

[1] Wulf, *op. cit.* p. 23.

in the dome arches on three sides—the eastern dome arch being prolonged to form the bema. The dome arches have arcades communicating with the ambulatory on the north, south, and west. The vaulting is executed either with barrel or with cross-groined vaults. These churches are evidently planned from a centre, not, like the domed basilicas, from a longitudinal axis. At the same time the absence of any cross

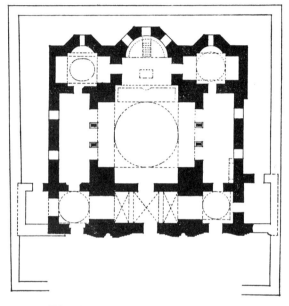

FIG. 5.—THE CHURCH OF THE KOIMESIS, NICAEA (Wulf).

arms differentiates them from the domed cross churches. S. Andrew, which still retains its western arcade, dates from at least the sixth century, so that the type was in use during the great period of Byzantine architecture. Indeed, we should be inclined to regard S. Andrew as a square form of SS. Sergius and Bacchus, but without galleries. The type is a natural development from the octagonal domed church with its surrounding ambulatory.

The typical late Byzantine church is a development from the domed cross plan. In three examples in Constantinople, S. Theodosia (pp. 170, 172), S. Mary Diaconissa (p. 185), and SS. Peter and Mark (p. 193), we can trace the gradual disappearance of the galleries. S. Theodosia, as has already been mentioned, has galleries in all three cross arms. In S. Mary Diaconissa they are confined to the four angles between the cross arms ; SS. Peter and Mark is a simple cross plan without galleries. In later times it became customary to build many small churches, with the result that the chambers at the

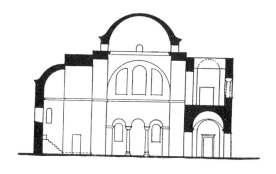

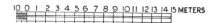

FIG. 6.—THE CHURCH OF THE KOIMESIS, NICAEA (Rott).

angles of the cross, of little account even in a large church, were now too diminutive to be of any value, and the question how to provide as much room as possible for the worshippers became paramount. Accordingly the dome piers were reduced to mere columns connected with the outer walls of the building by arches ; and thus was produced the typical late Byzantine plan—at the ground level a square, enclosing four columns ; above, a Greek cross with a dome on the centre.

From its distinguishing feature this type has been styled the 'four column' plan. It appears in many Constantinopolitan churches, as, for example, S. Theodore (p. 248) and S. Saviour Pantepoptes (p. 214). The cross arms are not always equal, and may be covered with barrel vaults (p. 214) or with cross-groined vaults (p. 198). The bema is usually a bay added to the eastern arm. The angle chambers have either cross-groined vaults or flat dome vaults. In general the churches of this type in Constantinople do not differ from the numerous churches of the same class in the provinces.[1]

A lobed cruciform plan is found in only one church in Constantinople, that of S. Mary of the Mongols (p. 277). Here the central dome is supported on four piers set across the angles of the square, so that the pendentives do not come to a point as usual, but spring from the face of the piers. Against each side of the square a semidome is set, thus producing a quatrefoil plan at the vaulting level.

Both trefoiled and quatrefoiled churches are not uncommon in Armenia, such as the cathedral at Etschmiadzin;[2] trefoiled churches of a later date are found in the western provinces, and examples have been published from Servia,[3] Salonica,[4] and Greece.[5]

An unusual form of the cross plan is seen in the building known as Sanjakdar Mesjedi (p. 267), where a cross is placed within an octagon. Probably the building was not originally a church. It resembles the octagon near the Pantokrator (p. 270), and may, like it, have been a library.

Single Hall Churches.—The plans hitherto considered have all been characterised by the presence of aisles, galleries, or other spaces adjoining the central area. The churches of the present class consist simply of an oblong hall, terminating in an apse, and either roofed in wood, or covered with domes placed longitudinally, and resting to north and south on wall arches. Examples of this plan are found in Monastir Mesjedi (p. 264), S. Thekla (p. 211), Bogdan Serai (p. 284), and in the memorial chapels attached to the Pantokrator (p. 235), and the Chora (p. 309). In

[1] For local variations in late churches in Greece, see Traquair's 'Churches of Western Mani,' *Annual of British School at Athens*, xv. 1908.
[2] Strzygowski, 'Das Etschmiadzin Evangeliar,' *Byzant. Denkmäler*, i., 1891.
[3] Ravanica, F. Kanitz, *Serbiens byzantische Monumente*, Wien, 1862.
[4] Pullan and Texier, *S. Elias.*
[5] G. Lampakis, *Les Antiquités chrétiennes de la Grèce*, Athens, 1902.

the case of these two memorial chapels, their narrow, long-stretched plan is evidently due to the desire to keep their eastern apses in line with the east end of the churches they adjoin, and at the same time to bring the western end to the narthex from which they were entered. They are covered with two domes, a system perhaps derived from S. Irene (p. 94). Kefelé Mesjedi (p. 257), which at first sight resembles a single hall church roofed, in wood, was a refectory. Its plan may be compared with that of the refectory at the monastery of S. Luke at Stiris.[1]

II. Architectural Features and Details

Apses.—A fully developed Byzantine church terminated in three apses : a large apse, with the bema or presbytery, in the centre ; on the right, the apse of the prothesis where the sacrament was prepared ; on the left, the apse of the diaconicon, where the sacred vessels were kept. Although there is proof that the prothesis and the diaconicon were in use at a very early period, yet many churches of the great period, as for example S. John of the Studion, SS. Sergius and Bacchus, and S. Sophia, dispensed with these chambers as distinct parts of the building. They were also omitted in small churches of a late date, where they were replaced by niches on either side of the bema. The three apses usually project from the east wall of the church, but occasionally (p. 248) the two lateral apses are sunk in the wall, and only the central apse shows on the exterior. As a rule the apses are circular within and polygonal without. It is rare to find them circular on both the interior and the exterior (p. 203), and in Greece such a feature is generally an indication of late date. An octagonal plan, in which three sides of the octagon appear, sometimes with short returns to the wall, is the most common ; but in later churches polygons of more sides are used, especially for the central apse, and these are often very irregularly set out. Some of the churches of Constantinople show five, and even seven sides.

[1] Schultz and Barnsley, *The Monastery of S. Luke at Stiris*, p. 13, fig. 6.

Bema.—The bema is rectangular, and sometimes has concave niches on each side (p. 130). It is covered either with a barrel or with a cross-groined vault, and communicates with the prothesis and the diaconicon.

Prothesis and Diaconicon.—These chambers are either square (p. 214) or have a long limb to the east resembling a miniature bema (p. 214). They are lower than the central apse and the cross arms, so that the cruciform figure of the church shows clearly above them on the exterior,[1] though in some churches with galleries small chapels overlooking the bema are placed above them at the gallery level (S. Theodosia). They have usually a niche on three sides, and are either dome vaulted or have cross-groined vaults. The combination of a cross-groined vault with four niches springing from the vaulting level is particularly effective. In S. Saviour in the Chora (p. 307) these chambers are covered with drum domes, pierced with windows, but this treatment is quite exceptional.

The Gynecaeum.—In the development of church building, the gynecaeum, or gallery for women, tends to become less and less important. In S. Sophia, S. Irene, and S. Theodosia, the gallery is a part of the structure. In S. Mary Diaconissa (p. 185) it is reduced to four boxes at the angles of the cross, while in S. Mary Pammakaristos and SS. Peter and Mark it is absent (pp. 149, 193). But though no longer a structural part of the church, a gynecaeum appears over the narthex in the latest type of church (p. 215). It is generally vaulted in three bays, corresponding to the three bays of the narthex below, and opens by three arches into the centre cross arm of the church and into the aisles.

The Narthex.—Unlike the gynecaeum, the narthex tends in later times to become of greater importance, and to add a narthex was a favourite method of increasing the size of a church. In basilican churches, like S. John of the Studion, the narthex was a long hall in three bays annexed to the west side of the building, and formed the east side of the atrium. In domed cross churches with galleries the passage under the western gallery was used as a narthex, being cut

---

[1] See, however, North Church in S. Mary, Panachrantos, p. 128.

off from the central area by the screen arcade which
supported the gallery. Such a narthex has been styled a
'structural narthex,' as forming an essential part of the
central building. It occurs in several of the churches of
the city (p. 114).

In domed cross churches without galleries, and in
churches of the 'four column' type, neither narthex nor
gallery was possible within the cross, and accordingly the
narthex was added to the west end. It is usually in three
bays and opens into the aisles and central area. Frequently
the ends of the narthex terminate in shallow niches (p. 198).
In many churches a second narthex was added (p. 166) to the
first, sometimes projecting an additional bay at each end, and
communicating with halls or chapels on the north or south,
or on both sides of the church (p. 128). S. Mark's at Venice
presents a fine example of such an extension of the narthex.

When a church could not be sufficiently enlarged by
additional narthexes, a second church was built alongside
the first, and both churches were joined by a narthex which
extended along the front of the two buildings. S. Mary
Panachrantos (p. 128) is a good example of how a church
could be thus enlarged from a simple square building into a
maze of passages and domes.

The Interior.—The natural division, in height, of an
early church, whether basilican or domical, was into three
stories—the ground level, the gallery level, and the clearstory or vault level. In the West these structural divisions
were developed into the triple composition of nave-arcade,
triforium, and clearstory. In the East, in conjunction with
the dome, these divisions survive in many examples of the
later period. Still, Byzantine architecture was more concerned with spaces than with lines. Large surfaces for
marble, painting, or mosaic were of prime importance, and
with the disappearance of the gallery the string-course
marking the level of the gallery also tended to disappear.
In churches with galleries, like S. Theodosia (p. 170) and
S. Mary Diaconissa (p. 185), the string-courses fulfil their
function, the first marking the gallery level, the second the
springing of the vault. In SS. Peter and Mark (p. 193),

which has no gallery, there is only one string-course, corresponding in level to the original gallery string-course ; accordingly the main arches are highly stilted above it. The absence of the second string-course is a faulty development, for a string-course at the vault level would be a functional member, whereas at the gallery level it is meaningless.

In the Panachrantos (p. 130), as well as in other churches without a gallery, the gallery string-course is omitted by a more logical development, and the string-course at the springing of the vault is retained. Openings which do not cut into the vault are then frankly arched, without impost moulding of any kind. Simple vaulted halls, narthexes, and passages have usually a string-course at the vaulting level, broken round shallow pilasters as at the Chora, S. Theodosia, and the Myrelaion. Sometimes the string-courses or the pilasters or both are omitted, and their places are respectively taken by horizontal and vertical bands. Decorative pilasters flush with the wall are employed in the marble incrustation of S. Sophia.

In churches of the 'four column' type the full triple division is common but with a change in purpose. A gallery in a church of this character is not possible, for the piers between which the gallery was placed have dwindled into single shafts. Hence the first string-course ceases to mark a gallery level and becomes the abacus level of the dome columns, as in the north and in the south churches of the Pantokrator. It is then carried round the building, and forms the impost moulding of the side arches in the bema and of the east window. Sometimes, however, it does not extend round the bema and apse but is confined to the central part of the church, as in the Myrelaion, S. Theodore, and the Pantepoptes. On the other hand, in at least one case, the parecclesion of the Pammakaristos, the central part of the chapel is designed in the usual three tiers, but the apse and bema vaults spring from the lower or abacus string-course, leaving a lunette in the dome arch above pierced by a large window. A corresponding lunette at the west end opens into the gynecaeum of the chapel. In S. John in Trullo the two string-courses coalesce and the arches connecting the columns with the walls cut into the stilted part of the dome arches, with the result that all the structural arches and vaults spring from the same level.

Arches.—Though the pointed arch was known and employed in cisterns, as in the Cistern of the One Thousand and One Columns, Bin-bir-derek, the circular arch is invariably found in work meant to be seen. The difficulty attending this form, in which arches of unequal breadth do not rise to the same height, was overcome, as in the West, by stilting, that is, by raising the smaller arches on straight 'legs' to the required height. The stilted arch, indeed, seems to have been admired for its own sake, as we find it used almost universally both in vaulting and in decorative arches even where it was not structurally required. In windows and in the arches connecting the dome columns to the wall stilting is sometimes carried to extremes.

Domes.—The eastern dome of S. Irene, erected about 740 A.D., is generally considered to be the first example of a dome built on a high drum, though S. Sophia of Salonica, an earlier structure, has a low imperfect drum. After this date the characteristics of the Byzantine dome are the high drum divided by ribs or hollow segments on the interior, polygonal on the exterior, and crowned by a cornice which is arched over the windows.[1]

Drumless domes are sometimes found in the later churches, as in the narthexes of the Panachrantos and S. Andrew, the angle domes of S. Theodosia, and in Bogdan Serai. These are ribless hemispherical domes of the type shown in Fig. 8, and are in all cases without windows. The earlier system of piercing windows through the dome does not occur in the later churches, though characteristic of Turkish work.

The three diagrams (Figs. 8, 9, and 10) illustrate the development of the dome : firstly, the low saucer dome or dome-vault in which dome and pendentives are part of the

---

[1] Strzygowski's views as to the early date of the drum-dome are not universally accepted. The examples he produces seem rather octagons carried up from the ground to give a clearstory under the dome than true drums interposed between the dome and its pendentives.

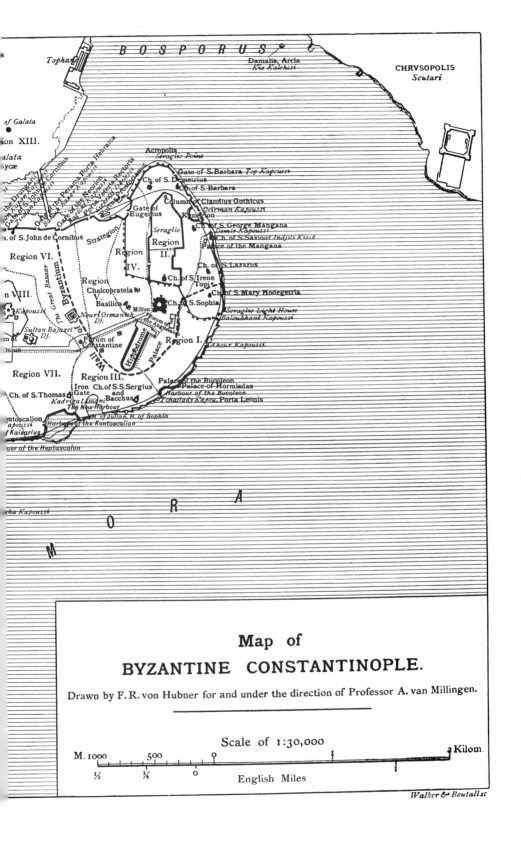

Map of
BYZANTINE CONSTANTINOPLE.

Drawn by F. R. von Hubner for and under the direction of Professor A. van Millingen.

Scale of 1:30,000

M. 1000   500   0   Kilom.

½   ¼   0

English Miles

Walker & Boutall sc

same spherical surface ; secondly, the hemispherical dome on pendentives ; and thirdly, the hemispherical dome with a drum interposed between it and the pendentives.

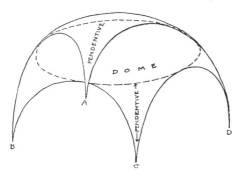

FIG. 8.—THE SAUCER DOME OR DOME-VAULT.

Flat external cornices on the dome are not uncommon in the later churches of Byzantine Greece, as in S. Sophia at Monemvasia.[1]   In Constantinople only one dome with a flat cornice can be regarded as original, that of S. John in Trullo, a church which is exceptional also in other respects.   The many other domes in the churches of Constantinople on high drums and with flat cornices are Turkish either in whole or in part. The high ribless domes of the Panachrantos, for instance, circular in plan within and without, with square-headed windows, plain stone sill, and flat cornice in moulded plaster, may be regarded as typical Turkish drum-domes. As will appear in the sequel, the dome over the north church of the Pantokrator and the domes of SS. Peter and Mark, the Diaconissa, and S. Theodosia, are also Turkish.

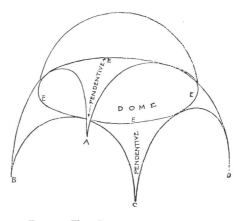

FIG. 9.—THE DOME ON PENDENTIVES.

[1] *Annual B.S.A.* xii. 1905-6.   See also Schultz and Barnsley, *Monastery of S. Luke at Stiris*.

It is most unfortunate that the domes of these three domed cross churches have been altered, especially as the domes of S. Mary Diaconissa and S. Theodosia are larger than any of the later domes except the large oval dome on the central church of the Pantokrator which is almost of the same size. It is therefore now difficult to say what was the precise form of the original domes. Most probably they were polygonal drum-domes, and their collapse owing to their size may well have led to the small drum-domes of later times.

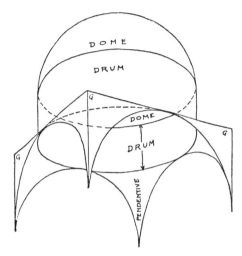

FIG. 10.—THE DRUM DOME.

Though not strictly Byzantine these Turkish domes are of interest as showing the development of Byzantine forms under Turkish rule, and that reversion to the earlier drumless dome which is so marked a feature of the imperial mosques of the city.

Domes are either eight, twelve, or sixteen sided, and usually have a window in each side. These numbers arise naturally from setting a window at each of the cardinal points and then placing one, two, or three windows between, according to the size of the dome. Internally the compartments are separated by broad, flat ribs, or are concave and form a series of ridges on the dome which die out towards the crown. In sixteen-sided domes of the latter type the alternate sides sometimes correspond to the piers outside, so that the dome which has sixteen sides within shows only eight sides without, as in the narthex of S. Theodore (p. 246). The octagonal dome of the Myrelaion

c

(p. 198) seems to have had only four windows from the beginning.

The ribs of a Byzantine dome are not constructive in the same way as are the ribs of a Gothic vault. They were built along with the rest of the dome and of the same material, and are in no way separate from the infilling, though they no doubt strengthened the shell of the dome by their form.[1] On the outside a circular shaft with a very simple cap is often placed at the angles of the piers, and from these shafts the brick cornice springs in a series of arches over the windows. Sometimes the angle is formed by a point between two half-shafts, as in the domes of the narthex in S. Theodore (p. 246).

External Treatment.—In the older churches the exterior seems to have been left in simple masses of brickwork, impressive only by their size and proportion. Probably even this effect was not considered of great importance. In later times a very beautiful system of decoration with slender shallow niches was introduced and was applied in particular to the east end and to the apses. The finest examples of this system on a large scale are seen at the Pantokrator (p. 235) and S. Theodosia (p. 173). Carefully considered or elaborate external compositions are rare, and the only examples in Constantinople are the side chapel of the Pammakaristos (p. 154) and the narthex of S. Theodore (p. 246).

External Marble and Mosaic.—Marble and mosaic, we have reason to know, were occasionally used on the exterior of churches,[2] though no fragments remain. On the south side of the Pantepoptes (p. 216) the string-course does not correspond to the line of the walls, but projects in a manner which shows that marble must have been employed to line the large windows. A similar projection of the string-course or cornice is not uncommon elsewhere, though not so evident as in the Pantepoptes, and may have been made to receive a marble or mosaic lining.

[1] See p. 154.
[2] Dome of the Rock at Jerusalem. S. Mary Peribleptos ; see *Vida de Gran Tamorlan y itinerario del Ruy Gonzalez de Clavijo*, p. 52.

Doors and Windows.—It is a primary rule in Byzantine architecture that all constructive openings are arched. Whatever may be the eventual form of a door or window the opening is first built in brick with a semicircular head, and into this opening the marble jambs and lining are fitted leaving a semicircular lunette above. Doors are square-headed, with heavily moulded architraves and cornice, and the lintel is mitred into the jambs instead of having the more constructive horizontal joint used in the West.

The doors made of wood or of wood lined with bronze, swing on top and bottom pivots which turned in bronze-lined sockets in lintel and threshold. They closed with a rebate in the jambs and against the raised threshold. Windows were sometimes filled in a similar manner, as in the palace of the Porphyrogenitus and in the north gallery of S. Saviour in the Chora (Fig. 100). In the latter double windows or shutters were employed, opening inwards in the same way as did the doors. These shutters may perhaps be regarded as domestic, for in the churches, as is still seen in S. Sophia though the arrangement has vanished elsewhere, the entire arched opening was usually filled in with a pierced marble grille.

In addition to the simple round-headed windows double and triple windows are found. Double windows were naturally formed by dividing the single arch by a central pier. This method presented two varieties : either the pier was continued up to the containing arch, thus giving two pointed lights, or the two lights were covered by separate arches within the main arch. Both methods are used in the narthex of S. Theodore (p. 247). Another variety was produced by placing two single lights together, with a shaft between them instead of the central pier. But as double windows are not very satisfactory, triple windows are more common. In this case both the methods just described of forming the windows were adopted. A large semicircular opening divided by two piers will give an arched light between two pointed lights, or three arched lights, as in the narthex of S. Theodore. In the former case, if shafts are substituted for the piers, a little adjustment will produce the beautiful form found in the side-chapels of the Pammakaristos (p. 152), and of S. Saviour in the Chora (p. 310), where the two side lights are covered by half-arches whose crowns abut on the capitals of the shafts, while between and above them rises the semicircular head of the central light.

The method of grouping three arched windows of the same height is adopted in apse windows, each of them occupying one side of the exterior. As the deep, narrow mullions are set radiating, the arch is narrower inside than outside. But this difficulty was overcome, partly by lowering the inner crowns, so that the arch is conical, partly by winding the surface. In the Pantokrator (p. 238), instead of radiating to the centre of the apse, the side and mullions are placed parallel to the axis of the church, thus obviating all difficulty. Generally the centre to which the mullions radiate is considerably beyond the apse, so that any necessary little adjustment of the arch could easily be made.

Triple windows supported on circular columns are not infrequent in the north and south cross arms. Sometimes the central light is larger than the lateral lights, at other times, as in the Pantepoptes, the three lights are equal. The lower part of these windows was probably filled in with a breastwork of carved slabs, as in S. Sophia, while the upper part was filled by a pierced grille. At present the existing examples of these windows have been built up to the abaci of the capitals, but in the church of S. Mary Diaconissa (p. 186) the columns still show the original form on the inside.

Vaulting.—All Byzantine churches of any importance are vaulted in brick. The only exception to this rule in Constantinople is the little church known as Monastir Mesjedi (p. 264). The different systems of Byzantine vaulting have been so fully treated by Choisy and other authorities, that in the absence of any large amount of new material it is not necessary to give here more than a few notes on the application of these systems in Constantinople. It should always be kept in view that, as these vaults were constructed with the lightest of centering, the surfaces and curves must have been largely determined by the mason as he built, and would not necessarily follow any definite geometrical development. " Il serait illusoire," remarks Choisy, " d'attribuer à toutes les voutes byzantines un trace géométrique rigoureusement défini." [1]

The vaults commonly found are the barrel vault, the cross-groined vault, and the dome-vault. The first is frequently used over the cross arms and the bema, and sometimes over the narthex in conjunction with the groined vault (Diaconissa). It is the simplest method of covering an oblong space, but it does not easily admit of side windows above the springing.

A very beautiful form of cross-groined vault is found in S. Sophia and in SS. Sergius and Bacchus, in which the crown is considerably domed, and the groins, accordingly, lose themselves in the vaulting surface. This form is found in Greek churches of late date, but does not occur in the later churches of Constantinople. A full description of the form and construction is given by Choisy [2] and by Lethaby and Swainson.[3]

The cross-groined vault as found in the Myrelaion and many other churches of the city is level in the crown, with clearly marked groins. It is sometimes used with transverse arches resting on pilasters, or without these adjuncts.

One of the most interesting of the vault forms is the dome-vault, a shallow dome with continuous pendentives. It is distinguished in appearance from the groined vault, as found in S. Sophia, by the absence of any groin line, and is completely different in construction.

The geometrical construction is that of the pendentives of all domes. The four supporting arches intersect a hemispherical surface whose diameter is equal to the diagonal of the supporting square. The pendentives produce at the crown line of the arches a circular plan which is filled in by a saucer dome of the same radius as the pendentives, constructed of circular brick rings, the joints of

[1] L'Art de bâtir chez les Byzantins, p. 57.   [2] Ibid. p. 99.
[3] Sancta Sophia, p. 219.

which radiate to the centre. If the space to be covered is
not square the broader arches intersect at a higher level,
while the narrow arches are not stilted, but kept down so
as to receive the dome surface, and in this case the narrow
arches are not semicircular, but segmental. Where the
difference in size between the two sides was not great,
the difficulty presented was easily overcome by the
Byzantine builder, who in the later buildings, at any rate,

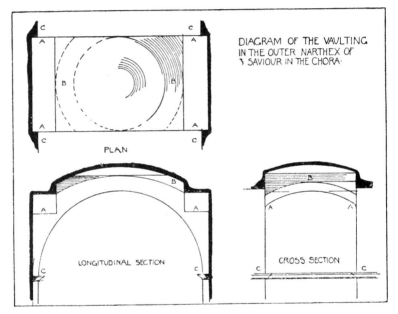

DIAGRAM OF THE VAULTING
IN THE OUTER NARTHEX OF
S SAVIOUR IN THE CHORA·

PLAN

LONGITUDINAL SECTION

CROSS SECTION

FIG. 11.

rarely built anything within four inches of its geometrical
position. Where the difference was too great it was
frankly accepted, and we find segmental arches at the
narrow ends.

The vaulting of the outer narthex of S. Saviour in the
Chora illustrates this fully (Fig. 11). Though some of the
bays of that narthex are oblong and others almost square
all are covered with dome vaults. The almost square bays,
although their sides vary considerably, are covered precisely

as if their sides were exactly equal.   But in two of the oblong
bays, which are nearly three times as long as they are broad,
such a method could not be applied.   Longitudinal arches
(AA) were accordingly thrown between the transverse arches
(CC) and made to rest on their spandrils.   The oblong
form of the intervening space was thus very much reduced,
and over it flat domes are thrown.   Their rings are true
circles, and as the space they cover is still somewhat oblong
they descend lower, with additional segments of rings (BB),
at the ends than at the sides.   In the remaining two oblong
bays of the narthex, the result of introducing the longitudinal arches is to convert a decidedly oblong space in
one direction into a slightly oblong space in the opposite
direction, an additional proof, if any were needed, that the
exact shape of plan with this form of vault was a matter
of comparative indifference to the builder.

In S. Sophia the vault springs from the intrados of the
transverse arches, that is, from the lower edge.   In SS.
Sergius and Bacchus it springs from a point so slightly
raised as to be hardly noticeable.   In the later vaults, however, the transverse arches, when present, are boldly shown,
and the vault springs from the extrados or outer edge
(e.g. S. Saviour in the Chora, S. Theodore).

Construction.—Most of the churches of the city are
covered with thick coats of plaster and whitewash, both
within and without.   Only in a few cases, where these
coatings have fallen away through neglect, or in some remote corner of a building to which these coatings were
never applied, can the construction and the laying of the
brickwork be studied.   The two-storied chapel, known
as Bogdan Serai (p. 283), is almost denuded of plaster,
and is therefore of importance in this connection.   The
bricks of the wall arches on which its dome rests are laid
considerably flatter than the true radiating line, leaving a
triangular piece to be filled in at the crown.   On the other
hand, the bricks of the transverse arches under the dome
radiate to the centre.

It has been supposed that the method followed in the wall
arches was employed in order to economise centering, since

bricks could gradually be worked out over the space, each course simply sticking to the one below. This is undoubtedly the case in some examples. But here centering could not have been of any service in the wall arches, and the transverse arches are laid without flattening of the courses, though that arrangement might have been useful in their case. It is therefore more probable that the flattening of the courses in the wall arches is simply a piece of careless workmanship. The pendentives, like all pendentives that could be examined, were formed of horizontal courses corbelled out to the circle. The dome, bema, and the barrel vault in the lower story (p. 285) seem to be laid with true radiating joints. The springing of the barrel vault is formed of four courses of stone laid horizontally and cut to the circle, and above them the entire barrel is of brick. The dome arches of the Sanjakdar Mesjedi (p. 270) are formed of three distinct rings, not bonded into one another. They radiate to the true centre, and the pendentives are, as usual, in horizontal courses. The transverse arches of the outer narthex in S. Saviour in the Chora are also built with true radiating courses.

The gynecaeum of the side-chapel of the Pammakaristos (p. 153) has never been plastered, and consequently the laying of the brickwork can be seen there to advantage. The little stair leading up to the gallery is covered with a sloping barrel vault built in segments perpendicular to the slope of the stair and could easily have been built without centering. The same remark applies to the cross vault at the head of the stair, which is similarly constructed in 'slices' parallel to each side (p. 154). The arches of the gynecaeum itself, the vaults, and the two little domes, seem to have true radiating joints. The ribs of the domes are formed in the brickwork, and are not structurally separate. In these last examples, and in all door and window openings, in which the joints invariably radiate from the centre, a certain amount of centering was inevitable.

On the other hand a little passage in S. Saviour in the

Chora between the church and the parecclesion (p. 311), is covered with a barrel vault evidently built without centering. The space is first narrowed by two corbelled courses of stone and, above them, by three projecting courses of brick. From this springs the vault, built from each end in strongly inclined segments. These segments meet in the middle, leaving a diamond-shaped space filled in with longitudinal courses. Like the stairs in the Pammakaristos, this passage is very narrow, some 85 cm., yet the builders thought it necessary to corbel out five courses before venturing to throw a vault without centering.

Near the Pantokrator is an octagonal building, now Suleiman Aga Mesjedi but generally regarded as a Byzantine library, which has on each side a large wall arch strongly elliptical in form (p. 270). Two arches of somewhat similar form and apparently original are found in the south end of the gynecaeum of the Pantokrator (p. 237). These arches may have been built in this manner to economise centering. Still, in the library they are wall arches easily constructed without centering.

Failing the examination of a larger number of buildings in Constantinople we can hardly judge of the later methods of vault and arch construction, but one point may be further noticed. The wall internally is often set back slightly at each spring-course, so that with the projection of the course a considerable ledge or shelf is left. On this ledge centering could easily be supported and would have required no further framework to the ground. Centering seems to have been used for domes, arches, vaults, and door and window openings. It was not used in small vaults. But it is difficult to imagine any method of constructing such groined vaults as those found in the narthexes of the Pantokrator without a very considerable amount of centering.

Ties.—As a general rule tie rods or beams were used, either of iron or wood. In the latter case they were painted with leaf or fret ornaments, and were evidently considered as natural features. But large vaults are often found without such ties as in the narthex of the Pantokrator. Many churches have ties to the dome-arches, and none to the main vault ; but it is difficult to lay down a fixed rule. The enormous amount of mortar in the walls must have made them yield to a certain degree when newly built, and some of the larger vaults would have been the better for rods.

Abutments.—The system of abutments in the Byzantine churches of the great period has been carefully studied by M. Choisy.[1] In early examples the dome springs directly from the pendentives on the inside, but is thickened externally over the haunches, producing a double curve and an apparent drum. This is seen very clearly in SS. Sergius and Bacchus. In S. Sophia the numerous windows are cut through this drum, so that it resembles rather a series of small abutments. The object was to support the crown of the dome by adding weight over the haunches. In both these churches the thrust of the dome and its supporting arches is taken by the two-storied galleries, which form, in fact, flying buttresses within the buildings, and are adapted to their architectural requirements. The square plan and the enormous size of the dome in S. Sophia demanded the great buttresses on the sides ; while in SS. Sergius and Bacchus the eight buttresses show only on the outside of the dome and are not carried over the aisles as they are in S. Sophia. Below the roof the arches and piers of the galleries and aisles are arranged so as to carry the thrust to the external walls, and following the tradition of Roman vaulting all buttressing is internal. In S. Irene, where the true drum dome first appears, the buttresses between the windows of the dome still remain, though much reduced in size. A dome raised on a drum can evidently no longer exercise a thrust against the dome-arches ; its thrust must be taken by the drum, and only its weight can rest on the arches.

The weight of the drum and dome rests on the pendentives and dome-arches. Their thrust is neutralized by the use of ties and by the barrel vaults of the cross arms, and these in their turn depend on the thickness of the walls.

[1] *L'Art de bâtir chez les Byzantins,* p. 135.

The lower buildings attached to the church in the form of side-chapels and the narthex also helped to stiffen and buttress the cross walls. The system is by no means perfect in these late churches. It was apparently found impossible to construct drum domes of any size, except at the extreme risk of their falling in, and probably it is for this reason that many of the larger domes in late churches, like SS. Peter and Mark, S. Theodosia, the Chora, have fallen. No system of chainage appears to have been used for domes in Constantinople.

Flying buttresses probably of the ninth century are used at the west end of S. Sophia. The double-flying buttress to the apse of the Chora does not bond with the building and is certainly not original. It may be set down as part of the Byzantine restoration of the church in the fourteenth century. In any case, such external flying abutments are alien to the spirit of Byzantine architecture, and may be regarded as an importation from the West. Flying buttresses, it may here be noted, are not uncommon in the great mosques of the city. They are found in Sultan Bayazid, Rustem Pasha, Sultan Selim, the Suleimanieh, and the Shahzadé. But they are generally trifling in size, and are rather ornaments than serious attempts to buttress the dome.

Walls.—The walls of the earlier churches are built of large thin bricks laid with mortar joints at least as thick as the bricks, and often of greater thickness. Stone is used only in special cases, as in the main piers of S. Sophia, but monolithic marble columns are an important part of the structure. In the later churches stone is used in courses with the bricks to give a banded effect, and herring-bone, diamond, and radiating patterns are frequently introduced. The palace of the Porphyrogenitus, the parecclesion of the Pammakaristos, and Bogdan Serai, exhibit this style of work. As illustrations of the method adopted in the construction of walls the following measurements may be given, the sizes being in centimetres :

	Brick.	Joint.
Parecclesion of the Pammakaristos .	.08	.04
4 courses brick, 5 joints . .	.46	...
S. John in Trullo	.03	.07 to .09
Refectory of the Monastery of Manuel	.04	.04 to .06
4 course stone, 3 joints . . .	.78	...
4 courses brick, 5 joints . .	.30	...
Bogdan Serai	.0375 / .035 / .04	.052 / .035 / .04
4 courses stone, 8 joints . .	...	.55 to .60
4 courses brick, 5 joints . .	...	.43 to .47
Sanjakdar, brick	.045	...

Building Procedure.—The first step in the erection of a building was to obtain the necessary marble columns with their capitals and bases. These seem to have been largely supplied ready made, and Constantinople was a great centre for the manufacture and export of stock architectural features. Then the main walls were built in brick, the columns were inserted as required, the vaults were thrown, and the whole building was left to settle down. Owing to the enormous amount of mortar used this settling must have been very considerable, and explains why hardly a plumb wall exists in Constantinople, and why so many vaults show a pronounced sinking in at the crown or have fallen in and have been rebuilt. After the walls had set the marble facings, mosaic, and colour were applied and could be easily adapted to the irregular lines of the walls.

Byzantine architecture made little use of mouldings. The great extension of flat and spacious decoration rendered unnecessary, or even objectionable, any strong line composition. External cornices are in coursed brick, the alternate courses being laid diagonally so as to form the characteristic dentil. The richest form is that found in the Pammakaristos, S. Theodosia, and S. Thekla, where the small dentil cornice is supported on long tapering corbels, a design suggested by military machicolations.

The stone ogee, cavetto, or cavetto and bead cornice is common, but seems in every case to be Turkish work and is very common in Turkish buildings. Internal cornices and string-courses are in marble, and are all of the same type, a splay and fillet. The splayed face is decorated with upright leaves or with a guilloche band, either carved (in the Pantepoptes) or painted (in the Chora), the carving as in classic work, serving only to emphasise the colour. The splay is sometimes slightly hollowed, sometimes, as in the Chora, worked to an ogee.

Doors.—Doors often have elaborately moulded architraves and cornice. In S. John of the Studion (p. 61), the oldest example, the jamb-moulding has a large half-round on the face, with small ogees and fillets, all on a somewhat massive scale. The doors of S. Sophia are very similar. The later mouldings are lighter but the half-round on the face remains a prominent feature. It is now undercut and reduced in size, and resembles the Gothic moulding known as the bowtell. This is combined with series of fillets, small ogees, and cavettos into jamb-moulds of considerable richness. The cornices are often simply splayed or are formed of a series of ogees, fillets, and cavettos. The jamb-mouldings are cut partly on a square and partly on a steep splayed line. In some, the portion forming the ingo seems to have been regarded as a separated piece though cut from the solid. If in the doors of the Pantokrator or the Pantepoptes the line of the inner jamb be continued through the rebate, it will correspond on the outside with the bowtell moulding, as though the inner and outer architrave had been cut from one square-edged block, placing the bowtell at the angle and adding the rebate. This formation is not followed in S. John of the Studion.

Carving.—Carving is slight, and is confined to capitals, string-courses, and the slabs which filled in the lower parts of screens and windows. Fragments of such slabs are found everywhere. They are carved with geometrical interlacing and floral patterns, often encircling a cross or sacred monogram, or with simply a large cross. Such slabs may be seen still in position in S. Sophia and in the narthex of S. Theodore. In the latter they are of verd antique, and are finely carved on both sides. In later times the embargo on figure sculpture was considerably relaxed. Little figures are introduced in the cornices of the eikon frames in the Diaconissa (p. 186), and both in the parecclesion and the outer narthex of the Chora are found many small busts of angels, saints, and warriors carved with great delicacy. The carving in the Chora is the finest work of the kind excepting that in S. Sophia.

Capitals.—The development of the capital from the Roman form, which was suitable only for the lintel, to the impost capital shaped to receive an arch has been well explained by Lethaby and Swainson. According to these authors Byzantine capitals exhibit seven types.

I. The Impost capital.—It is found in SS. Sergius and Bacchus, the outer narthex of the Chora, the inner narthex of S. Andrew and elsewhere. A modification of this type is used in windows. It was employed throughout the style but especially in early times up to the sixth century, and again in the twelfth, thirteenth, and fourteenth centuries.

II. The Melon type.—This is seen on the columns of the lower order in SS. Sergius and Bacchus and on the columns of the narthex of S. Theodore, where they have been taken from an older building. The melon capital was probably not in use after the sixth century.

III. The Bowl capital.—This type is used in the great order of S. Sophia at Constantinople. It has been thought peculiar to this church, but the capitals from S. Stephen at Triglia in Bithynia resemble those of S. Sophia closely. Only the peculiar volutes of the S. Sophia capitals are absent.[1]

IV. The Byzantine or 'Pseudo-Ionic.'—This is found in the upper order of SS. Sergius and Bacchus, and in the narthex of S. Andrew. It is an early type, not used after the sixth century, and its occurrence in S. Andrew favours the early date assigned to that church.

V. The Bird and Basket.—Found in Constantinople, only in S. Sophia.

VI. The Byzantine Corinthian.—This is the commonest

[1] Hasluck, 'Bithynica,' *Annual B.S.A.* XIII. 1906-7.

form of capital in the later churches, and must have been in continuous use from the earliest date. It occurs in S. John of the Studion, the Diaconissa, the Chora, and in many other churches. Here the classic form is accurately adhered to, but, as the curved abacus was unsuitable to the arch, a large splayed abacus or impost block is placed above the capital. It is a general feature of the Byzantine capital that it projects at no point beyond the impost line of the arch, thus differing both from the classic and the Gothic forms.

VII. The Windblown Acanthus.—This is found in the churches of Salonica and Ravenna. Three examples are mentioned as seen in Constantinople, two near the Diaconissa, forming bases for the posts of a wooden porch to a house ; one is the cistern commonly known as the cistern of Pulcheria.

Window Capitals.—In shafted window of several lights, the impost piers between the arches are of the full thickness of the wall, but are very narrow from side to side. Similarly the shafts are almost slabs placed across the wall, and sometimes, as in the Pammakaristos, are carved on their narrow faces. The capitals are cubical, of slight projection at the sides, but spreading widely at the ends, while the bases closely resemble capitals turned upside down. As with columns, the joints at base and necking are bedded in sheet lead.

Floors.—The floors are usually of thick red brick tiles, some .31 cm. square, or, as in S. Theodore, hexagonal, .34 cm. across by 45 cm. from point to point. Marble floors were used when possible, inlaid with patterns, or in slabs surrounded by borders of coloured marbles, as is still seen in a portion of the floor in the Pantokrator (Fig. 76).

Decoration.—Of the churches of Constantinople only S. Sophia, S. Mary Diaconissa, the South Church of the Pantokrator, and the Chora, retain any considerable part of their original decoration. The first is beyond our present scope, but from the general tone and atmosphere which still linger there we are able to appreciate the effect of the same style of decoration where it survives in less complete form.

The accepted method, as may be observed in the Chora and the Diaconissa, was to split marble slabs so as to form patterns in the veining, and then to place them upright on the wall. It is probable that the finest slabs were first placed in the centre points of the wall, and that other slabs or borders were then arranged round them. The centre slabs in the Chora are of exceptional beauty. The usual design consists of a dado of upright slabs surmounted by panelling to the cornice level, the panels being outlined with plain or carved beads. In the Diaconissa the notched dentil form is used for the beads ; in the Chora, a 'bead and reel.' The arches have radiating voussoirs, or, in the Diaconissa, a zigzag embattled design, found also in S. Demetrius of Salonica, though two hundred years must have separated the buildings. In the Chora the arch spandrils and cornice are inlaid with scroll and geometrical designs in black, white, and coloured marbles.

The surfaces above the cornice and the interior of the domes gleamed with mosaic, representing, as seen in the Chora, figures on a gold background. The mosaic cubes are small, measuring 5 mm. to 7 mm., and are closely set. This is about the same size as the mosaic cubes in S. Sophia, but smaller than those at Ravenna, which measure about 10 mm.

Painting.—In the majority of churches this full decoration with marble and mosaic must have been rendered impossible by the expense, and accordingly we find examples like the parecclesion at the Chora decorated with painting, following exactly the tradition of marble and mosaic. This painting is in tempera on the plaster, and is executed with a free and bold touch.

Conclusion.—Byzantine architecture is essentially an art of spaces. 'Architectural' forms, as we are accustomed to think of them, are noticeably absent, but as compensation, colour was an essential and inseparable part of the architecture. The builder provided great uninterrupted spaces broken only by such lines and features as were structurally necessary—capitals, columns, string-courses, and over these spaces the artist spread a glittering robe of marble or mosaic.

No school has ever expressed its structure more simply, or given fuller scope to the artist, whether architect or painter.

Byzantine architecture is not only a school of construction, it is also a school of painting. Most of the churches of Constantinople have unfortunately lost the latter part of their personality. They are mere ghosts, their skeletons wrapped in a shroud of whitewash. Still the Greek artist retained his skill to the last, and the decorative work of S. Saviour in the Chora will stand comparison even with the similar work in S. Sophia.

In Byzantine times the greatness of S. Sophia tended to crush competition. No other ecclesiastical building approached the 'Great Church.' But structural ability was only latent, and displayed its old power again in the erection of the imperial mosques of the early Turkish Sultans, for they too are monuments of Greek architectural genius.

The origins of Byzantine architecture have been discussed at great length by Strzygowski, Rivoira, and many other able writers. Much work still remains to be done in the investigation of the later Roman and early Byzantine work ; nor does it seem probable that the difficult questions of the Eastern or the Western origin of Byzantine art will ever be finally settled.

The beginnings of Byzantine architecture have never been satisfactorily accounted for. With S. Sophia it springs almost at once into full glory ; after S. Sophia comes the long decline. It may, however, be noted that the 'endings' of Roman architecture are similarly obscure. Such buildings as the Colosseum, in which the order is applied to an arched building, are evidently transitional, the Roman construction and the Greek decoration, though joined, not being merged into one perfect style. Even in the baths and other great buildings of Imperial Rome the decoration is still Greek in form and not yet fully adapted to the arched construction. At Spalatro, in such parts as the Porta Aurea, a developed style seems to be on the point of emerging, but it is not too much to say that in no great Roman building do we find a perfect and homogeneous style.

D

There is nothing in either the planning or the construction of S. Sophia which cannot be derived from the buildings of the Roman Imperial period, with the exception of the pendentive, a feature which had to be evolved before the dome could be used with freedom on any building plan on a square. The great brick-concrete vaulted construction is that of the Roman baths, and with this is united a system of decoration founded on the classic models, but showing no trace of the Greek beam tradition which had ruled in Rome.

S. Sophia then may be regarded as the culminating point of one great Roman-Byzantine school, of which the art of classic Rome shows the rise, and the later Byzantine art the decline. This view is in accord with history, for Constantinople was New Rome, and here, if anywhere, we should expect to find preserved the traditions of Old Rome.

The division of Western Mediaeval Architecture into the two schools of Romanesque and Gothic presents a parallel case. It is now realised that no logical separation can be made between the two so-called styles. Similarly we may continue to speak of the Classic Roman style and of the Byzantine style, although the two really belong to one great era in the history of art.

CHAPTER II

THE CHURCH OF S. JOHN THE BAPTIST OF THE STUDION, EMIR AHOR JAMISSI

THE mosque Emir Ahor Jamissi, situated in the quarter of Psamathia, near the modern Greek church of S. Constantine, and at short distance from the Golden Gate (Yedi Koulé), is the old church of S. John the Baptist, which was associated with the celebrated monastery of Studius, ἡ μονὴ τοῦ Στουδίου. It may be reached by taking the train from Sirkiji Iskelessi to Psamathia or Yedi Koulé.[1]

In favour of the identification of the building, there is, first, the authority of tradition,[2] which in the case of a church so famous may be confidently accepted as decisive. In the next place, all indications of the character and position of the Studion, however vague, point to Emir Ahor Jamissi as the representative of that church. For the mosque presents the characteristic features which belonged to the Studion as a basilica of the fifth century, and stands where that sanctuary stood, in the district at the south-western angle of the city,[3] and on the left hand of the street leading from S. Mary Peribleptos (Soulou Monastir) to the Golden Gate.[4] Furthermore, as held true of the Studion, the mosque is in the vicinity of the Golden Gate,[5] and readily

---

[1] The Latin thesis of Eugenius Marin, *De Studio coenobio Constantinopolitano*, Paris, 1897, is a most useful work.

[2] Gyllius, *De top. C.P.* p. 313.

[3] *Itinéraires russes en Orient*, p. 306, *traduits pour la Société de l'Orient Latin par Mdme. B. de Khitrovo*.

[4] *Ibid.* p. 231. For all questions concerning the walls of the city I refer, once for all, to my work, *Byzantine Constantinople : the Walls and adjoining Historical Sites*, published in 1889 by John Murray, London.

[5] *Paschal Chronicle*, p. 726.

accessible from a gate and landing (Narli Kapou) on the shore of the Sea of Marmora.[1]

According to the historian Theophanes,[2] the church was erected in the year 463 by the patrician Studius, after whom the church and the monastery attached to it were named. He is described as a Roman of noble birth and large means who devoted his wealth to the service of God,[3] and may safely be identified with Studius who held the consulship in 454 during the reign of Marcian.[4]

If we may trust the Anonymus,[5] the church erected by Studius replaced a sanctuary which stood at one time, like the Chora, outside the city. Seeing the territory immediately beyond the Constantinian fortifications was well peopled before its inclusion within the city limits by Theodosius II., there is nothing improbable in the existence of such extra-mural sanctuaries, and as most, if not all, of them would be small buildings, they would naturally require enlargement or reconstruction when brought within the wider bounds of the capital. According to Suidas,[6] the building was at first a parochial church ; its attachment to a monastery was an after-thought of its founder.

The monastery was large and richly endowed, capable of accommodating one thousand monks.[7] Its first inmates were taken from a fraternity known as the Akoimeti, ' the sleepless ' ; so named because in successive companies they

[1] Constantine Porphyrogenitus, De ceremoniis, pp. 462-3.
[2] P. 175. But according to Epigram 4 in the Anthologia Graeca epigrammatum (Stadt-Mueller, 1894) Studius became consul after the erection of the church and as a reward for its erection. Under the heading εἰς τὸν ναὸν τοῦ Προδρόμου ἐν τοῖς Στουδίου it says τοῦτον Ἰωάννῃ, Χριστοῦ μεγάλῳ θεράποντι, Στούδιος ἀγλαὸν οἶκον ἐδείματο. καρπαλίμως δὲ τῶν κάμων εὕρετο μισθὸν ἐλὼν ὑπατηίδα ῥάβδον. In Suidas is a similar epigram in honour of the erection by Studius of another church ; τοῦ ἀρχιστρατηγοῦ Νακωλείας in Phrygia.
[3] Theodori Studitae vita, Migne, Patrologia Graeca, tome 99.
[4] Pasch. Chron. p. 591.
[5] Banduri, i. p. 54. In the recent excavations carried on in the Studion by the Russian Archaeological Institute of Constantinople, the foundations of an earlier building were discovered below the floor of the church. The line of the foundations ran through the church from north-east to south-west, parallel to the wall of the cistern to the south-west of the church. Perhaps it is too soon to determine the character of the earlier building.
[6] s.v. : ἡ τῶν Στουδιτῶν μονὴ πρότερον καὶ καθολικῆς ἐκκλησίας ἦν, ὕστερον δε μετῆλθεν εἰς μονήν. The reading is doubtful. A proposed emendation is, τῶν καθολικῶν ἐκκλησία ἦν.
[7] Codinus, De aed. p. 102.

celebrated divine service in their chapels day and night without ceasing, like the worshippers in the courts of heaven.

> ' Even thus of old
> Our ancestors, within the still domain
> Of vast cathedral or conventual church
> Their vigils kept : where tapers day and night
> On the dim altar burned continually.
> In token that the House was ever more
> Watching to God. Religious men were they ;
> Nor would their reason, tutored to aspire
> Above this transitory world, allow
> That there should pass a moment of the year
> When in their land the Almighty's service ceased.'

But this devout practice does not seem to have been long continued at the Studion ; for we never hear of it in any account of the discipline of the House. The monks of the Studion should therefore not be identified with the Akoimeti who took up such a determined and independent attitude in the theological conflicts under Zeno, Basiliscus, and Justinian the Great.[1]

In the course of its history the church underwent noteworthy repairs on two occasions. It was first taken in hand for that purpose, soon after the middle of the eleventh century,[2] by the Emperor Isaac Comnenus (1057-58), who was interested in the House because he and his brother had received part of their education in that ' illustrious and glorious school of virtue.'[3] What the repairs then made exactly involved is unfortunately not stated. But, according to Scylitzes, they were so extensive that ' to tell in detail what the emperor and empress did for the embellishment of the church would surpass the labour of Hercules.'[4] Probably they concerned chiefly the decoration of the edifice.

The next repairs on record were made about the year 1290, in the reign of Andronicus II., by his unfortunate brother Constantine Porphyrogenitus. Owing to the neglect

---

[1] Theophanes, pp. 187, 218 ; Evagrius, cc. 18, 19, 21. In the list of the abbots who subscribed one of the documents connected with the Synod held at Constantinople in 536, the two establishments are clearly distinguished. They are distinguished also by Antony of Novgorod in 1200, *Itin. russes*, pp. 97, 100.

[2] Scylitzes, p. 650.

[3] Nicephorus Bryennius, p. 181.   [4] Cedrenus, ii. p. 650.

of the building during the Latin occupation the roof had
fallen in, the cells of the monks had disappeared, and
sheep grazed undisturbed on the grass which covered the
grounds. Constantine, rich, generous, fond of popularity,
did all in his power to restore the former glory of the
venerated shrine. The new roof was a remarkable piece
of work ; large sums were spent upon the proper accommodation of the monks, and the grounds were enclosed
within strong walls.[1]

Like other monastic institutions, the Studion suffered
greatly at the hands of the iconoclast emperors. Under
Constantine Copronymus, indeed, the fraternity was scattered
to the winds and practically suppressed, so that only twelve
old members of the House were able to take advantage of
the permission to return to their former home, upon the
first restoration of eikons in 787 by the Empress Irene.
Under these circumstances a company of monks, with the
famous abbot Theodore at their head, were eventually
brought from the monastery of Saccudio to repeople the
Studion, and with their advent in 799 the great era in the
history of the House began, the number of the monks rising
to seven hundred, if not one thousand.[2]

Theodore had already established a great reputation for
sanctity and moral courage. For when Constantine VI.
repudiated the Empress Maria and married Theodote, one
of her maids of honour, Theodore, though the new empress
was his relative, denounced the marriage and the priest who
had celebrated it, insisting that moral principles should
govern the highest and lowest alike, and for this action he
had gladly endured scourging and exile. The Studion had,
therefore, a master who feared the face of no man, and who
counted the most terrible sufferings as the small dust of the
balance when weighed against righteousness, and under him
the House became illustrious for its resistance to the tyranny
of the civil power in matters affecting faith and morals.
When the Emperor Nicephorus ordered the restoration of

[1] Nicephorus Gregoras, i. p. 190 ; Stephen of Novgorod, who saw the church in
1350, refers to its 'very lofty roof,' *Itin. russes*, p. 123.
[2] Theoph. p. 747 ; *Life of S. Theodore*, Migne, *P.G.* tome 99.

the priest who had celebrated the marriage of Constantine VI. with Theodote, not only did Theodore and his brother Joseph, bishop of Thessalonica, and their venerable uncle Plato, endure imprisonment and exile, but every monk in the Studion defied the emperor. Summoning the fraternity into his presence, Nicephorus bade all who would obey his order go to the right, and all who dared to disobey him go to the left. Not a single man went to the right. Under the very eyes of the despot all went to the left, and in his wrath Nicephorus broke up the community and distributed the monks among various monasteries. Upon the accession of Michael I. the exiled monks and Theodore were allowed indeed to return to the Studion, peace being restored by the degradation of the priest who had celebrated the obnoxious marriage. But another storm darkened the sky, when Leo V., the Armenian, in 813, renewed the war against eikons. Theodore threw himself into the struggle with all the force of his being as their defender. He challenged the right of the imperial power to interfere with religious questions ; he refused to keep silence on the subject ; and on Palm Sunday, in 815, led a procession of his monks carrying eikons in their hands in triumph round the monastery grounds. Again he was scourged and banished. But he could not be subdued. By means of a large and active correspondence he continued an incessant and powerful agitation against the iconoclasts of the day. Nor would he come to terms with Michael II., who had married a nun, and who allowed the use of eikons only outside the capital. So Theodore retired, apparently a defeated man, to the monastery of Acritas[1]; and there, 'on Sunday, 11 November 826, and about noon, feeling his strength fail, he bade them light candles and sing the 119th psalm, which seems to have been sung at funerals. At the words : " I will never forget Thy commandments, for with them Thou hast quickened me," he passed away.' He was buried on the island of Prinkipo, but eighteen years later, when eikons were finally restored in the worship of the

---

[1] The modern Touzla at the northern head of the gulf of Nicomedia. See the articles by Mr. Siderides and Mr. Meliopoulos in the *Proceedings of the Greek Syllogos of Constantinople*, vol. xxxi., 1907-8.

Orthodox Church, his body was transferred to the Studion, and laid with great ceremony in the presence of the Empress Theodora beside the graves of his uncle Plato and his brother Joseph, in sign that after all he had conquered.[1] *Tandem hic quiescit.*

NOTE

His remains were interred at the east end of the southern aisle, where his uncle Plato and his brother Joseph had been buried before him, and where Naucratius and Nicholas, his successors as abbots of the Studion, were laid to rest after him. πρὸς τῷ δεξιῷ μέρει ἐν τῷ κατ᾽ ἀνατολὰς τοῦ Προδρομικοῦ τεμένους πανδόξῳ καὶ ἱερῷ τῶν μαρτύρων σηκῷ, ἔνθα δὴ καὶ τοῦ ὁσίου πατρὸς ἡμῶν Θεοδώρου ἡ πανευκλεὴς καὶ πανσέβαστος τιμία θήκη καθίδρυται (*Vita S. Nicolai Studitae*, Migne, *P.G.* tome 105).

There, in fact, during the recent Russian exploration of the church, three coffins were discovered : one containing a single body, another four bodies, and another three bodies. The grave had evidently been disturbed at some time, for some of the bodies had no head, and all the coffins lay under the same bed of mortar. No marks were found by which to identify the persons whose remains were thus brought to view. But there can be no doubt that five of the bodies belonged to the five persons mentioned above. To whom the three other bodies belonged is a matter of pure conjecture. They might be the remains of three intimate friends of Theodore, viz. Athanasius, Euthemius, Timotheus, or more probably of the abbots, Sophronius (851-55), Achilles (858-63), Theodosius (863-64). Cf. *Itin. russes,* p. 100.

It would be a mistake, however, to think of Theodore only as a controversalist and defier of the civil authority. He was a deeply religious man, a pastor of souls, and he revived the religious and moral life of men, far and wide, not only in his own day, but long after his life on earth had closed. He made the Studion the centre of a great spiritual influence, which never wholly lost the impulse of his personality or the loftiness of his ideal. The forms of mediæval piety have become antiquated, and they were often empty and vain, but we must not be blind to the fact that they were frequently filled with a passion for holy living, and gave scope for the creation of characters which, notwithstanding their limitations, produced great and good men.

[1] The English reader should consult the *Life of Theodore of Studium*, by Miss Alice Gardner, for an excellent presentation of the man and his work.

Speaking of Eastern monks and abbots, especially during the eighth and ninth centuries, Mr. Finlay, the historian, justly remarks that ' the manners, the extensive charity, and the pure morality of these abbots, secured them the love and admiration of the people, and tended to disseminate a higher standard of morality than had previously prevailed in Constantinople. This fact must not be overlooked in estimating the various causes which led to the regeneration of the Eastern Empire under the iconoclast emperors. While the Pope winked at the disorders in the palace of Charlemagne, the monks of the East prepared the public mind for the dethronement of Constantine VI. because he obtained an illegal divorce and formed a second marriage. The corruption of monks and the irregularities prevalent in the monasteries of the West contrast strongly with the condition of the Eastern monks.' Certainly to no one is this tribute of praise due more than to the brotherhood in the monastery of Studius.

The monks of the Studion, like most Greek monks, lived under the rules prescribed by S. Basil for the discipline of men who aspired to reach ' the angelic life.' Theodore, however, quickened the spirit which found expression in those rules, and while inculcating asceticism in its extremest form, showed greater consideration for the weakness of human nature. The penalties he assigned for transgressions were on the whole less Draconian than those inflicted before his time.

According to the moral ideal cherished in the monastery, the true life of man was to regard oneself but dust and ashes, and, like the angels, to be ever giving God thanks. If a monk repined at such a lot, he was to castigate himself by eating only dry bread for a week and performing 500 acts of penance. The prospect of death was always to be held in view. Often did the corridors of the monastery resound with the cry, ' We shall die, we shall die ! ' The valley of the shadow of death was considered the road to life eternal. A monk could not call even a needle his own. Nor were the clothes he wore his personal property. They were from time to time thrown into a heap with the clothes of the other members of the House, and every monk then took from the pile the garment most convenient to his hand. Female animals were forbidden the monastery. A monk was not allowed to kiss his mother, not even at Easter, under penalty of excommunication for fifty days. Daily he attended seven services, and had often to keep vigil all night long. There was only one set meal a day ; anything more in the way of food consisted of the fragments which a monk laid aside from that meal. No meat was eaten unless by special permission for reasons of health.

If a brother ate meat without permission he went without fish, eggs, and cheese for forty days. The ordinary food consisted of vegetables cooked in oil. Fish, cheese, and eggs were luxuries. Two, sometimes three, cups of wine were permitted. If a brother was so unfortunate as to break a dish, he had to stand before the assembled monks at dinner time with covered head, and hold the broken article in view of all in the refectory.[1] It was forbidden to a monk to feel sad. Melancholy was a sin, and was to be overcome by prayer, one hundred and fifty genuflexions, and five hundred Kyrie Eleisons a day. The monks were required to read regularly in the monastery library.[2] The task of copying manuscripts occupied a place of honour, and was under strict regulations. Fifty genuflexions were the penalty prescribed for not keeping one's copy clean ; one hundred and fifty such acts of penance for omitting an accent or mark of punctuation ; thirty, for losing one's temper and breaking his pen ; fasting on dry bread was the fate of the copyist guilty of leaving out any part of the original, and three days' seclusion for daring to trust his memory instead of following closely the text before him.[3]

Ignatius of Smolensk[4] found Russian monks in the monastery employed in transcribing books for circulation in Russia. Stephen of Novgorod[5] met two old friends from

---

[1] According to Stephen of Novgorod (*Itin. russes*, p. 121) the refectory was an unusually fine hall, situated near the sea.

[2] At a short distance beyond the north-eastern end of the church are some ruined vaults which the Turks have named Kietab Hané, the library. See Plate III.

[3] For the Constitution and *Epitamia* of the Studion, see Migne, *P.G.* tome 99.

[4] *Itin. russes*, p. 136.

[5] *Ibid.* p. 122 'on envoyait beaucoup de livres de ce couvent en Russie, des

his town busy copying the Scriptures. A good monastic scriptorium rendered an immense service ; it did the work of the printing-press.

Yet, notwithstanding all restrictions, men could be happy at the Studion. One of its inmates for instance congratulates himself thus on his lot there, ' No barbarian looks upon my face ; no woman hears my voice. For a thousand years no useless (ἄπρακτος) man has entered the monastery of Studius ; none of the female sex has trodden its court. I dwell in a cell that is like a palace ; a garden, an oliveyard, and a vineyard surround me. Before me are graceful and luxuriant cypress trees. On one hand is the city with its market-place ; on the other, the mother of churches and the empire of the world.' [1]

Hymnology was likewise cultivated at the Studion, many hymns of the Greek Church being composed by Theodore and his brother Joseph.

Two abbots of the monastery became patriarchs : Antony (975),[2] and Alexius (1025),[3] the latter on the occasion when he carried the great relic of the Studion, the head of John the Baptist, to Basil II. lying at the point of death.[4]

At least as early as the reign of Alexius I. Comnenus, the abbot of the Studion held the first place among his fellow-abbots in the city. His precedence is distinctly recognised in a Patriarchal Act of 1381 as a right of old standing.[5]

The spirit of independence which characterized the monastery did not die with the abbot Theodore. The monks of the Studion were the most stubborn opponents of the famous Photius who had been elevated to the patriarchal throne directly from the ranks of the laity, and in the course of the conflict between him and the monks during the first

règlements, des triodions et autres livres.' Many members of the Studion were Russians.
    [1] Marin, *De Studio*, p. 11. See Marin, *Les Moines de Constantinople*, for the monastic institutions of the city in general.
    [2] Cedren. ii. p. 147.   [3] *Ibid.* p. 212.   [4] *Ibid.* p. 479.
    [5] *Acta et diplomata patriarchatus Constantinop.* t. ii. p. 12 ἐν ταῖς ἱεραῖς τε καὶ συνοδικαῖς συνελεύσεσι· πρῶτον μὲν γὰρ πάντων τὸν ἀρχιμανδρίτην τῶν Στουδίου καὶ ὁ χρόνος κατέστησε καὶ τὸ δίκαιον αὐτό.

tenure of his office for ten years, the abbots of the House were changed five times. Indeed, when Photius appointed Santabarenus as the abbot, a man accused of being a Manichaean, and who professed to be able to communicate with departed spirits, many of the monks, if not all of them, left their home. Nor was this the last assertion of the freedom of conscience for which this monastery was distinguished, and which makes it memorable in history.

Like other monasteries the Studion often served as a place of correction for offenders whom it was expedient to render harmless without recourse to the extreme rigour of the law. Santabarenus, who has just been mentioned, was sent in his wild youth, after narrowly escaping a sentence of death at the hands of the Caesar Bardas, to this monastery in the hope of being reformed in the orthodox atmosphere of the House. In the reign of Leo VI. (826-912), an official named Mousikos was sent hither to be cured of the propensity to accept bribes.[1] In 912, Gregoras and Choirosphacta were obliged to join the brotherhood to repent at leisure for having favoured the attempt of Constantine Ducas, domestic of the Scholae, to usurp the throne of Constantine VII. Porphyrogenitus when seven years of age.[2]

Several emperors sought the shelter of the Studion as a refuge from danger, or as a retreat from the vanity of the world. Thither, in 1041, Michael V. and his uncle Constantine fled from the popular fury excited by their deposition of the Empress Zoe and the slaughter of three thousand persons in the defence of the palace. The two fugitives made for the monastery by boat, and betook themselves to the church for sanctuary. But as soon as the place of their concealment became known, an angry crowd forced a way into the building to wreak vengeance upon them, and created a scene of which Psellus has left us a graphic account. Upon hearing the news of what was going on, he and an officer of the imperial guard mounted horse and galloped to the Studion. A fierce mob was madly attempting to pull down the structure, and it was with the utmost difficulty that the two friends managed to enter the church and

---

[1] Theoph. Cont. p. 362.　　　　[2] *Ibid.* p. 384.

make their way to the altar. The building seemed full of
wild animals, glaring with eyes on fire at their victims, and
making the air resound with the most terrible cries.
Michael was on his knees clasping the holy table;
Constantine stood on the right; both were dressed like
monks, and their features were so transformed by terror as
to be almost beyond recognition. The spectacle of greatness
thus brought low was so pathetic that Psellus burst into
tears and sobbed aloud. But the crowd only grew more fierce,
and drew nearer and nearer to the fugitives as though to rend
them in pieces. Only a superstitious dread restrained it
from laying hands upon them in a shrine so sacred and
venerated. The uproar lasted for hours, the mob content
meanwhile with striking terror and making flight impossible.
At length, late in the afternoon, the prefect of the city
appeared upon the scene, accompanied by soldiers and
followed by large crowds of citizens. He came with instructions to bring Michael and Constantine out of the church.
In vain did he try the effect of mild words and promises of
a gentle fate. The fallen emperor and his uncle clung to the
altar more desperately. The prefect then gave orders that
the two wretched men should be dragged forth by main force.
They gripped the altar yet more tightly, and in piteous
tones invoked the aid of all the eikons in the building. The
scene became so heartrending that most of the spectators in-
terfered on behalf of the victims of misfortune, and only by
giving solemn assurance that they would not be put to death
was the prefect allowed to proceed to their arrest. Michael
and Constantine were then dragged by the feet as far as the
Sigma, above S. Mary Peribleptos (Soulou Monastir), and
after having their eyes burnt out were banished to different
monasteries, to muse on the vanity of human greatness and
repent of their misdeeds.[1]

The Studion appears in the final rupture of the Eastern
and Western Churches.[2] The immediate occasion was a

[1] Glycas, p. 592; Cedrenus, ii. p. 539; Psellus, pp. 87-93; *Byzantine
Texts*, edited by Prof. Bury; cf. Schlumberger, *Épopée byzantine à la fin du
dixième siècle*, p. 372.
[2] See Cedrenus, ii. p. 555; Will, *Commemoratio brevis*, p. 150; Schlumberger,
op. cit. chapitre viii.

letter sent by the Archbishop of Achrida, in 1053, to the Bishop of Trani, condemning the Church of Rome for the use of unleavened bread in the administration of the Holy Communion, and for allowing a fast on Saturday. Nicetas Stethetos (Pectoratus), a member of the House renowned for his asceticism, and for his courage in reproving the scandalous connection of Constantine IX. with Sklerena, wrote a pamphlet, in Latin, in which, in addition to the charges against Rome made by the Archbishop of Achrida, the enforced celibacy of the clergy was denounced. The pamphlet was widely circulated by the Patriarch Kerularios, who wished to bring the dispute between the Churches to an issue. But the emperor not being prepared to go so far, invited the Pope to send three legates to Constantinople to settle the differences which disturbed the Christian world. Cardinal Humbert, one of the legates, replied to Nicetas in the most violent language of theological controversy, and to bring matters to a conclusion an assembly, which was attended by the Emperor Constantine, his court, and the Papal legates, met at the Studion on the 24th of June 1054. A Greek translation of the pamphlet composed by Nicetas was then read, and after the discussion of the subject, Nicetas retracted his charges and condemned all opponents of the Roman Church. His pamphlet was, moreover, thrown into the fire by the emperor's orders, and on the following day he called upon the Papal legates, who were lodged at the palace of the Pegé (Baloukli), and was received into the communion of the Church he had lately denounced. But the patriarch was not so fickle or pliant. He would not yield an iota, and on the 15th of July 1054 Cardinal Humbert laid on the altar of S. Sophia the bull of excommunication against Kerularios and all his followers, which has kept Western and Eastern Christendom divided to this day.

When Michael VII. (1067-78) saw that the tide of popular feeling had turned against him in favour of Nice-phorus Botoniates, he meekly retired to this House, declining to purchase a crown with cruelty by calling upon the Varangian guards to defend his throne with their battle-axes.   Michael was appointed bishop of Ephesus, but after paying one visit to his diocese he returned to Constantinople and took up his abode in the monastery of Manuel (p. 257).[1]

To the Studion, where he had studied in his youth and which he had embellished, the Emperor Isaac Comnenus retired, when pleurisy and the injuries he received while boar-hunting made him realize that he had but a short time to live.   In fact, he survived his abdication for one year only, but during that period he proved a most exemplary monk, showing the greatest deference to his abbot, and besides performing other lowly duties acted as keeper of the monastery gate.   How thoroughly he was reconciled to the exchange of a throne for a cell appears in the remark made to his wife, who had meantime taken the veil at the Myrelaion, ' Acknowledge that when I gave you the crown I made you a slave, and that when I took it away I set you free.'   His widow commemorated his death annually at the Studion, and on the last occasion surprised the abbot by making a double offering, saying, ' I may not live another year,' a presentiment which proved true.   According to her dying request, Aecatherina was buried in the cemetery of the Studion, ' as a simple nun, without any sign to indicate that she was born a Bulgarian princess and had been a Roman empress.' [2]

On the occasion of the triumphal entry of Michael Palaeologus into the city in 1261, the emperor followed the eikon of the Theotokos Hodegetria, to whom the recovery of the Empire was attributed, on foot as far as the Studion ; and there, having placed the eikon in the church, he mounted horse to proceed to S. Sophia.[3]

One of the sons of Sultan Bajazet was buried at the Studion.[4]   The prince had been sent by the Sultan as a hostage to the Byzantine Court, and being very young attended school in Constantinople with John, the son of the Emperor Manuel.   There he acquired a taste for Greek letters, and became a convert to the Christian faith ; but for fear of the

[1] Attaliotes, pp. 304, 306 ; Glycas, p. 617 ; Scylitzes, pp. 738-39.
[2] Scylitzes, pp. 649-51 ; Bryennius, p. 20.
[3] Acropolita, p. 197.
[4] Ducas, p. 99 πλησίον τοῦ ναοῦ ἐντὸς τῆς πύλης.

Sultan's displeasure he was long refused permission to be baptized. Only when the young man lay at the point of death, in 1417, a victim to the plague raging in the city, was the rite administered, his schoolmate and friend acting as sponsor.

A tombstone from the cemetery of the monastery is built into the Turkish wall at the north-eastern corner of the church. It bears an epitaph to the following effect :—' In the month of September of the year 1387, fell asleep the servant of God, Dionysius the Russian, on the sixth day of the month.' The patrician Bonus, who defended the city against the Avars in 627, while the Emperor Heraclius was absent dealing with the Persians, was buried at the Studion.[1]

On the festival of the Decapitation of S. John the Baptist, the emperor attended service at the Studion in great state. Early in the morning the members of the senate assembled therefore at the monastery, while dignitaries of an inferior rank took their place outside the gate (Narli Kapou) in the city walls below the monastery, and at the pier at the foot of the steep path that descends from that gate to the shore of the Sea of Marmora, all awaiting the arrival of the imperial barge from the Great Palace. Both sides of the path were lined by monks of the House, holding lighted tapers, and as soon as the emperor disembarked, the officials at the pier and the crowd of monks, with the abbot at their head, swinging his silver censer of fragrant smoke, led the way up to the gate. There a halt was made for the magistri, patricians, and omphikialioi (ὀμφικιάλιοι) to do homage to the sovereign and join the procession, and then the long train wended its way through the open grounds attached to the monastery (διὰ τοῦ ἐξαέρου), and through covered passages (διὰ τῶν ἐκεῖσε διαβατικῶν),[2] until it reached the south-eastern end of the narthex (εἰσέρχονται διὰ τοῦ πρὸς ἀνατολικὴν δεξιοῦ μέρους τοῦ νάρθηκος). Before the entrance at that point, the emperor put on richly embroidered robes, lighted tapers, and then followed the clergy into the church, to take his

[1] *Pasch. Chron.* pp. 726-27.

[2] Mr. Pantchenko of the Russian Institute at Constantinople has found evidence that cloisters stood along the east and south sides of the great cistern to the south-west of the church.

stand at the east end of the south aisle.   The most important
act he performed during the service was to incense the head
of John the Baptist enshrined on the right hand of the bema.
At the conclusion of the Office of the day, he was served
by the monks with refreshments under the shade of the
trees in the monastery grounds (ἀναδενδράδιον); and, after a
short rest, proceeded to his barge with the same ceremonial
as attended his arrival, and returned to the palace.[1]

The church was converted into a mosque in the reign
of Bajazet II. (1481-1512) by the Sultan's equerry, after
whom it is now named.

Architectural Features

The church of S. John the Baptist of the Studion is a
basilica, and is of special interest because the only surviving
example of that type in Constantinople, built while the
basilica was the dominant form of ecclesiastical architecture
in the Christian world.   It has suffered severely since the
Turkish conquest, especially from the fire which, in 1782,
devastated the quarter in which it stands, and from the fall
of its roof, a few winters ago, under an unusual weight of
snow.   Still, what of it remains and the descriptions of its
earlier state given by Gyllius, Gerlach, and other visitors,
enable us to form a fair idea of its original appearance.
The recent explorations conducted by the Russian Institute
at Constantinople have also added much to our knowledge
of the building.

It is the oldest church fabric in the city, and within its
precincts we stand amid the surroundings of early Christian
congregations.   For, partly in original forms, partly in
imitations, we still find here a basilica's characteristic features :
the atrium, or quadrangular court before the church ; on three
of its sides surrounded by *cloisters* ; in its centre, the marble
phialé or fountain, for the purification of the gathering
worshippers ; the *narthex*, a pillared porch along the western
façade, where catechumens and penitents, unworthy to enter

---

[1] Constant. Porphyr. *De cer.* ii. pp. 562-3.

E

the sanctuary itself, stood afar off; the interior area divided into *nave* and *aisles* by lines of columns ; the semicircular *apse* at the eastern extremity of the nave for altar and clergy ; and *galleries* on the other sides of the building to provide ample accommodation for large assemblies of faithful people.

NOTE

Gyllius (*De Top. Constant.* l. iv. c. 9) describes the church as follows : 'Quod (monasterium) nunc non extat ; aedes extat, translata in religionem Mametanam ; in cujus vestibulo sunt quatuor columnae cum trabeatione egregie elaborata ; in interiore parte aedium utrinque columnae sunt septem virides, nigris maculis velut fragmentis alterius generis lapidum insertis distinctae, quarum perimeter est sex pedum et sex digitorum.   Denique earum ratio capitulorum, epistyliorum opere Corinthio elaborata, eadem est quae columnarum vestibuli.   Supra illas sex existunt totidem columnae in parte aedis superiore.   In area aedis Studianae est cisterna, cujus lateritias cameras sustinent viginti tres columnae excelsae Corinthiae.'

Gerlach (*Tagebuch*, p. 217 ; cf. pp. 359, 406) describes it under the style of the church of S. Theodore, for he confounds the monastery of Studius with that of the Peribleptos at Soulou Monastir : 'Das ist eine sehr hohe und weite Kirche (wie die unsern) ; hat zwei Reyhen Marmel-steiner Säulen mit Corinthischen Knäufen (capitellis), auff einer jeden Seiten sieben ; auff deren jeden wieder ein andere Säule stehet.   Der Boden ist mit lauter buntem von Vögeln und anderen Thieren gezierten Marmel auff das schönste gepflästert.' (This is a very lofty and broad church (like our churches). It has two rows of marble columns with Corinthian capitals, on either side seven ; over each of which stands again another column.   The floor is paved in the most beautiful fashion entirely with variegated marble, adorned with figures of birds and other animals.)

Choiseul Gouffier (*Voyage pittoresque en Grèce*, ii. p. 477), French ambassador to the Sublime Porte (1779-92), speaks of the church in the following terms : 'Dans l'intérieur sont de chaque côté sept colonnes de vert antique, surmontées d'une frise de marbre blanc parfaitement sculptée, qui contient un ordre plus petit et très bien proportionné avec le premier.   Je ne sais de quel marbre sont ces secondes colonnes, parce que les Turcs qui défigurent tout ont imaginé de les couvrir de chaux.'

Ph. Bruun (*Constantinople, ses sanctuaires et ses reliques au commencement du XVᵉ siècle*, Odessa, 1883) identifies with the Studion one of the churches dedicated to S. John, which Ruy

Gonzalez de Clavijo visited in Constantinople when on his way to the Court of Tamerlane. But that church was 'a round church without corners,' 'una quadra redonda sin esquinas,' and had forty-eight columns of verd antique, 'veinte é quatro marmoles de jaspe verde, . . . é otros veinte é quatro marmoles de jaspe verde.' What church the Spanish ambassador had in view, if his description is correct, it is impossible to say. No other writer describes such a church in Constantinople. See the Note at the end of this chapter for the full text of the ambassador's description.

The northern wall of the atrium is original, as the crosses in brick formed in its brickwork show. The trees which shade the court, the Turkish tombstones beneath them, and the fountain in the centre, combine to form a very beautiful approach to the church, and reproduce the general features and atmosphere of its earlier days.

The narthex is divided into three bays, separated by heavy arches. It is covered by a modern wooden roof, but shows no signs of ever having been vaulted. The centre bay contains in its external wall a beautiful colonnade of four marble columns, disposed, to use a classical term, ' in antis.' They stand on comparatively poor bases, but their Corinthian capitals are exceptionally fine, showing the richest Byzantine form of that type of capital. The little birds under the angles of the abaci should not be overlooked.

The entablature above the columns, with its architrave, frieze, and cornice, follows the classic form very closely, and is enriched in every member. Particularly interesting are the birds, the crosses, and other figures in the spaces between the modillions and the heavy scroll of the frieze. The drill has been very freely used throughout, and gives a pleasant sparkle to the work.

In the second and fourth intercolumniations there are doorways with moulded jambs, lintels, and cornices, but only the upper parts of these doorways are now left open to serve as windows.

The cornice of the entablature returns westwards at its northern and southern ends, indicating that a colonnade, with a smaller cornice, ran along the northern and southern sides of the atrium, if not also along its western side. The cloisters behind the colonnades, were connected at their west end with the narthex by two large and elaborately moulded doorways still in position.

Five doors lead from the narthex into the church ; three opening into the nave, the others into the aisles.

The interior of the church, now almost a total ruin, was divided into nave and two aisles by colonnades of seven columns of verd antique marble. But only six of the original columns have survived the injuries which the building has sustained ; the other columns are Turkish, and are constructed of wood with painted plaster covering.

The colonnades supported an entablature of late Corinthian type, which, as the fall of the Turkish plaster that once covered it has revealed, had the same moulding as the entablature in the narthex. The architrave was in three faces, with a small bead ornament to the upper two, and finished above with a small projecting moulding. The frieze was an ogee, bellied in the lower part. Of the cornice only the bed mould, carved with a leaf and tongue, remains.

Above each colonnade stood another range of seven [1] columns connected, probably, by arches. Along the northern, southern, and western sides of the church were galleries constructed of wood. Those to the north and south still exist in a ruined condition, and many of the stone corbels which supported the beams remain in the walls. Only scanty vestiges of the gallery above the narthex can be now distinguished. Its western wall, the original outer wall of the upper part of the church, has totally disappeared. Its eastern arcade has been replaced by the Turkish wall which constitutes the present outer wall of that part of the church. But beyond either end of that wall are visible, though built up, the old openings by which the gallery communicated with its companion galleries ; while to the west of the wall project the ragged ends of the Byzantine walls which formed the gallery's northern and southern sides. The nave rose probably to a greater height than it does now, and had a roof at a higher level

[1] Gyllius says six.

than the roofing of the aisles.   It doubtless resembled the basilican churches at Salonica, either with clearstory windows, as in S. Demetrius, or without such windows, as in Eski Juma Jamissi.

The nave terminates in a large apse, semicircular within and showing three sides on the exterior.   Only the lower part is original ; the Turkish superstructure is lower and on a smaller scale than the Byzantine portion it has replaced. There are no side chapels.   Under the bema the Russian explorers discovered a small cruciform crypt.   The large quantity of mosaic cubes found in the church during the recent Russian excavations proves that the church was decorated with mosaics, while the remains of iron plugs in the western wall for holding marble slabs show that the building had the customary marble revetment.   But what is curious is to find the mortar pressed over the face of the stones, and broad decorative joints formed by ruled incised lines and colour.   Mr. W. S. George suggests that this was a temporary decoration executed pending some delay in the covering of the walls with marble.   He also thinks that the importance given to the joint in late Byzantine work and in Turkish work may be a development from such early treatment of mortar.

The floor of the church was paved with pieces of marble arranged in beautiful patterns, in which figures of animals and scenes from classic mythology were inlaid.   Gerlach[1] noticed the beauty of the pavement, and Salzenberg[2] represents a portion of it in his work on S. Sophia.   But the members of the Russian Institute of Constantinople have had the good fortune to bring the whole pavement to light.

A noticeable feature is the number of doors to the church, as in S. Irene.   Besides the five doors already mentioned, leading into the interior from the narthex, there is a door at the eastern end of each aisle, and close to each of these doors is found both in the southern and northern walls of the building an additional door surmounted by a

[1] See passage from his *Tagebuch* quoted on page 50.
[2] *Altchristliche Baudenkmäler von Konstantinopel*, Blatt iv.

window. The latter doors and their windows have been walled up.

The exterior is in two stories, corresponding to the ground floor and the galleries. It has two ranges of eight large semicircular-headed windows in the northern and southern walls, some of them modified, others built up, since the building became a mosque. The five windows in the gable of the western wall are, like the wall itself, Turkish. Pilasters are placed at the angles and at the apse.

On the south side of the church is a cistern, the roof or which rests on twenty-three columns crowned by beautiful Corinthian capitals.

Note

The full text of the description given of the church of S. John, mentioned by Ruy Gonzalez de Clavijo, reads as follows :—

É la primera parte (puerta?) de la Iglesia es muy alta é de obra rica, é delante desta puerta está un grand corral y luego al cuerpo de la Iglesia, é el qual cuerpo es una quadra redonda sin esquinas muy alta, é es cerrada al derredor de tres grandes naves, que son cubiertas da un cielo ellas y la quadra. É ha en ella siete altares, é el cielo desta quadra é naves é las paredés es de obra de musayca muy ricamente labrada, é en ello muchas historias, é la quadra está armada sobre veinte é quatro marmoles de jaspe verde, é las dichas naves son sobradadas, é los sobrados dellas salen al cuerpo de la Iglesia, é alli avia otros veinte é quatro marmoles de jaspe verde, é il cielo de la quadra é las paredes e de obra musayca, é los andamios de las naves salen sobre el cuerpo de la Iglesia, é alli do avia de aver verjas avia marmoles pequenos de jaspe.[1]

With the kind help or Professor Cossio of Madrid, the Spanish text may be roughly translated as follows :—

And the first part (door?) of the church is very lofty and richly worked. And before this door is a large court beside the body of the church ; and the said body is a round hall without corners (or angles), very lofty, and enclosed round about by three large naves, which are covered, they and the hall, by one roof. And it (the church) has in it seven altars ; and the roof of the hall and naves and the walls are or mosaic work very richly wrought, in which are (depicted) many histories. And the (roof of the) hall is placed on

---

[1] *Vida del Gran Tamorlan y itinerario*, pp. 55-56 (Madrid, 1782).

twenty-four marble columns of green jasper (verd antique). And the said naves have galleries, and the galleries open on the body of the church, and these have other twenty-four marble columns of green jasper ; and the roof of the hall and the walls are of mosaic work. And the elevated walks of the naves open over the body of the church,[1] and where a balustrade should be found there are small marble columns of jasper.

Outside the church, adds the ambassador, was a beautiful chapel dedicated to S. Mary, remarkable for its mosaics.

---

[1] *I.e.* From the elevated floors of the galleries one could look over the church.

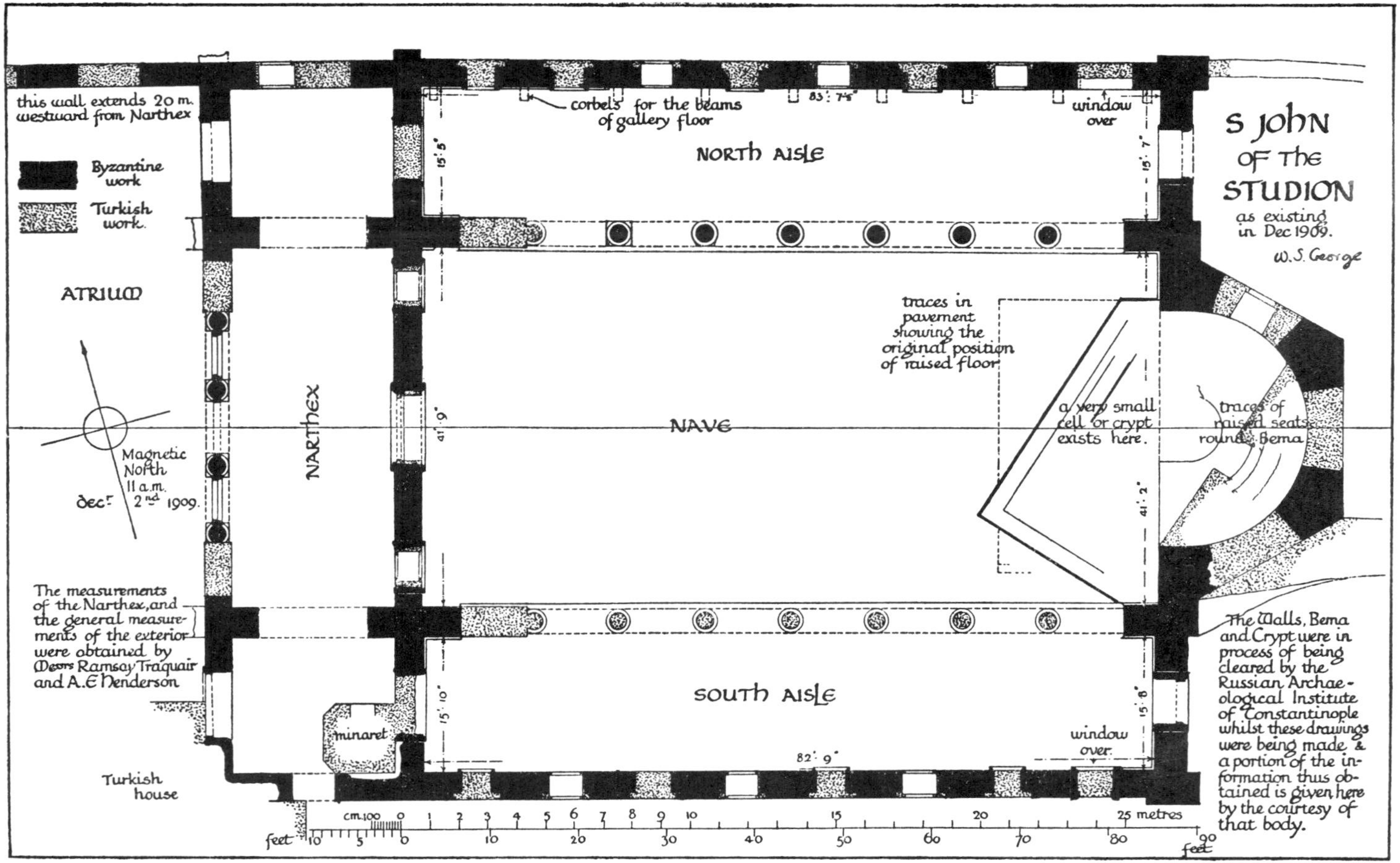

S JOHN OF THE STUDION

as existing in Dec 1906.

W. S. George

The Walls, Bema and Crypt were in process of being cleared by the Russian Archaeological Institute of Constantinople whilst these drawings were being made & a portion of the information thus obtained is given here by the courtesy of that body.

traces of raised seats round the Bema

a very small cell or crypt exists here.

41':2'

window over

15':6'

82':9'

traces in pavement showing the original position of raised floor

83':1½'

NORTH AISLE

corbels for the beams of gallery floor

window over

15':5'

NAVE

15':10'

SOUTH AISLE

41':9'

NARTHEX

minaret

ATRIUM

Magnetic North 11 a.m. Dec.r 2.nd 1909.

this wall extends 20 m. westward from Narthex

Byzantine work.

Turkish work.

The measurements of the Narthex, and the general measurements of the exterior were obtained by Messrs Ramsay, Traquair and A. E. Henderson

Turkish house

metres 25 80 70 20 60 15 50 40 10 30 20 5 10 0 cm.100 50 feet 10 5

FIG. 12.

56

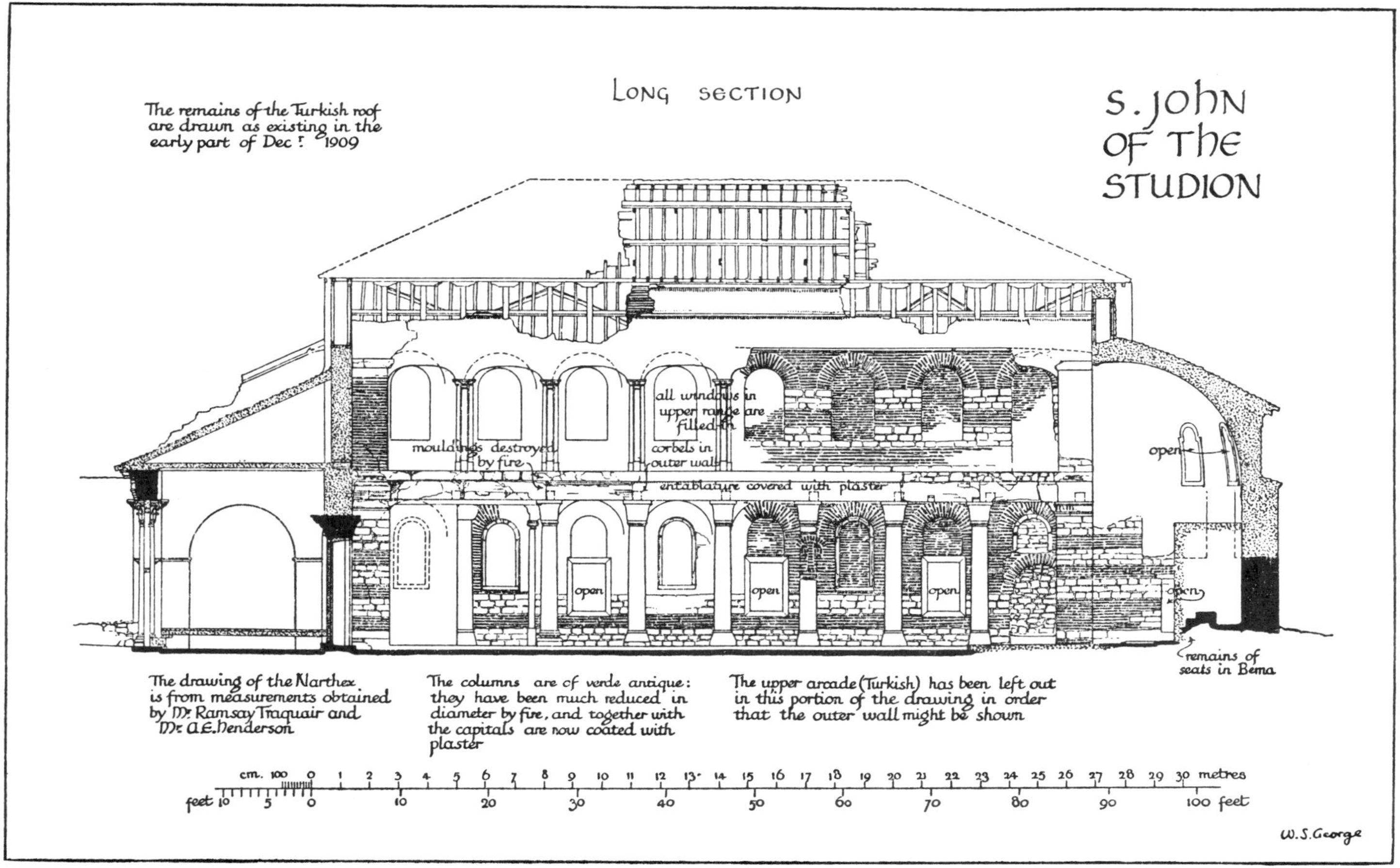

S. JOHN
OF THE
STUDION

LONG SECTION

The remains of the Turkish roof
are drawn as existing in the
early part of Dec.r 1909

The drawing of the Narthex
is from measurements obtained
by Mr Ramsay Traquair and
Dr A.E.Henderson

The columns are of verde antique:
they have been much reduced in
diameter by fire, and together with
the capitals are now coated with
plaster

all windows in
upper row are
filled

corbels in
outer wall

mouldings destroyed
by fire

entablature covered with plaster

The upper arcade (Turkish) has been left out
in this portion of the drawing in order
that the outer wall might be shown

open

open

open

open

open

open

remains of
seats in Bema

W.S.George

cm. 100   0   1   2   3
feet 10   5   0

10   20   30   40   50   60   70   80   90   100 feet
1 2 3 4 5 6 7 8 9 10 11 12 13 14 15 16 17 18 19 20 21 22 23 24 25 26 27 28 29 30 metres

FIG. 13.

57

S JOHN OF THE STUDION

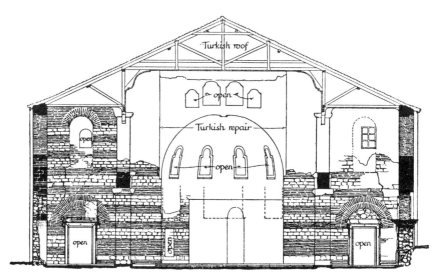

CROSS SECTION LOOKING EAST

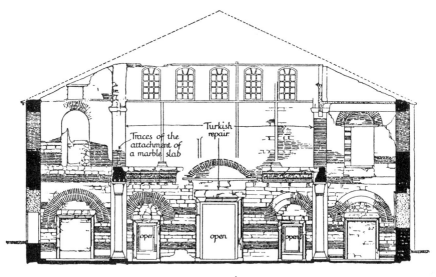

CROSS SECTION LOOKING WEST

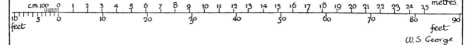

W. S. George

FIGS. 14 AND 15.

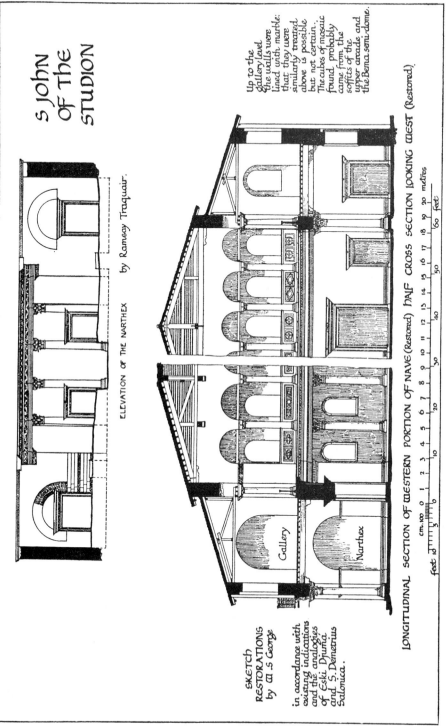

S JOHN OF THE STUDION

ELEVATION OF THE NARTHEX

by Ramsay Traquair.

SKETCH RESTORATIONS by W. S George

in accordance with existing indications and the analogies of Eski Djuma and S. Demetrius Salonica.

Up to the gallery level the walls were lined with marble: that they were similarly treated above is possible but not certain. The cubes of mosaic found probably came from the soffits of the upper arcade and the Bema semi-dome.

Gallery

Narthex

LONGITUDINAL SECTION OF WESTERN PORTION OF NAVE (Restored)   HALF CROSS SECTION LOOKING WEST (Restored).

cm. 100   0   1   2   3   4   5   6   7   8   9   10 metres
feet 10   0   10   20   30   40   50   60 feet

FIGS. 16 AND 17.

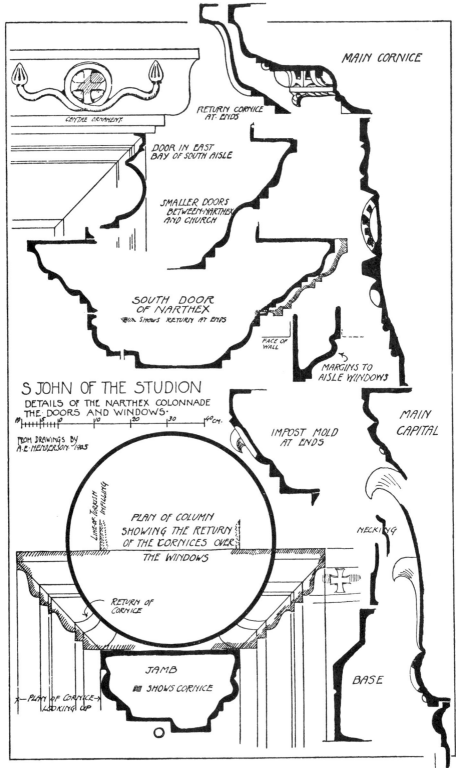

MAIN CORNICE

CENTRE ORNAMENT.

RETURN CORNICE AT ENDS

DOOR IN EAST BAY OF SOUTH AISLE

SMALLER DOORS BETWEEN NARTHEX AND CHURCH

SOUTH DOOR OF NARTHEX

▨ SHOWS RETURN AT ENDS

FACE OF WALL

MARGINS TO AISLE WINDOWS

S JOHN OF THE STUDION

DETAILS OF THE NARTHEX COLONNADE THE DOORS AND WINDOWS.

10   5   0   10   20   30   40 CM.

FROM DRAWINGS BY A·E·HENDERSON· 1905·

IMPOST MOLD AT ENDS

MAIN CAPITAL

LINE OF TURKISH INFILLING

PLAN OF COLUMN SHOWING THE RETURN OF THE CORNICES OVER THE WINDOWS

NECKING

RETURN OF CORNICE

JAMB

▨ SHOWS CORNICE

← PLAN OF CORNICE → LOOKING UP

BASE

60

FIG. 18.

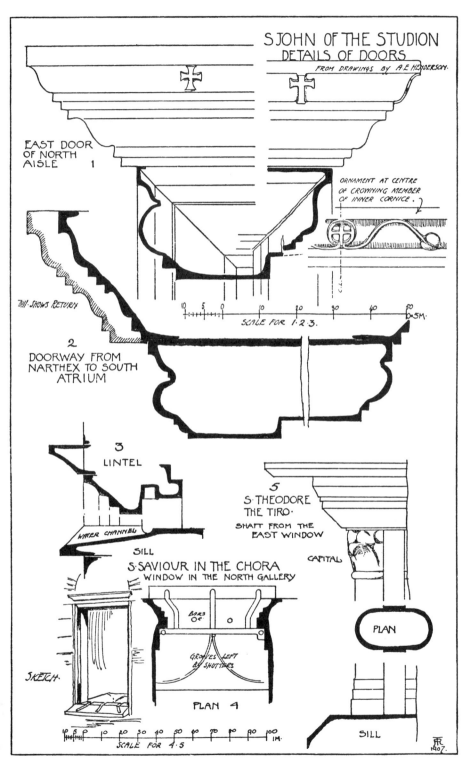

S.JOHN OF THE STUDION
DETAILS OF DOORS
FROM DRAWINGS BY A.E.HENDERSON.

EAST DOOR
OF NORTH
AISLE   1

ORNAMENT AT CENTRE
OF CROWNING MEMBER
OF INNER CORNICE.

THIS SHOWS RETURN

SCALE FOR 1.2.3.

2
DOORWAY FROM
NARTHEX TO SOUTH
ATRIUM

3
LINTEL

WATER CHANNEL

SILL

5
S.THEODORE
THE TIRO.

SHAFT FROM THE
EAST WINDOW

CAPITAL

S.SAVIOUR IN THE CHORA
WINDOW IN THE NORTH GALLERY

BARS
OF

GROOVES LEFT
BY SHUTTERS

SKETCH.

PLAN 4

PLAN

SILL

SCALE FOR 4.5

1M.

FIG. 19.   61

CHAPTER III

THE CHURCH OF SS. SERGIUS AND BACCHUS, KUTCHUK AYA SOFIA

On the level tract beside the Sea of Marmora, to the south of the Hippodrome, and a few paces to the north-west of Tchatlady Kapou, stands the ancient church of SS. Sergius and Bacchus. It is commonly known as the mosque Kutchuk Aya Sofia, Little S. Sophia, to denote at once its likeness and its unlikeness to the great church of that name. It can be reached by either of the two streets descending from the Hippodrome to the sea, or by taking train to Koum Kapou, and then walking eastwards for a short distance along the railroad.

There can be no doubt in regard to its identity. For the inscription on the entablature of the lower colonnade in the church proclaims the building to be a sanctuary erected by the Emperor Justinian and his Empress Theodora to the honour of the martyr Sergius. The building stands, moreover, as SS. Sergius and Bacchus stood, close to the site of the palace and the harbour of Hormisdas.[1] When Gyllius visited the city the Greek community still spoke of the building as the church of SS. Sergius and Bacchus— 'Templum Sergii et Bacchi adhuc superest, cujus nomen duntaxat Graeci etiam nunc retinent.'[2]

The foundations of the church were laid in 527, the year of Justinian's accession,[3] and its erection must have been completed before 536, since it is mentioned in the

---

[1] Procop. *De aed.* i. c. 4 ; Banduri, iii. p. 45.
[2] *De top.* ii. c. 14.　　　　　　　　[3] Cedren. ii. pp. 642-43.

proceedings of the Synod held at Constantinople in that year.[1] According to the Anonymus, indeed, the church and the neighbouring church of SS. Peter and Paul were founded after the massacre in the Hippodrome which suppressed the Nika Riot. But the Anonymus is not a reliable historian.[2]

The church did not stand alone. Beside it and united with it, Justinian built also a church dedicated to the Apostles Peter and Paul,[3] so that the two buildings formed a double sanctuary, having a common court and a continuous narthex. They were equal in size and in the richness of the materials employed in their construction, and together formed one of the chief ornaments of the palace and the city. There was, however, one striking difference between them ; SS. Sergius and Bacchus was a domical church, while SS. Peter and Paul was a basilica. Styles of ecclesiastical architecture destined soon to blend together in the grandeur and beauty of S. Sophia were here seen converging towards the point of their union, like two streams about to mingle their waters in a common tide. A similar combination of these styles occurs at Kalat-Semân in the church of S. Symeon Stylites, erected towards the end of the fifth century, where four basilicas forming the arms of a cross are built on four sides of an octagonal court.[4]

The saints to whom the church was dedicated were brother officers in the Roman army, who suffered death in the reign of Maximianus,[5] and Justinian's particular veneration for them was due, it is said, to their interposition in his behalf at a critical moment in his career. Having been implicated, along with his uncle, afterwards Justin I., in a plot against the Emperor Anastasius, he lay under sentence of death for

---

[1] Mansi, viii. col. 1010.

[2] Banduri, iii. p. 45. The church was visited by Russian pilgrims in 1200, 1350, 1393.—*Itin. russes*, pp. 160, 120, 164.

[3] Procop. *De aed.* i. p. 186. S. Peter 'near the palace' is mentioned in the list of abbots at the Synod of C.P. in 536. Mansi, viii. col. 930, col. 939. Another document of the same Synod, col. 1010, is signed by Peter, hegoumenos of SS. Peter and Paul and of the holy martyrs SS. Sergius and Bacchus.

[4] Diehl, *Manuel d'art byzantin*, p. 31. Antoniadi has drawn my attention to the junction of a basilica and a hexagonal building in a baptistery at Tivoli. See Dehio und Bezold, *Atlas*, plate i. fig. 10.

[5] Synax, Oct. 7.

high treason ; but on the eve of his execution, a formidable figure, as some authorities maintain,[1] or as others affirm, the saints Sergius and Bacchus, appeared to the sovereign in a vision and commanded him to spare the conspirators. Thus Justinian lived to reach the throne, and when the full significance of his preservation from death became clear in the lustre of the imperial diadem, he made his deliverers the object of his devout regard. Indeed, in his devotion to them he erected other sanctuaries to their honour also in other places of the Empire.[2] Still this church, founded early in his reign, situated beside his residence while heir-apparent, and at the gates of the Great Palace, and withal a gem of art, must be considered as Justinian's special thankoffering for his crown.

With the church of SS. Sergius and Bacchus was associated a large monastery known, after the locality in which it stood, as the monastery of Hormisdas, ἐν τοῖς Ὁρμίσδου. It was richly endowed by Justinian.[3]

NOTE

There is some obscurity in regard to the church of SS. Peter and Paul. According to Theophanes,[4] the first church in Constantinople built in honour of those apostles was built at the suggestion of a Roman senator Festus, who on visiting the eastern capital, in 499, was astonished to find no sanctuary there dedicated to saints so eminent in Christian history, and so highly venerated by the Church or the West. As appears from a letter addressed in 519 to Pope Hormisdas by the papal representative at the court of Constantinople, a church of that dedication had been recently erected by Justinian while holding the office of Comes Domesticorum under his uncle Justin I. 'Your son,' says the writer, 'the magnificent Justinian, acting as becomes his faith, has erected a basilica or the Holy Apostles, in which he wishes relics of the martyr

---

[1] Du Cange, iv. p. 135.

[2] Cedren. i. p. 635 ; Procop. *Secret History*, c. 6 ; Procop. *De aed.* ii. p. 234 ; Theoph. p. 339 ; Theoph. Cont. p. 154.

[3] Cedren. i. pp. 642-43. The Synaxaria (Sirmondi) speak of three churches of S. Sergius, in or near Constantinople ; ἐν ταῖς Σοφίαις, Oct. 7 ; πλησίον τῆς Ἀετίου κινστέρνης, Nov. 9 (near Monastery of Manuel, p. 258) ; πέραν ἐν Ῥουφινιαναῖς, May 29 (near Kadikeui).

[4] Page 220.

S. Laurentius should be placed.' 'Filius vester magnificus vir
Justinianus, res convenientes fidei suae faciens, basilicam sanctorum
Apostolorum in qua desiderat Sancti Laurentii martyris reliquias
esse, constituit.' [1]   We have also a letter to the Pope from Justinian
himself, in which the writer, in order to glorify the basilica which
he had built in honour of the apostles in his palace, begs for some
links of the chains which had bound the apostles Peter and Paul,
and for a portion of the gridiron upon which S. Laurentius was
burnt to death.[2]   The request was readily granted in the same year.

The description of the basilica, as situated in the palace then
occupied by Justinian, leaves no room for doubt that the sanctuary to
which the letters just quoted refer was the church of SS. Peter
and Paul which Procopius describes as near ($\pi\alpha\rho\acute{\alpha}$) the palace of
Hormisdas.   In that case the church of SS. Peter and Paul was
built before the church of SS. Sergius and Bacchus, for the inscription
on the entablature in the latter church, not to mention Cedrenus,
distinctly assigns the building to the time when Justinian and
Theodora occupied the throne.   This agrees with the fact that
Procopius [3] records the foundation of SS. Peter and Paul before
that of SS. Sergius and Bacchus, and if this were all he did the
matter would be clear.   But, unfortunately, this is not all Procopius
has done.   For after recording the erection of SS. Sergius and
Bacchus, he proceeds to say that Justinian subsequently ($\check{\epsilon}\pi\epsilon\iota\tau\alpha$)
joined another ($\check{\alpha}\lambda\lambda o$) church,[4] a basilica, to the sanctuary dedicated
to those martyrs, thus leaving upon the reader's mind the impression
that the basilica was a later construction.   To whom that basilica
was consecrated Procopius does not say.   Was that basilica the
church of SS. Peter and Paul which Procopius mentioned before
recording the erection of SS. Sergius and Bacchus ?   Is he speaking
of two or of three churches ?   The reply to this question must take
into account two facts as beyond dispute : first, that the church of
SS. Peter and Paul, as the letters cited above make clear, was earlier
than the church of SS. Sergius and Bacchus ; secondly, that the basilica
united to the latter sanctuary was dedicated to the two great apostles ;
for scenes which, according to one authority,[5] occurred in S. Peter's
took place, according to another authority,[6] in the church of SS.
Sergius and Bacchus.   In the face of these facts, Procopius is either
mistaken in regard to the relative age of the two sanctuaries, or he

---

[1] Baronius, *Annales ecclesiastici*, tom. ix. p. 253, Luccae, 1741 : 'quam basilicam eorum hic in domo nostra sub nomine praedictorum venerabilium con-
structam, illustrare et illuminare large dignemini.'

[2] *Ibid.* p. 254.   [3] *De aed.* i. p. 186.

[4] *Ut supra*, καὶ ἔπειτα καὶ τέμενος ἄλλο ἐκ πλαγίου τούτῳ παρακείμενον (i.e.
SS. Sergius and Bacchus).

[5] Baronius, x. p. 43.   [6] Theoph. p. 349 ; Malalas, p. 485.

has not expressed his meaning as clearly as he might have done. To suppose that two sanctuaries dedicated to the great apostles were built by Justinian within a short time of each other in the same district, one within the palace, the other outside the palace, is a very improbable hypothesis. The question on which side of SS. Sergius and Bacchus the basilica of SS. Peter and Paul stood, seems decided by the fact that there is more room for a second building on the north than on the south of Kutchuk Agia Sofia. Furthermore, there are traces of openings in the north wall of the church which could serve as means of communication between the two adjoining buildings. Ebersolt, however, places SS. Peter and Paul on the south side of SS. Sergius and Bacchus.[1]

A remarkable scene was witnessed in the church in the course of the controversy which raged around the writings known in ecclesiastical history as ' The Three Chapters,' the work of three theologians tainted, it was alleged, with the heretical opinions of Nestorius. Justinian associated himself with the party which condemned those writings, and prevailed upon the majority of the bishops in the East to subscribe the imperial decree to that effect. But Vigilius, the Pope of the day, and the bishops in the West, dissented from that judgment, because the authors of the writings in question had been acquitted from the charge of heresy by the Council of Chalcedon. To condemn them after that acquittal was to censure the Council and reflect upon its authority. Under these circumstances Justinian summoned Vigilius to Constantinople in the hope of winning him over by the blandishments or the terrors of the court of New Rome. Vigilius reached the city on the 25th of January 547, and was detained in the East for seven years in connection with the settlement of the dispute. He found to his cost that to decide an intricate theological question, and above all to assert ' the authority of S. Peter vested in him' against an imperious sovereign and the jealousy of Eastern Christendom, was no slight undertaking. Pope and Emperor soon came into violent collision, and fearing the consequences Vigilius sought sanctuary in the

---

[1] Le Grand Palais. Epigram 8 in the *Anthologia Graeca epigrammatum* (vol. i. Stadt-Mueller) celebrates the erection by Justinian of SS. Peter and Paul, εἰς τὸν ναὸν τῶν ἁγίων ἀποστόλων πλησίον τοῦ ἁγίου Σεργίου εἰς τὰ Ὁρμίσδου.

church of S. Peter[1] as he styles it, but which Byzantine writers[2] who record the scene name S. Sergius.

Justinian was not the man to stand the affront. He ordered the praetor of the city to arrest the Pope and conduct him to prison. But when that officer appeared, Vigilius grasped the pillars of the altar and refused to surrender. Thereupon the praetor ordered his men to drag the Pope out by main force. Seizing Vigilius by his feet, holding him by his beard and the hair of his head, the men pulled with all their might, but they had to deal with a powerful man, and he clung fast to the altar with an iron grip. In this tug-of-war the altar at length came crashing to the ground, the Pope's strong hands still holding it tight. At this point, however, the indignation and sympathy of the spectators could not be restrained ; the assailants of the prostrate prelate were put to flight, and he was left master of the situation. Next day a deputation, including Belisarius and Justin, the heir-apparent, waited upon Vigilius, and in the emperor's name assured him that resistance to the imperial will was useless, while compliance with it would save him from further ill-treatment. Yielding to the counsels of prudence, the Pope returned to the palace of Placidia,[3] the residence assigned to him during his stay in the capital.

Probably at this time arose the custom of placing the churches of SS. Peter and Paul, and SS. Sergius and Bacchus at the service of the Latin clergy in Constantinople, especially when a representative of the Pope, or the Pope himself, visited the city. The fact that the church was dedicated to apostles closely associated with Rome and held in highest honour there, would make it a sanctuary peculiarly

---

[1] Baronius, x. p. 43 'ex domo Placidiana, ubi degebat, confugit ad ibi proxime junctam ecclesiam S. Petri' ; cf. Vigilius' letter, *Ep.* vii. t. i. *Ep. Rom. pont.*

[2] Theoph. p. 349 ; Malalas, p. 485.

[3] *Notitia.* Two palaces bearing similar names stood in the First Region of the city, the *Palatium Placidianum* and the *Domus Placidiae Augustae.* Vigilius refers to the palace in his circular letter, giving an account of his treatment at Constantinople. There also the legates of Pope Agatho were lodged in 680, on the occasion of the First Council in Trullo, and there likewise Pope Constantine in 710, when he came to the East at the command of Justinian II., took up his abode.—Anastasius Bibliothecarius, pp. 54, 65.

acceptable to clergy from Western Europe. This, however, did not confer upon Roman priests an exclusive right to the use of the building, and the custom of allowing them to officiate there was often more conspicuous in the breach than in the observance. Still the Roman See always claimed the use of the church, for in the letter addressed in 880 by Pope Julius VIII. to Basil I., that emperor is thanked for permitting Roman clergy to officiate again in SS. Sergius and Bacchus according to ancient custom : 'monasterium Sancti Sergii intra vestram regiam urbem constitutum, quod sancta Romana Ecclesia jure proprio quondam retinuit, divina inspiratione repleti pro honore Principis Apostolorum nostro praesulatui reddidistis.' [1]

The most distinguished hegoumenos of the monastery was John Hylilas, better known, on account of his learning, as the Grammarian, and nicknamed Lecanomantis, the Basin-Diviner, because versed in the art of divination by means of a basin of polished brass. He belonged to a noble family of Armenian extraction, and became prominent during the reigns of Leo V., Michael II., and Theophilus as a determined iconoclast. His enemies styled him Jannes, after one of the magicians who withstood Moses, to denote his character as a sorcerer and an opponent of the truth. Having occasion, when conducting service in the imperial chapel to read the lesson in which the prophet Isaiah taunts idolaters with the question, 'To whom then will ye liken God, or to what likeness will ye compare him ?' John, it is said, turned to Leo V., and whispered the significant comment, 'Hearest thou, my lord, the words of the prophet? They give thee counsel.' He was a member of the Commission charged by that emperor to collect passages from the Holy Scriptures and the Fathers of the Church that condemned the use of images in worship. Prominent iconodules were interned in the monastery of Hormisdas in the hope that he would turn them from the error of their ways by his arguments and influence. He directed the education of Theophilus and supported the iconoclastic policy pursued by that pupil when upon the throne.

[1] Epistola ccli. See Du Cange, *Const. Christ.* iv. p. 116.

Theophilus appointed his tutor syncellus to the Patriarch Antony, employed him in diplomatic missions,[1] and finally, upon the death of Antony, created him patriarch. The name of John can still be deciphered under somewhat curious circumstances, in the litany which is inscribed on the bronze doors of the Beautiful Gate at the south end of the inner narthex of S. Sophia. When those doors were set up in 838, Theophilus and his empress had no son, and accordingly, in the threefold prayer inscribed upon the doors, the name of John was associated with the names of the sovereigns as a mark of gratitude and esteem. But in the course of time a little prince, to be known in history as Michael III., was born and proclaimed the colleague of his parents. It then became necessary to insert the name of the imperial infant in the litany graven on the Beautiful Gate of the Great Church, and to indicate the date of his accession. To add another name to the list of names already there was, however, impossible for lack of room ; nor, even had there been room, could the name of an emperor follow that of a subject, though that subject was a patriarch. The only way out of the difficulty, therefore, was to erase John's name, and to substitute the name of the little prince with the date of his coming to the throne ; the lesser light must pale before the greater. This was done, but the bronze proved too stubborn to yield completely to the wishes of courtiers, and underneath Michael's name has kept fast hold of the name John to this day. The original date on the gate also remains in spite of the attempt to obliterate it.

SS. Sergius and Bacchus was one of the sanctuaries of the city to which the emperor paid an annual visit in state.[2] Upon his arrival at the church he proceeded to the gallery and lighted tapers at an oratory which stood in the western part of the gallery, immediately above the Royal Gates, or principal entrance to the church. He went next to the chapel dedicated to the Theotokos, also in the

---

[1] 'Under the microscope of modern historical criticism, . . . it is not surprising to find that the famous embassy of John the Grammarian to the court of Baghdad must be rejected as a fiction irreconcilable with fact.'—Prof. Bury in the *English Historical Review*, April 1909. But he was sent on other embassies.

[2] Constant. Porphyr. pp. 87-88.

gallery, and after attending to his private devotions there, took his place in the parakypticon (ἐν τῷ παρακυπτικῷ τοῦ θυσιαστηρίου), at the north-eastern or south-eastern end of the gallery, whence he could overlook the bema and follow the public service at the altar.[1] In due course the Communion elements were brought and administered to him in the chapel of the Theotokos ; he then retired to the metatorion (a portion of the gallery screened off with curtains), while the members of his suite also partook of the Communion in that chapel. At the close of the service he and his guests partook of some light refreshments, biscuits and wine, in a part of the gallery fitted up for that purpose, and thereafter returned to the palace.

Architectural Features

In the description of the architectural features of the church and for the plans and most of the illustrations in this chapter I am under deep obligation to Mr. A. E. Henderson, F.S.A. The information gained from him in my frequent visits to the church in his company, and from his masterly article on the church which appeared in the *Builder* of January 1906, has been invaluable.

In design the church is an octagonal building roofed with a dome and enclosed by a rectangle, with a narthex along the west side. This was a favourite type of ecclesiastical architecture, and is seen also in another church of the same period, San Vitale of Ravenna, in which Justinian and Theodora were interested. There, however, the octagonal interior is placed within an octagonal enclosure. The adoption of a rectangular exterior in the Constantinopolitan sanctuary is a characteristic Byzantine feature.[2] S. Vitale was founded in 526, a year before SS. Sergius and Bacchus.

As an examination of the plan will show, the architect's

---

[1] Similar to the parakypticon at the east end of the southern gallery in S. Sophia. Reiske (*Comment. ad Constant. Porphyr.* p. 195) defines it as ' Fenestra, quae in sacrificatorium despicit e catechumeniis.' Cf. on the whole subject, Antoniadi, Ἔκφρασις τῆς Ἁγίας Σοφίας, vol. ii. p. 291, note 101 ; p. 331, note 190 ; p. 332.

[2] The plan of SS. Sergius and Bacchus is similar to that of the cathedral of Bosra (511-12), which was also dedicated to the same saints. Fergusson, *History of Ancient and Mediaeval Architecture*, vol. i. p. 432.

design has not been followed with strict accuracy, and the result is that both the enclosing square and the interior octagon are very irregular figures.   Furthermore, the two portions of the building have not the same orientation, so that the octagon stands askew within its rectangular frame. How this lack of symmetry should be explained, whether due to sloven work or the result of the effort to adapt the church to the lines of the earlier church of SS. Peter and Paul, with which it was united, is difficult to decide.

The court which stands before the Turkish portico in front of the west side of the building represents the old atrium of the church, and to the rear of the portico is still found the ancient narthex.   At the south end of the narthex is a stone staircase leading to the gallery.   The arch at the foot of the staircase is built of fragments from the old ciborium or eikonostasis of the church.   The great height (0.24 metre or 9 inches) of the steps is found, according to Mr. Antoniadi, also in S. Sophia.

The exterior walls, which are mostly in brick and rubble masonry, exhibit poor workmanship, and have undergone considerable repair, especially on the east.   On the south there are two thicknesses of walling.   The outer thickness has arched recesses at intervals along its length, corresponding to openings in the inner thickness, and thus while buttressing the latter also enlarges slightly the area of the church.   The length of the rectangular enclosure from west to east is 101 feet, with an average breadth of $77\frac{1}{2}$ feet from north to south, excluding the recesses in the latter direction.

All the windows of the church have been altered by Turkish hands, and are rectangular instead of showing semi-circular heads.

The passage intervening between the rectangular enclosure and the octagon is divided into two stories, thus providing the church with an ambulatory below and a gallery above.

The domed octagon which forms the core of the building stands at a distance of some $18\frac{1}{2}$ feet from the rectangle within which it is placed.   It measures $53\frac{1}{2}$ feet by $50\frac{1}{2}$ feet. The eight piers at its angles rise to a height of $33\frac{1}{2}$ feet from the floor to the springing of the dome arches. The archways thus formed, except the bema arch, are filled in with two pairs of columns in two stories set on the outer plane of the piers. The lower colonnade is surmounted, after the classic fashion, by a horizontal entablature profusely carved ; while the upper columns are bound by arches, thus making seven sides of the octagon a beautiful open screen of fourteen columns and as many triple arcades, resplendent with marbles of various hues and rich with carved work. The mass of the piers is relieved by their polygonal form, a fluted cymatium along their summit, and a repeating design of a flower between two broad leaves below the entablature. Though the flower points upwards it has been mistaken for a cluster of grapes.[1] At the four diagonal points the sides of the octagon are semicircular, forming exhedrae, an arrangement which gives variety to the lines of the figure, widens the central area, secures more frontage for the gallery, and helps to buttress the dome. The same feature appears in S. Sophia, whereas in San Vitale all the sides of the octagon, excepting the eastern side, are semicircular. The extension of the interior area of a building (square or octagonal) by means of niches at the angles or in the sides, or both at the angles and in the sides, was a common practice.[2]

There is considerable difference in the size of the piers and the dome arches. The eastern piers stand farther apart than their companions, and consequently the arch over them, the triumphal arch of the sanctuary, is wider and loftier than the other arches. The bays to the north-east and the south-east are also wider than the bays at the opposite angles. The apse is semicircular within, and shows three sides on the exterior. As in S. Sophia and S. Irene, there is no prothesis or diaconicon.

The pairs of columns, both below and above, are

---

[1] Gyllius, *De Top. C.P.* ii. c. 16. If the design represented vine leaves and grapes, it surely did not allude to the god Bacchus, but to the vine in the gospel of S. John. The small columns on the piers are Turkish.

[2] Antoniadi, *S. Sophia*, vol. ii. pp. 7-9, draws attention to the development of buildings with sides turned into exhedrae, from their simplest form to their culmination in S. Sophia. He refers for illustrations to plans in Dehio und Bezold. *Die kirchliche Baukunst des Abendlandes*, vol. i. pp. 23-31 ; *Atlas*, vol. i. plate i. figures 1, 2, 3, 4, 7 ; plate iii. figures 1, 2, 7.

alternately verd antique and red Synnada marble, resting on bases of the blue-veined white marble from the island of Marmora. The capitals on the lower order are of the beautiful type known as the 'melon capital,' a form found also in San Vitale at Ravenna and in the porch of S. Theodore in Constantinople (p. 246). The neckings are worked with the capitals, and enriched by 'egg-and-dart' pointing upwards. In the centre of the capitals was carved the monogram of Justinian or that of Theodora. Most of the monograms have been effaced, but the name of the empress still appears on the capital of the western column in the south bay, while that of Justinian is found on the first capital in the south-western bay ; on both capitals in the north-western bay, accompanied by the title Basileus ; and, partially, on the last capital in the north-eastern bay.

In the soffit of the architrave are sunk panels of various patterns, the six-armed cross occurring twice. The beadings of the fasciae are enriched with the designs commonly known as ' rope,' ' bead-and-reel,' ' egg-and-dart,' and again ' bead-and-reel.'

The frieze is in two heights. The lower portion is a semicircular pulvinar adorned with acanthus leaves, deeply undercut ; the upper portion is occupied by a long inscription in raised ornamental letters to the honour of Justinian, Theodora, and S. Sergius. The cornice is decorated with dentils, ' bead-and-reel,' projecting consols, ' egg-and-dart,' and leaves of acanthus.

The inscription (Fig. 20) may be rendered thus : Other sovereigns, indeed, have honoured dead men whose labour was useless. But our sceptred Justinian, fostering piety, honours with a splendid abode the servant of Christ, Creator of all things, Sergius ; whom nor the burning breath of fire, nor the sword, nor other constraints of trials disturbed ; but who endured for the sake of God Christ to be slain, gaining by his blood heaven as his home. May he in all things guard the rule of the ever-vigilant sovereign, and increase the power of the God-crowned Theodora whose mind is bright with piety, whose toil ever is unsparing efforts to nourish the destitute.

The inscription is not mere flattery to the founders of the church. Justinian and Theodora were devout after the fashion of their day, and took a deep interest in the poor. The empress erected an asylum for fallen women, hostels for strangers, hospitals for the sick, and homes for the destitute. 'On the splendid piece of tapestry embroidered in gold which formed the altar cloth of S. Sophia, she was represented with Justinian as visiting hospitals and churches.'[1]

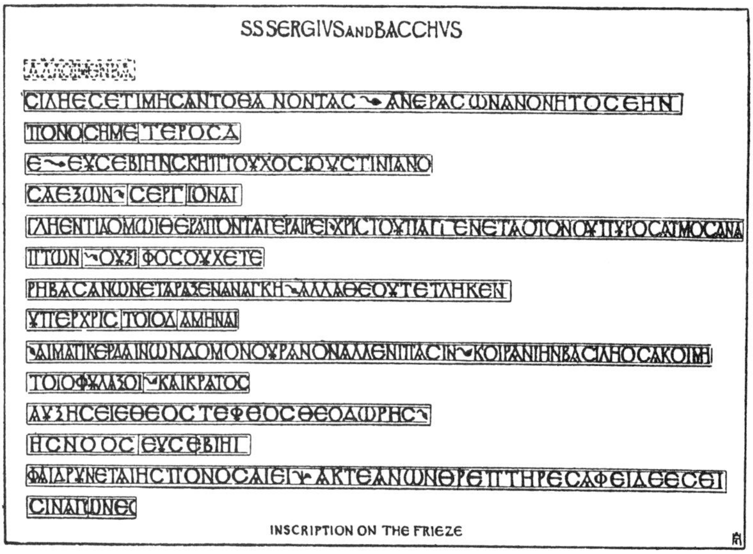

SS SERGIVS AND BACCHVS

INSCRIPTION ON THE FRIEZE

FIG. 20.

To the rear of the southern straight side of the octagon two columns stand under the gallery, with wide fillets worked on both sides of their bases, shafts, and capitals, showing that a frame of stone or wood was once affixed to them. The capitals are of the ordinary cushion type and bear on opposite faces the monograms Justinian, Basileus.

Two feet above the cornice, or twenty feet from the floor of the church, the level of the gallery is reached.[2]

[1] C. Diehl, *Theodora*, pp. 242, 342.
[2] The ratio of the height of the gallery above the floor of the church to the height of the summit of the dome is, according to Antoniadi, $\frac{1}{3\cdot5}$, the same as in S. Sophia as built by Anthemius.

Here the columns are smaller than those below, and are bound together by arches instead of by an architrave. Their capitals represent the type known as the 'Pseudo-Ionic' or cushion capital, in view of its broad head. It appears appropriately here as the form of capital required to carry the impost of an arch upon a capital. At one time, indeed, that demand was met by placing upon the capital a distinct block of stone, a fragment, so to speak, of the horizontal architrave. It is the device adopted in San Vitale at Ravenna, S. Demetrius of Salonica, and elsewhere, but never it would seem in Constantinople, except in the underground cisterns of the city. It was, however, too inartistic to endure, and eventually was superseded by capitals with a broad flattened head on which the wide impost of an arch could rest securely.[1]

A free form of acanthus, deeply undercut on the face towards the central area of the church, covers the capitals, and in the centre of that face, on all the capitals except the eighth (counting from the north-east) is carved the monogram of the title Basileus, or of Justinian, or of Theodora.

In the south side of the gallery stand two columns corresponding to the two columns in the aisle below. They are poor in design and not original. The western capital is 'Pseudo-Ionic,'[2] with a plain cross on the northern face. The eastern capital is in the basket form with roundels on the four faces. Two additional columns are found in the western portion of the gallery. They are of verd antique and larger than the other columns in this story of the church, and have sunk crosses in them. The splendour of the interior decoration has certainly been dimmed, for the walls of the edifice once gleamed with marbles and glittered with mosaics. 'By the sheen of its

---

[1] 'Pulvins,' says Rivoira (*Lombardic Architecture*, p. 11, English translation), 'serve the purpose of providing the springers of the arches with a base corresponding to the wall which they carry, while allowing the support beneath to be much slighter without injuring the stability of the structure.'

[2] Rivoira, *ut supra*, p. 62 : 'The volutes in the Pseudo-Ionic capital intended to conceal the abruptness of the transition from the square of the pulvin to the round.'

marbles,' says Procopius,[1] 'it was more resplendent than the sun, and everywhere it was filled profusely with gold.' When Ferguson examined the building, remains of frescoes or of mosaics, which have disappeared since his time, could be distinguished in the narthex. The soffit, both of the upper and of the lower cymatium on the piers, projects sufficiently to admit the application of the customary marble incrustation. The proportions of the building are marred by the boarded floor which rises seventeen centimeters above the original pavement, disguising the real elevation of the dome and of the columns in the lower colonnade. But notwithstanding all changes for the worse the building is still a beautiful structure. Very effective especially is the happy combination of the various lines and forms here brought together—the rectilinear and the semicircular sides of the octagon, the octagonal fabric and the round dome that crowns it, the horizontal entablature stretched along the summit of the lower story of columns and the arches that leap from column to column in the gallery. This harmonious variety of form has also a historical significance. An old order in architecture and a new order here meet and embrace before the earlier, having served its age, passes away and the later comes triumphant to fill another era of the world with fresh beauties. Here in the tide of time we look before and after.

To the student of architecture the dome of this church is specially interesting. In the application of the dome to the octagon no pendentives are employed. The octagon is carried up to the base of the dome, which is built in sixteen longitudinal compartments that impinge upon one another and form groins giving to the dome its strength and sweep. On the groins is a plaster moulding, probably Byzantine. The eight compartments directly above the dome arches are flat, and flush with the inner face of the octagon, and in each of them is a semicircular-headed window. They rise perpendicular to a point a little above the windows, and then curve with a radius to the centre of the dome. On the other hand the eight compartments directly above the angles of the octagon are narrower than the preceding

[1] *De aed.* i. p. 187.

compartments ; they have no windows, and, what is of special importance to note, they are deeply concave.[1]   Such marked hollowness is found in later domes as a decorative feature, but here it is primarily and supremely a constructive device. By its means the concave compartments are set slightly back

FIG. 21.—VIEW OF THE EXTERIOR OF THE DOME OF SS. SERGIUS AND BACCHUS.

from the octagon's inner face, leaving, at the springing line, portions of the wall-head to appear as little flat ledges on each side of the angles.   This is a most skilful expedient,

---

[1] 'The centres of the radii of these concave compartments are formed by having three points given the groins on either side and the angle of the octagon in the centre.   With these points for each compartment the radius is given, and an arc turned giving the concavity required for each web at its springing.'—A. E. Henderson in the *Builder*, January 1906, p. 4.

and compares favourably with the methods employed elsewhere to apply the dome to the octagon.[1] In the octagonal church of S. Lorenzo at Milan the octagon is turned into the circle by the introduction of squinches. In San Vitale a considerable walling is built between the line of the octagon and the springing line of the dome, while the bed for the dome is formed by introducing, in the space over the angles of the octagon, niches which are worked above to the circle on plan. On the other hand, it is interesting to compare with these methods the method employed in the baptistery of S. Sophia, now a Sultan's Turbé, near the southern entrance to the inner narthex. Although the walls of the building describe a square on the exterior, they form an octagon on the interior with semicircular bays at the diagonals, as in SS. Sergius and Bacchus. But in the application of the dome the true pendentive is used. The baptistery was erected shortly before S. Sophia, and in view of the erection of the great church.

The curvature of the dome of SS. Sergius and Bacchus has three zones, which have respectively a radius of m. 8, (drawn from the centre of the octagon), m. $3\frac{1}{4}$, and m. $9\frac{1}{2}$, (centre about m. 2, below the springing of the dome). The first extends to a point a little above the heads of the dome windows ; the second about m. 2 higher ; the third to the crown of the dome. The groins stop short a little below the dome's apex, where they are arched into one another, leaving a saucer-shaped crown now capped by a Turkish finial. The dome is covered with lead, and presents an undulating surface owing to the protuberance of its eight concave compartments.[2]

---

[1] In S. George of Ezra in Syria (515), as Mr. E. M. Antoniadi informs me, the dome overhangs or oversails the angles of the octagon.

[2] 'The dome stands within a polygon of sixteen sides, that rises four metres above the springing line, keeping the dome taut and weighting the haunches. Against this polygonal casing are set buttresses formed by the extension of the piers of the octagon to within m. $1\frac{1}{2}$ from the cornice of the dome. These buttresses are in their turn respectively strengthened, on the rear, by two small buttresses ; of which those on the north, south, east, and west sides rest on an arch of the gynecaeum, and carry the thrust to the outer walls of the church, while the others rest on the exhedrae and the vaulting of the gynecaeum. Furthermore, from the summit of the buttresses formed by the piers of the octagon a small buttress is set against the cupola itself up to the cornice.' This marshalling of the

The system of weighting and buttressing the dome displays great skill, and will be best understood by studying Mr. Henderson's geometrical and constructive sections of the systems (Figs. 28, 29).

buttresses around the dome in three tiers, while securing the stability of the structure, is moreover strikingly artistic.   See Fig. 21.

At east end of south aisle.

In the gallery.

Fig. 22.—Brick Stamps in SS. Sergius and Bacchus.
(From rubbings by Mr. A. E. Henderson.)

S.S. SERGIVS AND BACCHVS.

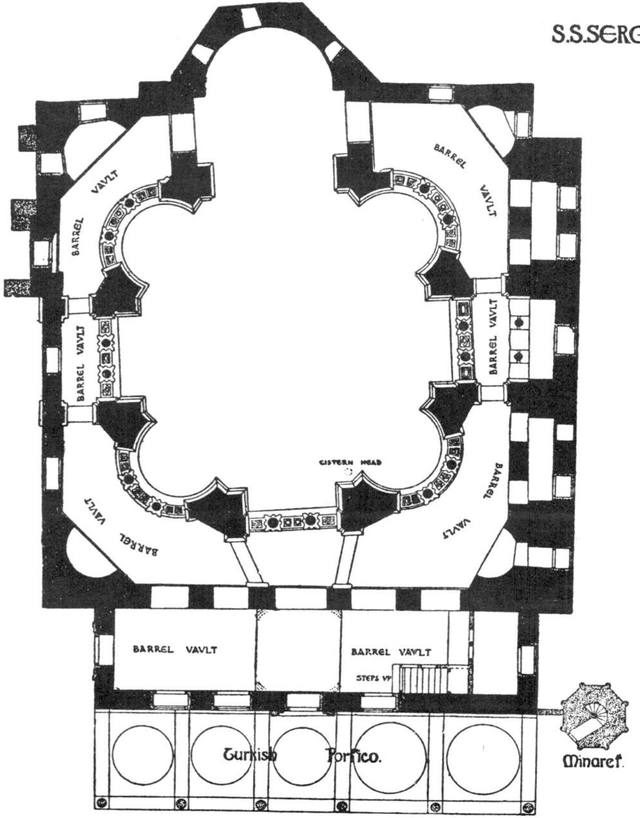

GROUND PLAN
LOOKING UP
SCALE 10 5 0   10   20   30
SCALE 100 0 100

FIG. 23.

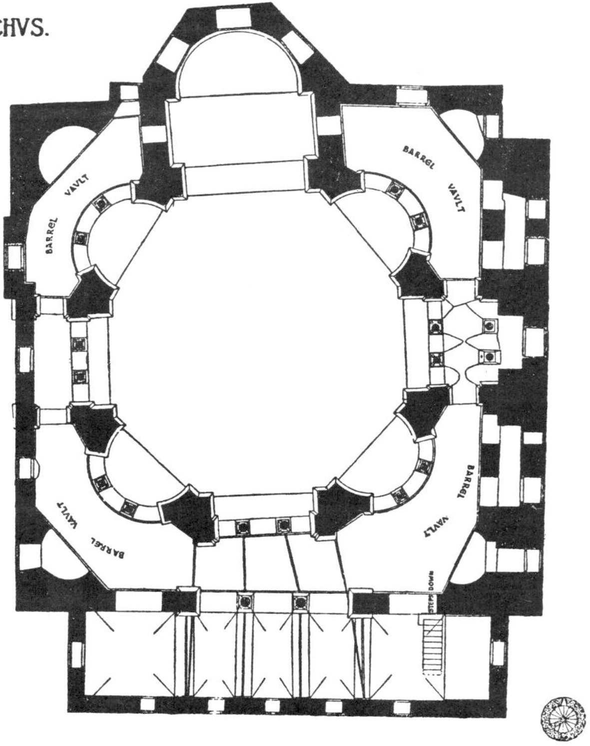

GYNAECEVM PLAN
LOOKING UP
90   100 FEET
30.00 OF METRES

THE WALLS TINTED GREY
ARE TURKISH WORK

AUTHUR E HENDERSON FSA.

FIG. 24.

BARREL VAVLT

Minaret.

Curniss Portico.

BARREL VAVLT

BARREL VAVLT

STEPS VP

CISTERN HEAD

80

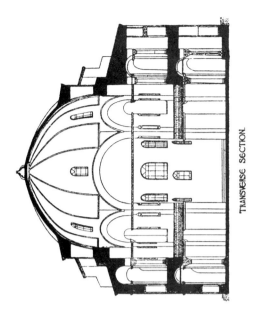

TRANSVERSE SECTION.

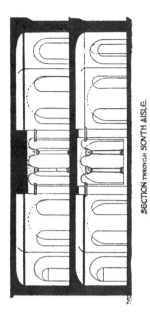

SECTION THROUGH SOUTH AISLE.

ARTHUR E HENDERSON F.S.A

SCALE OF FEET
100

90 80 70 60 50 40 30 20 10 5 0

3000 2500 2000 1500 1000 500

SCALE OF METRES

FIGS. 25, 26, AND 27

PLAN AT BASE OF DOME,
DOTTED LINES LOOKING UP

81

G

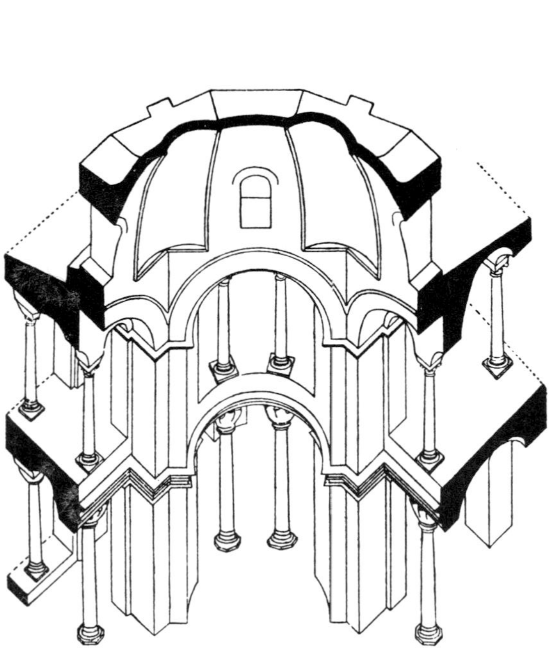

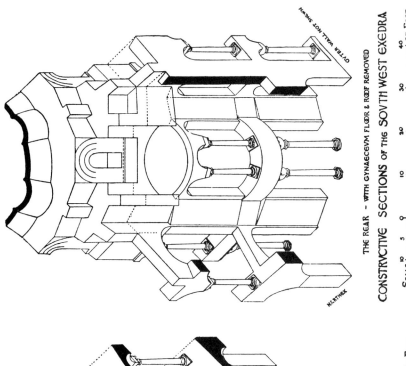

THE INTERIOR ARRANGEMENT
SHEWING GYNAECEVM FLOOR VAVLTING ROOF AND
SPRINGING OF DOME

FIG. 28.

THE REAR - WITH GYNAECEVM FLOOR & ROOF REMOVED

CONSTRVCTIVE SECTIONS OF THE SOVTH WEST EXEDRA

FIG. 29.

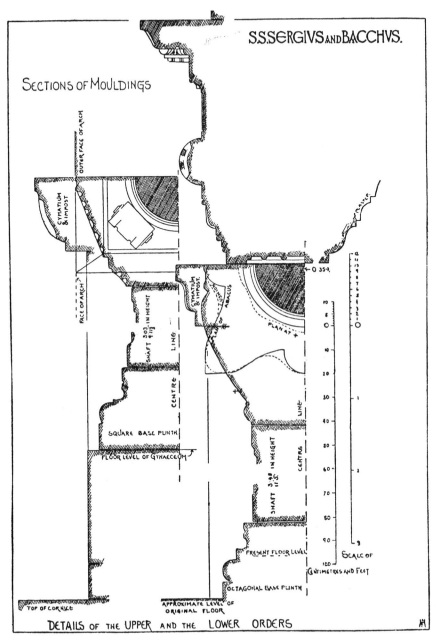

S.S. SERGIVS AND BACCHVS.

SECTIONS OF MOULDINGS

OUTER FACE OF ARCH

CYMATIUM & IMPOST

FACE OF ARCH?

SHAFT 3.03 IN HEIGHT 9'11½"

CENTRE LINE

SQUARE BASE PLINTH

FLOOR LEVEL OF GYNAECEUM

TOP OF CORNICE

← 0.35 →

CYMATIUM & IMPOST

ABACUS

PLAN AT ✛

CENTRE LINE

SHAFT 3.58 IN HEIGHT 11'5"

PRESENT FLOOR LEVEL

OCTAGONAL BASE PLINTH

APPROXIMATE LEVEL OF ORIGINAL FLOOR

0 1 2 3 4 5 6 7 8 9 10 11 12

10
5
0
10
20
30
40
50
60
70
80
90
100

SCALE OF CENTIMETRES AND FEET

DETAILS OF THE UPPER AND THE LOWER ORDERS

FIG. 30.   83

CHAPTER IV

THE CHURCH OF S. IRENE

THE church of S. Irene stands at a short distance to the north-east of S. Sophia, in the first court of the Seraglio. Its identity has never been questioned, for the building was too much in the public eye and too near the centre of the ecclesiastical affairs of the city to render possible any mistake concerning its real character. It is always described as close to S. Sophia.[1] According to the historian Socrates,[2] it was originally one of the Christian sanctuaries of the old town of Byzantium, a statement we may well believe, seeing Byzantium was the seat of a bishop before the foundation of Constantinople. The designation of the church as 'the Ancient' or 'the Old Church,' Ecclesia Antiqua, ἡ παλαιά,[3] and the special regard cherished for the church during the earlier history of the city, are also thus best explained. The original sanctuary was small,[4] but when Byzantium became the capital of the East the old fabric was enlarged and beautified by Constantine the Great to harmonize with its grander surroundings, and was dedicated to Peace, in honour of the rest and quiet which settled upon the Roman world when the founder of the city had vanquished all his rivals after eighteen years of civil war.[5]

---

[1] Socrates, ii. c. 6 ; *Corpus juris civilis,* Nov. iii. c. 3. 2 ; *Itin. russes,* p. 119.
[2] Socrates, ii. c. 16. So also the author of the *Vita Pauli Patr. C.P.* The Church of S. Irene, which the Anonymus (Banduri, ii. p. 31) says had once been a heathen temple, was the church of S. Irene, τὸ πέραμα.
[3] *Notitia, regio secunda* ; Codin. *De aed.* p. 73.
[4] Socrates, *loc. cit.*
[5] *Ibid.*

NOTE

Other churches of the same name were found in Constantinople :
S. Irene in the Seventh Region, according to the *Notitia.* S. Irene
in Sykai (Galata), πέραν ἐν Συκαῖς ; Theophanes, p. 353.   S. Irene by
the Sea, πρὸς θάλασσαν ; Nicetas Choniates, p. 269 ; Synax., Jan. 10.
The last was also known as the New, Νέα ; Synax., Jan. 23.   Erected
in the reign of the Emperor Marcian, it was partially restored by
the Emperor Manuel Comnenus after its destruction by fire ; Nicet.
Chon. *ut supra.*   It was styled likewise ' at the Ferry,' τὸ πέραμα ;
Codinus, *De aed.* p. 89 ; Banduri, ii. p. 31.

Until the year 360, when the church of S. Sophia was
opened to public worship by the Emperor Constantius,
S. Irene appears to have been the cathedral of the city.
Hence, probably, the name sometimes given to it, the
Patriarchate, τὸ πατριαρχεῖον.[1]   Nor did the church lose its
primacy altogether even after the erection of S. Sophia.
On the contrary, the two churches were regarded as forming
one sanctuary ; they were enclosed within the same court,
served by the same clergy, and known by the same name,
' the Great Church,' ἡ Μεγάλη ᾿Εκκλησία.[2]   S. Irene was
again the sole cathedral building, while S. Sophia lay in ruins
for eleven years after being set on fire in 404, on the
occasion of the final banishment of John Chrysostom.

S. Irene comes prominently into view during the fierce
struggle between the adherents of the Nicene Creed and the
Arians, in the half-century which followed the inauguration
of New Rome.   Having been persuaded that the point at
issue between the two theological parties was not essential,
and that the agitation of the question was due to love of
disputation, Constantine the Great, who valued peace at
almost any price, attempted to suppress the controversy
by his authority, and accordingly ordered the Patriarch
Alexander to admit Arius, then present in the city, to the
Holy Communion.   With this order Alexander, a champion
of the Nicene Creed, refused to comply.   Whereupon the
followers of Arius decided to have recourse to violence.   But
on the very eve of the day fixed to carry out their purpose,
Arius was taken suddenly ill in the Forum of Constantine

[1] Banduri, ii. p. 52.   [2] Socrates, ii. c. 16.

and died on the spot. The historian Socrates regards the event as the act of God, for when the patriarch heard what the heretics intended to do, he retired to the church of S. Irene, and there for many days and nights, with fasting and tears, and with his lips pressed to the altar, implored divine succour in his terrible extremity. 'If the opinions of Arius be true,' the patriarch prayed, 'let me die ; but if they are false let him be judged.' The tragic end of Arius was considered the answer to that prayer.

Upon the death of Alexander in 343, at the age of ninety-eight, the two parties came into collision in regard to the question of his successor. The deceased prelate had recommended two persons as suitable to fill his place : the presbyter Paul, because of his abilities ; the deacon Macedonius, on account of his age and venerable appearance. The Arians favoured Macedonius, as more in sympathy with their opinions ; the orthodox, however, carried the election and installed Paul in S. Irene. The defeated party seems to have submitted, but the Emperor Constantius, a violent Arian, quashed the election, and appointed Eusebius of Nicomedia, a prominent upholder of the views of Arius, bishop of the capital. Upon the death of Eusebius in 346 the theological combatants again seized the opportunity to try their strength. The orthodox recalled Paul ; the Arians consecrated Macedonius. Incensed by these proceedings, Constantius, then at Antioch, ordered Hermogenes, the magister militum in Thrace, to proceed to Constantinople and drive Paul from the city. But no sooner did Hermogenes attempt to execute his instructions than the populace rose, burnt his house to the ground, and after dragging him along the streets, killed him. The emperor was furious. He hurried back to Constantinople, banished Paul, and reduced by one-half the amount of free bread daily distributed among the citizens. Nor did he fully recognize Macedonius as bishop. Under these circumstances Paul made his way to Rome, and, having secured the support of the Pope, reappeared in Constantinople as the rightful bishop of the see. But the emperor, again in Syria, was not to be baffled. More angry than ever, he

sent peremptory orders to Philip, the prefect of Constantinople, to expel Paul and to recognize Macedonius.
By skilful arrangements Paul was quietly removed from the
scene. But to install Macedonius was a more difficult
undertaking. The prefect, however, ordered his chariot,
and with Macedonius seated by his side made for S. Irene,
under an escort of troops carrying drawn swords. The
sharp, naked weapons alarmed the crowds in the streets,
and without distinction of sect or class men rushed for the
church, everybody trying to outstrip his neighbour in the
race to get there first. Soon all the approaches to the
building were packed to suffocation ; no one stirred back-
wards or forwards, and the prefect's chariot was unable to
advance. What seemed a hostile barricade of human beings
welded together obstructed his path. In vain did the
soldiers brandish their swords in the hope of frightening the
crowd to disperse. The crowd stood stock still, not because
it would not, but because it could not move. The soldiers
grew angry, resorted to their weapons, and cut a way to the
church through that compact mass of humanity at the cost
of 3150 lives ; some of the victims being crushed to death,
others killed at the point of the sword. So was Macedonius
conducted to his throne in the temple of Peace.[1] But the conflict between the opposite parties continued, and after six years
spent in efforts to recover his position, Paul was restored to
office through the intervention of the Pope of Rome, of the
Emperor Constans, and of the Synod of Sardica. It was a
brief triumph. In 350 Paul was exiled for life to Cucusus,
and Macedonius ruled once more in his stead.[2] For the
next thirty years S. Irene with the other churches of the
capital remained in the hands of the Arians.

During that period the Nicene faith was preached by
Gregory of Nazianzus only in a small chapel, subsequently
dedicated to S. Anastasia.[3] But with the accession of
Theodosius the Great the adherents of the Creed of Nicaea
prevailed, and the Second General Council, held in Constantinople in 381, adopted that creed as the true faith of the
Christian Church.

[1] Socrates, ii. c. 16.   [2] *Ibid.* ii. 13, 15, 16.   [3] *Ibid.* v. 7.

According to the biographer of S. Stephen the Younger, who enumerates the six ecumenical councils, and indicates, in most cases, where each met, that famous Council met in the church of S. Irene.[1] But Theodore Lector[2] says the Council assembled in the church of Homonoia, and explains the name of that church as commemorative of the harmony which prevailed among the bishops who gathered there on that occasion. As a matter of fact, one of the churches of the city bore the name Homonoia.[3] Possibly the discrepancy between the statements of the authors just mentioned may be due to a confusion arising from a similar meaning of the names of the two churches.

According to the Anonymus,[4] the usurper Basiliscus took refuge with his wife and children in S. Irene, when he was overthrown in 477, and the Emperor Zeno recovered the throne. But, according to the *Paschal Chronicle*,[5] Basiliscus fled on that occasion to the great baptistery of S. Sophia. As that baptistery stood between S. Irene and S. Sophia and may have served both churches, the difference between the two statements is not serious.

After standing for two centuries the Constantinian edifice was burnt to the ground by the fire which the rebel factions in the Nika Riot set to the offices of the prefect on Friday, the 16th of January 532. The building had narrowly escaped the same fate in the fire which destroyed S. Sophia earlier in the course of the riot, and might have survived also the conflagration in which it actually perished, but for the strong wind which carried the flames from the praetorium to the church, devouring on their way the bath of Alexander, a part of the hospice of Eubulus, and the hospital of Sampson with its patients.

The restoration of the church was included in the

---

[1] *Vita S. Stephani Junioris,* Migne, *P.G.* 100, col. 1144, ἡ δευτέρα ἐν Κπλει ἐν τῷ ναῷ τῆς ἁγίας Εἰρήνης.

[2] Theodore Lector, ed. Valesius (1748), p. 533. Eutychius afflicted by the divine anger went ἐν τῷ εὐαγεῖ εὐκτηρίῳ ἔνθα πεπίστευται ἀναπαύεσθαι μέρος ἱερῶν λειψάνων τῶν θεσπεσίων Πανταλέοντος καὶ Μαρίνου, ἐπικαλουμένου τοῦ τόπου Ὁμόνοια ἐκ τοῦ ἐκεῖ συνελθόντας τοὺς ἑκατὸν πεντήκοντα ἐπισκόπους ἐπὶ Θεοδοσίου τοῦ μεγάλου βασιλέως. The passage is preserved in John Damascene, *De imaginibus,* book iii.

[3] *Notitia, Regio nona,* 'continet in se ecclesias duas, Cenopolim et Omonaeam.'   [4] Banduri, ii. p. 25.   [5] *Ad annum* 478.

magnificent scheme of Justinian the Great to build on the wilderness of ashes created by his rebel subjects the finest monuments of his empire. And so S. Irene rose from its ruins, the largest sanctuary in Constantinople, except S. Sophia.[1] The bricks bearing the mark ' the Great Church,' Μεγάλη Ἐκκλησία, which are built into a raised bank against the northern wall of the atrium, afford no indication of the date when S. Irene was rebuilt. The bank is of comparatively recent origin.[2]

In the month of December 564, the thirty-seventh year of Justinian's reign, another great fire threatened to destroy the buildings which that emperor had erected in the quarter of the city beside S. Sophia. The hospital of Sampson was again burnt down ; the atrium of the Great Church, known as the Garsonostasion, suffered ; two monasteries close to S. Irene perished, and, what most concerns us, the atrium and part of the narthex of S. Irene itself were consumed.[3] How soon these injuries were repaired is not recorded.

During the 176 years that followed the reconstruction of the church by Justinian, S. Irene does not appear in history. But in 740 it was injured by the earthquake which shook Constantinople in the last year of the reign of Leo III. the Isaurian.[4] Theophanes[5] is very precise in regard to the time when the disaster occurred ; it was on the 26th of October, the ninth indiction, on a Wednesday, at eight o'clock. The damage done both in the city and in the towns of Thrace and Bithynia was terrible. In Nicaea only one church was left standing, while Constantinople deplored the ruin of large portions of the landward fortifications and the loss of many churches, monasteries, and public monuments. S. Irene was then shaken, and, as the examination of the building by Mr. George has proved, sustained most serious injuries. The Emperor Leo died about six months after the disaster, and it is therefore uncertain whether the church was rebuilt before his death. His first attention was

---

[1] Procop. De aed. i. c. 2 ; Pasch. Chron. p. 622.
[2] For this information I am indebted to Mr. W. S. George.
[3] Theoph. p. 371.
[4] Patr. Nicephorus, in Breviario.   [5] Theoph. p. 634.

naturally directed to the reconstruction of the fortifications of the city, where his name still appears, with that of his son and successor Constantine Copronymus, as the rebuilder of the fallen bulwarks. But although there is no record of the precise date at which the ruined church was repaired, we may safely assume that if the work was not commenced while Leo III. sat upon the throne, it was undertaken soon after the accession of Constantine Copronymus. S. Irene was too important to be long neglected, and was probably rebuilt during the ascendancy of the iconoclasts.

The church reappears for a moment in 857 during the dispute which raged around the persons of Ignatius and Photius as to which of them was the lawful patriarch. While the partisans of the latter met in the church of the Holy Apostles to depose Ignatius, the few bishops who upheld the claims of Ignatius assembled in S. Irene to condemn and depose Photius with equal vehemence.[1]

The church comes into view once more in connection with the settlement of the quarrel caused in 907 by the fourth marriage of Leo VI. the Wise. As the union was uncanonical, the Patriarch Nicholas deposed the priest who had celebrated the marriage ; he, moreover, refused the Communion to the emperor, and treated Zoe, the emperor's fourth wife, as an outcast. For such conduct Nicholas lost his office, and a more pliant ecclesiastic was appointed in his place. The inevitable result followed. The religious world was torn by a schism which disturbed Church and State for fifteen years. At length Romanus I. summoned a council of divines to compose the agitation, and peace was restored in 921, by a decree which condemned a fourth marriage, but allowed a third marriage under very strict limitations. So important was this decision regarded that it was read annually, in July, from the pulpit, and on that occasion the emperor, with the patriarch, attended service in S. Irene, and at its close took part in a procession from S. Irene to S. Sophia, on the way back to the Great Palace.[2]

---

[1] Mansi, xv. 211 ; xvi. p. 18. See *Basile I.* par Albert Vogt, p. 206.
[2] Const. Porphyr. *De cer.* p. 186 ; Cedren. ii. pp. 265, 275, 297. Readers of Russian are referred to D. Belaev, ' The Church of S. Irene and the Earthquake

On Good Friday the patriarch held a service for catechumens (κατήχησις) in S. Irene, which the patricians were
required to attend.[1]

The church of S. Irene has never been used as a mosque.
After its enclosure within the precincts of the Seraglio
soon after the Turkish conquest, it was converted into an
armoury, probably because it stood in the court occupied
by the body of Janissaries who formed the palace guard,
and it has served that military purpose, in contradiction to
its name, for the most part ever since. For several years it
contained the first collection of antiquities made by the
Turkish Government, and some of the objects in that
collection still remain to recall the use of the building as a
museum ; the most interesting of them being the chain
stretched across the mouth of the Golden Horn during the
siege of 1453, the monument to the charioteer Porphyrios,
and the pedestal of the silver statue of the Empress Eudocia,
which played a fatal part in the relations of that empress to
the great bishop of Constantinople, John Chrysostom. Since
the establishment of the constitutional régime in the Ottoman Empire the building has been turned into a Museum
of Arms.

Architectural Features

Until the recent establishment of constitutional government in Turkey it was impossible to obtain permission to
study this church in a satisfactory manner, so jealously was
even entrance into the building guarded. The nearest
approach to anything like a proper examination of the
building was when Salzenberg was allowed to visit the church
in 1848, while the church of S. Sophia was undergoing
repairs under the superintendence of the Italian architect
Fossati. But the liberty accorded to Salzenberg was not
complete, and, consequently, his plan of the church published

in C.P. 28 June 1894,' *Vizantisky Vreinennik*, i., St. Petersburg, 1894, parts
iii.-iv. section iii. pp. 769-798, and the article by the same author on the
'Interior and Exterior View of S. Irene' in the same periodical, 1895, parts i.
ii. section i. pp. 177-183. For the references to these articles I am indebted to
Mr. Norman E. Baynes, one of our younger Byzantine scholars.

[1] Const. Porphyr. *De Cer.* p. 179.

in his *Altchristliche Baudenkmäler von Konstantinopel* is marred by serious mistakes. Happily the new Government of the Empire is animated by an enlightened and liberal spirit, and at the request of His Excellency Sir Gerard Lowther, H.B.M. Ambassador to the Sublime Porte, permission was granted to the Byzantine Research and Publication Fund to have the church examined as thoroughly as its condition allowed, and to make all the plans, drawings, and photographs required in the interests of a scientific knowledge of its architectural character. The Byzantine Research and Publication Fund was fortunate in having as its president, Edwin Freshfield, LL.D., so long distinguished for his devotion to Byzantine archaeology, and it is mainly due to his generosity that the means necessary for carrying on the study of the church were provided. The society was, moreover, most happy in being able to secure the services of an architect in Mr. W. S. George, who already possessed considerable experience in the investigation of Byzantine buildings at Salonica and elsewhere. Fortunately, also, the building was at the same time placed under repair, in view of its conversion into a museum of arms, thus affording exceptional facilities for the erection of scaffolding and the removal of plaster and other obstructions. Mr. George gave nearly five months to the study of the church, and the results of his careful investigations will appear in a monograph to be published by the Byzantine Research and Publication Fund. But with great courtesy, in view of the fact that I was engaged on the present work, and also because I waived my own application for leave to study S. Irene in favour of the application made by the Byzantine Fund, I have been allowed to anticipate that monograph by making use of some of the results of Mr. George's investigations. For this permission I am very grateful, as it will add much to the value of this volume. I visited the church frequently while Mr. George was at work upon it, and my account of its architectural features is based entirely upon the information he then kindly supplied, and upon the notes he has communicated to me since his return to England.

The architectural feature which gives to this building a peculiar interest, in the study of the development of planning and construction, is the more complete fusion of the basilican type of plan with a domical system of roofing which it presents than is found in any other example of a similar combination.

On the west, where the ground retains its original level, stands the old atrium, though much modified by Turkish repairs and alterations. It had covered arcades on the north, south, and west sides, but only the outer walls of the northern and southern arcades, with some portions of their inner walls, and three complete vaulted bays at the northern end of the western arcade, are Byzantine. The walls, vaults, and piers in other parts of the arcades are Turkish. There is no trace of the west door which, under ordinary circumstances, would form the main entrance to the atrium, but a Byzantine doorway, now built up, is found close to the narthex, in the outer wall of the south arcade. The area of the atrium has been, moreover, greatly reduced by the erection, on its four sides, of an inner range of Turkish vaulting.

Five doors led from the atrium to the narthex, but only the central and the northernmost of these doors are now open, the latter entrance still retaining its original architrave and cornice of white marble, with the usual mouldings and a cross worked on the crowning member of the cornice. The present entrance to the church, however, is on the north side of the building, through a porch that leads down a sloping Turkish passage to the western end of the north aisle.

The narthex is in five bays, the two terminal bays having cross-groined vaults, the three central, vaults of a domical character with blunt rounded groins at the springing. The whole vaulting surface of the narthex was once covered with mosaics exhibiting mainly a geometrical pattern.

From the narthex three tall arched openings conducted to the nave, and one opening to each aisle. But the direct communication between the narthex and the northern aisle is now cut off by the insertion of the Turkish entrance to the church, although the old doorway to the aisle remains complete.

The nave is divided into two large bays of equal breadth but unequal length, the western bay being the shorter. In the latter the arches which support its roof are, to the east and west, semicircular, while those to north and south are roughly elliptical, springing from the same level and rising to the same height as the semicircular arches, but being of shorter span. These elliptical arches extend to the outer walls of the church, thus partaking of the character of short barrel vaults.

Upon these arches is raised what has been called an elliptical dome. But in no part has it the character of a true ellipse, nor does it spring from its supporting arches in the simple regular manner of a dome, but in the complex manner of a vault built upon arches of unequal curvature. It should therefore rather be called a domical vault. Where it shows above the roof it has the appearance of a modified and very low cone covering an irregular elliptical drum.

The eastern bay of the nave is square on plan, bounded by semicircular arches, all extended so as to form short barrel vaults. The western arch is joined to the eastern arch of the western bay, thus forming a short barrel vault common to both bays. The vault to the east runs to the semi-dome of the apse ; whilst the vaults to north and south, like the corresponding vaults in the western bay, extend to the outer walls and cover the eastern portions of the aisles and galleries. Above the supporting arches regular pendentives are formed, and above these there is a drum carrying a dome. The apse to the east of the nave is semicircular within and covered by a semi-dome.

Between that semi-dome and the eastern barrel vault of the nave a break is interposed, giving the bema arch two orders or faces, with their external and internal angles rounded off, and the whole surface of the semi-dome and of the bema arch is covered with mosaic. At one time the mosaic extended also over the surface of the barrel vault. The decoration in the semi-dome consists of a large cross in black outline upon a gold ground ; below the cross there are three steps set upon a double band of green that runs round the base of the semi-dome. A geometrical border bounds the semi-dome, and then comes the following inscription, an extract from Psalm lxv. verses 5, 6 (the lxiv. in the Septuagint version), on the inner face of the arch :

(ΔΕΥΤ ΕΙ)CΟΜΕΘΑ ΕΝ ΤΟῖC ΑΓΑΘΟῖC ΤΟΥ ΟῖΚΟΥ CΟΥ, ΑΓΙΟC Ο ΝΑΟC CΟΥ ΘΑΥΜΑCΤΟC ΕΝ ΔΙΚΑΙΟCΥΝΗ ΕΠΑΚΟΥCΟΝ ΗΜΩΝ Ο Θ[ΕΟ]C Ο C[ΩΤ]ΗΡ ΗΜΩΝ Η ΕΛΠΙC ΠΑΝΤΩΝ ΤΩΝ ΠΕΡΑΤΩΝ ΤΗC ΓΗC ΚΑΙ ΤΩΝ ΕΝ ΘΑΛΑCCΗ ΜΑΚ(ΡΑ)[Ν].

(Come we will go ?) in the good things of thy house. Holy is thy temple. Thou art wonderful in righteousness. Hear us, O God our Saviour ; the hope of all the ends of the earth and of them who are afar off upon the sea.

The letters enclosed within curved brackets and the accents [1] above them are paint only ; the letters within square brackets are not in the inscription, but are supplied where evident contractions render that course necessary. The remaining letters are in unrestored mosaic.

Probably (Δεῦτ᾽ εἰσ)όμεθα is a mistake of the restorer for the word πλησθησόμεθα in the original text. ʻWe shall be filled with the goodness (or the good things) of thy house.ʼ

Three other geometrical patterns in mosaic succeed, after which follows a broad wreath of foliage on the outer face of the bema arch and the words :

(Ο Ο)ΙΚΟΔΟΜΩΝ ΕΙC Τ(ΟΝ ΟΙΚΟΝ CΟΥ ΚΑΙ) ΑΝΑΒΑCΙΝ ΑΥΤΟΥ, ΚΑΙ ΤΗΝ ΕΠΑΓΓΕΛΙΑΝ (ΤΟΥ ΑΓΙΟΥ ΠΝΕΥΜΑΤΟC ΕΥ ΗΜΑC ΗΛΠΕΙCΑΜΕΝ ΕΙC ΤΟ Ο)ΝΟΜΑ Α(ΥΤΟΥ).

The mosaic above the crown of the semi-dome has been injured and restored imperfectly in plaster, paint, and gilt. Hence the large black patch in it which includes the upper arm of the cross.

The letters enclosed within curved brackets are in paint and are manifestly the work of a restorer who has spoiled the grammatical construction of the words and obscured the meaning of the inscription. The remaining letters are in unrestored mosaic.

---

[1] Only some of the accents are indicated in the transcription.

I venture to suggest that the original text was a quotation from Amos ix. 6, with possibly some variations :

ὁ οἰκοδομῶν εἰς τὸν οὐρανὸν ἀνάβασιν αὐτοῦ καὶ τὴν ἐπαγγελίαν αὐτοῦ ἐπὶ τῆς γῆς θεμελιῶν.

'He who builds his ascent up to the heaven and his command on the foundations of the earth.'

The words, ἠλπείσαμεν εἰς τὸ ὄνομα αὐτοῦ, 'we have hoped in his name,' may be original (Psalm xxxii. 21 ; Isaiah xxvi. 8).

With these inscriptions may be compared the beautiful collect used at the consecration of a church :

Ἀκολουθία εἰς ἐγκαίνια ναοῦ.

Ναὶ Δέσποτα Κύριε ὁ Θεὸς ὁ Σωτὴρ ἡμῶν, ἡ ἐλπὶς πάντων τῶν περάτων τῆς γῆς, ἐπάκουσον ἡμῶν τῶν ἁμαρτωλῶν δεομένων σου καὶ κατάπεμψον τὸ πανάγιόν σου Πνεῦμα τὸ προσκυνητὸν καὶ παντοδυνάμενον καὶ ἁγίασον τὸν οἶκον τοῦτον.

'Yea, Lord God Almighty our Saviour, the hope of all the ends of the earth, hear us sinners when we call upon thee, and send thy Holy Spirit, the worshipful and all powerful, and sanctify this house.'

Below the windows of the apse are ranges of seats for the clergy, forming a sloping gallery, and consisting of eleven risers and eleven treads, so that, according to the method of seating adopted, there are five or six or eleven rows of seats. There is no vestige of a special episcopal seat in the centre, but the stonework has been disturbed ; for some of the seats are built with portions of the moulded base of the marble revetment of the building. Underneath the seats runs a narrow semicircular passage originally well lighted through openings [1] in the riser of one range of seats, and having a doorway at each end.

On either side of the nave, towards the eastern end of each aisle, there is an approximately square compartment covered with a domical vault, and having an opening communicating with the nave immediately to the west of the bema. To the east of these compartments stands what was the original eastern wall of the church, and in it, in the north aisle, a large doorway retaining its architrave and

---

[1] These openings are now covered with Turkish wooden staging, and the passage is therefore quite dark.

cornice, is still found. Of the corresponding doorway in the
south aisle only the threshold is left. These doorways
must have communicated with the outer world to the east
of the church, like the doorways which occupy a similar
position in the Studion (p. 53). The northern compartment
had an opening, which is still surmounted by architrave and
cornice, also in its north wall. There are, moreover, four
other openings or recesses in the northern wall of the
church, and two in the southern.

The main portions of the aisles are divided from the
nave by light screens of columns, the eastern and western
portions being connected by passages driven through the
dome piers. In the eastern nave bay there are four columns,
giving five aisle bays on each side. The columns are very
slender, without any base moulding, and stand upon square
pedestals, now framed round with Turkish woodwork. On
opening one of these frames the pedestal was found to be a
mutilated and imperfectly squared block of stone. Such
blocks may have served as the core of a marble lining, or
may be damaged material re-used.

The capitals are of the ' Pseudo-Ionic' type, with roughly
cut Ionic volutes. The sinking on their lower bed is too
large for the necks of the columns. Towards the aisles they
bear the monograms of Justinian and Theodora, identical
with the monograms of these sovereigns in S. Sophia,
while on the side towards the nave they have a cross in low
relief. Usually monograms are placed in the more conspicuous position.

Above the capitals the vaulting that covers the aisles
and supports the galleries is of an uncommon type. Towards
the nave the arches are narrow and raised upon very high
stilts ; from each capital a semicircular arch is thrown
across to the outer wall, where is a range of windows, each
of which has an extrados at a slightly higher level than
the extrados of the corresponding nave arch ; and thus a
long narrow space is left between the four arches of each
vault compartment that could be filled, wholly or in part,
without the use of centering. The result is a narrow,
irregularly curved vault, shaped to the backs of each of its

H

surrounding arches, and having, in the main, the character of a spherical fragment.

The western portion of each aisle is divided from the nave by an irregular arcade supported by a pier and one column, and, consequently, there are three aisle bays to the western nave bay, and not four as shown by Salzenburg.

The whole interior surfaces of the walls, up to the level of the springing of the gallery vaulting, and the nave walls, up to the gallery level, were once faced with marble. This is proved by the presence in the walls of many marble plugs and some iron holdfasts, as well as by remains of the moulded base of the facing.

At the eastern extremity of the aisles there are chambers formed by walls built, as the vertical straight joints and difference of materials employed indicate, at various periods. The chamber at the end of the northern aisle has an arch-way, now built up, in its eastern wall, and seems to have served as a vestibule. It is in these chambers that Salzenberg supposes the staircases leading to the galleries stood, but it is evident from the character of the walls and vaulting that no such staircases could ever have existed there.

The galleries extend over the narthex and over the whole length of the aisles. Access to them is now obtained by a wooden staircase and landing of Turkish construction, but how they were reached in Byzantine times is not evident. Possibly the fragments of wall on the exterior face of the south wall of the narthex and the traces of vaulting beside them may be the remains of a staircase. Or a staircase may have stood to the west of the narthex over the vaulting of the atrium, where projecting spurs of walls appear.

The vaulting of the gallery over the narthex was originally similar to that of the narthex itself, but only the cross-groined vaults at the corners are Byzantine ; the three central compartments are Turkish. Five windows in the western wall looked into the atrium, and as many openings in the eastern wall into the nave and side galleries. Below the former range is a string-course corresponding to that which runs round the interior of the building at gallery level.

The gallery over each aisle consists of two open portions under the dome arches, divided from each other by the dome piers, which are pierced to connect the different parts of the gallery with each other, and with the gallery over the narthex. In the side walls there is a range of windows at gallery level; five on each side of the eastern nave bay, three in the south wall of the western nave bay, but none, at present, in its northern wall. Above these windows are two ranges of windows in each lunette under the dome arches, a system of five and three in the eastern bay, and of four and two in the western bay. All these windows, now square-headed, had originally semicircular heads. The lunette filling the western dome arch had doubtless a similar window arrangement, though at present it has only one window.

The eastern ends of the side galleries have been formed into separate chambers since the Turkish occupation. Of the additions beyond the original east wall of the church, that to the north was connected with the gallery by a tall wide arch, while that to the south was divided off from the gallery with only a small door as a means of communication. The southern addition was divided into two chambers as on the ground floor.

The walls above gallery level and the large vaulting surfaces of the building are now covered with plaster, but a close examination proves that if any mosaic or marble revetment ever existed above gallery level, none of it, excepting the mosaic in the apse, remains.

Looking next at the exterior of the building, it is to be observed that the ground on the north, south, and east has been raised as much as fifteen feet. In many places the walls have undergone Turkish repair. The apse shows three sides. The drum of the dome is pierced by twenty semicircular-headed windows (of which only five are now open), and as their arches and the dome spring at about the same level the heads of the windows impinge upon the dome's surface. Two low shoulders cover the eastern pendentives. The plan of the drum is peculiar. From the shoulders, just mentioned, to the windows, it is a square with rounded corners, one side of the square being joined with and buried in the drum of the western dome vault ; but upon reaching the base of the windows it becomes an accurate circle in plan, and at the springing of the window arches is set back, leaving a portion of the piers to appear as buttresses. The upper portion of the drum is carried well up above the springing of the dome, leaving a large mass of material properly disposed so as to take the thrusts produced.

The careful examination of the building by Mr. George has proved that the fabric is not the work of one age, but consists of parts constructed at different periods. For the full evidence on the subject we must await the forthcoming monograph on the church. Here, only the main results of Mr. George's survey can be presented.

Up to the level of the springing of the aisle vaults, the walls of the main body of the building, excepting the narthex and the additions at the east end of the church, are built of large well-squared stones laid in regular courses, and are homogeneous throughout.

Above that level the walls are built in alternate bands of brick and stone, five courses of brick to five courses of stone being the normal arrangement. The stones in this portion of the walls are smaller and much more roughly squared than those below the springing of the aisle vaults. This brick and stone walling is, so far as could be ascertained, homogeneous right up to the domical vault and the dome. As usual the arches and vaults are in brick. A point to be noted is that the recesses or openings in the lower part of the north and south walls of the church do not centre with the windows and vaulting above them ; sometimes, indeed, the head of an opening comes immediately below a vaulting arch or rib. Again, at the north-eastern external angle of the apse the wall up to the level of the springing of the aisle vaulting is in stone, but above that level in brick, and the two portions differ in the angle which they subtend. Evidently there has been rebuilding from a level coinciding

with the springing of the aisle vaulting. Projecting above
the ground at the same place is a square mass of stonework
that was left unbuilt upon when that rebuilding took place.
The narthex is built of brick, with bands of large stone at
wide intervals, and is separated by distinct joints from the
upper and lower walls of the body of the church. Furthermore, while the two eastern bays on each side of the western
portion of the nave continue and belong to the unusual
system of vaulting followed in the aisles, the bay on each
side immediately adjoining the narthex belongs to the vaulting system found in the narthex, and has, towards the nave,
an arch precisely similar to the arches between the nave and
the narthex. The division between the two systems is well
marked, both in the nave and in the aisles, and points clearly
to the fact that the narthex and the body of the church are
of different dates.

Thus the architectural survey of the building shows that
the principal parts of the fabric represent work done upon it
on three great occasions, a conclusion in striking accord with
the information already derived from history. For we have
seen (p. 89) that after the destruction of the original Constantinian church by fire in the Nika Riot, Justinian the Great
erected a new sanctuary upon the old foundations ; that
later in his reign another fire occurred which necessitated the
reconstruction of the narthex of that sanctuary ; and that
some two centuries later, towards the close of the reign of Leo
the Isaurian, the church was shaken by one of the most violent
earthquakes known in Constantinople, and subsequently
restored probably by that emperor or by his son and successor Constantine Copronymus. Accordingly, leaving minor
changes out of account, it is safe to suggest that the walls of
the body of the church, up to the springing of the aisle vaults,
belong to the new church built by Justinian after the Nika
Riot in 532 ; while the narthex, the aisle vaults immediately
adjoining it, and the upper portion of the western end of
the south wall, represent the repairs made probably by the
same emperor after the injuries to the fabric caused by
the fire of 564. The earthquake of 740 must therefore
have shaken down or rendered unstable all the upper part

of the building, but left standing the narthex, the gallery above it, and the lower part of the walls of the church. Consequently, the upper part of the building, the apse, the dome-arches, the dome-vault, and the dome with its drum, belong to the reconstruction of the church after that earthquake.

The buttresses to the apse where it joins the main eastern wall are later additions, and still later, but before Turkish times, are the short walls at the north and south-eastern corners forming the small eastern chambers.

Of the building erected by Constantine the Great the only possible vestige is the square projection at the north-eastern angle of the apse, but that is an opinion upon which much stress should not be laid.

In harmony with these conclusions is the evidence afforded by the mosaics found in the church. Those of the narthex are of the same character as the mosaics in S. Sophia, Constantinople, and may well have been executed under Justinian. On the other hand, the mosaics in the apse are characteristic of the iconoclastic period, the chief decoration there being a simple cross. For, as Finlay [1] has remarked, Leo the Isaurian ' placed the cross on the reverse of many of his gold, silver, and copper coins, and over the gates of his palace, as a symbol for universal adoration.' A similar iconoclastic decoration and a portion of the same verses from Psalm lxv. formed the original decoration of the apse in S. Sophia, Salonica.

Thus also is the presence of capitals bearing the monograms of Justinian and Theodora explained, seeing those sovereigns were intimately connected with the church. And thus also is a reason suggested why those monograms face the aisles instead of the nave ; it was a position which would be assigned to them by a later restorer of the church who was obliged to use old material, and at the same time felt anxious to conceal the fact as much as possible, lest the glory of the previous benefactors of the church should eclipse his own renown.

The conclusion that in the present building we have

[1] *History of the Byzantine Empire*, p. 34, Everyman Edition.

parts representing different periods solves also the problem
of the elliptical domical vault. For it is difficult to imagine
that a Byzantine architect with a free hand would choose to
build such a vault. But given the supports Mr. George
believes were left standing after the earthquake of 740, and
given also the narthex on the west, the architect's liberty was
limited, and he would be forced to cover the space thus
bounded in the best way the circumstances allowed.

How the western portion of the church was roofed in
Justinian's time it is impossible to say with certainty.
There are buttress slips in the south wall at gallery level
and in the nave below, where the break occurs in the arcade,
that suggest the existence, in the church as originally built
by Justinian, of a narthex carrying a gallery. In that case
the length of the barrel vault over the western part of the
church would be about the length of the barrel vault over
the eastern part, and the church would then show in plan a
regular cross with a dome at the centre, two lateral doors,
one of which is now built up, giving access to the ends of
the narthex.

The dates here assigned to the different parts of the
building simplify the problem of the tall drum below the
main dome. That this could have been built by Justinian,
as has been supposed, is difficult of belief if the large domes
which are known to have been built by him are carefully
examined. It is true that the drum dome of S. Sophia,
Salonica, has also been claimed for Justinian, but that drum
is low and only partially developed, and although its date is
not known, the consensus of opinion is against its being so
early. The whole question of the development of the drum
still awaits treatment at the hands of an investigator who has
thoroughly studied the buildings themselves, and perhaps
the publication of the results obtained by Mr. George at
S. Sophia, Salonica, and S. Irene, Constantinople, two crucial
examples, will throw some light on the subject. For the
present the date here given for the drum of S. Irene (*i.e.*
towards the middle of the eighth century) is an inherently
probable one.

In the foregoing description of S. Irene there is no

pretence to an exhaustive statement of facts, or any claim that the conclusions reached are final. There is still too much plaster on the walls to permit a complete examination of the building. But the conclusions here suggested are those which agree best with the evidence which has been brought to light by Mr. George under present circumstances.

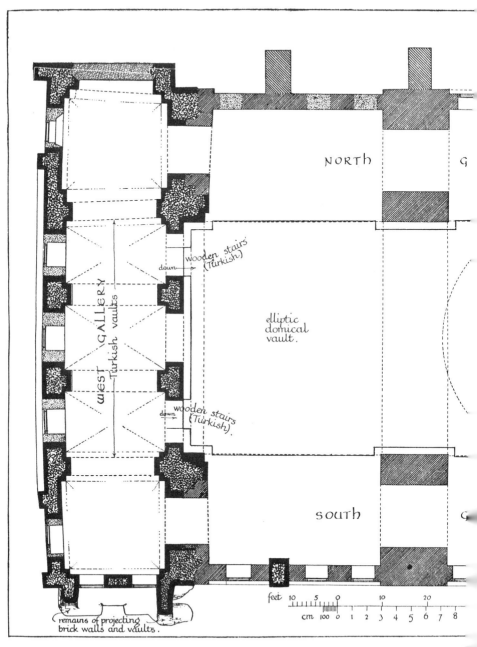

NORTH G

WEST GALLERY Turkish vaults

wooden stairs (Turkish)
down

elliptic domical vault.

wooden stairs (Turkish)
down

SOUTH G

remains of projecting brick walls and vaults.

feet 10 5 0 10 20

cm 100 0 1 2 3 4 5 6 7 8

F

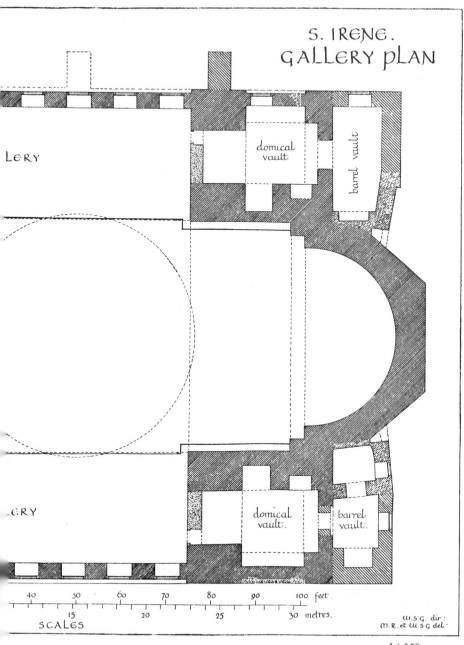

S. IRENE.
GALLERY PLAN

LERY

domical
vault

barrel vault

LERY

domical
vault.

barrel
vault.

SCALES

40   50   60   70   80   90   100 feet.

15   20   25   30 metres.

ա.ѕ.Ԍ. dir:
ጠ.R.et ա.ѕԌ del.

I : 250

The existing square-headed Turkish windows
are shown within the original semicircular-headed openings.
The pedestals below the columns of nave arcade are at
present cased in wood ; one of these was uncovered, and
was found to be a roughly-squared stone block : there is
evidence that two others are similar.

S. IRENE
LONGITUOINAL SECTION

SCALES

w.s.g.dir. m.r. et w.s.g. del.

I : 250

33.

The general wall-surfaces are more or less covered with plaster, but where the construction beneath has been ascertained, it is shown : the existing square-headed Turkish windows are indicated within the original semicircular-headed openings.

feet 10 5 0   10   20   30   40   50 feet
cm 100 0 1 2 3 4 5 6 7 8 9 10   15 metres

SCALES

present ground le

floor level

FIG.

S. IRENE
SOUTH ELEVATION

(external)

in South Aisle.

W.S.G dir.
M.R. et W.S.G del.

I : 250

To face page 104.

SCALES

feet
10 5   0   10   20   30 feet

cm 100 0 1 2 3 4 5 6 7 8 9 10 metres

repair

Turkish
repair

Turkish
repair

W.S.G. dir. M.R. et W.S.G del.

1 : 250

FIG. 35.

CHAPTER V

THE CHURCH OF S. ANDREW IN KRISEI, HOJA MUSTAPHA PASHA MESJEDI

THAT the old Byzantine church now converted into the mosque styled Hoja Mustapha Pasha Mesjedi, in the quarter of Juma Bazaar, at a short distance to the east of the Gate of Selivria was the church of S. Andrew in Krisei (Μονὴ τοῦ Ἁγίου Ἀνδρέου ἐν Κρίσει)[1] can be established, by the indications which Byzantine writers have given of the site of that famous church, and by the legend which is still associated with the mosque. According to Stephen of Novgorod[2] (c. 1350) the church dedicated to S. Andrew of Crete, who was buried, as other authorities[3] inform us, in the district named Krisis, stood at a short distance to the north of the monastery of the Peribleptos. It lay, therefore, to the north of the Armenian church of S. George (Soulou Monastir) in the quarter of Psamathia, which represents the church of S. Mary Peribleptos. The mosque Hoja Mustapha Pasha Mesjedi lies in the same direction. Again, according to Pachymeres,[4] the church of S. Andrew in Krisei was near the monastery of Aristina. That monastery, another authority states,[5] was opposite the

---

[1] Pachym. ii. pp. 35, 123.   [2] *Itin. russes*, p. 122.
[3] Synax., October 17.   [4] Pachym. ii. p. 133.
[5] Typicon of George Kappodokes, quoted by the late lamented Père J. Pargoire in his masterly article on the 'Suburb and the Churches of S. Mamas,' published in the *Proceedings of the Institut archéologique russe à Constantinople*, vol. ix. fasc. 1, 32, 1904. In that article the writer demonstrates the erroneousness of the commonly received opinion, maintained, I regret, also in *Byzantine Constantinople*, pp. 89-90, that the suburb of S. Mamas was situated near Eyoub to the west of the Blachernae quarter. Père Pargoire proves that the suburb stood

106

church of S. Mamas. The church of S. Mamas was on the road between the Studion and the church of S. Andrew.[1] Hence the church of S. Andrew stood to the north of the Studion, the situation occupied by Hoja Mustapha Pasha Mesjedi. Once more, the site of the mosque corresponds to the position assigned to the church of S. Andrew on the map of Bondelmontius (1420), to the east of the Gate of Selivria. Finally, the old church is more definitely identified by the legend of the judicial procedure which clings to the building. In the picturesque courtyard of the mosque, where the colour of the East is still rich and vivid, there stands an old cypress tree around whose bare and withered branches a slender iron chain is entwined like the skeleton of some extinct serpent. As tradition would have it, the chain was once endowed with the gift of judgment, and in cases of dispute could indicate which of the parties concerned told the truth. One day a Jew who had borrowed money from a Turk, on being summoned to pay his debt, replied that he had done so already. To that statement the Turk gave the lie direct, and accordingly, debtor and creditor were brought to the chain for the settlement of the question at issue. Before submitting to the ordeal, however, the Jew placed a cane into the hands of the Turk, and then stood under the cypress confident that his honour for truthfulness and honesty would be vindicated. His expectation proved correct, for the chain touched his head to intimate that he had returned the money he owed. Whereupon taking back his cane he left the scene in triumph. Literally, the verdict accorded with fact ; for the cane which the Jew had handed to his creditor was hollow and contained the sum due to the latter. But the verdict displayed such a lack of

on the European shore of the Bosporus near Beshiktash. He also shows that the church of S. Mamas, near the Gate Xylokerkou, stood within the landward walls, somewhere between the Studion and S. Andrew in Krisei. Cf. *Itinéraires russes*, p. 102.

[1] The Anonymus (Banduri, iii. p. 54) places S. Mamas, τὰ Ξυλοκέρκου, within the city, between the monastery of Gastria and that of S. Saviour in the Chora. The suburb of S. Mamas he places (*ut supra*, pp. 57-58) outside the city between Galata and the Diplokionion (Beshiktash). This is only one proof of the correctness of Père Pargoire's position. See Pargoire, *ut supra*.

insight, and involved so gross a miscarriage of justice, that from that day forth the chain lost its reputation and has hung ever since a dishonoured oracle on the dead arms of the cypress, like a criminal on a gibbet. Although this tale cannot be traced to its Byzantine source, it is manifestly an echo of the renown which the precincts of the mosque once enjoyed as a throne of judgment before Turkish times, and serves to prove that Hoja Mustapha Pasha Mesjedi is indeed the old church of S. Andrew in Krisei.

The earliest reference to the locality known as Krisis occurs in the narrative of the martyrdom of S. Andrew of Crete given by Symeon Metaphrastes,[1] who flourished in the latter part of the ninth century. A devoted iconodule, S. Andrew, came from his native island to Constantinople, in the reign of Constantine Copronymus (740-775), expressly to rebuke the emperor for opposing the use of eikons in religious worship. As might have been anticipated, the zeal and courage of the saint only incurred cruel and insulting treatment, and at length a martyr's death. For, while his persecutors were dragging him one day along the streets of the city in derision, a half-witted fisherman stabbed him dead with a knife. So strong was the feeling prevalent at the time against the champion of the cause of eikons that his body was flung among the corpses of murderers and thieves ; but eventually his admirers succeeded in removing it from its foul surroundings and buried it 'in a sacred place which was named Krisis' (εἰς ἕνα ἱερὸν τόπον ὁ ὁποῖος ἐπωνομάζετο Κρίσις).[2] It is evident from this statement that the name Krisis was applied to the locality before the interment of S. Andrew there ; how long before, it is impossible to say, but probably from early times. The body of the martyr was laid in or beside one of the two churches dedicated to saints also named S. Andrew, which stood on the Seventh Hill of the city already in the sixth century.[3]

[1] Migne, *Patr. Graec.* tom. 115, Mensis Octobr. p. 1128.
[2] Synax., October 17.
[3] Mansi, *Sacrorum conciliorum nova et amplissima collectio*, viii. p. 906.

NOTE

One of these churches was dedicated to S. Andrew the Apostle, and stood 'near the column,' πλησίον τοῦ στύλου; [1] the other to S. Andrew, not otherwise identified, was near the Gate of Saturninus, πλησίον τῆς πόρτας τοῦ Σατουρνίνου.[2] It is difficult to decide which church is represented by the mosque. For there were two columns on the Seventh Hill of the city : the Column of Constantine the Great, which stood outside the city bounds, giving name to the extramural district of the Exokionion now Alti Mermer ; and the Column of Arcadius now Avret Tash. Nor can the position of the Gate of Saturninus be determined more accurately than that it was an entrance in the portion of the Constantinian Walls which traversed the Seventh Hill, the Xerolophos of Byzantine days. On the whole, however, the indications favour the view that Hoja Mustapha Pasha Mesjedi represents the church of S. Andrew near the Gate of Saturninus. A church in that position, though outside the Constantinian fortification, was still so near them that it could be, very appropriately, described as near one of the city gates. Again the Russian pilgrim [3] who visited the shrines of Constantinople in the second quarter of the fifteenth century found two churches dedicated to S. Andrew in this part of the city, one to S. Andrew the Strategos, the other to S. Andrew 'mad with the love of God' ('God-intoxicated'). In proceeding northwards from the church of S. Diomed, which stood near the Golden Gate (Yedi Koulé), the Russian visitor reached first the sanctuary dedicated to S. Andrew the Strategos, and then the church dedicated to S. Andrew the 'God-intoxicated,' which lay still farther to the north. But this order in the positions of the two churches implies that Hoja Mustapha Pasha Mesjedi represents the church of S. Andrew the Strategos, a martyr of the fourth century, viz. the church which the documents of the sixth century describe as near the Gate of Saturninus, without specifying by what title its patron saint was distinguished. This agrees, moreover, with what is known regarding the site of the church of S. Andrew the Apostle. It stood to the west of the cistern of Mokius,[4] the large ruined Byzantine reservoir, now Tchoukour Bostan, to the north of Hoja Mustapha Pasha Mesjedi.

The church does not appear again in history, under the designation ἐν κρίσει, until the reign of Andronicus II. (1282-

---

[1] Mansi, *Sacrorum conciliorum nova et amplissima collectio*, p. 882.
[2] *Itin. russes*, p. 232.   [3] *Ibid.*
[4] Theoph. Cont. p. 323.

1328), when it was found, like so many other churches which survived the Latin occupation of the city, in a state demanding extensive repair. It was then embellished and enlarged by the protovestiarissa Theodora,[1] a lady who occupied a prominent position in the society of the day, both as the emperor's cousin, and on account of her accomplishments and character. In her early youth she was married to George Muzalon,[2] the favourite counsellor and trusted friend of Theodore II. Ducas of Nicaea. What confidence Muzalon enjoyed may be inferred from the fact that he was associated with the Patriarch Arsenius as guardian of the emperor's son, John Lascaris, when left the heir to the throne of Nicaea, as a child eight years old.[3] Had Muzalon not met with an untimely end he might have become the colleague of his ward, and Theodora might have worn the imperial crown. The tragic murder of her husband by his political opponents, while celebrating the obsequies of the Emperor Theodore, provoked a terrible outburst of indignation and grief on her part,[4] and so vehement was her condemnation of the criminals that her uncle, the treacherous Michael Palaeologus, threatened she would share her husband's fate if she did not control her feelings.[5] After the accession of Michael Palaeologus to the throne, her hand was bestowed on the protovestiarius Raoul, and hence she is generally known by his name and title as Raoulaina the protovestiarissa (ἡ Ῥαούλαινα πρωτοβεστιάρισσα). One of her beautiful daughters became the wife of Constantine Palaeologus, the ill-fated brother of Andronicus II. But, as already stated, Theodora was not only highly connected. Like many noble ladies in Byzantine society, she cultivated learning,[6] and took a deep interest in the theological discussions and ecclesiastical affairs of her day. She was a devoted adherent of the party attached to the person and memory of the Patriarch Arsenius; the party that never forgave Michael Palaeologus for blinding the young John Lascaris and robbing him of the throne, the party that

---

[1] Pachym. ii. p. 85 ; Niceph. Greg. i. pp. 167, 178.
[2] Niceph. Greg. i. pp. 167, 168.   [3] Pachym. i. p. 39.
[4] Ibid. pp. 55-63.   [5] Ibid. i. p. 108.   [6] Niceph. Greg. i. p. 178.

opposed the subjection of the Eastern Church to the Papal
See, and which maintained the freedom of the Church from
the political interference of the emperor. Whatever its
faults, that party certainly represented the best moral life of
the period.

To heal the schism caused by the attitude of the Arsenites 'was the serious labour of the Church and State' for
half a century. And in pursuance of the policy of concilia-
tion, Andronicus II. allowed the body of Arsenius to be
brought to Constantinople from the island of Proconessus,
where he had died in exile and been buried. The whole
city gathered to welcome the remains of the venerated prelate, and saw them borne in solemn and stately procession
from the landing at the Gate of Eugenius (Yali Kiosk) to
the church of S. Sophia. There, robed in pontifical vestments, the body was first seated upon the patriarchal
throne, then laid before the altar, while the funeral service
was intoned, and finally placed on the right hand of the bema
in a chest locked and sealed for safe keeping. Once a week,
however, the body was exposed to public view, and all strife
seemed hushed in a common devotion to the memory of the
saint. It was soon after this event that Theodora restored
the church and monastery of S. Andrew, and upon the
completion of the work she besought the emperor to allow
the remains of Arsenius to be transferred to that shrine.
The request was granted, and the body was carried to the
church of St. Andrew with as great pomp and ceremony as
attended its arrival in the capital. There it was kept until
the patriarchate of Niphon (1311-1314), when it was again
taken to S. Sophia to appear in the final conclusion of
peace between the friends and foes of the deceased.[1] Standing beside the remains, Niphon pronounced, in the name
and by the authority of the dead man, a general absolution
for all offences committed in connection with the quarrels
which had raged around the name of Arsenius ; and so long
as S. Sophia continued to be a Christian sanctuary the
remains were counted among the great treasures of the
cathedral. 'There,' to quote the words of a devout visitor

[1] Niceph. Greg. i. p. 262.

shortly before the Turkish conquest, 'is found the body
of the holy patriarch Arsenius, whose body, still intact,
performs many miracles.' [1]

During the closing years of her life Theodora made the
monastery or convent of S. Andrew in Krisei her home.[2]
To retire thus from the troubled sea of secular life to the
haven of a monastery, and there prepare for the voyage
beyond earthly scenes, was a common practice in the fashion-
able world of the men and women of Byzantine days.   And
it was natural for a wealthy traveller to leave at the port of
call some splendid token of devotion and gratitude.   The
protovestiarissa was still an inmate of the monastery in 1289,
when her friend the Patriarch Gregory, to whom she was
bound by many ties, was compelled to resign.[3]   He was one
of the most learned men of his time and took an active part
in the efforts to reconcile the Arsenites.   It was during his
tenure of office that the body of Arsenius was brought
to the capital, and subsequently transferred from S. Sophia
to the church of S. Andrew ; he also opposed the union of
the Churches, and in the controversy regarding the 'Procession of the Holy Ghost' which divided Christendom,
he vigorously defended the doctrine of the Greek Communion against Veccus, who championed the Latin Creed.

Strongly attached to her friends, and quick to resent any
injustice to them, Theodora came forward in the hour of
the patriarch's disgrace and offered him a refuge in the monastery of Aristina, which stood, as we have seen, near the
church of S. Andrew and in the immediate neighbourhood
of her own residence.[4]   It was a fortunate arrangement, for
Gregory soon fell seriously ill and required all the sympathy
and generous kindness which Theodora was able to extend
to him.[5]   Upon his death, ten short months after his retirement, Theodora determined to show again her admiration
for the man and his work by honouring his memory with
a funeral befitting the position he had held in the Church.

---

[1] *Itin. russes,* p. 226 ; cf. pp. 117, 135, 161, 201.
[2] Pachym. ii. p. 132.   [3] *Ibid. ut supra.*
[4] Pachym. ii. p. 133 ; Niceph. Greg. p. 178.   According to the latter historian, Theodora erected a special residence for Gregory near her monastery.
[5] Pachym. *ut supra.*

She was prevented from carrying out her intention only by the peremptory and reiterated commands of the emperor, that Gregory should be buried as a private person.[1]

After the death of Theodora we have only occasional glimpses of the church and monastery. In 1350 Stephen of Novgorod came 'to kiss' the relics of S. Andrew of Crete, and describes the convent as 'very beautiful.'[2] Once, at least, a sister proved too frail for her vocation;[3] sometimes a devout and wealthy inmate, such as Theognosia,[4] would provide an endowment to enable poor girls to become her heirs in religion ; or the sisterhood was vexed by the dishonesty of parties who had rented the lands from which the convent derived its revenues.[5] Towards the end of its Byzantine period another Russian pilgrim[6] came to honour the remains of S. Andrew the Strategos, and bring the Christian history of the church to a close. It was converted into a mosque by Mustapha Pasha, Grand Vizier in the reign of Selim I. (1512-1520).[7] The custom of illuminating the minarets of the mosques on the eve of the Prophet's birthday was introduced first at this mosque.[8]

Architectural Features

On account of the serious changes made in the building and its surroundings when it became a mosque, and after the earthquake of 1765, its real character is not immediately apparent. The present entrance is in the northern side, where a fine Turkish arcade has been erected. The mihrab is on the south side, a greater change for the correct orientation of a mosque than is usually necessary in the adaptation of a church to the requirements of a sanctuary in which the worshippers turn towards Mecca. To the east a hall has been added for the accommodation of women who attend the services ; while on the west is another hall, where the dervishes of the Teké attached to the mosque

---

[1] Pachym. *ut supra*, p. 152.
[2] *Itin. russes*, p. 122.
[3] Miklosich et Müller, i. p. 548, year 1371.
[4] *Ibid.* ii. p. 353, year 1400.
[5] *Ibid.* ii. p. 506, year 1401.
[6] *Itin. russes*, p. 232.
[7] Paspates, Βυζαντιναὶ Μελέται, p. 319.
[8] *Ibid.* p. 320.

I

hold their meetings. The north aisle also has been much altered and is covered with Turkish domes.

The first impression produced by the interior of the building is that we have here a church on the trefoil plan, similar to S. Mary of the Mongols (p. 272) or S. Elias of Salonica, for the central area is flanked by two semi-domes, which with the eastern apse form a lobed plan at the vaulting level. A closer examination of the building, however, will prove that we are dealing with a structure whose original features have been concealed by extensive Turkish alterations, and that the trefoil form is a superficial disguise.

The arches supporting the central dome on the north and south sides are filled in with semi-domes which rest on arches thrown diagonally across the 'aisles' on each side of the central dome. These arches are very clumsily set to the sides of an irregular hexagon, with the central wall arch much larger than the side arches. They have no responds, and have every appearance of being makeshifts.

The eastern dome arch is prolonged into a barrel-vaulted bema, flanked by shallow niches leading to the prothesis and diaconicon, and beyond the bema is the semi-circular apse. Only the diaconicon now remains, covered by a cross-groined vault, and its apse pierced by a door leading to the hall of the Teké. The place of the prothesis has been taken by a similar door and a small Turkish dome.

The western dome arch is filled in with a triple arcade resting on two marble columns with finely carved cubical capitals. Above the arcade is a group of three windows whose heads are circular on the inside, but pointed on the outside. To the west of this arcade is an oblong passage corresponding to the 'inner narthex' of S. Theodosia. It is in three bays. The central long bay is barrel-vaulted; the two outer bays open into the north and south 'aisles'; the bay to the north is covered by a Turkish dome, while that to the south has a cross-groined vault which seems to be original.

Beyond this to the west is the outer narthex, a fine piece of work, and, from the character of its details, of the same period as the western dome arcade. It is in five bays.

The three central bays correspond to the ' inner narthex ' ; the middle bay is covered by a low saucer dome on pendentives, and is separated from the two side bays by columns set against flat pilasters. The latter bays are covered by groined vaults springing from the imposts of the capitals, which are of the Byzantine Ionic type, with high carved imposts. They resemble the capitals in the gallery of SS. Sergius and Bacchus, and are worthy of particular notice.

The two outer bays are separated from the central compartment of three bays by strongly projecting pilasters. They are covered by low saucer domes similar to the dome over the central bay, and communicate on the east with the ' aisles.' Both outer and inner narthexes are in one story, above which rise the windows of the western dome arch and the semi-domes on north and south.

Turning now to the exterior, the south wall is the only outer wall which is exposed at the ground level. It is faced with finely dressed and polished stone, with thin joints, no tiles, and a stone-moulded cornice. The windows are covered with four centred Turkish arches and are evident insertions. Above the stone cornice rise the low drums of the semi-domes. These, as well as the square base of the dome and the dome itself, are faced with polished stone alternating with courses of three bricks set in thick beds of mortar. The angles are plain, without shafts, and the drums, dome base, and dome are crowned with stone cornices moulded to a reversed ogee.

The north and south semi-domes are each pierced by three large windows, which on the interior cut through the curved surface of the domes, and on the exterior appear as dormers in the roof above the cornice. Accordingly they are double glazed, with one glazed frame on the inside corresponding to the curved dome surface, and a second upright glazed frame on the outside. The roofs are covered with lead.

The central dome is circular inside, with a high drum pierced by eight windows. On the outside it is octagonal, with a window on each side. These have circular arched heads, but have no moulding, shaft, or inset to either arches or sides. The dome is crowned by a moulded stone cornice of the same type as that of the other walls.

In attempting to reconstruct the original form of the church we may first note those features which are evidently Turkish. None of the exterior masonry is Byzantine, as the use of polished ashlar with fine joints, of pointed arches, and of moulded stone cornices clearly proves. The absence of shafts at the angles of the dome drums and the unrecessed windows are additional proofs of this fact, and we may conclude that the entire exterior was refaced in Turkish times.

The diagonal arches under the north and south semidomes are peculiar. Furthermore, in lobed Byzantine churches the lateral apses project beyond the square outer walls. Here they are contained within the walls.[1]

Nor are the semi-domes themselves Byzantine in character. The large windows in the dome surface and the lead-covered dormers placed above the flat moulded cornice betray a Turkish hand; for windows in the dome are universal in the great Turkish mosques, and the method of protecting them on the exterior with wooden dormers is quite foreign to Byzantine ideas. The form of the drums and cornices should be compared with the minor domes of the mosque of Sultan Bayazid.

A careful examination of the building has led to the following conclusions. The lateral semi-domes with their supporting arches are a Turkish addition. The central dome, including the drum, is probably entirely Turkish, and takes the place of an original ribbed dome. The two easternmost domes in the north 'aisle' and those over the inner narthex and the prothesis are also Turkish, and, as already stated, the exterior of the entire building. On the other hand, the eastern apse, the dome arches, the arcade, and the windows above it on the west side of the dome, the inner narthex with the ground vault to the south of it, and the entire outer narthex, are parts of the original building, dating probably from the sixth or seventh century.

---

[1] *E.g.* S. Elias, Salonica ; Churches on Mt. Athos ; S. Mary of the Mongols, Constantinople. See plan, p. 279.

It should be particularly noticed that the windows over the western dome arcade are circular-headed inside, though they have been provided with pointed heads on the outside in the process of refacing.

If we stand in the northern lateral apse and face the mihrab the reason for the alterations is evident. The original Christian orientation is ignored, and the apses, in place of being lateral, are terminal. To the left is the old apse left unaltered ; to the right, the original filling of the dome arch forms a ' nave-arcade ' similar to that of the mosque of Sultan Bayazid ; while by means of the additional apses the building has been converted into a miniature imperial mosque of the S. Sophia type, a distinctly clever piece of Turkish alteration.

In its original form the central dome was surrounded by an ' ambulatory ' of one story formed by the aisles and ' inner narthex.' Such a plan is common to both the domed basilica type and the domed cross type, the difference depending upon the treatment of the cross arms above. In both types, however, the side dome arches are invariably filled in with arcades similar to that filling in the western arch of S. Andrew. We are therefore justified in restoring such arcades here. The type thus restored differs from the domed cross church in that the cross arms do not extend to the outer walls, and from the domed basilica in that the western dome arch is treated in a similar manner to the lateral arches. To this type the term ' ambulatory church ' may be applied.

Adjoining the west end of the church is the fine cloister of the Teké of dervishes, probably on the lines of the old monastery. All the columns around the court are Byzantine, and one of them bears the inscription : the (column) of, Theophane—ἡ τῆς Θεωφάνης (Fig. 69). In the south wall is built a beautiful Byzantine doorway having jambs and lintel decorated on the face with a broad undercut scroll of flat leaves and four-petalled flowers, running between two rows of egg and dart, while on the intrados are two bands of floral ornaments separated by a bead moulding. One of the bands is clearly a vine scroll. The method employed here, of joining leaves to a centre so as to form spiral rosettes, is found also on some of the small capitals in S. Sophia. Similar rosettes appear in the decoration of the doorway to the Holy Sepulchre on the ivory in the Trivulce collection at Milan.[1]

[1] See figure 26 in Diehl's *Manuel d'art byzantin*, p. 74. That author (pp. 313-14) assigns the church of S. Andrew to the seventh century, but recognizes in it also features of the sixth century.

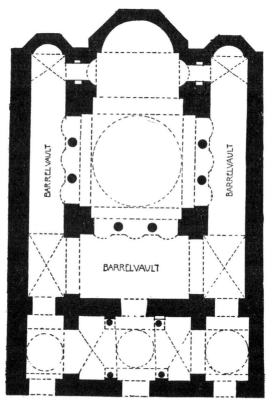

FIG. 36.—THE CHURCH OF S. ANDREW IN KRISEI (RESTORED PLAN).

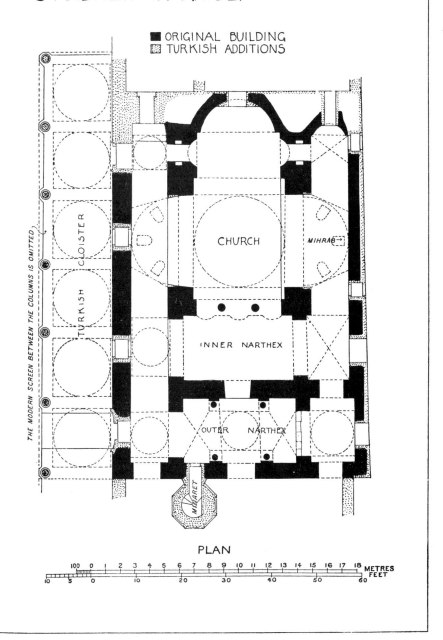

S·ANDREW IN KRISEI

■ ORIGINAL BUILDING
▨ TURKISH ADDITIONS

THE MODERN SCREEN BETWEEN THE COLUMNS IS OMITTED

TURKISH CLOISTER

CHURCH

MIHRAB →

INNER NARTHEX

OUTER NARTHEX

MINARET

PLAN

100 0 1 2 3 4 5 6 7 8 9 10 11 12 13 14 15 16 17 18 METRES
FEET
10 5 0 10 20 30 40 50 60

Fig. 37.

119

S·ANDREW IN KRISEI

■ ORIGINAL BUILDING
▨ TURKISH ADDITIONS

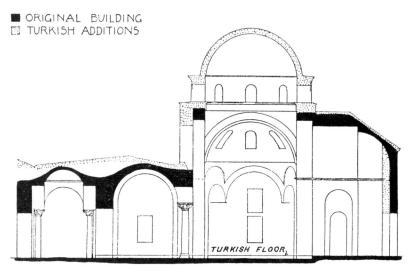

LONGITUDINAL SECTION

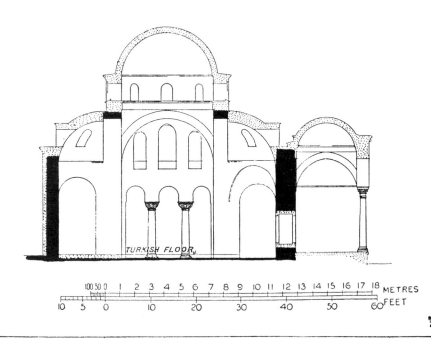

FIGS. 38 AND 39.

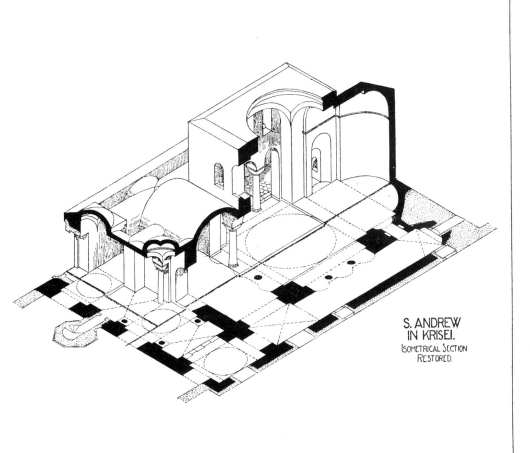

S. ANDREW
IN KRISEI.
Isometrical Section
Restored.

Fig. 40.   121

CHAPTER VI

THE CHURCH OF S. MARY (PANACHRANTOS) OF LIPS, PHENERÉ ISA MESJEDI

THE old Byzantine church, now Pheneré Isa Mesjedi, in the valley of the Lycus, to the south of the mosque of Sultan Mehemed, should be identified as the church of the Theotokos of Lips, although the Patriarch Constantius,[1] Scarlatus Byzantius and Paspates[2] identify that church with Demirjilar Mesjedi, a building which lay to the east of the mosque of Sultan Mehemed, but fell in the earthquake of 1904. According to the writers just cited, Pheneré Isa Mesjedi is the church of the Theotokos Panachrantos which appears in connection with certain incidents in the history of the Patriarch Veccus. In this view there is a curious mingling of truth and error. For, as a matter of fact, Constantinople did possess a church dedicated to the Panachrantos which had no connection with the monastery of Lips. But that church was not the building in the valley of the Lycus ; it stood in the immediate vicinity of S. Sophia. Furthermore, while it is certain that there was in the city a church of the Panachrantos which had nothing whatever to do with the monastery of Lips, it is equally true that the sanctuary attached to that monastery was also dedicated to the Theotokos under the same style. In other words, Pheneré Isa Mesjedi was the sanctuary attached to the monastery

---

[1] *Ancient and Modern C.P.* pp. 70, 79.
[2] Pp. 322, 325.

of Lips and was dedicated to the Theotokos Panachrantos, but was not the church of that name with which it has been identified by the authorities above mentioned.[1]

The correctness of these positions can be readily established. First, that a monastery of the Panachrantos and the monastery of Lips were different Houses is evident from the express statements of the pilgrim Zosimus to that effect. For, according to that visitor to the shrines of the city, a monastery, 'de Panakhran,'[2] stood near S. Sophia, 'non loin de Sainte Sophie.' Stephen of Novgorod refers to the monastery of the 'Panacrante'[3] also in the same connection. And the proximity of the House to the great cathedral may be inferred likewise from the statements of the pilgrim Alexander[4] and of the anonymous pilgrim.[5] On the other hand, Zosimus speaks of the monastery of Lips, 'couvent de femmes Lipesi,'[6] as situated in another part of the city. It was closely connected with the monastery of Kyra Martha,[7] from which to S. Sophia was a far cry. The distinction of the two monasteries is, moreover, confirmed by the historians Pachymeres[8] and Nicephorus Gregoras,[9] who employ the terms Panachrantos and Lips to designate two distinct monastic establishments situated in different quarters of the capital.

In the next place, the monastery of Lips did not stand at the point marked by Demirjilar Mesjedi. The argument urged in favour of its position at that point is the fact that the monastery is described as near the church of the Holy Apostles ($\pi\lambda\eta\sigma\acute{\iota}o\nu$ $\tau\hat{\omega}\nu$ $\acute{\alpha}\gamma\acute{\iota}\omega\nu$ $\acute{\alpha}\pi o\sigma\tau\acute{o}\lambda\omega\nu$). But while proximity to the Holy Apostles must mark any edifice claiming to be the monastery of Lips, that proximity

[1] To Mühlmann and Mordtmann, *Esq. top.* paragraph 127, belongs the credit of the identification of Pheneré Isa Mesjedi with the monastery of Lips. But I have not seen any full statement of their reasons for that opinion.

[2] *Itin. russes*, p. 202.

[3] *Ibid.* p. 119.

[4] *Ibid.* p. 162.

[5] *Ibid.* p. 230.

[6] *Ibid.* p. 205.

[7] Phrantzes, pp. 141 ; *Itin. russes*, pp. 205, 122, 234.

[8] i. p. 455 ; ii. p. 19.

[9] i. p. 160.

alone is not sufficient to identify the building.   Pheneré[1]
Isa Mesjedi satisfies that condition equally well.   But what
turns the balance of evidence in its favour is that it satisfies
also every other condition that held true of the monastery
of Lips.   That House was closely associated with the
monastery of Kyra Martha, as Phrantzes[2] expressly declares,
and as may be inferred from the narratives of the Russian
pilgrims.[3]   That being so, the position of Kyra Martha

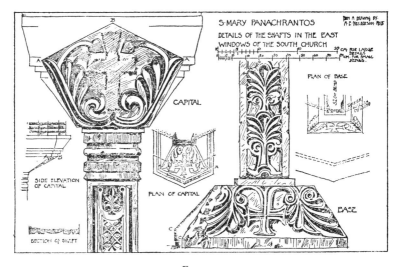

FIG. 41.

will determine likewise that of the monastery of Lips.
Now, Kyra Martha lay to the south of the Holy Apostles.
For it was reached, says the anonymous pilgrim of the
fifteenth century[4] ' en descendent (du couvent) des
Apôtres *dans la direction du midi* ' ;   while Stephen of
Novgorod[5] reached the Holy Apostles in proceeding
northwards from the Kyra Martha.   Hence the monastery
of Lips lay to the south of the Holy Apostles, as
Pheneré Isa Mesjedi stands to the south of the mosque

---

[1] Theoph. Cont. p. 371.   [2] Page 141.
[3] *Itin. russes*, pp. 205, 234.   [4] *Ibid.* p. 234.
                    [5] *Ibid.* p. 122.

of Sultan Mehemed, which has replaced that famous church.

With this conclusion agrees, moreover, the description given of the district in which the monastery of Lips stood.   It was a remote and quiet part of the city, like the district in which Pheneré Isa Mesjedi is situated to-day ; πρὸς τὰ τοῦ Λίβα μέρη, τόπον ἀποκισμένον καὶ ἥσυχον.[1] Furthermore, the monastery of Lips borrowed its name from its founder or restorer, Constantine Lips ;[2] and in harmony with that fact we find on the apse of one of the two churches which combine to form Pheneré Isa Mesjedi an inscription in honour of a certain Constantine.[3]   Unfortunately the inscription is mutilated, and there were many Constantines besides the one surnamed Lips.   Still, the presence of the principal name of the builder of the monastery of Lips on a church, which we have also other reasons to believe belonged to that monastery, adds greatly to the cumulative force of the argument in favour of the view that Constantine Lips is the person intended.   But, if necessary, the argument can be still further strengthened.   The church attached to the monastery of Lips was dedicated to the Theotokos, as may be inferred from the circumstance that the annual state visit of the emperor to that shrine took place on the festival of the Nativity of the Virgin.[4]   So likewise was the sanctuary which Pheneré Isa Mesjedi represents, for the inscription it bears invokes her blessing upon the building and its builder (Fig. 42).   Would that the identity of all the churches in Constantinople could be as strongly established.

It remains to add in this connection that while the monastery of Lips and that of the Panachrantos associated with Veccus were different Houses, the churches of both monasteries were dedicated to the Theotokos under the

---

[1] Du Cange, iv. p. 93, quoting the Life of Nicholas of the Studion.   The district was named Μερδοσαγάρη, Leo Gramm. p. 280.

[2] Theoph. Cont. p. 371.

[3] See inscription, p. 131.

[4] Codinus, De officiis, p. 80.

same attribute—Panachrantos, the Immaculate. The in-
vocation inscribed on Pheneré Isa Mesjedi addresses the
Theotokos by that epithet. But to identify different
churches because of the same dedication is only another
instance of the liability to allow similarity of names to
conceal the difference between things.

The distinction thus established between the two
monasteries is important not only in the interests of
accuracy ; it also throws light on the following historical
incidents. In 1245 permission was granted for the trans-
ference of the relics of S. Philip the Apostle from the
church of the Panachrantos to Western Europe. The
document authorising that act was signed by the dean of
the church and by the treasurer of S. Sophia.[1] The
intervention of the latter official becomes more intelligible
when we know that the monastery of the Panachrantos
stood near S. Sophia, and not, as Paspates maintains, at
Pheneré Isa Mesjedi. Again, the Patriarch Veccus took
refuge on two occasions in the monastery of the Panachrantos, once in 1279 and again in 1282. He could do
so readily and without observation, as the case demanded,
when the shelter he sought stood in the immediate vicinity
of his cathedral and official residence. To escape to a
monastery situated in the valley of the Lycus was, under
the circumstances, impracticable.

Constantine Lips was an important personage during
the reign of Leo the Wise (886-912) and of Constantine
VII. Porphyrogenitus (912-956). Under the former
emperor he held the offices of protospatharius and domestic
of the household. He also went on several missions to the
Prince of Taron, in the course of which romance mingled
with politics, with the result that the daughter of Lips
became engaged to the son of the prince.[2] Upon the
accession of Constantine Porphyrogenitus, Lips came under
a cloud, on suspicion of being implicated in the plot to raise
Constantine Ducas to the throne, and was obliged to flee

---

[1] Du Cange, iv. p. 93.
[2] Const. Porphyr. *De adm. imp.* c. 43.

the capital.[1]   Eventually he was restored to favour, and
enjoyed the dignities of patrician, proconsul, commander
of the foreign guard, and drungarius of the fleet.[2]   He
fell in battle in the war of 917 between the Empire and the
Bulgarians under Symeon.[3]

The monastery of Lips was restored in the reign of
Leo the Wise ; the festival of the dedication of the church
being celebrated in the year 908, in the month of June.[4]
The emperor honoured the occasion with his presence, and
attended a banquet in the refectory of the monastery.   But
the happy proceedings had not gone far, when they were
suddenly interrupted by a furious south-west wind which
burst upon the city and shook houses and churches with
such violence that people feared to remain under cover and
imagined that the end of the world had come, until the
storm was allayed by a heavy downpour of rain.   As the
south-west wind was named Lips, it is not clear whether
the historians who mention this incident intend to explain
thereby the origin of Constantine's surname, or simply
point to a curious coincidence.

Near the church Lips erected also a xenodocheion for
the reception of strangers.[5]   The monastery is mentioned
by the Anonymus of the eleventh century,[6] but does not
appear again until the recovery of the Empire from the
Latins in 1261.   In the efforts then made to restore all
things, it underwent repairs at the instance of the Empress
Theodora,[7] the consort of Michael Palaeologus, and from
that time acquired greater importance than it had previously
enjoyed.   Within its precincts, on the 16th of February
1304, a cold winter day, Theodora herself was laid to rest
with great pomp, and amid the tears of the poor to whom
she had been a good friend.[8]   There, two years later, a
splendid service was celebrated for the benefit of the soul of
her son Constantine Porphyrogenitus,[9] as some compensation

---

[1] Theoph. Cont. p. 384.   [2] Const. Porphyr. *ut supra.*
[3] Theoph. Cont. p. 389.   [4] *Ibid.* p. 371.
[5] Banduri, iii. p. 52.   [6] *Ut supra.*
[7] Niceph. Greg. i. p. 162.   [8] Pachym. i. p. 378.
                [9] *Ibid.* p. 425.

for the cruel treatment he had suffered at the hands of his
jealous brother Andronicus.   There, that emperor himself became a monk two years before his death,[1] and there
he was buried on the 13th of February 1332.   The
monastery contained also the tomb of the Empress Irene,[2]
first wife of Andronicus III., and the tomb of the Russian
Princess Anna[3] who married John VII. Palaeologus while
crown prince, but died before she could ascend the throne,
a victim of the great plague which raged in Constantinople
in 1417.   The monastery appears once more as the scene
of a great religious revival, when a certain nun Thomais,
who enjoyed a great reputation for sanctity, took up her
residence in the neighbourhood.   So large were the crowds
of women who flocked to place themselves under her rule
that 'the monastery of Lips and Martha' was filled to
overflowing.[4]

The church was converted into a mosque by Pheneré
Isa, who died in 1496, and has undergone serious alterations since that time.[5]

Architectural Features

The building comprises two churches, which, while
differing in date and type, stand side by side, and communicate with each other through an archway in their common
wall, and through a passage in the common wall of their
narthexes.   As if to keep the two churches more closely
together, they are bound by an exonarthex, which, after
running along their western front, returns eastwards along
the southern wall of the south church as a closed cloister or
gallery.

The North Church.—The north church is of the normal
'four column' type.   The four columns which originally
supported the dome were, however, removed when the
building was converted into a mosque in Turkish times,
and have been replaced by two large pointed arches which

---

[1] Niceph. Greg. i. p. 461.   [2] Cantacuz. i. p. 193.
[3] Phrantzes, p. 110.   [4] *Ibid.* p. 141.
[5] Paspates, p. 325.

span the entire length of the church. But the old wall arches of the dome-columns are still visible as arched piercings in the spandrils of the Turkish arches. A similar Turkish 'improvement' in the substitution of an arch for the original pair of columns is found in the north side of the parecclesion attached to the Pammakaristos (p. 152). The dome with its eight windows is likewise Turkish. The windows are lintelled and the cornice is of the typical Turkish form. The bema is almost square and is covered by a barrel vault formed by a prolongation of the eastern dome arch ; the apse is lighted by a lofty triple window. By what is an exceptional arrangement, the lateral chapels are as lofty both on the interior and on the exterior as is the central apse, but they are entered by low doors. In the normal arrangement, as, for instance, in the Myrelaion, the lateral chapels are low and are entered by vaults rising to the same height as those of the angle chambers, between which the central apse rises higher both externally and internally.

The chapels have niches arched above the cornice on three sides, and are covered by cross-groined vaults which combine with the semicircular heads of the niches to produce a very beautiful effect. To the east they have long bema arches flanked by two small semicircular niches, and are lighted by small single windows.

The church is preceded by a narthex in three bays covered by cross-groined vaults supported on strong transverse arches. At either end it terminates in a large semicircular niche. The northern one is intact, but of the southern niche only the arched head remains. The lower part of the niche has been cut away to afford access to the narthex of the south church. This would suggest that, at least, the narthex of the south church is of later date than the north church.

Considered as a whole the north church is a good example of its type, lofty and delicate in its proportions.

The South Church.—The narthex is unsymmetrical to the church and in its present form must be the result of extensive alteration. It is in two very dissimilar bays. That to the

K

north is covered with a cross-groined vault of lath and plaster, probably on the model of an original vault constructed of brick. A door in the eastern wall leads to the north aisle of the church. The southern bay is separated from its companion by a broad arch. It is an oblong chamber reduced to a figure approaching a square by throwing broad arches across its ends and setting back the wall arches from the cornice. This arrangement allows the bay to be covered by a low drumless dome. Two openings, separated by a pier, lead respectively to the nave and the southern aisle of the church.

The interior of the church has undergone serious alterations since it has become a mosque, but enough of the original building has survived to show that the plan was that of an 'ambulatory church.'

Each side of the ambulatory is divided into three bays, covered with cross-groined vaults whose springings to the central area correspond exactly to the columns of such an arcade as that which occupies the west dome bay of S. Andrew (p. 114). We may therefore safely assume that triple arcades originally separated the ambulatory from the central area and filled in the lower part of the dome arches. The tympana of these arches above were pierced to north, south, and west by three windows now built up but whose outlines are still visible beneath the whitewash which has been daubed over them. The angles of the ambulatory are covered by cross vaults.

The pointed arches at present opening from the ambulatory to the central area were formed to make the church more suitable for Moslem worship, as were those of the north church. In fact we have here a repetition of the treatment of the Pammakaristos (p. 151), when converted into a mosque. The use of cross-groined vaults in the ambulatory is a feature which distinguishes this church from the other ambulatory churches of Constantinople and connects it more closely with the domed-cross church. The vaults in the northern portion of the ambulatory have been partially defaced in the course of Turkish repairs.

The central apse is lighted by a large triple window.

It is covered by a cross-groined vault and has on each side a tall shallow segmental niche whose head rises above the springing cornice. Below this the niches have been much hacked away. The passages leading to the lateral chapels are remarkably low, not more than 1.90 m. high to the crown of the arch.

The southern chapel is similar to the central apse, and is lighted by a large triple window. The northern chapel is very different. It is much broader ; broader indeed than

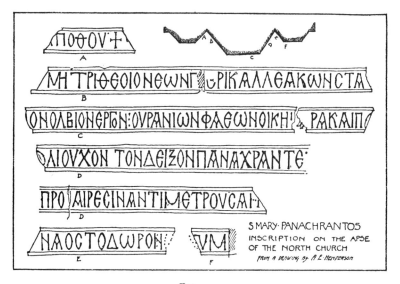

FIG. 42.

From love for the mother of God . . . beautiful temple . . . Constantine ; which splendid work . . . of the shining heaven an inhabitant and citizen him show O Immaculate One ; friendliness recompensing . . . the temple . . . the gift.

the ambulatory which leads to it, and is covered by barrel vaults. The niches in the bema only rise to a short distance above the floor, not, as on the opposite side, to above the cornice. It is lighted by a large triple window similar to those of the other two apses.

The outer narthex on the west of the two churches and

the gallery on the south of the south church are covered with cross-groined vaults without transverse arches. The wall of the south church, which shows in the south gallery, formed the original external wall of the building. It is divided into bays with arches in two and three orders of brick reveals, and with shallow niches on the broader piers.

The exterior of the two churches is very plain. On the west are shallow wall arcades in one order, on the south similar arcades in two orders. The northern side is inaccessible owing to the Turkish houses built against it.

On the east all the apses project boldly. The central apse of the south church has seven sides and shows the remains of a decoration of niches in two stories similar to that of the Pantokrator (p. 235); the other apses present three sides. The carved work on the window shafts is throughout good. An inscription commemorating the erection of the northern church is cut on a marble string-course which, when complete, ran across the whole eastern end, following the projecting sides of the apses. The letters are sunk and marked with drill holes.

Wulff is of opinion that the letters were originally filled in with lead, and, from the evidence of this lead infilling, dates the church as late as the fifteenth century. But it is equally possible that the letters were marked out by drill holes which were then connected with the chisel, and that the carver, pleased by the effect given by the sharp points of shadow in the drill holes, deliberately left them. The grooves do not seem suitable for retaining lead.

In the course of their history both churches were altered, even in Byzantine days. The south church is the earlier structure, but shows signs of several rebuildings. The irregular narthex and unsymmetrical eastern side chapels are evidently not parts of an original design. In the wall between the two churches there are indications which appear to show the character of these alterations and the order in which the different buildings were erected.

As has already been pointed out, the north side of the ambulatory in the south church, which for two-thirds of its length is of practically the same width as the southern and western sides, suddenly widens out at the eastern end and opens into a side chapel broader than that on the opposite side. The two large piers separating the ambulatory from the central part of the north church are evidently formed by building the wall of one church against the pre-existing wall of the other. The easternmost pier is smaller and, as can be seen from the plan, is a continuation of the wall of the north church. Clearly the north church was already built when the north-eastern chapel of the south church was erected, and the existing wall was utilised. As the external architectural style of the three apses of the south church is identical, it is reasonable to conclude that this part of the south church also is later in date than the north church. For if the entire south church had been built at the same time as the apses, we should expect to find the lateral chapels similar. But they are not. The vaulting of the central apse and of the southern lateral chapel are similar, while that of the northern chapel is different. On the same supposition we should also expect to find a similar use of the wall of the north church throughout, but we have seen that two piers representing the old wall of the south church still remain. The narthex of the south church, however, is carried up to the line of the north church wall.

The four column type is not found previous to the tenth century. The date of the north church was originally given on the inscription, but is now obliterated. Kondakoff dates it in the eleventh or twelfth century. Wulff would put it as late as the fifteenth. But if the view that this church was attached to the monastery of Lips is correct, the building must belong to the tenth century.

The ambulatory type appears to be early, and the examples in Constantinople seem to date from the sixth to the ninth century. It may therefore be concluded that, unless there is proof to the contrary, the south church is the earlier. In that case the southernmost parts of the two large piers which separate the two churches represent the old outer wall of the original south church, whose eastern chapels were then symmetrical. To this the north church was added, but at some subsequent date the apses of the south church demanded repair and when they were rebuilt, the north-eastern chapel was enlarged by the cutting away of the old outer wall. To this period also belongs the present inner narthex. The fact that the head of the terminal niche at the south end of the north narthex remains above the communicating door shows that the south narthex is later. The outer narthex and south gallery are a still later addition.

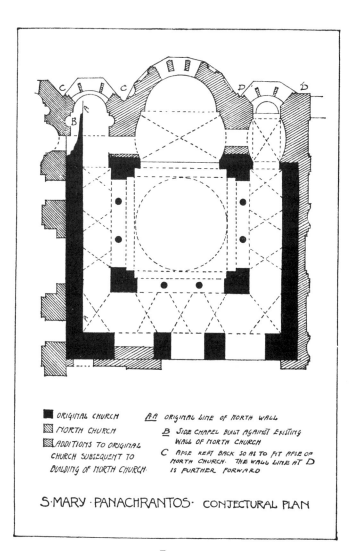

ORIGINAL CHURCH   _A A_ ORIGINAL LINE OF NORTH WALL

NORTH CHURCH   _B_ SIDE CHAPEL BUILT AGAINST EXISTING
WALL OF NORTH CHURCH

ADDITIONS TO ORIGINAL   _C_ APSE KEPT BACK SO AS TO FIT APSE OF
CHURCH SUBSEQUENT TO   NORTH CHURCH. THE WALL LINE AT _D_
BUILDING OF NORTH CHURCH.   IS FURTHER FORWARD

S·MARY·PANACHRANTOS· CONJECTURAL PLAN

FIG. 43.

135

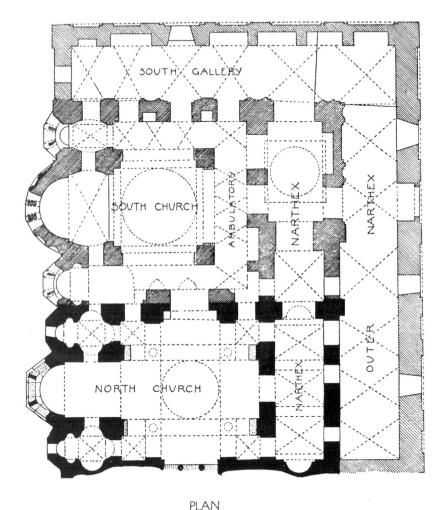

S·MARY PANACHRANTOS

SOUTH GALLERY

SOUTH CHURCH

AMBULATORY

NARTHEX

NARTHEX

NORTH CHURCH

NARTHEX

OUTER

PLAN

100 0 1 2 3 4 5 6 7 8 9 10 11 12 13 14 15 16 17 18 19 20 METRES

FEET

10 5 0   10   20   30   40   50   60   70

■ NORTH CHURCH   ▨ BYZANTINE ADDITIONS

▧ SOUTH CHURCH   ▩ TURKISH WORK

A.E·HENDERSON·MENS

1906

S·MARY
PANACHRANTOS

SECTION THROUGH NORTH CHURCH

■ ORIGINAL NORTH CHURCH
▨ SOUTH CHURCH
▨ BYZANTINE ADDITIONS
▨ TURKISH WORK

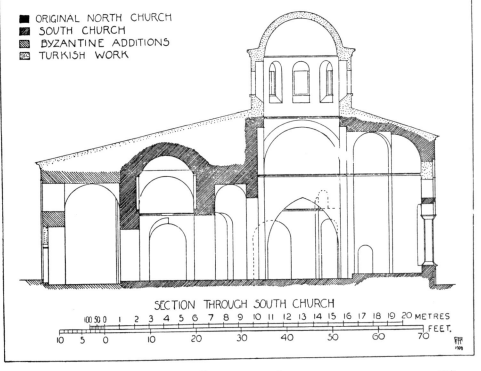

SECTION THROUGH SOUTH CHURCH

FIGS. 45 AND 46.

CHAPTER VII

THE CHURCH OF THE THEOTOKOS PAMMAKARISTOS, FETIYEH JAMISSI

The Byzantine church, now Fetiyeh Jamissi, overlooking the Golden Horn from the heights of the Fifth Hill, was the church of the Theotokos Pammakaristos (the All Blessed), attached to the monastery known by that name.

Regarding the identity of the church there can be no manner of doubt, as the building remained in the hands of the Greek community for 138 years after the conquest, and was during that period the patriarchal cathedral.

The questions when and by whom the church was founded cannot be so readily determined. According to a manuscript in the library of the Greek theological college on the island of Halki (one of the small group of islands known as the Princes' Islands in the Sea of Marmora), an inscription in the bema of the church ascribed the foundation of the building to John Comnenus and his wife Anna.[1] The manuscript perished in the earthquake which reduced the college to a heap of ruins in 1894, but the inscription had fortunately been copied in the catalogue of the library before that disaster occurred. It read as follows :

Ἰωάννου φρόντισμα Κομνηνοῦ τόδε
Ἄννης τε ῥίζης Δουκικῆς τῆς συζύγου.
οἷς ἀντιδοῦσα πλουσίαν, ἁγνή, χάριν
τάξαις ἐν οἴκῳ τοῦ θεοῦ μονοτρόπους.[2]

---

[1] See the masterly articles of Mr. Siderides in the *Proceedings of the Greek Syllogos of C.P.* ; supplement to vols. xx.-xxii. pp. 19-32 ; vol. xxix. pp. 265-73. I beg to acknowledge my great indebtedness to their learned author.

[2] 'This is the thoughtful deed of John Comnenus and of his consort Anna of

The legend cannot refer to the Emperor John Comnenus (1118-1143), for his consort was neither named Anna nor related to the family of Ducas. She was a Hungarian princess, who, on becoming the emperor's bride, assumed the name Irene. Mr. Siderides, therefore, suggests that the persons mentioned in the inscription were that emperor's grandparents, the curopalates and grand domestic John Comnenus and his wife, the celebrated Anna Dalassena, who bore likewise the title of Ducaena. In that case, as the curopalates and grand domestic died in 1067, the foundation of the church cannot be much later than the middle of the eleventh century. But whether the term φρόντισμα should be understood to mean that the church was founded by the illustrious persons above mentioned, or was an object already in existence upon which they bestowed their thought and care, is not quite certain. Mr. Siderides is prepared to adopt the latter meaning, and the architecture of the church allows us to assign the foundation of the building to an earlier date than the age of the grandparents of the Emperor John Comnenus. But while the connection of the church with those personages must not be overlooked, the building underwent such extensive repairs in the thirteenth century that the honour of being its founder was transferred to its restorer at that period. Pachymeres[1] speaks of the monastery as the monastery of Michael Glabas Tarchaniotes (τὴν ἰδίαν μονήν). While the poet Philes (1275-1346), referring to a figure portrayed on the walls of the church, asks the spectator,

Seest thou, O stranger, this great man? He is none other than the protostrator, the builder of this monastery, the wonder of the world, the noble Glabas.

ὁρᾷς τὸν ἄνδρα τὸν πολὺν τοῦτον, ξένε;
ἐκεῖνος οὗτός ἐστιν ὁ πρωτοστράτωρ,
ὁ δημιουργὸς τῆς μονῆς τῆς ἐνθάδε,
τὸ θαῦμα τῆς γῆς, ὁ Γλαβᾶς ὁ γεννάδας.[2]

---

the family Ducas. Grant to them, O Pure One, rich grace and appoint them dwellers in the house of God.'

[1] Vol. ii. p. 183.
[2] *Carmina Philae*, vol. i. ode 237, lines 21-23. Codex Paris, p. 241.

In accordance with these statements, Gerlach[1] saw depicted on the walls of the church two figures in archducal attire, representing the founder of the church and his wife, with this legend beside them:

Michael Ducas Glabas Tarchaniotes, protostrator and founder ; Maria Ducaena Comnena Palaeologina Blachena,[2] protostratorissa and foundress.

Μιχαὴλ Δούκας Γλαβᾶς Ταρχανιώτης, ὁ πρωτοστράτωρ καὶ κτήτωρ· Μαρία Δούκαινα Κομνηνὴ Παλαιολογίνα Βλάκαινα,[2] ἡ πρωτοστρατόρισσα καὶ κτητώρισσα.

Michael Glabas was created protostrator in 1292, and acquired the right to appoint the abbot of the monastery before 1295. Consequently the completion of the repair of the church at his instance must be assigned to the interval between these dates.

The protostrator Michael Glabas Ducas Tarchaniotes, who must not be confounded with his namesake the protovestiarius Michael Palaeologus Tarchaniotes,[3] enjoyed the reputation of an able general and wise counsellor in the reign of Andronicus II., although, being a victim to gout, he was often unable to serve his country in the former capacity. He was noted also for his piety and his interest in the poor, as may be inferred from his restoration of the Pammakaristos and the erection of a xenodocheion.[4] His wife was a niece of the Emperor Michael Palaeologus, and related, as her titles imply, to other great families in the country. A pious woman, and devoted to her husband, she proved the sincerity of her affection by erecting to his memory, as will appear in the sequel, the beautiful chapel at the south-east end of the church. Before her death she

---

[1] M. Crusius, *Turcograecia*, p. 189.

[2] It should read, Βράναινα. See Siderides, in the *Proceedings of the Greek Syllogos of C.P.* vol. xxix. p. 267.

[3] For the protovestiarius, see Pachym. i. pp. 205, 469 ; ii. pp. 68, 72, 210 ; for the protostrator, see Pachym. ii. pp. 12, 445. The former died in 1284, the latter about 1315. Cf. Siderides, *ut supra*. See on this subject the article of A. E. Martini in *Atti della R. Academia di archeologia, lettere e belle arti*, vol. xx., Napoli, 1900.

[4] *Carmina Philae*, vol. i. Codex Florent. ode 95, lines 280-82.

retired from the world and assumed the name Martha in religion.[1]

In addition to the figures of the restorers of the church, portraits in mosaic of the Emperor Andronicus and his Empress Anna, as the legends beside the portraits declared, stood on the right of the main entrance to the patriarchate.[2]

✠ Ἀνδρόνικος ἐν Χῷ τῷ θῷ πιστὸς βασιλεὺς καὶ αὐτοκράτωρ Ῥωμεῶν ὁ παλαιόλογος.

✠ Ἄννα ἐν Χῷ τῷ θῷ πιστὴ αὐγούστα ἡ παλαιολογίνα.

As both Andronicus II. and his grandson Andronicus III. were married to ladies named Anna, it is not clear which of these imperial couples was here portrayed. The fact that the consort of the former emperor died before the restoration of the church by the protostrator Michael is certainly in favour of the view supported by Mr. Siderides that the portraits represented the latter emperor and empress.[3] Why these personages were thus honoured is not explained.

Having restored the monastery, Michael Glabas entrusted the direction of its affairs to a certain monk named Cosmas, whom he had met and learned to admire during an official tour in the provinces. In due time Cosmas was introduced to Andronicus II., and won the imperial esteem to such an extent as to be appointed patriarch.[4] The new prelate was advanced in years, modest, conciliatory, but,

[1] See *Carmina Philae*, edited by E. Miller, odes 54, 57, 59, 92, 164, 165, 219, 237, for references to the protostrator, or to his wife, or to the Pammakaristos.

[2] Hans Jacob Breüning, *Orientalische Reyss*, chap. xvii. p. 66. He visited Constantinople 1579-80. The portraits stood 'Im Eingang auff der rechten Seiten,' or, as another authority has it, 'in patriarchica porta exteriore, in pariete dextero ab ingredientibus conspiciuntur,' *Turcograecia*, p. 75.

[3] Gerlach refers to these portraits, but without mentioning the names of the persons they represented. The legends were communicated to M. Crusius (*Turcograecia*, p. 75) by Theodosius Zygomalas, the protonotarius of the patriarch in the time of Gerlach.

[4] Pachym. ii. pp. 182-89. When Cosmas was appointed patriarch a curious incident occurred. A monk of the monastery of the Pantepoptes protested against the nomination, because it had been revealed to him that the person who should fill the vacant office would bear the name John. Such was the impression made by this prediction that matters were so arranged that somehow Cosmas was able to claim that name also. Whereupon the monk went on to predict how many years Cosmas would hold office, and that he would lose that position before his death.

withal, could take a firm stand for what he considered right. On the other hand, the piety of Andronicus was not of the kind that adheres tenaciously to a principle or ignores worldly considerations. Hence occasions for serious differences between the two men on public questions were inevitable, and in the course of their disputes the monastery of the Pammakaristos, owing to its association with Cosmas, became the scene of conflicts between Church and State.

No act of Andronicus shocked the public sentiment of his day more painfully than the political alliance he cemented by giving his daughter Simonis, a mere child of six years, as a bride to the Kraal of Servia, who was forty years her senior, and had been already married three times, not always, it was alleged, in the most regular manner.[1] Cosmas did everything in his power to prevent the unnatural union, and when his last desperate effort to have an audience of the emperor on the subject was repelled, he left the patriarchal residence and retired to his old home at the Pammakaristos. There, during the absence of the emperor in Thessalonica, where the objectionable marriage was celebrated, Cosmas remained for two years, attending only to the most urgent business of the diocese.[2] Upon the return of Andronicus to the capital, Cosmas was conspicuous by his refusal to take part in the loyal demonstrations which welcomed the emperor back. Andronicus might well have seized the opportunity to remove the patriarch from office for discourtesy so marked and offensive, but, instead of doing so, he sent a friendly message to the Pammakaristos, asking Cosmas to forget all differences and resume his public duties. Achilles in his tent was not to be conciliated so easily. To the imperial request Cosmas replied by inviting Andronicus to come to the Pammakaristos, and submit the points at issue between the emperor and himself to a tribunal of bishops and other ecclesiastics specially convened for the purpose. He furthermore declared that he would return to the patriarchal residence only if the verdict of the court

[1] Pachym. ii. pp. 271-77.   [2] *Ibid.* pp. 278-84.

was in his favour, otherwise he would resign office. The public feeling against Andronicus was so strong that he deemed it expedient to comply with this strange demand, going to the monastery late at night to escape notice. The tribunal having been called to order, Cosmas produced his charges against the emperor : the Servian marriage ; oppressive taxes upon salt and other necessaries of life, whereby a heavy burden was laid upon the poor, on one hand, and imperial prodigality was encouraged on the other ; failure to treat the petitions addressed to him by Cosmas with the consideration which they deserved. The defence of Andronicus was skilful. He maintained that no marriage of the Kraal had violated Canon Law as some persons claimed. He touched the feelings of his audience by dwelling upon the sacrifice he had made as a father in bestowing the hand of a beloved daughter on such a man as the Servian Prince ; only reasons of State had constrained him to sanction a union so painful to his heart. The taxes to which objection had been taken were not imposed, he pleaded, to gratify any personal love of money, but were demanded by the needs of the Empire. As to love of money, he had reasons to believe that it was a weakness of which his accuser was guilty, and to prove that statement, he there and then sent two members of the court to the treasurer of the palace for evidence in support of the charge. In regard to the accusation that he did not always favour the petitions addressed to him by the patriarch, he remarked that it was not an emperor's duty to grant all the petitions he received, but to discriminate between them according to their merits. At the same time he expressed his readiness to be more indulgent in the future. Moved by these explanations, as well as by the entreaties of the emperor and the bishops present at this strange scene, held in the dead of night in the secrecy of the monastery, Cosmas relented, and returned next day to the patriarchate.[1]

But peace between the two parties was not of long duration. Only a few weeks later Andronicus restored to office a bishop of Ephesus who had been canonically deposed. Cosmas

---

[1] Pachym. ii. pp. 292-98.

protested, and when his remonstrances were disregarded, he withdrew again to the Pammakaristos,[1] and refused to allow his seclusion to be disturbed on any pretext. To the surprise of everybody, however, he suddenly resumed his functions—in obedience, he claimed, to a Voice which said to him, ' If thou lovest Me, feed My sheep.' [2] But such conduct weakened his position. His enemies brought a foul charge against him. His demand for a thorough investigation of the libel was refused. And in his vexation he once more sought the shelter of the Pammakaristos, abdicated the patriarchal throne, and threw the ecclesiastical world into a turmoil.[3] Even then there were still some, including the emperor, who thought order and peace would be more speedily restored by recalling Cosmas to the office he had laid down. But the opposition to him had become too powerful, and he was compelled to bid farewell to the retreat he loved, and to end his days in his native city of Sozopolis, a man worsted in battle.[4]

Of the life at the Pammakaristos during the remainder of the period before the Turkish conquest only a few incidents are recorded. One abbot of the monastery, Niphon, was promoted in 1397 to the bishopric of Old Patras, and another named Theophanes was made bishop of the important See of Heraclea. An instance of the fickleness of fortune was brought home to the monks of the establishment by the disgrace of the logothetes Gabalas and his confinement in one of their cells, under the following circumstances :—In the struggle between John Cantacuzene and Apocaucus for ascendancy at the court of the Dowager Empress Anna of Savoy and her son, John VI. Palaeologus, Gabalas[5] had been persuaded to join the party of the latter politician by the offer, among other inducements, of the hand of Apocaucus' daughter in marriage. But when Gabalas urged the fulfilment of the promise, he was informed that the young lady and her mother had meantime taken a violent aversion to him on account of his corpulent figure.

[1] Pachym. ii. pp. 298-300.   [2] Ibid. ii. p. 303.
[3] Ibid. pp. 341-43.   [4] Ibid. 347-85.
[5] Cantacuzene, ii. pp. 442-48 ; Niceph. Greg. pp. 701, 710, 726.

Thereupon Gabalas, like a true lover, had recourse to a method of banting recommended by an Italian quack. But the treatment failed to reduce the flesh of the unfortunate suitor ; it only ruined his health, and made him even less attractive than before. Another promise by which his political support had been gained was the hope that he would share the power which Apocaucus should win. But this Apocaucus was unwilling to permit, alleging as an excuse that his inconvenient partisan had become obnoxious to the empress. The disappointment and anxiety caused by this information wore so upon the mind of the logothetes as to alter his whole appearance. He now became thin indeed, as if suffering from consumption, and in his dread of the storm gathering about him he removed his valuable possessions to safe hiding. Whereupon the wily Apocaucus drew the attention of the empress to this strange behaviour, and aroused her suspicions that Gabalas was engaged in some dark intrigue against her. No wonder that the logothetes observed in consequence a marked change in the empress's manner towards him, and in his despair he took sanctuary in S. Sophia, and assumed the garb of a monk. The perfidy of Apocaucus might have stopped at this point, and allowed events to follow their natural course. But though willing to act a villain's part, he wished to act it under the mask of a friend, to betray with a kiss. Accordingly he went to S. Sophia to express his sympathy with Gabalas, and played the part of a man overwhelmed with sorrow at a friend's misfortune so well that Gabalas forgot for a while his own griefs, and undertook the task of consoling the hypocritical mourner. Soon an imperial messenger appeared upon the scene with the order for Gabalas to leave the church and proceed to the monastery of the Pammakaristos. And there he remained until, on the charge of attempting to escape, he was confined in a stronger prison.

Another person detained at the Pammakaristos was a Turkish rebel named Zinet, who in company with a pretender to the throne of Mehemed I., had fled in 1418 to Constantinople for protection. He was welcomed by the

L

Byzantine Government, which was always glad to receive refugees whom it could use either to gratify or to embarrass the Ottoman Court, as the varying relations between the two empires might dictate. It was a policy that proved fatal at last, but meanwhile it often afforded some advantage to Byzantine diplomats. On this occasion it was thought advisable to please the Sultan, and while the pretender was confined elsewhere, Zinet, with a suite of ten persons, was detained in the Pammakaristos. Upon the accession of Murad II., however, the Government of Constantinople thought proper to take the opposite course. Accordingly the pretender was liberated, and Zinet sent to support the Turkish party which disputed Murad's claims. But life at the Pammakaristos had not won the refugee's heart to the cause of the Byzantines. The fanatical monks with whom he was associated there had insulted his faith ; his Greek companions in arms did not afford him all the satisfaction he desired, and so Zinet returned at last to his natural allegiance. The conduct of the Byzantine Government on this occasion led to the first siege of Constantinople, in 1422, by the Turks.

The most important event in the history of the monastery occurred after the city had fallen into Turkish hands. The church then became the cathedral of the patriarchs of Constantinople. It is true that, in the first instance, the conqueror had given the church of the Holy Apostles to the Patriarch Gennadius as a substitute for the church of S. Sophia. But the native population did not affect the central quarters of the city, preferring to reside near the Golden Horn and the Sea of Marmora. Furthermore, the body of a murdered Turk was discovered one morning in the court of the Holy Apostles, and excited among his countrymen the suspicion that the murder had been committed by a Christian hand.[1] The few Greeks settled in the neighbourhood were therefore in danger of retaliation, and Gennadius begged permission to withdraw to the Pammakaristos, around which a large colony of Greeks, who came from other cities to repeople the capital, had settled.[2]

---

[1] Ducas, pp. 117-21, 134, 139-42, 148-52, 176.   [2] *Historia politica*, p. 16.

The objection that nuns occupied the monastery at that moment was easily overcome by removing the sisterhood to the small monastery attached to the church of S. John in Trullo (Achmed Pasha Mesjedi) in the immediate vicinity,[1] and for 138 years thereafter the throne of seventeen patriarchs of Constantinople stood in the church of the Pammakaristos, with the adjoining monastery as their official residence.[2]

As the chief sanctuary of the Greek community, the building was maintained, it would appear, in good order and displayed considerable beauty. 'Even at night,' to quote extravagant praise, 'when no lamp was burning, it shone like the sun.' But even sober European visitors in the sixteenth century agree in describing the interior of the church as resplendent with eikons and imperial portraits. It was also rich in relics, some of them brought by Gennadius from the church of the Holy Apostles and from other sanctuaries lost to the Greeks. Among the interesting objects shown to visitors was a small rude sarcophagus inscribed with the imperial eagle and the name of the Emperor Alexius Comnenus.[3] It was so plain and rough that Schweigger speaks of it as too mean to contain the dust of a German peasant.[4] But that any sarcophagus professing to hold the remains of Alexius Comnenus should be found at the Pammakaristos is certainly surprising. That emperor was buried, according to the historian Nicetas Choniates, in the church of S. Saviour the Philanthropist,[5] near the palace of Mangana, on the east shore of the city. Nor could the body of a Byzantine autocrator have been laid originally in a sarcophagus such as Breüning and Schweigger describe. These difficulties in the way of regarding the monument

---

[1] Phrantzes, p. 307.

[2] See Gerlach's description in *Turcograecia*, pp. 189-90.

[3] Breüning, *Orientalische Reyss*, p. 68, 'zur rechten an der Mauren Imp. Alexii Comneni monumentum von Steinwerck auffs einfältigste und schlechteste.'

[4] Salomon Schweigger, *Ein newe Reyssbeschreibung auss Deutschland nach Constantinopel* pp. 119-20, Chaplain for more than three years in Constantinople, at the Legation of the Holy Roman Empire, 1581. He gives the inscription on the sarcophagus : Ἀλέξιος αὐτοκράτωρ τῶν Ῥωμαίων. There is an eagle to the right of the legend.

[5] P. 12, εἰς ἣν ἐκεῖνος ἐδείματο Χριστῷ τῷ φιλανθρώπῳ μονήν.

as genuine are met by the suggestion made by Mr. Siderides, that when the church of Christ the Philanthropist was appropriated by the Turks in connection with the building of the Seraglio, some patriotic hand removed the remains of Alexius Comnenus from the splendid coffin in which they were first entombed, and, placing them in what proved a convenient receptacle, carried them for safe keeping to the Pammakaristos. The statement that Anna Comnena, the celebrated daughter of Alexius Comnenus, was also buried in this church rests upon the misunderstanding of a passage in the work of M. Crusius, where, speaking of that princess, the author says : 'Quae (Anna) anno Domini 1117 vixit ; filia Alexii Comneni Imp. cujus sepulchrum adhuc exstat in templo patriarchatus Constantinopli a D. Steph. Gerlachio visum.'[1]

But *cujus* (whose) refers, not to Anna, but to Alexius. This rendering is put beyond dispute by the statement made by Gerlach in a letter to Crusius, that he found, in the Pammakaristos, 'sepulchrum Alexii Comneni αὐτοκράτορος,' the tomb of the Emperor Alexius Comnenus.[2]

The church was converted into a mosque under Murad III. (1574-1592), and bears the style Fetiyeh, 'of the conqueror,' in honour of the conquest of Georgia and Azerbaijan during his reign. According to Gerlach, the change had been feared for some time, if for no other reason, because of the fine position occupied by the church. But quarrels between different factions of the Greek clergy and between them and Government officials had also something to do with the confiscation of the building.[3] When the cross, which glittered above the dome and gleamed far and wide, indicating the seat of the chief prelate of the Orthodox Communion, was taken down, 'a great sorrow befell the Christians.'[4] The humble church of S. Demetrius Kanabou, in the district of Balat, then became the patriarchal seat until 1614, when that honour was conferred upon the church

---

[1] *Turcograecia*, p. 46, where the tomb is further described ; 'est id lapideum, non insistens 4 basibus, sed integro lapide a terra surgens, altius quam mensa, ad parietem templi.'

[2] *Turcograecia*, p. 189.

[3] Patr. Constantius, p. 72.

[4] *Historia politica*, p. 178.

which still retains it, the church of S. George in the quarter of Phanar.

Architectural Features

Owing to the numerous additions and alterations introduced into the original fabric, both before and since the Turkish conquest, the original plan of the building is not immediately apparent. Nor does the interior, with its heavy piers, raised floor, and naked walls correspond to the accounts given of its former splendour and beauty. A careful study will, however, unravel the tangled scheme which the actual condition of the church presents, and detect some traces of the beauty which has faded and passed away. The building might be mistaken for a domed church with four aisles, two narthexes, and a parecclesion. But notwithstanding all the disguises due to the changes it has undergone, the original church was unquestionably an 'ambulatory' church. It had, moreover, at one time a third narthex, of which now only the foundations remain on the west side of the church. The present outer narthex is in five bays, covered by dome vaults on transverse arches, and is paved with hexagonal tiles. The centre bay is marked by transverse arches of greater breadth and projects slightly on the outside, forming a plain central feature. At the north end a door led to the third narthex, but has now been built up; at the south end is a door inserted in Turkish times. To the south of the central bay the exterior is treated with plain arcades in two orders of brick; to the north these are absent, probably on account of some alterations. At the south end the narthex returns round the church in two bays, leading to the parecclesion.

The inner narthex is in four bays covered with cross-groined vaults without transverse arches, and is at present separated from the body of the church by three clumsy hexagonal piers, on to which, as may be seen in the photograph (Plate XXXVII.), the groins descend in a very irregular manner.

In the inner part of the church is a square central area covered by a lofty drum-dome of twenty-four concave compartments, alternately pierced by windows. The intermediate compartments correspond to the piers, and the dome is therefore twelve-sided on the exterior with angle half columns and arches in two orders. Internally the dome arches are recessed back from the lower wall face and spring from a heavy string-course. They were originally pierced on the north, south, and west sides by three windows similar to those in the west dome arch of S. Andrew (p. 114).

The west side is now occupied by the wooden balcony of a Turkish house built over the narthex, but there are no indications of any gallery in that position.

Below the dome arches the central area communicates with the surrounding ambulatory on the north, west, and south sides by large semicircular arches corbelled slightly out from the piers.

On the east side the dome arch is open from floor to vault, and leads by a short bema to a five-sided space covered by a dome and forming a kind of triangular apse, on the south-eastern side of which is the mihrab. As is clearly shown by the character of its dome windows and masonry, this structure is a Turkish addition taking the place of the original three eastern apses, and is a clever piece of planning to alter the orientation of the building.

The ambulatory on the three sides of the central square is covered by barrel vaults on the sides and with cross-groined vaults at the angles. To the east it opened into the eastern lateral chapels, now swept away, though the passage from the prothesis to the central apse still remains.

On the north side of the church is a passage in three bays covered by dome vaults on transverse arches, communicating at the west end with the inner narthex, and at the east terminating in a small chapel covered by an octagonal drum dome. The upper part of the apse of the chapel is still visible on the exterior, but the lower part has been destroyed and its place taken by a Turkish window.

The floor of the eastern part of the church is raised a step above the general level, this step being carried diagonally across the floor in the centre part so as to line with the side of the apse containing the mihrab.

In considering the original form of the church there is yet another important point to be noted. It will be seen from the plan that at the ground level the central area is not cruciform, but is rather an oblong from east to west with large arches on the north and south sides. This oblong is, however, reduced to a square at the dome level by arches thrown across the east and west ends, and this, in conjunction with the setting back of the dome arches already mentioned, produces a cruciform plan at the springing level. The oblong character of the central area is characteristic of the domed basilica and distinguishes this church from S. Andrew or S. Mary Panachrantos. The employment of barrel vaults in the ambulatory is also a point of resemblance to the domed basilica type, though the cross groin is used on the angles.[1] In this feature S. Mary Pammakaristos resembles S. Andrew and differs from S. Mary Panachrantos. We are probably justified in restoring triple arcades in all the three lower arches similar to the triple arcade which still remains in S. Andrew. The present arches do not fit, and are evidently later alterations for the purpose of gaining internal space as at the Panachrantos.

The hexagonal piers between the ambulatory and the inner narthex are not original, as is evident from the clumsy manner in which the vaulting descends on to them. They are the remains of the old western external wall of the church left over when it was pierced through, probably in Turkish times, to include the narthex in the interior area of the building. The piers between the ambulatory and the gallery on the north side of the church also seem to be due to openings made for a similar reason in the old northern wall of the church when that gallery was added in Byzantine days. The dotted lines on the plan show the original form of the piers and wall, as shown by the outline of the vault springings above. The inner narthex is later than the central church and is of inferior workmanship. The restored plan shows the probable form of the church at that date. The outer narthex was added at a subsequent period.

---

[1] A barrel vault is, however, used under the west gallery of S. Theodosia though cross-groined vaults are used in the side 'aisles.'

The Parecclesion.—The parecclesion forms a complete church of the 'four column' type with a narthex and gynecaeum on the west. On the north side the two columns supporting the dome arches have been removed, and their place is taken by a large pointed Turkish arch which spans the chapel from east to west as is done in the north church

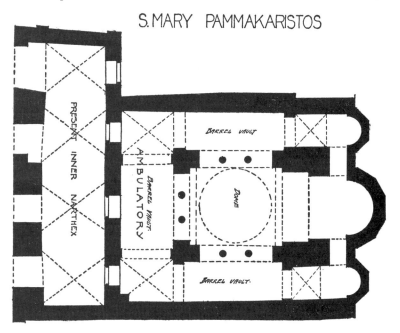

S. MARY PAMMAKARISTOS

PROBABLE ORIGINAL PLAN

Fig. 47.

of the Panachrantos (p. 129). The southern columns are of green marble with bases of a darker marble and finely carved capitals both bedded in lead. One of these columns, that to the east, has been partly built into the mihrab wall. The arms of the cross and the western angle compartments are covered with cross-groined vaults, while the eastern angle compartments have dome vaults. The bema and the two lateral chapels have cross-groined vaults. As usual the apse is semicircular within and shows to the exterior seven sides, the three centre sides being filled with a triple window with carved oblong shafts and cubical capitals.

Internally the church is divided by string-courses at the abacus level of the columns and at the springing level of the vaults into three stories. The lowest story is now pierced by Turkish windows but was originally plain ; the middle story is pierced by single-light windows in each of the angle compartments, and in the cross arm by a three-light window of two quarter arches and a central high semi-circular arch, similar to those in the narthex of the Chora. The highest story has a single large window in the cross arm.

To the east the bema arch springs from the abacus level and all three apses have low vaults, a somewhat unusual arrangement. This allows of an east window in the tympanum of the dome arch above the bema.

The dome is in twelve bays, each pierced by a window and separated by flat projecting ribs. It retains its mosaics, representing Christ in the centre surrounded by twelve prophets. Each prophet holds in his hand a scroll inscribed with a characteristic quotation from his writings. The drawing, for which I am indebted to the skill and kindness of Mr. Arthur E. Henderson, gives an excellent idea of the scheme of the mosaics.

Speaking of these mosaics, Diehl remarks that we have here, as in the Chora, indications of the Revival of Art in the fourteenth century. The Christ in the centre of the dome is no longer represented as the stern and hard Pantokrator, but shows a countenance of infinite benignity and sweetness. The twelve prophets grouped around Him in the flutings of the dome reveal, in the variety of their expressions, in their different attitudes, in the harmonious colours and elegant draping of their robes, an artist who seeks to escape from traditional types and create a living work of his own.[1]

The narthex is in three bays covered by cross-groined vaults without transverse arches. The lower window is a Turkish insertion, and above it, rising from the vaulting

---

[1] *Manuel d'art byzantin*, p. 742.

string-course at the level of the abacus course in the church,
is a triple window of the type already described.

Above the narthex and approached by a narrow stair in

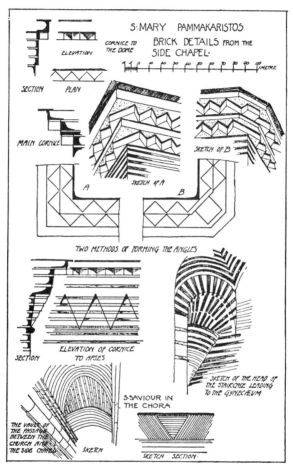

FIG. 48.
(For other details see Fig. 68.)

the thickness of the west wall is the small gynecaeum.
It is in three bays, separated by strong transverse arches
resting on pilasters, each bay having a deep recess to east
and west. The centre bay is covered by a cross-groined

vault, and overlooks the church by a small window pierced in the west cross arm. Each of the side bays is covered by a drum dome of sixteen concave bays pierced with eight windows and externally octagonal. The plaster has fallen away from these bays, allowing us to see that they are built in regular courses of brick with thick mortar joints and without any special strengthening at the lines of juncture or ribs between the compartments. Such domes, therefore, are not strictly ribbed domes but rather domes in compartments. The 'ribs' no doubt do, by their extra thickness, add to the strength of the vault, but here, as in most Byzantine domes, their purpose is primarily ornamental.

The exterior of the chapel, like the façade of S. Theodore (p. 247), presents a carefully considered scheme of decoration, characteristic of the later Byzantine school both here and in the later schools outside Constantinople. The southern wall is divided externally as it is also internally, into three stories, and forms two main compartments corresponding to the narthex and to the cross arm. They are marked by high arches of two orders, which enclose two triple windows in the upper story of the narthex and of the cross arm. The clue to the composition is given by the middle story, which contains the two large triple windows of the narthex and of the cross arm, and the two single lights of the angle compartment, one on each side of the cross arm triple light. These windows are enclosed in brick arches of two orders and linked together by semicircular arched niches, of which those flanking the narthex window are slightly larger than the rest, thus giving a continuous arcade of a very pleasant rhythmic quality.

In the lower story the piers of the arches round the triple windows are alone carried down through the inscribed string-course which separates the stories and forms the window-sill. The system of niches is repeated, flat niches being substituted for the angle compartment windows above.

The highest story contains the large single windows which light the cross arm and the gynecaeum, the former flanked by two semicircular niches, the latter by two brick roundels with radiating joints. Between them, above the west angle compartment window, is a flat niche with a Turkish arch. It is possible that there was originally a break here extending to the cornice, and that this was filled up during Turkish repairs. The cornice has two ranges of brick dentils and is arched over the two large windows. The domes on the building have flat angle pilasters supporting an arched cornice.

The masonry is in stripes of brick and stone courses, with radiating joints to the arched niches and a zigzag pattern in the spandrils of the first-story arches. At this level are four carved stone corbels with notches on the upper side, evidently to take a wooden beam. These must have supported the roof of an external wood cloister. The inscribed string-course already mentioned between the ground and first stories bears a long epitaph in honour of Michael Glabas Tarchaniotes.[1] (Fig. 49.)

The three apses at the east end are of equal height. The side ones are much worn but were apparently plain. The centre apse is in three stories with alternately flat and circular niches in each side. It is crowned by a machi-colated cornice similar to that on the east end of S. Theodosia.

The general composition, as will be seen from the description, arises very directly from the internal arrange-ments of the chapel and is extremely satisfactory. The ranges of arches, varying in a manner at first irregular, but presently seen to be perfectly symmetrical, give a rhythmic swing to the design. The walls are now heavily plastered and the effect of the horizontal bands of brick and stone is lost ; but even in its present state the building is a very delightful example of Byzantine external architecture.

Evidently the foundress of the chapel wished the monu-ment she reared to her husband's memory to be as beautiful both within and without as the taste and skill of the times could make it.

---

[1] The bands of marble on which the inscription is found were cut from marble slabs which once formed part of a balustrade, for the upper side of the bands is covered with carved work.

What information we have in regard to the chapel is little, but clear and definite, resting as it does on the authority of the two epitaphs which the poet Philes composed to be inscribed on the interior and exterior walls of the building. One of the epitaphs, if ever placed in position, has been destroyed or lies concealed under Turkish plaster. Of the other only fragments remain, forming part of the scheme of decoration which adorns the south wall of the chapel. But fortunately the complete

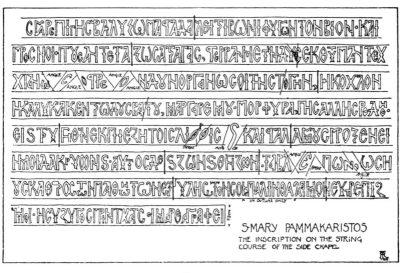

S·MARY PAMMAKARISTOS
THE INSCRIPTION ON THE STRING
COURSE OF THE SIDE CHAPEL

Fig. 49.

text of both epitaphs is preserved in the extant writings of their author, and affords all the information they were meant to record. The chapel was dedicated to Christ as the Logos[1] and was built after the death of the protostrator by his wife Maria, or Martha in religion, for a mausoleum in which to place his tomb.[2] As the protostrator died about 1315, the chapel was erected soon after that date. An interesting incident occurred in this chapel soon after

[1] *Carmina Philae*, i. pp. 115-16, lines 4, 7.
[2] *Ibid.* Heading to poem, and lines 10, 13-16. Second epitaph p. 117, lines 2, 5, 14.

the Turkish conquest. One day when the Sultan was riding through his newly acquired capital he came to the Pammakaristos, and upon being informed that it was the church assigned to the Patriarch Gennadius, alighted to honour the prelate with a visit. The meeting took place in this parecclesion, and the conversation, of which a summary account was afterwards sent to the Sultan, dwelt on the dogmas of the Christian Faith.[1]

The text of the epitaph, portions of which appear on the exterior face of the south wall of the parecclesion of the church of the Pammakaristos (*Carmina Philae*, ccxxiii. ed. Miller, vol. i. pp. 117-18) reads as follows :—

Ἄνερ, τὸ φῶς, τὸ πνεῦμα, τὸ πρόσφθεγμά μου,
καὶ τοῦτό σοι τὸ δῶρον ἐκ τῆς συζύγου ·
σὺ μὲν γὰρ ὡς ἄγρυπνος ἐν μάχαις λέων
ὑπνοῖς, ὑπελθὼν ἀντὶ λόχμης τὸν τάφον ·
5 ἐγὼ δέ σοι τέτευχα πετραίαν στέγην,
μὴ πάλιν εὑρὼν ὁ στρατός σε συγχέῃ,
κἂν δεῦρο τὸν χοῦν ἐκτινάξας ἐκρύβης,
ἢ τοῦ πάχους ῥεύσαντος ἡρπάγης ἄνω,
πᾶν ὅπλον ἀφεὶς ἐκκρεμὲς τῷ παττάλῳ ·
10 τὰς γὰρ ἐπὶ γῆς ἐβδελύξω παστάδας
ἐν εὐτελεῖ τρίβωνι φυγὼν τὸν βίον
καὶ πρὸς νοητοὺς ἀντετάξω σατράπας,
στερρὰν μετενδὺς ἐκ θεοῦ παντευχίαν.
ὡς ὄστρεον γοῦν ὀργανῶ σοι τὸν τάφον,
15 ἢ κόχλον ἢ κάλυκα κεντρώδους βάτου ·
μάργαρέ μου, πορφύρα, γῆς ἄλλης ῥόδον,
εἰ καὶ τρυγηθὲν ἐκπιέζῃ τοῖς λίθοις
ὡς καὶ σταλαγμοὺς προξενεῖν μοι δακρύων,
αὐτὸς δὲ καὶ ζῶν καὶ Θεὸν ζῶντα βλέπων
20 ὡς νοῦς καθαρὸς τῶν παθῶν τῶν ἐξ ὕλης
τὸν σὸν πάλιν θάλαμον εὐτρέπιζέ μοι ·
ἡ σύζυγος πρὶν ταῦτά σοι Μάρθα γράφει,
πρωτοστράτορ κάλλιστε καὶ τεθαμμένων.[2]

O my husband, my light, my breath, whom I now greet.
This gift to thee also is from thy wife.
For thou indeed who wast like a sleepless lion in battles
Sleepest, having to endure the grave, instead (of occupying) thy lair.

---

[1] *Turcograecia*, pp. 16, 109, ἔνδον τῆς μικρᾶς ἐκκλησίας καὶ ὡραίας τοῦ παρεκκλησίου.   [2] τεθαμμένε (Cod. Mon. fol. 102).

But I have erected for thee a dwelling of stone,
Lest the army finding thee again, should trouble thee,
Although here thou art hidden, having cast off thy (body of) clay,
Or, the gross flesh having dropped off, thou hast been transported above,
Leaving every weapon hung up on its peg.
For thou didst abhor the mansions in the world,[1]
Having fled from life in the cheap cloak (of a monk),
And didst confront invisible potentates,
Having received instead (of thine own armour) a strong panoply from God.
Therefore I will construct for thee this tomb as a pearl oyster shell,
Or shell of the purple dye, or bud on a thorny brier.
O my pearl, my purple, rose of another clime,
Even though being plucked thou art pressed by the stones
So as to cause me sheddings of tears.
Yet thou thyself, both living and beholding the living God,
As a mind pure from material passions,
Prepare for me again thy home.
Martha,[2] thy wife formerly, writes these things to thee,
O protostrator, fairest also of the dead !

The following epitaph in honour of the protostrator Glabas[3] was to be placed in the parecclesion of the church of the Pammakaristos (*Carmina Philae*, ccxix., ed. Miller, vol. i. pp. 115-16) :—

Ἐπίγραμμα εἰς τὸν ναὸν ὃν ᾠκοδόμησεν ἡ τοῦ πρωτοστράτορος
σύμβιος ἀποθανόντι τῷ ἀνδρὶ αὐτῆς.

ἡ μὲν διὰ σοῦ πᾶσα τῶν ὄντων φύσις
οὐ δύναται χωρεῖν σε τὴν πρώτην φύσιν·
πληροῖς γὰρ αὐτὴν ἀλλὰ καὶ πλείων μένεις,
Θεοῦ Λόγε ζῶν καὶ δρακὶ τὸ πᾶν φέρων,
5 κἂν σὰρξ ἀληθὴς εὑρεθεὶς περιγράφῃ,
ψυχαῖς δὲ πισταῖς μυστικῶς ἐνιδρύῃ
μονὴν σεαυτῷ πηγνύων ἀθάνατον·
οὐκοῦν δέχου τὸν οἶκον ὃν τέτευχά σοι
δεικνύντα σαφῶς τῆς ψυχῆς μου τὴν σχέσιν·
10 τὸν σύζυγον δὲ φεῦ τελευτήσαντά μοι
καὶ τῆς χοϊκῆς ἀπαναστάντα στέγης,

---

[1] Alludes to the retirement of Glabas from the world as a monk.
[2] Her name as a nun.
[3] In the superscription to this epigram in the Florentine and Munich MSS. the name Γλαβᾶς is given.

οἴκισον εἰς ἄφθαρτον αὐτὸς παστάδα,
κἀνταῦθα τηρῶν τὴν σορὸν τοῦ λειψάνου,
μή τις ἐνεχθῇ συντριβῇ τοῖς ὀστέοις.
15 πρωτοστράτορ καὶ ταῦτα σὴν δήπου χάριν
ἡ σύζυγος πρίν, ἀλλὰ νῦν Μάρθα γράφει.

The whole nature of existing things which thou hast made
Cannot contain Thee, the primordial nature,
For Thou fillest it, and yet remainest more than it ;
O Logos of God, living and holding all in the hollow of Thy hand,
Although as true flesh Thou art circumscribed,
And dwellest, mystically, in faithful souls,
Establishing for Thyself an immortal habitation,
Yet accept the house which I have built for Thee,
Which shows clearly the disposition of my soul.
My husband who, alas ! has died to me
And gone forth from his house of clay,
Do Thou Thyself settle in an incorruptible mansion,
Guarding also here the shrine of his remains,
Lest any injury should befall his bones.
O protostrator, these things, too, for thy sake I trow,
Writes she who erewhile was thy wife, but now is Martha.[1]

---

[1] In these translations I have been assisted chiefly by Sir W. M. Ramsay, Professor Bury, and Mr. E. M. Antoniadi.

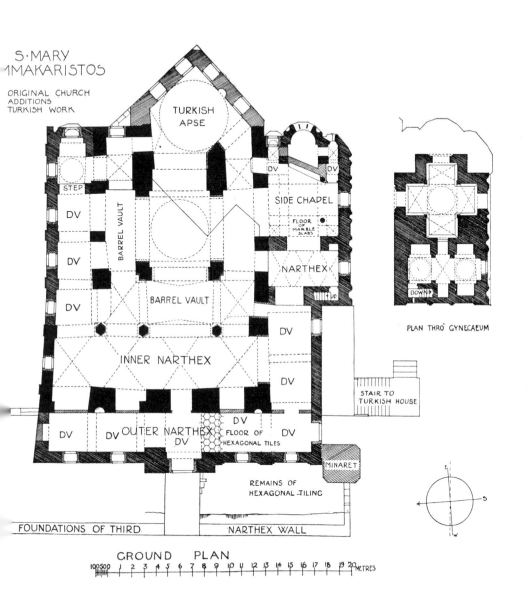

S·MARY
MMAKARISTOS

ORIGINAL CHURCH
ADDITIONS
TURKISH WORK

TURKISH
APSE

DV

STEP

DV

DV

BARREL VAULT

DV

DV

SIDE CHAPEL

FLOOR
OF
MARBLE
SLABS

NARTHEX

DV

DV

BARREL VAULT

INNER NARTHEX

DV

DV

STAIR TO
TURKISH HOUSE

DV

DV OUTER NARTHEX
DV

DV
FLOOR OF
HEXAGONAL TILES

DV

MINARET

REMAINS OF
HEXAGONAL TILING

PLAN THRO' GYNECAEUM

DOWN

FOUNDATIONS OF THIRD   NARTHEX WALL

GROUND   PLAN

100 50 0   1 2 3 4 5 6 7 8 9 10 11 12 13 14 15 16 17 18 19 20 METRES

F IG. 50.

To face page 160.

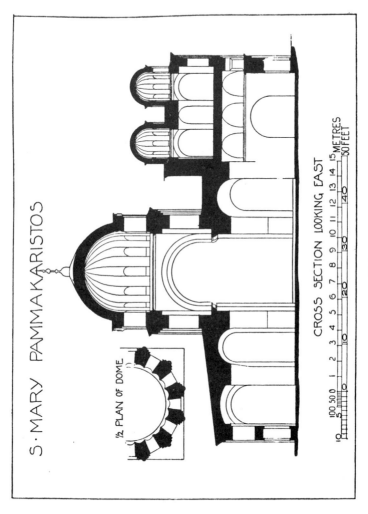

S·MARY PAMMAKARISTOS

½ PLAN OF DOME

CROSS SECTION LOOKING EAST

100 50 0   1   2   3   4   5   6   7   8   9   10 11 12 13 14 15 METRES
5   10   20   30   40   50 FEET

FIG. 51.

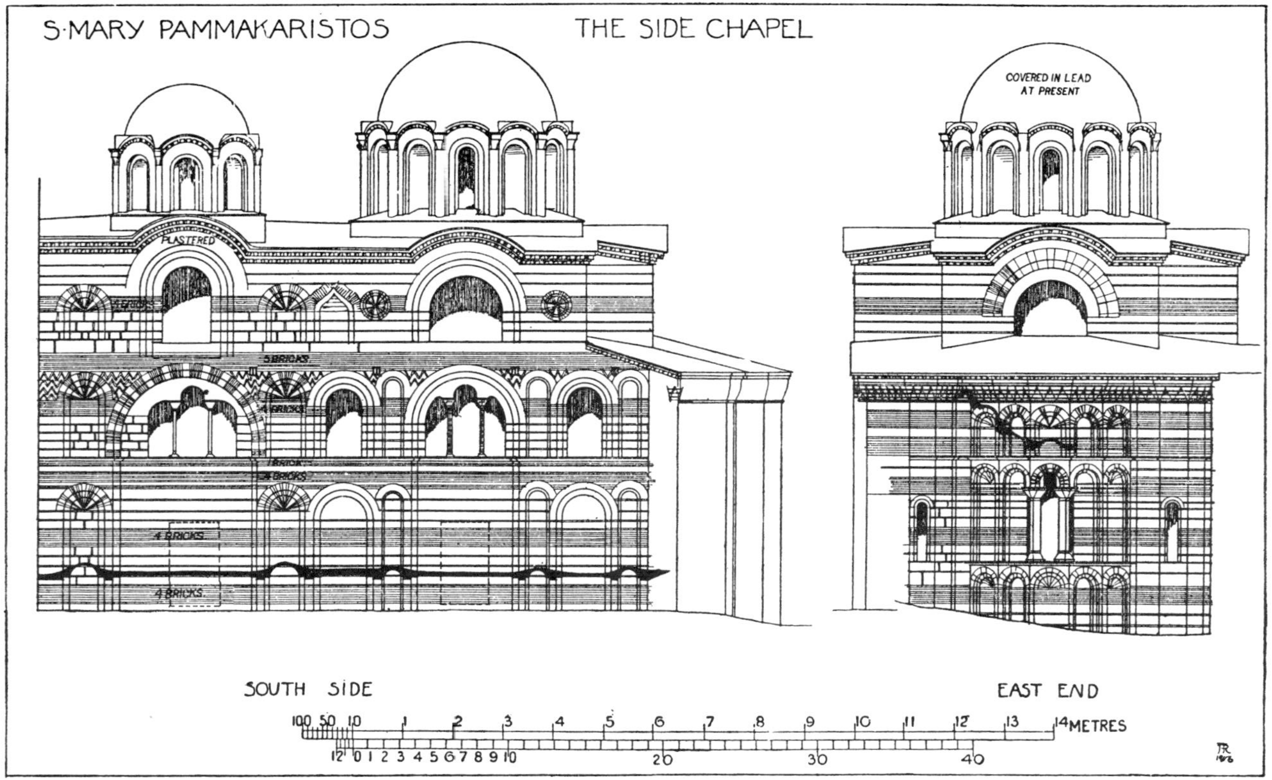
S·MARY PAMMAKARISTOS
THE SIDE CHAPEL
COVERED IN LEAD AT PRESENT
PLASTERED
5 BRICKS
1 BRICK
4 BRICKS
4 BRICKS
SOUTH SIDE
EAST END
METRES

FIG. 52.

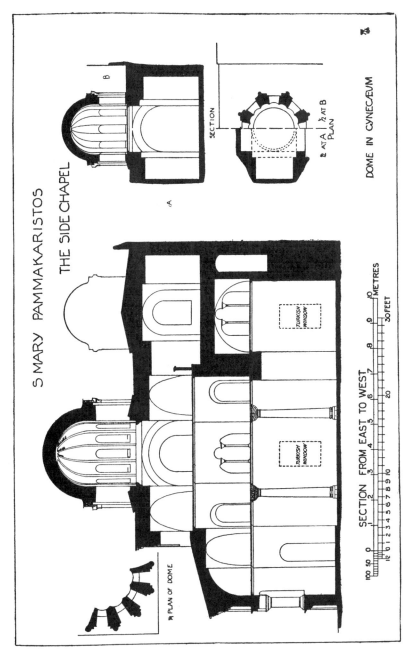

S MARY PAMMAKARISTOS

THE SIDE CHAPEL

SECTION FROM EAST TO WEST

DOME IN GYNECÆUM

FIG. 53.

CHAPTER VIII

CHURCH OF S. THEODOSIA, GUL JAMISSI

THERE can be no doubt that the mosque Gul Jamissi (mosque of the Rose), that stands within the Gate Aya Kapou, near the Golden Horn, was the Byzantine church of S. Theodosia. For Aya Kapou is the entrance styled in Byzantine days the Gate of S. Theodosia (πύλη τῆς ἁγίας Θεοδοσίας), because in the immediate vicinity of the church of that dedication.[1] This was also the view current on the subject when Gyllius[2] and Gerlach[3] visited the city in the sixteenth century. The Turkish epithet of the gate ' Aya,' Holy, is thus explained. Du Cange,[4] contrary to all evidence, places the church of S. Theodosia on the northern side of the harbour, or at its head, *ultra sinum*.

The saint is celebrated in ecclesiastical history for her opposition to the iconoclastic policy of Leo the Isaurian. For when that emperor commanded the eikon of Christ over the Bronze Gate of the Great Palace to be removed, Theodosia, at the head of a band of women, rushed to the spot and overthrew the ladder up which the officer, charged with the execution of the imperial order, was climbing to reach the image. In the fall the officer was killed. Whereupon a rough soldier seized Theodosia, and dragging her to the forum of the Bous (Ak Serai), struck her dead by driving a ram's horn through her neck. Naturally, when the cause for which she sacrificed her life triumphed, she was honoured

---

[1] Phrantzes, p. 254 ; Pusculus, iv. 190.
[2] *De Bosporo Thracio*, vi. c. 2.
[3] *Türkisches Tagebuch*, pp. 358, 454 ; Patr. Constantius, p. 13.
[4] Constant. Christ. iv. 190.

as a martyr, and men said, 'The ram's horn, in killing thee, O Theodosia, appeared to thee a new Horn of Amalthea.'[1]

The remains of the martyred heroine were taken for burial to the monastery of Dexiocrates (τὸ μοναστήριον τὸ ὀνομαζόμενον Δεξιοκράτους), so named either after its founder or after the district in which it was situated.[2] This explains why the Gate of S. Theodosia was also designated the Gate of Dexiocrates (Πόρτα Δεξιοκράτους).[3] The earliest reference to the church of S. Theodosia occurs in the account of the pilgrimage made by Anthony, Archbishop of Novgorod,[4] to Constantinople in 1200. Alluding to that shrine he says : 'Dans un couvent,' to quote the French translation of his narrative, ' de femmes se trouvent les reliques de sainte Théodosie, dans une châsse ouverte en argent.' Another Russian pilgrim from Novgorod,[5] Stephen, who was in Constantinople in 1350, refers to the convent expressly as the convent of S. Theodosia : 'Nous allâmes vénérer la sainte vierge Théodosie, que (pécheurs) nous baisâmes ; il y a là un couvent en son nom au bord de la mer.' The convent is again mentioned in the description of Constantinople by the Russian pilgrim[6] who visited the city shortly before the Turkish conquest (1424-53). 'De là (Blachernae) nous nous dirigeâmes vers l'est et atteignîmes le couvent de Sainte Théodosie ; la sainte vierge Théodosie y repose dans une châsse découverte.'

Two other Russian pilgrims, Alexander the scribe (1395), and the deacon Zosimus (1419-21), likewise refer to the relics of the saint, but they do so in terms which create some difficulty. Alexander saw the relics in the church of the Pantokrator,[7] while Zosimus found them in the convent of the 'Everghetis.'[8] The discrepancy between these statements may indeed be explained as one of the mistakes very easily committed by strangers who spend only a short time in a city, visit a multitude of similar objects during that

---

[1] Synax., May 29.—

Κέρας κριοῦ κτεῖνόν σε, Θεοδοσία,
ὤφθη νέον σοι τῆς Ἀμαλθείας κέρας.

[2] Banduri, ii. p. 34. [3] Codinus, De S. Sophia, p. 147.
[4] Itin. russes, p. 104. [5] Ibid. p. 125.
[6] Ibid. p. 233. [7] Ibid. p. 162. [8] Itin. russes, p. 205.

brief stay, and write the account of their travels at hurried moments, or after returning home.

It is on this principle that Mordtmann[1] deals with the statement that the relics of S. Theodosia were kept in the monastery of the 'Everghetis.' In his opinion Zosimus confused the monastery of S. Saviour Euergetes[2] with the church of S. Theodosia,[3] because of the proximity of the two sanctuaries. Lapses of memory are of course possible, but, on the other hand, the trustworthiness of a document must not be brushed aside too readily.

But the differences in the statements of the Russian pilgrims, as to the particular church in which the relics of S. Theodosia were enshrined, may be explained without charging any of the good men with a mistake, if we remember that relics of the same saint might be preserved in several sanctuaries ; that the calendar of the Greek church celebrates four saints bearing the name Theodosia ;[4] and, lastly, that churches of the same dedication stood in different quarters of the city. In fact, a church dedicated to the Theotokos Euergetes stood on the Xerolophos above the quarter of Psamathia.[5]

Stephen of Novgorod[6] makes it perfectly clear that he venerated the relics of S. Theodosia in two different sanctuaries of the city, one of them being a church beside the Golden Horn, the other standing on the heights above Psamathia. So does the anonymous pilgrim.[7] The scribe Alexander[8] found the relics of S. Theodosia both in the Pantokrator and in the church of Kirmarta, above the quarter of Psamathia. It is clear, therefore, that Zosimus,[9] who places the relics of S. Theodosia in the monastery of 'Everghetis,' has in mind the church of the Theotokos Euergetes above Psamathia, and not the church of S.

[1] *Esq. top.* parags. 68, 69.

[2] Pachym. vol. i. p. 365; *Chroniques græco-romaines*, pp. 96, 97.

[3] Nicet. Chon. p. 752.

[4] Synax. March 25, May 29 (a day sacred to two saints named Theodosia), July 8.

[5] *Itin. russes*, p. 205. Not far from the church and cistern of S. Mokius.

[6] *Ibid.* cf. pp. 122, 125.　　　　　　　　[7] *Ibid.* pp. 233, 234.

[8] *Ibid.* pp. 162, 163.

[9] *Ibid.* p. 205.

Saviour Euergetes which stood near S. Theodosia beside the Golden Horn.

NOTE

While Zosimus and Alexander agree in placing the relics of S. Theodosia in a church in the region of Psamathia, they differ as to the name of that church, the former naming it Everghetis, while the latter styles it Kirmarta. As appears from statements found on pages 108, 163, 205 of the *Itinéraires russes*, the two sanctuaries were closely connected. But however this discrepancy should be treated, there can be no doubt that relics of S. Theodosia were exhibited, not only in the church dedicated to her beside the Golden Horn, but also in a church in the south-western part of the city. Nor can it be doubted that a church in the latter quarter was dedicated to the Theotokos Euergetes.

That several churches should have claimed to possess the relics of the heroine who championed the cause of eikons, assuming that all the Russian pilgrims had one and the same S. Theodosia in mind, is not strange. Many other popular saints were honoured in a similar fashion.

The shrine of S. Theodosia was famed for miraculous cures. Her horn of plenty was filled with gifts of healing. Twice a week, on Wednesdays and Fridays, according to Stephen of Novgorod, or on Mondays and Fridays, according to another pilgrim, the relics of the saint were carried in procession and laid upon sick and impotent folk.[1] Those were days of high festival. All the approaches to the church were packed with men and women eager to witness the wonders performed. Patients representing almost every complaint to which human flesh is heir filled the court. Gifts of oil and money poured into the treasury; the church was a blaze of lighted tapers; the prayers were long; the chanting was loud. Meanwhile the sufferers were borne one after another to the sacred relics, 'and whoever was sick,' says the devout Stephen, 'was healed.' So profound was the impression caused by one of these cures in 1306, that Pachymeres[2] considered it his duty, as the historian of his day, to record the wonder; and his example may be followed to furnish an illustration of the beliefs and usages

---

[1] *Itin. russes*, pp. 225, 233. [2] Pachym. i. p. 365.

which bulked largely in the religious life witnessed in the churches of Byzantine Constantinople.

At the time referred to there dwelt in the city a deaf-mute, a well-known object of charity who supported himself by petty services in benevolent households. While thus employed by a family that resided near the church of the Holy Apostles, the poor man one night saw S. Theodosia in a dream, and heard her command to repair with tapers and incense to the church dedicated to her honour. Next morning the deaf-mute made his friends understand what had occurred during his sleep, and with their help found his way to the designated shrine. There he was anointed with the holy oil of the lamp before the saint's eikon, and bowed long in humble adoration at her feet. Nothing remarkable happened at the time. But on his homeward way the devout man felt a strange pain in his ear, and upon putting his hand to the sore place, what seemed a winged insect flew out and vanished from view. Wondering what this might mean, he entered the house in which he served, and set himself to prepare the oven in which the bread for the family was to be baked that day. But all his efforts to kindle the fire were in vain ; the wood only smoked. This went on so long that, like most persons under the same circumstances, the much-tried man lost his temper and gave way to the impulse to use bad language. Whereupon sonorous imprecations on the obstinate fuel shook the air. The bystanders could not believe their ears. They thought the sounds proceeded from some mysterious voice in the oven. But the deaf-mute protested that he heard his friends talking, and assured them that the words they heard were his own ; S. Theodosia had opened his ears and loosed his tongue. The news of the marvel spread far and wide and reached even the court. Andronicus II. sent for the young man, interrogated him, and was so deeply impressed by the recital of what had happened that he determined to proceed to the church of S. Theodosia in state, and went thither with the patriarch and the senate, humbly on foot, and spent the whole night before the wonder-working shrine in prayer and thanksgiving.

The last scene witnessed in this church as a Christian sanctuary was pathetic in the extreme. It was the vigil of the day sacred to the memory of the saint, May 29, 1453. The siege of the city by the Turks had reached its crisis. The morning light would see the Queen of Cities saved or lost. All hearts were torn with anxiety, and the religious fervour of the population rose to the highest pitch. Already, in the course of the previous day, a great procession had gone through the streets of the city, invoking the aid of God and of all His saints. The emperor and the leading personages of his court were in S. Sophia, praying, weeping, embracing one another, forgiving one another, all feeling oppressed by a sense of doom. In the terrible darkness the church of S. Theodosia, ablaze with lighted tapers, gleamed like a beacon of hope. An immense congregation, including many women, filled the building, and prayers ascended to Heaven with unwonted earnestness—when suddenly the tramp of soldiers and strange shouts were heard. Had the city indeed fallen ? The entrance of Turkish troops into the church removed all doubt, and the men and women who had gathered to pray for deliverance were carried off as prisoners of war.[1] According to the *Belgic Chronicle*, the body of the saint and other relics were thrown into the mire and cast to the dogs.[2]

Architectural Features

As the building has undergone extensive repairs since it became a mosque, care must be taken to distinguish between the original features of the fabric and Turkish changes and restorations. The pointed dome arches rest on pilasters built against the internal angles of the cross. The dome is windowless, has no internal drum, and externally is octagonal with a low drum and a flat cornice. Dome, arches, and pilasters are all evidently Turkish reconstructions. The gable walls of the transepts and the western wall are also Turkish. As the central apse coincided with the orientation of the mosque, it

---

[1] Ducas, p. 293.   [2] Du Cange, iv. p. 190.

has retained its original form and some portions of its Byzantine walls, but it also has suffered Turkish alterations. The cross arches in the south gallery and in the narthex are pointed, and, in their present form, unquestionably Turkish; but as the vault above them is Byzantine, their form may be due to cutting away in order to secure a freer passage round the galleries for the convenience of Moslem worshippers. The outer narthex is Turkish, but the old wall which forms its foundation and traces of an old pavement imply the former existence of a Byzantine narthex. In spite, however, of these serious changes the building preserves its original characteristic features, and is a good example of a domed-cross church, with galleries on three sides and domes over the four angle-chambers.

The galleries rest on a triple arcade supported by square piers. On the north and south the aisles are covered with cross-groined vaults on oblong compartments, while the passage or narthex under the western gallery has a barrel vault.

The chambers at the north-eastern and south-eastern angles of the cross are thrown into the side chapels, which thus consist of two bays covered with cross-groined vaults. Communication between the chapels and the bema was maintained by passages opening in the ordinary fashion into the eastern bays.

In the thickness of each of the eastern dome piers, and at a short distance above the floor, is a small chamber. The chamber in the north-eastern pier is lighted by a small opening looking southwards, and was reached by a door in the east side of the passage leading from the bema to the north-eastern chapel. The door has been walled up, and the chamber is consequently inaccessible. The chamber in the south-eastern pier is lighted by a window looking northwards, and has a door in the east side of the passage from the bema to the south-eastern chapel.

Over the door is a Turkish inscription [1] in gilt letters to this effect, 'Tomb of the Apostles, disciples of Jesus. Peace to him.' The chamber is reached by a short spiral

---

[1] Merkadi havariyoun eshabi Issa alaihusselam.

stairway of nine stone steps, and contains a small marble
tomb, which is covered with shawls, and has a turban
around its headstone.   On a bracket in the wall is a lamp
ready to be lighted in honour of the deceased.   The roof
of the chamber is perforated by an opening that runs into

FIG. 54.—S. THEODOSIA.   THE INTERIOR, LOOKING WEST.
(From a Photograph.)

the floor at the east end of the southern gallery, and over
the opening is an iron grating.

Access to the galleries is gained by means of a staircase in the northern bay of the passage under the
western gallery.   For some distance from the floor of the
church the staircase has wooden steps, but from the first
landing, where a door in the northern wall stands on a level

with the ground outside the church, stone steps are employed for the remainder of the way up. The wooden steps are Turkish, but may replace Byzantine steps of the same material. The stone steps are Byzantine, and could be reached directly from outside the church through the door situated beside the landing from which they start. Probably in Byzantine days the stone staircase could not be reached from the floor of the church, and furnished the only means of access to the galleries.

The galleries are covered by the barrel vaults of the cross arms. At the east end of the northern and the southern gallery are chapels covered with domes and placed above the prothesis and the diaconicon. As stated already, the aperture in the roof of the chamber in the south-eastern dome pier opens into the floor of the southern chapel, and probably a similar aperture in the roof of the corresponding chamber in the north-eastern pier opened into the floor of the chapel at the east end of the northern gallery. The presence of chapels in such an unusual position is explained by the desire to celebrate special services in honour of the saints whose remains were buried in the chambers in the piers, as though in crypts.

The domes over the chapels are hemispherical and rest directly on the pendentives. They are ribless and without drums. The arches on which they rest are semicircular and, with their infilling of triple windows, are Byzantine. We may safely set down all four angle domes as belonging to the original design, though the arches by which they communicate with the galleries are pointed, and are therefore Turkish insertions or enlargements.

On the exterior the eastern wall of the church is fairly well preserved. The three apses project boldly ; the central apse in seven sides, the lateral apses in three sides. Although the central apse is unquestionably a piece of Byzantine work it does not appear to be the original apse of the building, but a substitute inserted in the course of repairs before the Turkish conquest. This accounts for its plain appearance as compared with the lateral apses, which are decorated with four tiers of five niches, corresponding to the window height and the vaulting-level within the church. As on the apses of the Pantokrator (p. 235) the niches are shallow segments in plan, set back in one brick order, and without impost moulding. In the lowest tier three arches are introduced between pilasters, with a window in the central arch. Above the four tiers of niches is a boldly corbelled cornice, like that in the chapel attached to the Pammakaristos. One cannot help admiring how an effect so decidedly rich and beautiful was produced by very simple means.

Details of the tiled floor and of several carved fragments are given in Fig. 76.

For some time after the conquest the building was used as a naval store.[1] It was converted into a mosque in the reign of Sultan Selim II. (1566-74) by a wealthy courtier, Hassan Pasha, and was known as Hassan Pasha Mesjedi.[2] Its title, the mosque of the Rose, doubtless refers to its beauty, just as another mosque is, for a similar reason, styled Laleli Jamissi, the mosque of the Tulip.

Before leaving the church we may consider the claims of the tradition that the chamber in the south-eastern dome pier contains the tomb of the last Byzantine emperor. The tradition was first announced to the general public by the Patriarch Constantius in a letter which he addressed in 1852 to Mr. Scarlatus Byzantius, his fellow-student in all pertaining to the antiquities and history of Constantinople.[3] According to the patriarch, the tradition was accepted by the Turkish ecclesiastical authorities of the city, and was current among the old men of the Greek community resident in the quarter of Phanar ; he himself knew the tradition even in his boyhood. Furthermore, distinguished European visitors who inquired for Byzantine imperial tombs were directed by Turkish officials to the church of S. Theodosia, as the resting-place of the emperor who died with the Empire ; and the inscription over the door of the chamber referred to that champion of the Greek cause. Strangely enough, the patriarch said nothing about this tradition when treating of

---

[1] Paspates, p. 322. [2] Leunclavius, *Pand. Turc.* c. 128.
[3] Συγγραφαὶ αἱ Ἐλάσσονες.

the church of S. Theodosia in his book on *Ancient and Modern Constantinople*, published in 1844. In that work, indeed, he assigns the tomb in question to some martyr who suffered during the iconoclastic period.[1] This strange silence he explains in his letter written in 1852 as due to prudence ; he had reason then to ' put the seal of Alexander upon his lips.'

The tradition has recently received the honour of being

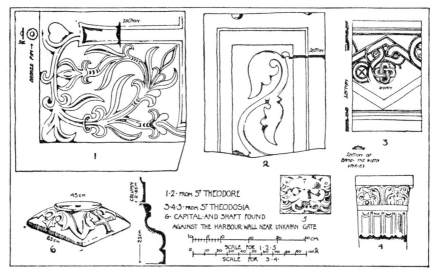

FIG. 55.

(For other details in the church see Fig. 76.)

supported by Mr. Siderides, to whom students of Byzantine archaeology are so deeply indebted. But while accepting it in general, Mr. Siderides thinks it is open to correction on two points of detail.

In his opinion the church of S. Theodosia was not the first sanctuary to guard the mortal remains of Constantine Palaeologus, but the second. Nor was the body of the fallen hero, when ultimately brought to this church, placed, as the

---

[1] "Μελέτης," Athens, 1908 : Κωνσταντίνου Παλαιολόγου θάνατος, τάφος, καὶ σπάθη.

patriarch supposed, in the chamber in the south-eastern pier, but in the chamber in the pier to the north-east. The reasons urged in favour of these modifications of the tradition, as reported by the Patriarch Constantius, are substantially the following :—In the first place, the body of the last Constantine, after its decapitation, was, at the express order of the victorious Sultan, buried with royal honours, μετὰ βασιλικῆς τιμῆς,[1] and therefore, so Mr. Siderides maintains, must have been interred in the church which then enjoyed the highest rank in the Greek community of the city, viz. the church of the Holy Apostles, the patriarchal cathedral after the appropriation of S. Sophia by the Turks. The church of the Holy Apostles, however, soon lost that distinction, and was torn down to make room for the mosque which bears the name of the conqueror of the city. Under these circumstances what more natural, asks Mr. Siderides, than that pious and patriotic hands should remove as many objects of historical or religious value as possible from the doomed shrine, and deposit them where men might still do them reverence—especially when there was every facility for the removal of such objects, owing to the fact that a Christian architect, Christoboulos, had charge of the destruction of the church and of the erection of the mosque.

Some of those objects were doubtless transferred to the church of the Pammakaristos,[2] where the Patriarch Gennadius placed his throne after abandoning the church of the Holy Apostles ; but others may have been taken elsewhere. And for proof that the church of S. Theodosia had the honour of being entrusted with the care of some of the relics removed from the Holy Apostles, Mr. Siderides points to the inscription over the doorway leading to the chamber in the south-eastern dome pier. According to the inscription that chamber is consecrated by the remains of Christ's apostles, i.e. the relics which

---

[1] Phrantzes, pp. 290-91, καὶ προστάξει αὐτοῦ οἱ εὑρεθέντες Χριστιανοὶ ἔθαψαν τὸ βασιλικὸν πτῶμα μετὰ βασιλικῆς τιμῆς.

[2] E.g., the column at which Christ was scourged stood in the church of the Holy Apostles before the conquest. It was found by Gerlach after the conquest in the Pammakaristos.—*Turcograecia*, p. 189.

formed the peculiar treasure of the church of the Holy Apostles.

This being so, Mr. Siderides argues, on the strength of the tradition under review, that the remains of the last Constantine also were brought from the church of the Holy Apostles to S. Theodosia under the circumstances described.

As to the position of the imperial tomb when thus transferred to the church of S. Theodosia, Mr. Siderides insists that it cannot be in the chamber in the south-eastern dome pier : first, because the religious veneration cherished by Moslems for the grave in that chamber is inconsistent with the idea that the grave contains the ashes of the enemy who, in 1453, resisted the Sultan's attack upon the city ; secondly, because the inscription over the doorway leading to the chamber expressly declares the chamber to be the resting-place of Christ's apostles. Hence Mr. Siderides concludes that if the tradition before us has any value, the tomb of the last Byzantine emperor was placed in the chamber in the north-eastern pier, and finds confirmation of that view in the absence of any respect for the remains deposited there.

To enter into a minute criticism of this tradition and of the arguments urged in its support would carry us far beyond our scope. Nor does such criticism seem necessary. The fact that the last Constantine was buried with royal honours affords no proof whatever that he was laid to rest in the church of the Holy Apostles. If he was ever buried in S. Theodosia, he may have been buried there from the first. The lateness of the date when the tradition became public makes the whole story it tells untrustworthy. Before a statement published in the early part of the nineteenth century in regard to the interment of the last Byzantine emperor can have any value, it must be shown to rest on information furnished nearer the time at which the alleged event occurred. No information of that kind has been produced. On the contrary, the only contemporary historian of the siege of 1453 who refers to the site of the emperor's grave informs us that the head of the last Constantine was interred in S. Sophia, and his mutilated body in Galata.[1] The patriarchal authorities of the sixteenth century, as Mr. Siderides admits, while professing to point out the exact spot where Constantine Palaeologus fell, were ignorant of the place where he was buried. In his work on the mosques of the city, written in 1620, Evlia Effendi not only knows nothing of the tradition we are considering, but says expressly that the emperor was buried elsewhere —in the church of the monastery of S. Mary Peribleptos, known by the Turks as Soulou Monastir, in the quarter of Psamathia. In 1852 a story prevailed that the grave of the last Constantine was in the quarter of Vefa Meidan.[2] From all these discrepancies it is evident that in the confusion attending the Turkish capture of the city, the real site of the imperial grave was soon forgotten, and that all subsequent indications of its position are mere conjectures, the offspring of the propensity to find in nameless graves local habitations for popular heroes.

NOTE

The first edition of *Ancient and Modern Constantinople* was published in 1824. In it there is no mention of any tomb in the church of S. Theodosia. The second edition of that work appeared in 1844, and there the author speaks of a tomb in the church, and suggests that it was the tomb of some martyr in the iconoclastic persecution. The patriarch's letter to Scarlatus Byzantius was written in 1852, and published by the latter in 1862. In that letter the patriarch reports for the first time the tradition that the tomb in S. Theodosia was the tomb of Constantine Palaeologus. In 1851 a Russian visitor to Constantinople, Andrew Mouravieff, who published an account of his travels, says that in the church of S. Theodosia he was shown a tomb which the officials of the mosque assured him was the tomb of the last Christian emperor of the city.[3] Lastly, but not least, in 1832 the church of S. Theodosia underwent repairs at the Sultan's orders, and then a neglected

---

[1] See the Muscovite's account in Dethier's *Collection of Documents relating to the Siege of 1453*, vol. ii. p. 1117.

[2] Achmed Mouktar Pasha, a recent Turkish historian of the siege of 1453, maintains that the emperor was buried in the church of the Pegé (Baloukli), outside the walls of the city. There is no persistency in the tradition that associates Constantine's tomb with the church of S. Theodosia.

[3] *Letters from the East* (in Russian), vol. ii. pp. 342-43, quoted by Mr. Siderides.

tomb was discovered in the church by the Christian architect who had charge of the work of restoration, Haji Stephen Gaitanaki Maditenou (see letter of the patriarch).[1] It is difficult to resist the impression that the discovery of the tomb at that time gave occasion for the fanciful conjectures current among Turks and Greeks in regard to the body interred in the tomb. See the article of Mr. Siderides, who gives the facts just mentioned, without drawing the inference I have suggested.

---

[1] Συγγραφαὶ αἱ Ἐλάσσονες.

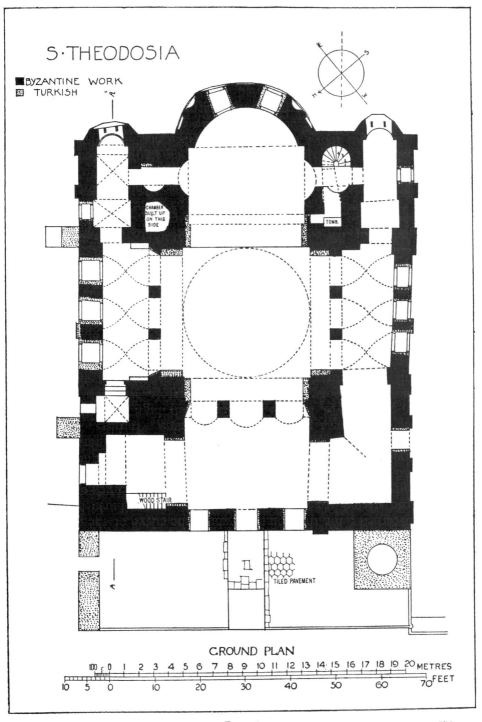

S·THEODOSIA

■ BYZANTINE WORK
▨ TURKISH

CHAMBER
BUILT UP
ON THIS
SIDE

TOMB.

WOOD STAIR

TILED PAVEMENT

GROUND PLAN

METRES
FEET

FIG. 56.

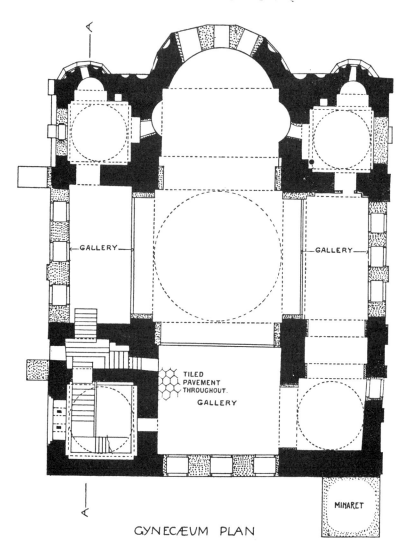

S·THEODOSIA

■ BYZANTINE WORK
▦ TURKISH

GALLERY

GALLERY

TILED
PAVEMENT
THROUGHOUT.

GALLERY

MINARET

GYNECÆUM PLAN

100 50 0 1 2 3 4 5 6 7 8 9 10 11 12 13 14 15 16 17 18 19 20 METRES
FEET.
10 5 0 10 20 30 40 50 60 70

FIG. 57.

S·THEODOSIA

■ BYZANTINE WORK
▨ TURKISH

SECTION THROVGH GYNECÆUM (A·A)

LONGITUDINAL SECTION

IRON TIE

FIGS. 58 AND 59.

181

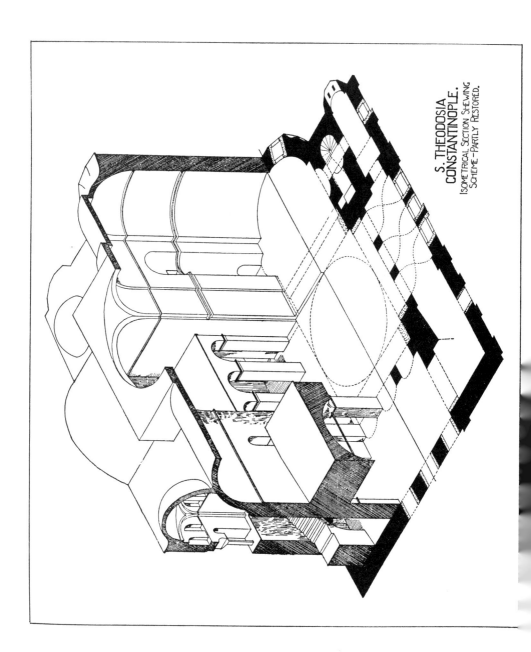

S. THEODOSIA
CONSTANTINOPLE.
ISOMETRICAL SECTION SHEWING
SCHEME – PARTLY RESTORED.

182

CHAPTER IX

THE CHURCH OF S. MARY DIACONISSA, KALENDER
HANEH JAMISSI

CLOSE to the eastern end of the aqueduct of Valens, and to the south of it, in the quarter of the mosque Shahzadé, is a beautiful Byzantine church, now known as Kalender Haneh Jamissi. It was visited by Gyllius,[1] who refers to its beautiful marble revetment—*vestita crustis varii marmoris*—but has, unfortunately, nothing to say concerning its dedication. Since that traveller's time the very existence of the church was forgotten by the Greek community of Constantinople until Paspates[2] discovered the building in 1877. But even that indefatigable explorer of the ancient remains of the city could not get access to the interior, and it was reserved for Dr. Freshfield in 1880 to be the first European visitor since Gyllius to enter the building, and make its interest and beauty known to the general public.[3]

The identity of the church is a matter of pure conjecture, for we have no tradition or documentary evidence on that point. Paspates[4] suggests that it may have been the sanctuary connected either with the 'monastery of Valens and Daudatus,' or with the 'monastery near the aqueduct,' establishments in existence before the age of Justinian the Great.[5] It cannot be the former, because the monastery of Valens and Daudatus, which was dedicated to

---

[1] *De top. C.P.* iii. c. 6.
[2] P. 351.
[3] *Archaeologia*, vol. lv. part 2, p. 431.
[4] P. 352.
[5] Their names appear in the Letter addressed to Menas, by the monks of the city, at the Synod of 536.

S. John the Baptist, stood near the church of the Holy
Apostles close to the western end of the aqueduct of
Valens. It might, so far as the indication 'near the
aqueduct' gives any clue, be the sanctuary of the latter
House, in which case the church was dedicated to S.
Anastasius.[1] But the architectural features of Kalender
Haneh Jamissi do not belong to the period before
Justinian. Mordtmann[2] identifies the building with the
church of the Theotokos in the district of the Deaconess
($\nu\alpha\grave{o}s$ $\tau\hat{\eta}s$ $\theta\epsilon o\tau\acute{o}\kappa o\upsilon$ $\tau\grave{\alpha}$ $\Delta\iota\alpha\kappa o\nu\acute{\iota}\sigma\sigma\eta s$), and in favour of this
view there is the fact that the site of the mosque
corresponds, speaking broadly, to the position which that
church is known to have occupied somewhere between the
forum of Taurus (now represented by the Turkish War
Office) and the Philadelphium (the area about the mosque
of Shahzadé), and not far off the street leading to the
Holy Apostles. Furthermore, the rich and beautiful
decoration of the church implies its importance, so that it
may very well be the church of the Theotokos Diaconissa,
at which imperial processions from the Great Palace to the
Holy Apostles stopped to allow the emperor to place a
lighted taper upon the altar of the shrine.[3]

Theophanes,[4] the earliest writer to mention the church
of the Diaconissa, ascribes its foundation to the Patriarch
Kyriakos (593-605) in the fourth year of his patriarchate,
during the reign of the Emperor Maurice. According to
the historical evidence at our command, that church was
therefore erected towards the close of the sixth century.
Dr. Freshfield,[5] however, judging by the form of the church
and the character of the dome, thinks that Kalender Haneh
Jamissi is 'not earlier than the eighth century, and not later
than the tenth.' Lethaby[6] places it in the period between
Justinian the Great and the eleventh century. 'The

---

[1] In the Epistle to Pope Agapetus the monastery 'near the aqueduct' is
described as 'Anastasii prope Agogum,' Mansi, viii. p. 907.

[2] *Esquisses top.* p. 70.

[3] Const. Porphr. *De cer.* i. p. 75.

[4] P. 428 ; Banduri, i. p. 18 ; viii. pp. 697-98.

[5] *Archaeologia*, vol. lv. part 2, p. 438.

[6] *Mediaeval Art*, p. 66.

church, now the Kalender mosque of Constantinople, probably belongs to the intermediate period. The similar small cruciform church of Protaton, Mount Athos, is dated *c.* 950.' Hence if Theophanes and his followers are not to clash with these authorities on architecture, either Kalender Haneh Jamissi is not the church of the Diaconissa, or it is a reconstruction of the original fabric of that sanctuary. To restore an old church was not an uncommon practice in Constantinople, and Kalender Haneh Jamissi has undoubtedly seen changes in the course of its history. On the other hand, Diehl is of the opinion that the building cannot be later than the seventh century and may be earlier.[1]

Architectural Features

The church belongs to the domed-cross type. The central area is cruciform, with barrel vaults over the arms and a dome on the centre. As the arms are not filled in with galleries this cruciform plan is very marked internally. Four small chambers, in two stories, in the arm angles bring the building to the square form externally. The upper stories are inaccessible except by ladders, but the supposition that they ever formed, like the similar stories in the dome piers of S. Sophia, portions of continuous galleries along the northern, western, and southern walls of the church is precluded by the character of the revetment on the walls. In the development of the domed-cross type, the church stands logically intermediate between the varieties of that type found respectively in the church of S. Theodosia and in that of SS. Peter and Mark.

The lower story of the north-western pier is covered with a flat circular roof resting on four pendentives, while the upper story is open to the timbers, and rises higher than the roof of the church, as though it were the base of some kind of tower. It presents no indications of pendentives or of a start in vaulting. The original eastern wall of the church has been almost totally torn down and replaced by

---

[1] *Manuel d'art byzantin*, p. 312.

a straight wall of Turkish construction. Traces of three apses at that end of the building can, however, still be discerned ; for the points at which the curve of the central apse started are visible on either side of the Turkish wall, and the northern apse shows on the exterior. The northern and southern walls are lighted by large triple windows, divided by shafts and descending to a marble parapet near the floor (Plate IV.). The dome, which is large in proportion to the church, is a polygon of sixteen sides. It rests directly on pendentives, but has a comparatively high external drum above the roof. It is pierced by sixteen windows which follow the curve of the dome. The flat, straight external cornice above them is Turkish, and there is good reason to suspect that the dome, taken as a whole, is Turkish work, for it strongly resembles the Turkish domes found in S. Theodosia, SS. Peter and Mark, and S. Andrew in Krisei. The vaults, moreover, below the dome are very much distorted ; and the pointed eastern arch like the eastern wall appears to be Turkish. When portions of the building so closely connected with the dome have undergone Turkish repairs, it is not strange that the dome itself should also have received similar treatment.

In the western faces of the piers that carry the eastern arch large marble frames of considerable beauty are inserted. The sills are carved and rest on two short columns ; two slender pilasters of verd antique form the sides ; and above them is a flat cornice enriched with overhanging leaves of acanthus and a small bust in the centre. Within the frames is a large marble slab. Dr. Freshfield thinks these frames formed part of the eikonostasis, but on that view the bema would have been unusually large. The more probable position of the eikonostasis was across the arch nearer the apse. In that case the frames just described formed part of the general decoration of the building, although, at the same time, they may have enclosed isolated eikons. Eikons in a similar position are found in S. Saviour in the Chora (Plate LXXXVI.).

The marble casing of the church is remarkably fine. Worthy of special notice is the careful manner in which the colours and veinings of the marble slabs are made to correspond and match. The zigzag inlaid pattern around the arches also deserves particular attention. High up in the western wall, and reached by the wooden stairs leading to a Turkish wooden gallery on that side of the church, are two marble slabs with a door carved in bas-relief upon them. They may be symbols of Christ as the door of His fold (Plate IV.).

The church has a double narthex. As the ground outside the building has been raised enormously (it rises 15-20 feet above the floor at the east end) the actual entrance to the outer narthex is through a cutting in its vault or through a window, and the floor is reached by a steep flight of stone steps. The narthex is a long narrow vestibule, covered with barrel vaults, and has a Turkish wooden ceiling at the southern end.

The esonarthex is covered with a barrel vault between two cross vaults. The entrance into the church stands between two Corinthian columns, but they belong to different periods, and do not correspond to any structure in the building. In fact, both narthexes have been much altered in their day, presenting many irregularities and containing useless pilasters.

Professor Goodyear refers to this church in support of the theory that in Byzantine buildings there is an intentional widening of the structure from the ground upwards. ' It will also be observed,' he says, 'that the cornice is horizontal, whereas the marble casing above and below the cornice is cut and fitted in oblique lines. . . . The outward bend on the right side of the choir is $11\frac{1}{2}$ inches in 33 feet. The masonry surfaces step back above the middle string-course. That these bends are not due to thrust is abundantly apparent from the fact that they are continuous and uniform in inclination up to the solid rear wall of the choir.'

But in regard to the existence of an intentional widening upwards in this building, it should be observed : First, that as the eastern wall of the church, ' the rear wall of the choir,' is Turkish, nothing can be legitimately inferred from the features of that wall about the character of

Byzantine construction. Secondly, the set back above the middle string-course on the other walls of the church is an ordinary arrangement in a Byzantine church, and if this were all 'the widening' for which Professor Goodyear contended there would be no room for difference of opinion. The ledge formed by that set back may have served to support scaffolding. In the next place, due weight must be given to the distortion which would inevitably occur in Byzantine buildings. They were fabrics of mortar with brick rather than of brick with mortar, and consequently too elastic not to settle to a large extent in the course of erection. Hence is it that no measurements of a Byzantine structure, even on the ground floor, are accurate within more than 5 cm., while above the ground they vary to a much greater degree, rendering minute measurements quite valueless. Lastly, as the marble panelling was fitted after the completion of the body of the building, it had to be adapted to any divergence that had previously occurred in the settling of the walls or the spreading of the vaults. The marble panelling, it should also be observed, is here cut to the diagonal at one angle, and not at the other.

Apart from the set back of the masonry at the middle string-course, this church, therefore, supplies no evidence for an intentional widening of the structure from the ground upwards. Any further widening than that at the middle string-course was accidental, due to the nature of the materials employed, not to the device of the builder, and was allowed by the architect because unavoidable. Such irregularities are inherent in the Byzantine methods of building.

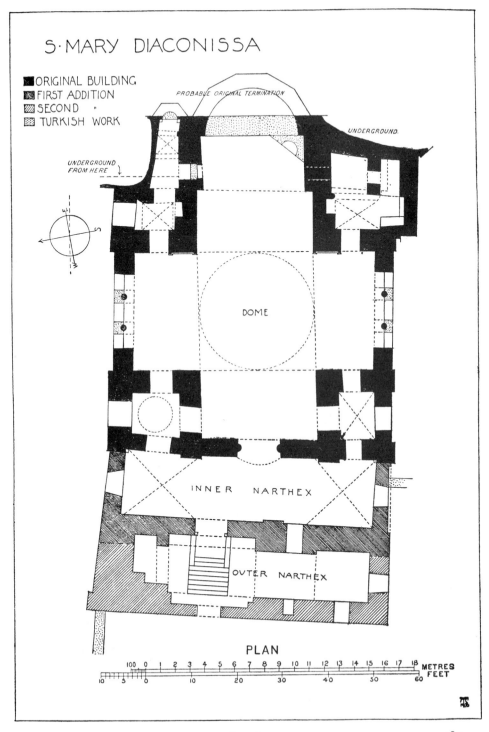

S·MARY DIACONISSA

- ■ ORIGINAL BUILDING
- ▩ FIRST ADDITION
- ▨ SECOND "
- ▧ TURKISH WORK

PROBABLE ORIGINAL TERMINATION

UNDERGROUND.

UNDERGROUND
FROM HERE

DOME

INNER NARTHEX

OUTER NARTHEX

PLAN

METRES
FEET

FIG. 61.

189

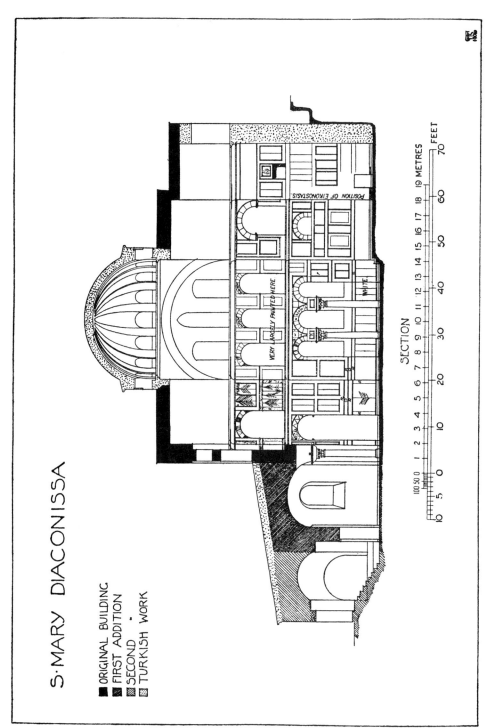

S·MARY DIACONISSA

■ ORIGINAL BUILDING
▨ FIRST ADDITION
▧ SECOND ·
▥ TURKISH WORK

POSITION OF EIKONOSTASIS.

VERY LARGELY PAINTED HERE

WHITE

SECTION

METRES
0 1 2 3 4 5 6 7 8 9 10 11 12 13 14 15 16 17 18 19

FEET
0 10 20 30 40 50 60 70

FIG. 62.

CHAPTER X

THE Byzantine church, now Hoja Atik Mustapha Jamissi,
situated in the Aivan Serai quarter, close to the Golden
Horn, is commonly regarded as the church of SS. Peter
and Mark, because it stands where the church dedicated to
the chief of the apostles and his companion stood, in the district of Blachernae (Aivan Serai) and near the Golden Horn.[1]
Such indications are too vague for a positive opinion on
the subject, but perhaps the Patriarch Constantius, who is
responsible for the identification, may have relied upon some
tradition in favour of the view he has made current.[2]

NOTE

Tafferner, chaplain to the embassy from Leopold I. of Austria
to the Ottoman Court, speaking of the patriarchal church in his day
(the present patriarchal church of S. George in the Phanar quarter),
says, 'Aedes haec in patriarchatum erecta est, postquam Sultan
Mehemet basilicam Petri et Pauli exceptam Graecis in moscheam
defoedavit' (*Caesarea legatio*, p. 89, Vien. 1668). Probably by
the church of SS. Peter and Paul he means this church of SS. Peter
and Mark. If so, the traditional name of the building is carried
back to the seventeenth century. The church of SS. Peter and
Mark, it is true, never served as a patriarchal church. That honour
belonged to the church of S. Demetrius of Kanabos, which is in the
immediate vicinity, and has always remained a Christian sanctuary.
Tafferner seems to have confused the two churches owing to their
proximity to each other. Or his language may mean that the

---

[1] Synax., July 2.   [2] *Ancient and Modern Constantinople*, p. 83.

patriarchal seat was removed from S. Demetrius when SS. Peter and Paul was converted into a mosque, because too near a building which had become a Moslem place of worship.

The church of SS. Peter and Mark was founded, it is said, by two patricians of Constantinople, named Galbius and Candidus, in 458, early in the reign of Leo I. (457-474). But the present building cannot be so old. It is a fair question to ask whether it may not be the church of S. Anastasia referred to in a chrysoboullon of John Palaeologus (1342), and mentioned by the Russian pilgrim who visited Constantinople in the fifteenth century (1424-53).[1]

The church of SS. Peter and Mark was erected as a shrine for the supposed tunic of the Theotokos, a relic which played an important part in the fortunes of Constantinople on several occasions, as 'the palladium of the city and the chaser away of all diseases and warlike foes.' As often happened in the acquisition of relics, the garment had been secured by a pious fraud—a fact which only enhanced the merit of the purloiners, and gave to the achievement the colour of a romantic adventure. In the course of their pilgrimage to the Holy Land, Galbius and Candidus discovered, in the house of a devout Hebrew lady who entertained them, a small room fitted up like a chapel, fragrant with incense, illuminated with lamps, and crowded with worshippers. Being informed that the room was consecrated by the presence of a chest containing the robe of the mother of their Lord, the pious men begged leave to spend the night in prayer beside the relic, and while thus engaged were seized by an uncontrollable longing to gain possession of the sacred garment. Accordingly they took careful measurements of the chest before them, and at Jerusalem ordered an exact facsimile of it to be made. Thus equipped they lodged again, on their homeward journey, at the house of their Galilean hostess, and once more obtained leave to worship in its chapel. Watching their opportunity they exchanged the chests, and forthwith despatched the chest containing the coveted treasure straight

---

[1] Νεολόγου ἑβδομαδιαία ἐπιθεώρησις, January 3, 1893, p. 205 ; *Itin. russes*, p. 233.

to Constantinople. They themselves tarried behind, as though loth to quit a spot still hallowed by the sacred robe. Upon their return to the capital the pious thieves erected a shrine for their prize on land which they owned in the district of Blachernae, and dedicated the building to SS. Peter and Mark instead of to the Theotokos, as would have been more appropriate, in the hope that they would thus conceal the precious relic from the public eye, and retain it for their special benefit. But the secret leaked out. Whereupon the emperor obliged the two patricians to surrender their treasure, and, after renovating the neighbouring church of the Theotokos of Blachernae, deposited the relic in that sanctuary as its proper home.

The site of that celebrated church lies at a short distance to the west of Hoja Atik Mustapha Jamissi, and is marked by the Holy Well which was attached to it. The well, in whose waters emperors and empresses were wont to bathe, is now enclosed by a modern Greek chapel, and is still the resort of the faithful.

Architectural Features

The plan of the church presents the simplest form of the domed-cross type without galleries. The dome, without drum, ribs, or windows, is almost certainly a Turkish reconstruction, but the dome arches and piers are original. The arms of the cross and the small chambers at its angles are covered with barrel vaults, and communicate with one another through lofty, narrow arches. In the treatment of the northern and southern walls of the building considerable architectural elaboration was displayed. At the floor level is a triple arcade ; higher up are three windows resting on the string-course ; and still higher a window divided into three lights. The arches in the church are enormously stilted, a feature due to the fact that the only string-course in the building, though structurally corresponding to the vaulting spring, has been placed at the height of what would properly be the column string-course. The three

o

apses, much altered by repairs, project boldly, all of them
showing three sides on the exterior. The roof and the
cornice are Turkish, and the modern wooden narthex has
probably replaced a Byzantine narthex. On the opposite
side of the street lies a cruciform font that belonged to
the baptistery of the church.

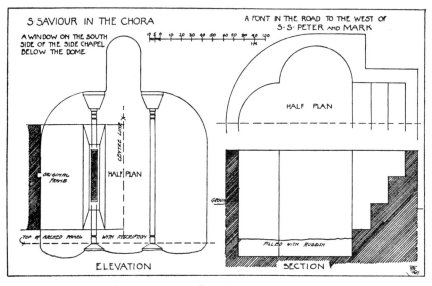

FIG. 63.

From a church of this type to the later four-columned
plan is but a step. The dome piers of SS. Peter and Mark
are still L-shaped, and form the internal angles of the cross.
As the arches between such piers and the external walls
increased in size, the piers became smaller, until eventually
they were reduced to the typical four columns of the late
churches.

S·S·PETER AND MARK

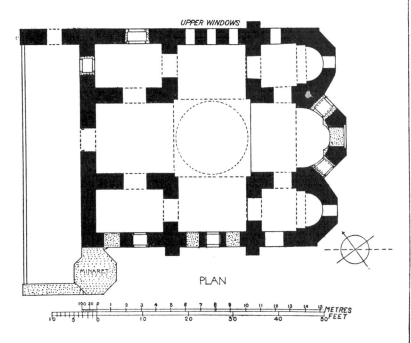

UPPER WINDOWS

MINARET

PLAN

SECTION

PRESENT WOOD FLOOR

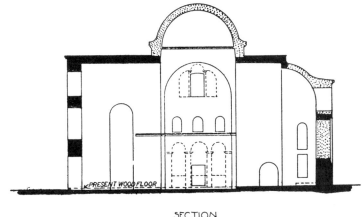

■ SHOWS ORIGINAL BUILDING
▨ " " TURKISH WORK

FIGS. 64 AND 65.

CHAPTER XI

THE identification of Bodroum Jamissi as the church attached to the monastery styled the Myrelaion rests upon the tradition current in the Greek community when Gyllius visited the city. According to that traveller, the church on the hill rising to the north of the eastern end of the gardens of Vlanga, the site of the ancient harbour of Theodosius, was known as the Myrelaion—' Supra locum hortorum Blanchae nuncupatorum, olim Portum Theodosianum continentium, extremam partem ad ortum solis pertinentem, clivus a Septentrione eminet, in quo est templum vulgo nominatum Myreleos.'[1] This agrees, so far, with the statement of the Anonymus[2] of the eleventh century, that the Myrelaion stood on the side of the city looking towards the Sea of Marmora. There is no record of the date when the monastery was founded. But the House must have been in existence before the eighth century, for Constantine Copronymus (740-775), the bitter iconoclast, displayed his contempt for monks and all their ways by scattering the fraternity, and changing the fragrant name of the establishment, Myrelaion, the place of myrrh-oil, into the offensive designation, Psarelaion, the place of fish-oil.[3] The monastery was restored by the Emperor Romanus I. Lecapenus (919-945), who devoted his residence in this district to that object.[4] Hence the monastery was sometimes described as 'in the palace of the Myrelaion,'[5] ἐν τοῖς παλατίοις τοῦ Μυρελαίου,

---

[1] *De top. C.P.* iii. c. 8.   [2] Banduri, iii. p. 48.   [3] *Ibid. ut supra.*
[4] Theoph. Cont. p. 402.   [5] Scylitzes, in Cedrenus, ii. p. 649.

and as 'the monastery of the Emperor Romanus,'.[1] Μονὴ
τοῦ βασιλέως Ῥωμανοῦ.   It was strictly speaking a convent,
and became noteworthy for the distinguished rank of some
of its inmates, and as the mausoleum in which the founder
and many members of his family were laid to rest.   Here
Romanus II. sent his sister Agatha to take the veil, when
he was obliged to dismiss her from the court to soothe the
jealousy of his beautiful but wicked consort Theophano.[2]
Upon the abdication of Isaac Comnenus, his wife
Aecatherina and her daughter Maria retired to the
Myrelaion, and there learned that a crown may be a badge
of slavery and the loss of it liberty.[3]   Here were buried
Theodora,[4] the wife of Romanus Lecapenus, in 923, and,
eight years later, his beloved son Christopher,[5] for whom he
mourned, says the historian of the event, with a sorrow
'greater than the grievous mourning of the Egyptians.'
Here also Helena, the daughter of Romanus Lecapenus,
and wife of Constantine VII. Porphyrogenitus, was laid to
rest, in 981, after an imposing funeral, in which the body
was carried to the grave on a bier of gold adorned with
pearls and other precious stones.[6]   To this monastery were
transferred, from the monastery of S. Mamas, near the
Gate of the Xylokerkou, the three sarcophagi, one of them a
fine piece of work, containing the ashes of the Emperor
Maurice and his children.   And here also Romanus
Lecapenus himself was interred in 948, his remains being
brought from the island of Proté, where his unfilial sons,
Stephen and Constantine, had obliged him to spend the last
years of his life as a monk.[7]

Architectural Features

The building is on the 'four column' plan.   The dome,
placed on a circular drum, is supported on four piers, and
divided into eight concave compartments, with windows in the

[1] Theoph. Cont. p. 404.
[2] *Ibid.* pp. 461, 757.
[3] Scylitzes, *ut supra*, pp. 648-49.
[4] Theoph. Cont. p. 402.
[5] *Ibid.* p. 420.
[6] *Ibid.* p. 473.
[7] *Ibid.* pp. 403-4.

alternate compartments. The arms of the cross, the chambers at the angles, and the bema are all covered with cross-groined vaults that spring, like those in the chapel of the Pammakaristos (p. 151), from the vaulting level. The apsidal chambers have dome vaults, a niche on the east recessed in an arch to form the apse, and a niche both on the north and the south rising above the vaulting string-course. In the lowest division of the south wall stood originally a triple arcade with a door between the columns. The arcade has been built up, but the moulded jambs and cornices of the door, and the arch above it, now contracted into a window, still show on the exterior, while the columns appear within the church. Above the column string-course is a range of three windows, the central window being larger than its companions ; higher up in the gable is a single light. The interior of the church has been much pulled about and cut away. The narthex is in three bays, separated by strong transverse arches, and terminates at either end in a high concave niche that shows on the outside. The central bay has a dome vault ; the other bays have cross-groined vaults. The church had no gynecaeum, although Pulgher indicates one in his plan. A striking feature of the exterior are the large semicircular buttresses that show beyond the walls of the church—six on the south side, one on either side of the entrance on the west, and two on the east, supporting the apsidal chambers. In the last case, however, where entire buttresses would have been at once too large and too close together, the buttresses are only half semicircles. The apses project with three sides. The northern side of the church and the roof are modern, for the building suffered severely in 1784 from fire.[1] The church stands on a platform, built over a small cistern, the roof of which is supported by four columns crowned by beautiful capitals. Hence the Turkish name of the mosque, Bodroum, signifying a subterranean hollow. Gyllius[2] is mistaken in associating this church with the

---

[1] Chevalier, *Voyage de la Propontide et du Pont Euxin*, vol. i. p. 108.
[2] *De top. C.P.* iii. c. 8, 'habens inter se cisternam, cujus camera lateritia sustinetur columnis marmoreis circiter sexaginta ' ; cf. *Die byzant. Wasserbehälter*,

large underground cistern situated lower down the slope of the hill close to the bath Kyzlar Aghassi Hamam.

Since the above was in print, the church has, unfortunately, been burnt in the great fire which destroyed a large part of Stamboul on the 23rd July 1912 (see Plates II., III.).

NOTE

Gyllius (*De top. C.P.* iii. c. 8) places the Horreum, the statue of Maimas, the house of Craterus, the Modius, and the arch bearing the two bronze hands, after passing which a criminal on the way to punishment lost all hope of reprieve, near this church ; basing that opinion on the statement of Suidas that these buildings stood near the Myrelaion. But there was a Myrelaion also (Codinus, *De aed.* p. 108) in the district in which the Shahzadé mosque is situated. The buildings above mentioned were near this second Myrelaion. On the other hand, the Chrysocamaron near the Myrelaion mentioned by Codinus (*De signis*, pp. 65-66) stood near the church under our consideration, for it was close to the church of S. Acacius in the Heptascalon. So also, doubtless, did the xenodocheion Myrelaion (Du Cange, iv. p. 160), possibly one of the many philanthropic institutions supported by Helena (Theoph. Cont. p. 458), the daughter of Romanus Lecapenus and wife of Constantine VII. Porphyrogenitus.

---

pp. 59, 222-23. The bath of Kyzlar Aghassi Hamam may represent the bath built by the eunuch Nicetas, in the reign of Theophilus, and was probably supplied with water from the cistern beside it (Banduri, vi. p. 133).

THE CHURCH OF THE MYRELAION

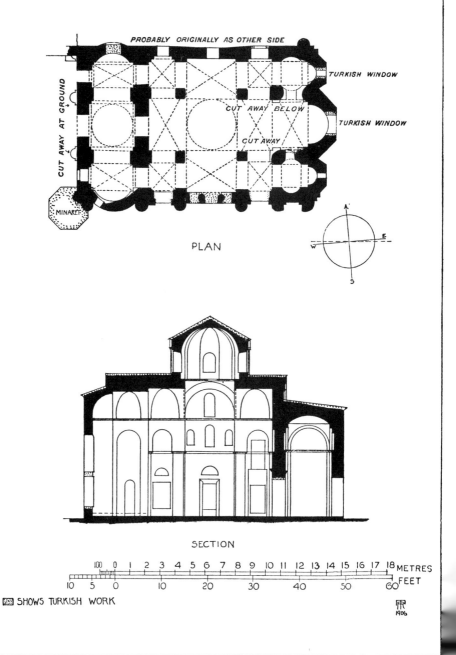

PROBABLY ORIGINALLY AS OTHER SIDE

TURKISH WINDOW

CUT AWAY AT GROUND

CUT AWAY BELOW

TURKISH WINDOW

CUT AWAY

MINARET

PLAN

SECTION

SHOWS TURKISH WORK

Figs. 66 and 67.

CHAPTER XII

THE CHURCH OF S. JOHN THE BAPTIST IN TRULLO, ACHMED PASHA MESJEDI

THE identification of the church of S. John the Baptist in Trullo (Μονὴ τοῦ ἁγίου προφήτου προδρόμου Ἰωάννου τοῦ ἐν τῷ Τρούλλῳ) with the mosque of Achmed Pasha Mesjedi is based on two reasons : first, because of their common proximity to the church of the Pammakaristos,[1] now Fetiyeh Jamissi ; secondly, on the ground of the tradition current in the Greek community on that point. The latter reason is in this case particularly strong, seeing the church of the Pammakaristos was the patriarchal cathedral almost immediately after the Turkish conquest, and retained that honour until 1591.[2] The highest Greek ecclesiastical authorities were therefore in a position to be thoroughly acquainted with the dedication of a church in their close vicinity. In 1578 the protonotarius of the patriarch showed Gerlach the site of the Trullus close to Achmed Pasha Mesjedi.[3]

The church is mentioned in history only by Phrantzes,[4] who informs us that when the Patriarch Gennadius trans-

---

[1] Phrantzes, p. 307.　　　　[2] Patr. Constantius, p. 80.

[3] *Tagebuch*, p. 456. On the way eastwards from the residence of the Moldavian agent (Bogdan Serai), says Gerlach, ' Auf diesem Spazier-weg hat mir Theodosius auch den Trullum auf der Seiten des Patriarchats gegen dem Sultan Selim gewiesen. Welches vor diesen ein sehr weiter Platz gewesen, nun aber nichts mehr da als ein rundes getäffeltes Haus, wie ein kleines Kirchlein ist.' Cf. his statement reported by Crusius in *Turcograecia*, p. 189 : ' Patriarchatui contiguum est monasteriolum Joannis Baptistae a Graecis sanctimonalibus inhabitatum.'

[4] Phrantzes, p. 307 ; cf. *Turcograecia*, p. 189.

ferred the patriarchal seat to the monastery and church of the Pammakaristos, certain nuns previously accommodated in that House were removed to the neighbouring monastery of S. John Baptist in Trullo. Phrantzes explains the designation of the church, 'in Trullo,' as derived from a palace named Trullus which once stood in the vicinity to the north of the Pammakaristos. It was the palace, adds the historian,[1] in which the Council of Constantinople, known as the Concilium Quinisextum (Πενθέκτη), or the second Concilium Trullanum, assembled in 692, in the reign of Justinian II. But the palace Trullus, in which the first Concilium Trullanum met in 680, was one of the group of buildings forming the Great Palace[2] beside the Hippodrome, and there the second Concilium Trullanum also held its meetings.[3] Phrantzes is therefore mistaken in associating the Council of 692 with a palace in the vicinity of the Pammakaristos and Achmed Pasha Mesjedi. But his mistake on that particular point does not preclude the existence of a palace named Trullus in the neighbourhood of the Pammakaristos. In fact, the existence of such a palace in that district is the only possible explanation of the attachment of the style 'in Trullo' to a church on the site of Achmed Pasha Mesjedi. Nor is it strange to find a name pertaining primarily to a building in the Great Palace transferred to a similar building situated elsewhere. The imperial residence at the Hebdomon, for example, was named Magnaura after one of the halls in the Great Palace.[4] There was an Oaton or Trullus in the palace of Blachernae,[5] and in the palace at Nicaea.[6] Consequently, a palace known as the Oaton or the Trullus might also be situated near the Pammakaristos, to command the fine view from

---

[1] It was also styled 'Ωάτον, 'the Oval,' after the form of its roof or of the body of the building itself (Synax., Sept. 14). *Vita Stephani.* For the 'Ωάτον, see Labarte, *Le Palais impérial de Cons'ple,* pp. 62, 121, 122, 186.

[2] *Vita Stephani Junioris,* Migne, *P.G.* tom. 100, col. 1144 ἐν τῷ ἱερῷ παλατίῳ, ἔνθα ἐπιλέγεται ὁ Τροῦλλος ὅπερ ἡμεῖς 'Ωάτον καλοῦμεν.

[3] Balsamon, vol. i. col. 501 ἐν τῷ Τρούλλῳ τοῦ βασιλικοῦ παλατίου.

[4] Theoph. p. 541.

[5] Pachym. i. p. 405.

[6] *Acta et diplomata Graeca,* iii. p. 65 ; cf. Paspates, *Great Palace,* p. 248, Metcalfe's translation.

that point of the city. Mordtmann,[1] indeed, maintains that the building to which Phrantzes refers was the palace at Bogdan Serai, the subsequent residence of the Moldavian hospodar in Turkish days, and that the church of S. John in Trullo was not Achmed Pasha Mesjedi, but the church of S. John in Petra (Kesmé Kaya) beside that palace. This opinion, however, is at variance with the statements of Phrantzes and Gerlach. Furthermore, the designation 'in

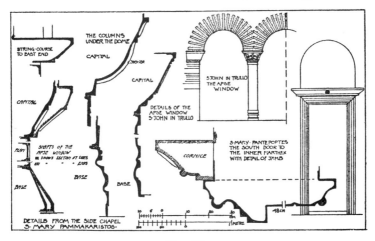

FIG. 68.

Petra' was so distinctive a mark of the church of S. John near Kesmé Kaya, that the church could scarcely have been recognised under another style.

Architectural Features

S. John in Trullo belongs to the ordinary 'four column' type of church building, and has a narthex. Its three apses are semicircular both within and without, presenting the only instance in Constantinople of apses semicircular on the

---

[1] *Proceedings of Greek Syllogos of C.P.*, Archaeological Supplement to vol. xvii. p. 8. His principal reason seems to be the fact that a company of nuns occupied some of the cells in the old monastery of S. John in Petra when Gerlach visited the city. But, according to Gerlach, another sisterhood was at the same time accommodated in the small convent of S. John the Baptist near the patriarchate. —*Turcograecia*, p. 189.

exterior. The central apse projects m. 3 beyond the body
of the building, and was lighted by a large but low window,
divided into three lights by two pilasters crowned with
carved capitals (for details see Fig. 68) ; the diaconicon has
been built up to form the mihrab of the mosque ; the prothesis, to the north, has a barrel vault.

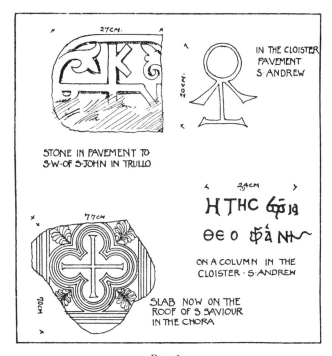

FIG. 69.

The drum dome is octagonal, with eight ribs and as
many windows. It seems large for the size of the church,
and is lower than usual inside. The windows do not cut
into the exterior cornice of the dome. Originally the dome
arches rested on four piers or columns, but these have been
removed in the course of Turkish repairs, and the dome
arches are now supported by beams running across the church,
under the impost of the arches.

The arms of the cross to the north and south have

barrel vaults, and the walls are pierced by triple windows. Two capitals built into the exterior face of the northern wall, and marked with a cross, were doubtless the capitals of the shafts which divided the northern window into three lights. The western arm of the cross is covered by the roof of the narthex, and lighted by a small round-headed window above it. The small narthex is in three bays, covered with cross-groined vaults.

It is not probable that the church was converted into a mosque before 1591, when the patriarchal seat was removed from the Pammakaristos to S. Demetrius beside the Xyloporta. Nor could the conversion have been later than 1598, the year in which Achmed Pasha—who converted the building into a mosque—died.[1]

[1] Cf. Paspates, p. 304.

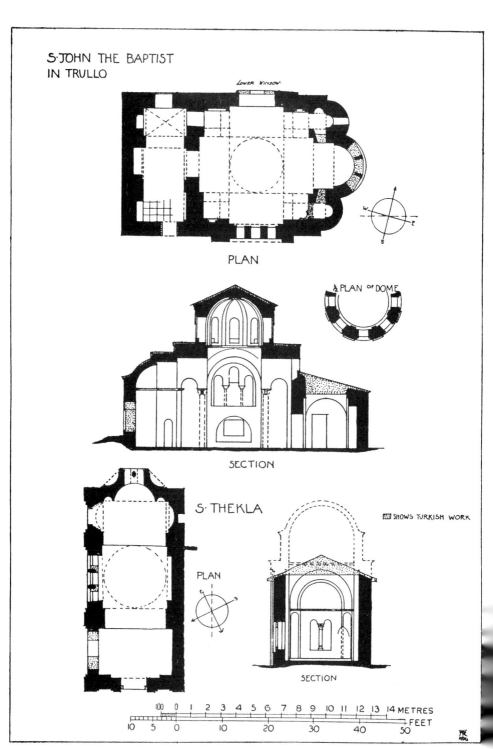

S·JOHN THE BAPTIST
IN TRULLO

LOWER WINDOW·

PLAN

½ PLAN OF DOME

SECTION

S· THEKLA

PLAN

SHOWS TURKISH WORK

SECTION

100 0 1 2 3 4 5 6 7 8 9 10 11 12 13 14 METRES

10 5 0 10 20 30 40 50 FEET

FIGS. 70 AND 71.

CHAPTER XIII

IN the quarter of Aivan Serai, a few paces to the rear of the Heraclian Wall, stands a small mosque known as Toklou Ibrahim Dedé Mesjedi, the architectural features of which proclaim it at once to be an old Byzantine chapel. There is no decisive tradition in regard to the identity of the building. The Patriarch Constantius is uncertain whether it should be recognised as the church of S. Nicholas or as the church of S. Thekla, two sanctuaries situated in the quarter of Blachernae. It cannot have been the former, inasmuch as the site of that church was near the Holy Well, still venerated by Christians and Moslems,[1] in the area enclosed between the Wall of Heraclius and the Wall of Leo the Armenian, now a picturesque Turkish cemetery. One argument for regarding the building as the church of S. Thekla, in this part of the city, is the striking similarity of its Turkish name Toklou to the Greek name Thekla, rendering it exceedingly probable that the former is a corruption of the latter, and a reminiscence of the original designation of the edifice.[2] Turkish authorities, however, have their own explanation of the name Toklou. In the *Historical and Geographical Dictionary* of Achmed Rifaat Effendi, we are told that a certain Toklou Dedé was the guardian of the tombs of the companions of Khaled, who took part in the first siege of Constantinople (673) by the Saracens. 'His real name was Ghazi Ismail ; Dogulu was his nickname. Now Dogh is the Persian for a drink named

---

[1] *Ancient and Modern C.P.* p. 46.   [2] Paspates, p. 359.

Airan (a mixture of curds and water), and he was called
Dogulu Dedé because during the siege his business was
to distribute that drink to the troops. At his request a
Christian church near Aivan Serai was converted into a
mosque. The church was formerly named after its founder,
Isakias.'[1] Another Turkish explanation of Toklou derives
the epithet from the rare Turkish term for a yearling lamb,
and accounts for its bestowal upon Ibrahim Dedé as a pet
name given in gratitude for his services to the thirsty soldiers
engaged in the siege of the city.[2] In keeping with these
stories is the tradition that the cemetery in the area between
the Walls of Heraclius and Leo V. the Armenian, is the
resting-place of Saracen warriors who fell in the siege of
673. But have we not here the fancy-bred tales which
Oriental imagination weaves to veil its ignorance of real
facts ? When etymology or history fails, romance is substituted. We may as well believe the tradition that the
body of Eyoub, the standard-bearer of Mahomet, lies buried
at the head of the Golden Horn, in the mosque of Eyoub,
where the Sultan girds the sword on his accession to the
throne. No Moslem graves could have been tolerated
between the lines of the city's fortification in Byzantine
days. The cemetery between the old walls near Toklou
Ibrahim Dedé Mesjedi must therefore be later than the
Turkish conquest. And as soon as Moslems were laid
there, it was almost inevitable that a church in the immediate
neighbourhood should either be destroyed or converted into
a mosque. By what name that mosque would thenceforth
become known was, of course, an open question. The new
name might be purely Turkish. But when it sounds like
the echo of a name which we know belonged to a Byzantine
building in this quarter of the city before Turkish times,
it is more reasonable to regard the new name as a trans-
formation of the earlier Greek term, than to derive it from
fine-spun etymological fancies and historical blunders. The
identification, therefore, of Toklou Ibrahim Dedé Mesjedi

---

[1] For this information I am indebted to Rev. H. O. Dwight, LL.D., late of
the American Board of Missions in Constantinople.
[2] Paspates, p. 357, *note.*

with the church of S. Thekla, on the ground of the similarity of the two names, has a strong presumption in its favour.

A second consideration in support of this identification is the statement made by Achmed Rifaat Effendi, that before the church became a mosque it was known by the name of its founder, 'Isakias.' . For it is a matter of history that the church of S. Thekla was restored by the Emperor Isaac Comnenus[1] in the eleventh century. The association of his name with the building was therefore perfectly natural, if the building is indeed the old church of S. Thekla, otherwise it is difficult to account for that association.

There is, however, one objection to this identification that must not be overlooked. According to Byzantine authorities, the church of S. Thekla stood in the palace of Blachernae ($\grave{\epsilon}\nu\tau\grave{o}s$ $\tau\hat{\omega}\nu$ $\beta\alpha\sigma\iota\lambda\epsilon\acute{\iota}\omega\nu$; $\grave{\epsilon}\nu$ $\tau\hat{\omega}$ $\pi\alpha\lambda\alpha\tau\acute{\iota}\omega$ $\tau\hat{\omega}\nu$ $B\lambda\alpha\chi\acute{\epsilon}\rho\nu\omega\nu$[2]). That palace occupied the heights above Aivan Serai, on which the quarter of Egri Kapou and the mosque of Aivas Effendi now stand, within the walls that enclose the western spur of the Sixth Hill. Toklou Ibrahim Dedé Mesjedi, however, does not stand within that enclosure, but immediately to the north of it, on the level tract that stretches from the foot of the Sixth Hill to the Golden Horn. If the reasons in favour of regarding the mosque as S. Thekla were less strong, this objection would, perhaps, be fatal. But the strip of land between the northern wall of the palace enclosure and the sea is so narrow, and was so closely connected with the life of the imperial residence, that a building on that tract might with pardonable inaccuracy be described, as 'in the palace.'[3]

The church is mentioned for the first time in the earlier half of the eighth century as a chapel ($\epsilon\mathring{v}\kappa\tau\acute{\eta}\rho\iota\rho\nu$) which Thekla, the eldest daughter of the Emperor Theophilus, restored and attached to her residence at Blachernae.[4] The

---

[1] Anna Comnena, vol. i. p. 168.

[2] Scylitzes, p. 647 (Cedrenus, vol. ii.) ; Zonaras, iii. p. 672.

[3] If the mosque Aivas Effendi could be proved to stand on the site of a church, the argument against the identification of Toklou Dedé Mesjedi with the church of S. Thekla would be stronger.

[4] Theoph. Cont. p. 147.

P

princess was an invalid, and doubtless retired to this part of
the city for the sake of its mild climate. To dedicate the
chapel to her patron saint was only natural. As already
intimated, the church was rebuilt from the foundations, in
the eleventh century, by Isaac Comnenus, in devout gratitude
for his escape from imminent death[1] in the course of his
campaign against the barbarous tribes beside the Danube,
when he was overtaken at the foot of the Lovitz mountain
by a furious tempest of rain and snow. The plain on which
his army was encamped soon became a sheet of water, and
many of his men and animals were drowned or frozen to
death. Thunder, lightning, and hurricane combined to
produce an awful scene, and there were moments when the
whole world seemed on fire. The emperor took shelter
under a large oak, but, fearing the tree might be thrown
down by the furious wind, he soon made for open ground.
Scarcely had he done so when the oak was torn up by the
roots and hurled to the earth. A few moments later the
emperor would have been killed. This narrow escape
occurred on the 24th September, the festival day of
S. Thekla, and, therefore, attributing his deliverance to her
intervention, Isaac rebuilt and greatly beautified the old
sanctuary dedicated to her in Blachernae, and frequently
attended services there in her honour. Anna Comnena[2]
speaks of the restored church in the highest terms.
According to her it was built at great cost, displayed
rare art, and was in every way worthy of the occasion which
led to its erection. Zonaras[3] is not so complimentary.
He describes the church as a monument of the niggardli-
ness of Isaac Comnenus. In any case, it was pulled down
and rebuilt in the following century by the Emperor John
Comnenus in splendid style, and dedicated to the Saviour.[4]
As the beauty and wealth of a Byzantine sanctuary were
exhibited in the lavish adornment of the interior, it is
possible that the church of S. Thekla, though small and
outwardly plain, may have been a beautiful and rich
building in its latest Christian character. It had then the

---

[1] Anna Comnena, vol. i. p. 168.   [2] *Ibid.* vol. i. p. 168.
[3] Zonaras, iii. p. 672.   [4] *Ibid. ut supra.*

honour of seeing among the worshippers before its altar Anna Dalassena, the mother of the Comneni. For, when charged with the government of the Empire during the absence of Alexius Comnenus from the capital, that able woman came often to pray in this church, 'lest she should be immersed in merely secular affairs.' [1]

Architectural Features

(For Plan see p. 206)

The building is an oblong hall, m. 13.55 by m. 5.4, divided into three compartments. It is now covered with a wooden roof, but the arrangements of the breaks or pilasters on the walls indicate that it had originally a dome. At the east end is a single apse, the usual side-apses being represented by two niches. The western compartment served as a narthex. During the repairs of the mosque in 1890, frescoes of the eikons which once decorated the walls were brought to view. On the exterior the apse shows three sides, crowned with a corbelled cornice. The central side is pierced by a window of good workmanship, divided by a shaft into two lights, and above the window are two short blind concave niches. High blind concave niches indent the other sides of the apse. In the northern wall are the remains of a triple window, divided by shafts built in courses. Above this is a row of three small windows.

[1] Anna Comnena, vol. i. p. 169.

CHAPTER XIV

THE CHURCH OF S. SAVIOUR PANTEPOPTES, ESKI IMARET MESJEDI

THE reasons which favour the identification of the mosque Eski Imaret Mesjedi, which is situated on the heights above Aya Kapou (Gate of S. Theodosia), with the church of S. Saviour Pantepoptes, the All-Seeing ($\pi\alpha\nu\tau\epsilon\pi\delta\pi\tau\eta\varsigma$), are the following : first, the tradition to that effect,[1] which in the case of a building so conspicuous can scarcely be mistaken ; secondly, the correspondence of its position to that of the Pantepoptes, on a hill commanding an extensive view of the Golden Horn ;[2] and finally, the architectural features which mark it to be what the church of the Pantepoptes was, a building of the Comnenian period. The church of the Pantepoptes was founded or restored by Anna Dalassena,[3] the mother of Alexius I. Comnenus (1081-1118), one of the most remarkable women in Byzantine history, combining to a rare degree domestic virtues with great political ambition and administrative ability. For twenty years she was associated with her son in the government of the Empire, and was the power behind the throne which he owed largely to her energy and devotion. About the year 1100 she laid aside the cares of state, and without renouncing altogether her royal style retired to rest in the monastery she had built, until her death, five years later, at an advanced age.[4] There is nothing of special importance

[1] Patr. Constantius, pp. 70-80.   [2] Nicet. Chon. p. 752.
[3] Glycas, p. 622.
[4] *Ibid.* For the career of this distinguished woman, see Diehl, *Figures byzantines.*

to record in the annals of the House. Its inmates were occasionally disturbed by the confinement among them of some dignitary who had offended the Government, or by the theological disputes that agitated the ecclesiastical circles of the capital.[1] But for the most part life at Pantepoptes was quiet and peaceful. Only once does the

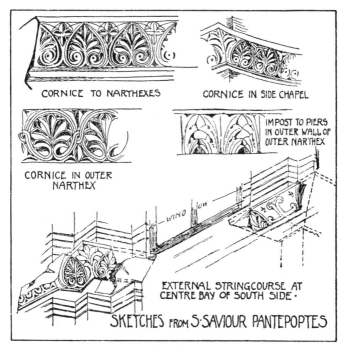

CORNICE TO NARTHEXES

CORNICE IN SIDE CHAPEL

CORNICE IN OUTER NARTHEX

IMPOST TO PIERS IN OUTER WALL OF OUTER NARTHEX

WIND OW

EXTERNAL STRINGCOURSE AT CENTRE BAY OF SOUTH SIDE.

SKETCHES FROM S·SAVIOUR PANTEPOPTES

FIG. 72.

monastery stand out conspicuous before the eyes of the world. When the Venetian ships under Henrico Dandolo, with the army of the Fourth Crusade on board, lined the shore of the Golden Horn from Ispigas and the church of S. Saviour the Benefactor to Blachernae (*i.e.* from Jubali Kapoussi to Aivan Serai) on Easter Monday, 12th April 1204, the Emperor Alexius Murtzuphlus established his headquarters beside the Pantepoptes. There he pitched

[1] Nicet. Chon. pp. 315-16 ; Pachym. i. pp. 314-15, ii. p. 185.

his vermilion tent, marshalled his best troops, and watched the operations of the enemy.   And thence he fled when he saw the walls on the shore below him carried by storm, and Flemish knights mounted on horses, which had been landed from the hostile fleet, advancing to assault his position.   So hurried was his flight that he left his tent standing, and under its shelter Count Baldwin of Flanders and Hainault slept away the fatigue of that day's victory.[1]   During the Latin occupation the church passed into the hands of the Venetians, and was robbed of many of its relics for the benefit of churches in the West.[2]   Upon the Turkish conquest it served for some time as an imaret or refectory for the students and teachers of the *medressé*,[3] then in course of construction beside the great mosque of Sultan Mehemed.   Hence its Turkish name.   After serving that purpose it was converted into a mosque later in the reign of the conqueror.

Architectural Features

In plan the church belongs to the 'four column' type, and has two narthexes.   The dome, placed on a drum, circular within and twelve-sided without, is carried on four piers which the Turks have reduced to an irregular octagonal form.   It is divided into twelve bays by square ribs, and is lighted by twelve semicircular-headed windows.   The cornice-string is adorned with a running leaf spray of a pleasing and uncommon design.   The arms of the cross have barrel vaults, while the chambers at its angles are covered with cross-groined vaults.   The apsidal chambers are small, with shallow niches on the north, south, and west, and a somewhat deeper niche on the east where the apse stands.   These niches are carried up through a vaulting string-course, carved with a repeating leaf ornament, and combine with the groined vault above them to produce a charming canopy.   The southern transept gable, though

---

[1] Villehardouin, *La Conquête de C.P.* pp. 141-44 ; *Chroniques gréco-romaines*, pp. 96, 97.
[2] Riant, *Exuviae sacrae*, p. 178.   [3] Paspates, p. 314.

much built up, still displays the design which occurs so frequently in Byzantine churches, namely, three windows in the lunette of the arch (the central light rising higher than the sidelights), and three stilted arches below the vaulting string-course, resting on two columns and containing three windows which are carried down to a breastwork of carved marble slabs between the columns. The floor of the church is paved with square red bricks, except in the apses, where marble is employed. The gynecaeum, above the inner narthex, is divided into three bays separated by broad transverse arches. The central bay, which is larger than its companions, is covered with a dome vault, and looks into the body of the church through a fine triple arcade in the lunette of the western arm of the cross. The smaller bays are covered with cross-groined vaults. As elsewhere, the vaulting-string in the gynecaeum is decorated with carved work. The inner narthex, like the gynecaeum above it, is divided into three bays covered with cross-groined vaults, and communicates with the church, as usual, by three doors. Its walls seem to have been formerly revetted with marble. In the northern wall is a door, now closed, which gave access to a building beyond that side of the church. The exonarthex is also divided in three bays, separated by transverse arches, and communicates with the inner narthex by three doors and with the outer world by a single door situated in the central bay. That bay has a low dome without windows, while the lateral bays have groined vaults. Turkish repairs show in the pilasters and the pointed arches which support the original transverse arches. The doors throughout the building are framed in marble jambs and lintels, adorned in most cases with a running ornament and crosses. In the case of the doors of the exonarthex a red marble, *brèche rouge*, is employed, as in the exonarthex of the Pantokrator, another erection of the Comnenian period. On the exterior the building is much damaged, but nevertheless preserves traces of considerable elaboration. The walls are of brick, intermixed with courses of stone, and on the three sides of the central apse there are remains of patterned brickwork. On the buttresses to the southern wall are roundels with radiating voussoirs in stone and brick, and if one may judge from the fact that the string-course does not fit the face of the wall, parts of the exterior of the church were incrusted with marble. The round-headed windows of the dome cut into its cornice. Under the church is a cistern[1] which Bondelmontius deemed worthy of mention.[2] Until some twenty years ago extensive substructures were visible on the north-east of the church, affording homes for poor Greek families.[3] They were probably the foundations of the lofty monastery buildings whose windows commanded the magnificent view of the Golden Horn that doubtless suggested the epithet Pantepoptes, under which the Saviour was worshipped in this sanctuary.

S. Saviour Pantepoptes is the most carefully built of the later churches of Constantinople. The little irregularities of setting out so common in the other churches of the city are here almost entirely absent. This accuracy of building, the carving of the string-courses, and the remains of marble decoration both within and on the exterior, prove exceptional care.

For details see Figs. 68, 72, 75.

[1] *Die byzantinischen Wasserbehälter von K.P.*, von Dr. P. Forcheimer und Dr. J. Strzygowski, pp. 106-7.
[2] *Librum insularum Archipelagi*, 65.   [3] Paspates, p. 314.

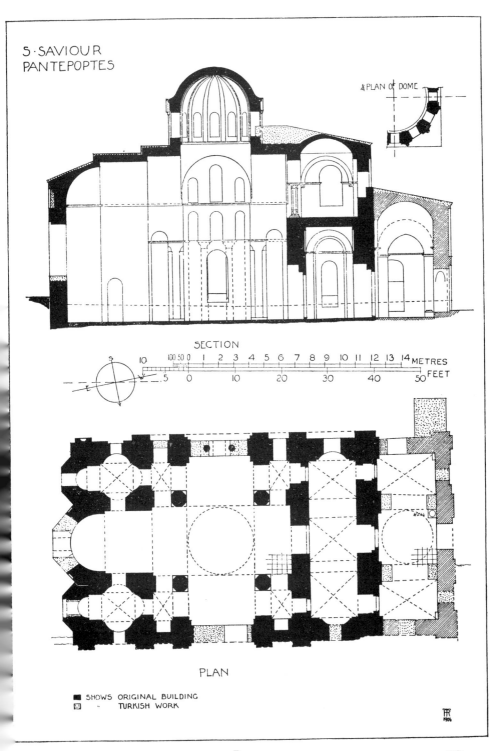

S·SAVIOUR
PANTEPOPTES

& PLAN OF DOME

SECTION

METRES

FEET

PLAN

■ SHOWS ORIGINAL BUILDING
▨   "   TURKISH WORK

FIG. 73.

217

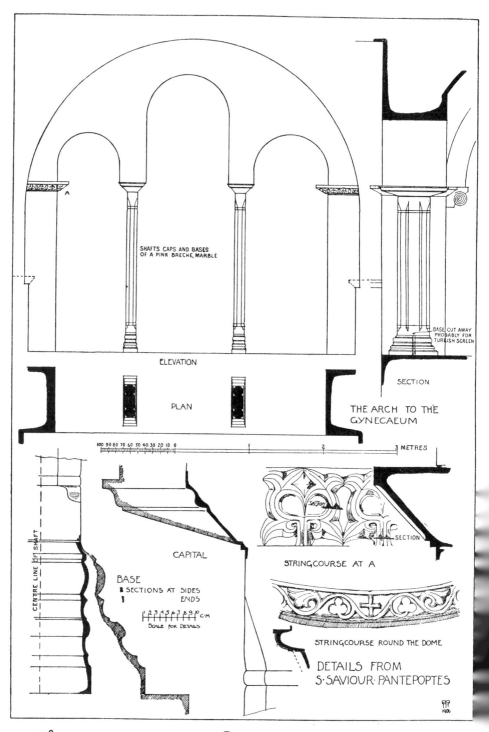

ELEVATION

SHAFTS CAPS AND BASES
OF A PINK BRECHE MARBLE

BASE CUT AWAY
PROBABLY FOR
TURKISH SCREEN

SECTION

PLAN

THE ARCH TO THE
GYNECAEUM

100 90 80 70 60 50 40 30 20 10 0   1   2   3 METRES

CENTRE LINE OF SHAFT

CAPITAL

BASE
SECTIONS AT SIDES
ENDS

1 2 3 4 5 6 7 8 9 10 C·M
SCALE FOR DETAILS

SECTION

STRINGCOURSE AT A

STRINGCOURSE ROUND THE DOME

DETAILS FROM
S·SAVIOUR· PANTEPOPTES

FIG. 74.

CHAPTER XV

THE CHURCH OF S. SAVIOUR PANTOKRATOR, ZEÏREK KILISSI JAMISSI

ACCORDING to the tradition current in the city when Gyllius[1] and Gerlach[2] explored the antiquities of Constantinople, the large Byzantine church, now the mosque Zeïrek Kilissi Jamissi, overlooking the Golden Horn from the heights above Oun Kapan, was the famous church of S. Saviour Pantokrator. There is no reason for doubting the accuracy of this identification. The church was so important, and so closely associated with events which occurred late in the history of the city, that its identity could not be forgotten by the Greek ecclesiastical authorities soon after the Turkish conquest. Moreover, all indications of the position of the church, although too vague to determine its precise site, are in harmony with the tradition on the subject. For, according to Russian pilgrims to the shrines of Constantinople, the Pantokrator could be reached most readily from the side of the city on the Golden Horn,[3] and stood in the vicinity of the church of the Holy Apostles[4]—particulars that agree with the situation of Zeïrek Kilissi Jamissi.

The church was founded by the Empress Irene,[5] the consort of John II. Comnenus (1118-1143), and daughter of Ladislas, King of Hungary. She came to Constantinople

[1] *De top. C.P.* iv. c. 2, p. 283, 'in supercilio quarti collis vergente ad solis ortum visitur templum Pantocratoris, illustre memoria recentium scriptorum.'
[2] *Tagebuch*, p. 157.
[3] *Itin. russes*, pp. 105, 233-34.
[4] Du Cange, *Const. Christ.* iv. p. 81; *Itin. russes*, pp. 123, 203-4.
[5] Synax., August 13; Cinnamus, p. 9; Phrantzes, p. 210.

shortly before 1105 as the Princess Pyrisca, a beautiful girl, 'a plant covered with blossoms, promising rich fruit,' to marry John Comnenus, then heir-apparent to the crown of Alexius Comnenus, and adorned eight years of her husband's reign by the simplicity of her tastes and her great liberality to the poor. The monastic institutions of the city also enjoyed her favour, and not long before her death in 1126 she assume the veil under the name of Xené. The foundations of the church were, probably, laid soon after her husband's accession to the throne, and to the church she attached a monastery capable of accommodating seven hundred monks ;[1] a xeno-docheion, a home for aged men, and a hospital.[2]

But the pious and charitable lady had undertaken more than she could perform, and was obliged to turn to the emperor for sympathy and assistance. Accordingly she took him, one day, to see the edifice while in course of erection, and falling suddenly at his feet, implored him with tears to complete her work. The beauty of the building and the devotion of his wife appealed so strongly to John Comnenus that he forthwith vowed to make the church and monas-tery the finest in the city, and altogether worthy of the Pantokrator to whom they were dedicated ;[3] and so well did he keep his promise, that the honour of being the founder of the church has been bestowed on him by the historian Nicetas Choniates.[4]

The imperial typicon or charter of the monastery,[5] granted in 1136, made the monastery an autonomous insti-tution, independent of the patriarch or the prefect of the city, and exempt from taxes of every description. At the same time it was provided with vineyards and richly endowed.

According to Scarlatus Byzantius[6] and the Patriarch Constantius,[7] a mosaic in the building portrayed the

---

[1] Du Cange, *C.P. Christ.* iv. p. 81, quoting Anselm, bishop of Havelsberg, who was in Constantinople as the ambassador of Lothair the Great to the Emperor John in 1145.

[2] MS. No. 85, in the Library of the Theological Seminary at Halki.

[3] Synax., 13th August.

[4] Pp. 66, 151.

[5] MS. No. 85, in the Library of the Theological Seminary at Halki.

[6] Vol. i. p. 555.   [7] *Ancient and Modern C.P.* p. 69.

Emperor Manuel Comnenus (1141-1180) in the act of presenting the model of the church to Christ. If that was the case the church was completed by that emperor. As will immediately appear, Manuel certainly enriched the church with relics.

The history of the Pantokrator may be conveniently divided into three periods : the period of the Comneni ; the period of the Latin Empire ; and the period of the Palaeologi.

During the first the following incidents occurred : Here, as was most fitting, the founders of the church and monastery were laid to rest, the Empress Irene in 1126,[1] the Emperor John Comnenus[2] seventeen years later. Here their elder son Isaac was confined, until the succession to the throne had been settled in favour of his younger brother Manuel. That change in the natural order of things had been decided upon by John Comnenus while he lay dying in Cilicia from the effects of a wound inflicted by the fall of a poisoned arrow out of his own quiver, when boar-hunting in the forests of the Taurus Mountains, and was explained as due to Manuel's special fitness to assume the care of the Empire, and not merely to the fact that he was a father's favourite son. But when the appointment was made Manuel was with his father in Cilicia, while Isaac was in Constantinople, in a position to mount the throne as soon as the tidings of John's death reached the capital.

The prospect that Manuel would wear the crown seemed therefore very remote. But Axuch, an intimate friend and counsellor of the dying emperor, started for Constantinople the moment Manuel was nominated, and travelled so fast, that he reached the city before the news of the emperor's death and of Manuel's nomination was known there. Then, wasting no time, Axuch made sure of the person of Isaac, removed him from the palace, and put him in charge of the monks of the Pantokrator, who had every reason to

---

[1] Cinnamus, p. 14 ; Guntherus Parisiensis in Riant's *Exuviae sacrae*, p. 105. The sarcophagus that forms part of a Turkish fountain to the west of the church is usually, but without any proof, considered to be the tomb of Irene. A long flight of steps near it leads to the cistern below the church.

[2] Cinnamus, p. 31.

be loyal to the wishes of the deceased sovereign. The wily courtier then set himself to win the leading men in the capital over to the cause of the younger brother, and, by the time Manuel was prepared to enter Constantinople, had secured for him a popular welcome and the surrender of Isaac's claims.[1]

In 1147, the famous eikon of S. Demetrius of Thessalonia was transferred from the magnificent basilica dedicated to the saint in that city to the Pantokrator. This was done by the order of Manuel Comnenus, at the request of Joseph, then abbot of the monastery, and in accordance with the wishes of the emperor's parents, the founders of the House.[2] It was a great sacrifice to demand of the Macedonian shrine, and by way of compensation a larger and more artistic eikon of S. Demetrius, in silver and gold, was hung beside his tomb. But Constantinople rejoiced in the greater sanctity and virtue of the earlier picture, and when tidings of its approach were received, the whole fraternity of the Pantokrator, with the senate and an immense crowd of devout persons, went seven miles out from the city to hail the arrival of the image, and to bear it in triumph to its new abode, with psalms and hymns, lighted tapers, fragrant incense, and the gleam of soldiers' spears. Thus, it was believed, the monastery gained more beauty and security, the dynasty of the Comneni more strength, the Roman Empire and the Queen of cities an invisible but mighty power to keep enemies afar off.

In 1158 Bertha, the first wife of Manuel Comnenus, and sister-in-law of the Emperor Conrad of Germany, was buried in the church.[3] Twenty-two years later, Manuel Comnenus himself was laid in its heroön in a splendid sarcophagus of black marble with a cover cut in seven protuberances.[4] Beside the tomb was placed the porphyry slab upon which the body of Christ was supposed to have been laid after His deposition from the cross. The slab was placed there in commemoration of the fact that when it was brought from Ephesus to Constantinople, Manuel

---

[1] Nicet. Chon. pp. 53, 56, 66. [2] Synax., October 26th.
[3] Nicet. Chon. p. 151. [4] Ibid. p. 289.

carried it on his broad shoulders all the way up the hill
from the harbour of the Bucoleon (at Tchatlady Kapou),
to the private chapel of the imperial residence near S. Sophia.[1]
Nicetas Choniates thought the aspect of the tomb and of its
surroundings very significant.   The seven protuberances on
its cover represented the seven-hilled city which had been
the emperor's throne ; the porphyry slab recalled the
mighty deeds which he whose form lay so still and silent in
the grave had wrought in the days of his strength ; while
the black marble told the grief evoked by his death.
Robert of Clari, who saw the tomb in 1203, extols its
magnificence.   'Never,' says he, 'was born on this earth
a holy man or a holy woman who is buried in so rich and
splendid a fashion as this emperor in this abbey.   There is
found the marble table on which Our Lord was laid when
taken down from the cross, and there are still seen the
tears which Our Lady shed upon it.'[2]

Some seven months after Manuel's death a strange
spectacle was witnessed at his tomb.   His cousin, Andronicus
Comnenus, the torment of his life and one of the worst
characters in Byzantine history, taking advantage of the
intrigues and disturbances which attended the minority of
Manuel's son and successor, Alexius II. Comnenus, left
his place of exile in Paphlagonia and appeared in Constantinople at the head of an army, as though the champion of
the young sovereign's cause.   No sooner had he reached
the city than he proceeded to visit Manuel's tomb, to show
the regard he professed to feel for a relative and sovereign.
At the sight of the dark sarcophagus Andronicus gave way
to the most violent paroxysms of grief.   So deep and
prolonged, indeed, did his distress seem, that his attendants
implored him to control his feelings and leave the sad spot.
But the mourner protested that he could not quit so hastily
a place hallowed by such sacred and tender associations.
Moreover, he had not yet said all he had to tell the dead.
Bending, therefore, again over the grave, Andronicus continued to address the deceased.   The words were inaudible,
but they seemed a fresh outpouring of sorrow, and deeply

[1] Nicet. Chon. p. 151.   [2] Riant, *Exuviae sacrae*, ii. p. 232.

affected many of the spectators, for, as the mourner had not lived on the best terms with his imperial cousin, his grief appeared to be the victory of a man's better nature. But those who knew Andronicus well interpreted his conduct as the performance of a consummate actor, and understood his whispers to mean curses and vows of vengeance upon his dead and helpless relative. Events justified this interpretation. For Andronicus ere long usurped the throne, murdered Alexius, insulted his remains, ordered his head to be cut off, and cast the mutilated corpse into the Sea of Marmora to the strains of music.[1]

During the Latin occupation the church was appropriated for worship according to the ritual of the Roman Communion, and many of its relics, its vessels of gold and silver, its jewels and vestments, were carried off to enrich S. Mark's at Venice, and other shrines of Western Christendom. How great a value was set upon such trophies, and by what strange methods they were secured, is seen in the account which Guntherus,[2] a contemporary historian, gives of the way in which some of the relics of the church were acquired. As soon as the Crusaders captured the city in 1204 and gave it over to pillage, a numerous band of looters made for the Pantokrator in search of spoil, having heard that many valuables had been deposited for safe keeping within the strong walls around the monastery. Among the crowd hastening thither was Martin, abbot of the Cistercian Abbey of Parisis in Alsace, who accompanied the Crusade as chaplain and chronicler. The fever of plunder raging about him was too infectious for the good man to escape. When everybody else was getting rich he could not consent to remain poor. His only scruple was not to defile his holy hands with the filthy lucre which worldlings coveted. To purloin sacred relics, however, was lawful booty. Entering, therefore, the Pantokrator with his chaplain, Martin accosted a venerable, white-bearded man who seemed familiar with the building, and in stentorian tones demanded where the relics of the church were to be found. The person addressed was, in fact, a

[1] Nicet. Chon. pp. 332-33, 354-55.　　[2] Riant, *Exuviae sacrae*, i. pp. 104 *seq.*

priest, though Martin had mistaken him for a layman on account of the strangeness of the Greek clerical garb. The priest did not understand Latin any more than the abbot understood Greek, and the situation became awkward, for the pitch of Martin's voice made it evident that he was not

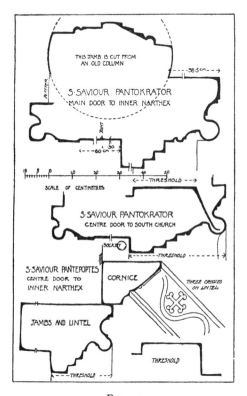

FIG. 75.

a person to be trifled with. The old man therefore tried what the Romance patois, which he had picked up from foreign residents in the city, could do to establish intelligible inter-course with the rough visitor. Fortunately the crusader also knew something of that patois, and made the purpose of his visit sufficiently clear. As soon as the iron safe con-taining the coveted relics was opened, abbot and chaplain plunged four greedy hands into the hoard and stowed relic

Q

after relic under the ample folds of their robes until there was no room for more. Thus laden, the pious thieves made as fast as they could for the ship in which they had come to Constantinople, not stopping to converse with friends on the way, and giving to all curious inquiries the brief and enigmatical reply, 'We have done well.' Upon reaching the ship Martin found himself the happy possessor of no less than sixty-two relics, including a piece of the Holy Cross, and drops of 'the blood shed for man's redemption.' Martin wished to start immediately for Alsace, but circumstances obliged him to remain in Constantinople for several months. Thanks, however, to the priest of the Pantokrator, whom the abbot had treated generously, Martin secured a small chapel where to conceal his spoils until an opportunity to return home should occur. A fellow-countryman, indeed, the only other person let into the secret, advised him to secure by means of the relics an abbotship, if not a bishopric, in the Holy Land. But Martin was above personal ambition, and notwithstanding all the difficulties involved in the attempt to carry the relics to the West, waited patiently till he could smuggle them out of the city. At length his chance came ; whereupon he embarked for Venice, and after a hard and tedious journey of eight months reached home safely. Again and again on the way he had narrowly escaped the loss of his treasures at the hands of pirates on the sea and of brigands upon land. But all toils and dangers were forgotten when, on the 24th of June 1205, at the head of the brotherhood of which he was the chief, Martin placed the relics purloined from the Pantokrator of Constantinople upon the high altar of the church of Parisis with a conqueror's pride and joy, while the people shouted, 'Blessed be the Lord God, the God of Israel, who only doeth wondrous things.' There is archaeology even in morals.

But while called thus to deplore the removal of many of its valued relics, the Pantokrator came during the Latin period into possession of a sacred object which compensated the house abundantly for all losses of that kind. The church became the shrine of the eikon of the Theotokos

Hodegetria. No relic was held in higher estimation. It was considered to be the portrait of the mother of our Lord painted by S. Luke, and was brought from Jerusalem to Constantinople by the Empress Eudocia, wife of Theodosius II., as a present to her sister-in-law Pulcheria. It led the hosts of the Empire to victory, and shared the honours of their triumphal entry into the capital. When enemies besieged the city, the eikon was carried in procession through the streets and around the fortifications, or was placed near the post of danger. After the capture of the city by the Latins the picture was first taken to S. Sophia, then the cathedral of the Venetian patriarchs of Constantinople. But the Venetian clergy of the Pantokrator claimed the sacred picture as their own, in virtue of a promise made to them by the Emperor Henry ; and when their claim was ignored, they persuaded the podesta of the Venetian community to break into S. Sophia and seize the eikon by force. In vain did the patriarch appear upon the scene with candle and bell to excommunicate the podesta, his council, and his agents for the sacrilegious act. The coveted prize was borne off in triumph to the Pantokrator. In vain did the Papal Legate in the city confirm the excommunication of the guilty parties, and lay their churches under interdict. In vain were those penalties confirmed by the Pope himself.[1] The eikon kept its place in the Pantokrator notwithstanding all anathemas until the fall of the Latin Empire, when it was removed from the church to lead the procession which came through the Golden Gate on the 15th August 1261, to celebrate the recovery of Constantinople by the Greeks.[2]

Towards the close of the Latin occupation the monastery became the residence of the Latin emperor, probably because the condition of the public exchequer made it impossible to keep either the Great Palace or the palace of Blachernae in proper repair. Money was not plentiful in Constantinople

---

[1] Belin, *Histoire de la latinité de Constantinople*, pp. 73-74, 113-14.

[2] Pachym. i. p. 160 ; Niceph. Greg. p. 87 ; G. Acropolita, pp. 196-97. The last writer says the eikon was taken from the monastery of the Hodegon, which was its proper shrine. The eikon may have been removed from the Pantokrator to the church of Hodegetria on the eve of the triumphal entry.

when Baldwin II., the last Latin ruler of the city, was compelled to sell the lead on the roof of his palace for a paltry sum, and to use the beams of his outhouses for fuel, nor when he had to leave his son and heir in the hands of the Capelli at Venice as security for a loan. Still, the selection of the monastery for the emperor's abode, even under these trying circumstances, implies the importance and comparative splendour of the building. Here Baldwin was in residence when the forces of Michael Palaeologus, under the command of Alexius Strategopoulos, approached the city, and here he received the intelligence, early in the morning of the 25th of July 1261, that the Greeks had entered the city by the Gate of the Pegé[1] (Selivri Kapoussi), and set fire to the capital at four points. Baldwin's first impulse was to make a brave stand. But his fleet and the greater part of his army were absent from the city, engaged in the siege of Daphnusium on the coast of the Black Sea. Meantime the fires kindled by the Greeks were spreading and drawing nearer and nearer to the Pantokrator itself. So casting off sword and helmet and every other mark of his station, Baldwin took ship and led the flight of the Latin masters of Constantinople back to their homes in the West.[2]

The first incident in the history of the Pantokrator after the restoration of the Greek Empire was not fortunate. The monastery then became the object upon which the Genoese, who had favoured that event, and been rewarded with the grant of Galata as a trading post, saw fit to vent the grudge they bore against certain Venetians who, in the course of the feud between the two republics, as competitors for the commerce of the East, had injured a church and a tower belonging to the Genoese colony at Acre. To destroy some building in Constantinople associated with Venice was thought to be the best way to settle the out-

[1] Niceph. Greg. i. p. 85. Cf. Canale, *Nuova Storia*, ii. p. 153, quoted by Belin, *Latinité de C.P.* p. 22, 'ov'erano la chiesa, la loggia, il palazzo dei Veneziani,' cf. Belin, p. 92.

[2] George Acropolita, p. 195. On the contrary, Pachymeres represents Baldwin as taking flight from the palace of Blachernae, and embarking at the Great Palace. See vol. i. of that historian's works, pp. 132-48.

standing account, and so a band of Genoese made for the Pantokrator, over which the banner of S. Mark had recently floated, and tore the monastery down to the ground, making it a greater ruin than the Venetians had made of the Genoese buildings in Syria. Then, not only to deprive the enemy of his property but to turn it also to one's own advantage, the scattered stones were collected and shipped to Genoa for the construction of the church of S. George in that city.[1]

In the reign of Michael Palaeologus, a member of the noble family of the princes of the Peloponnesus became abbot of the Pantokrator, and acquired great influence. He led, as we shall see, the mission which conducted the emperor's daughter Maria to the Mongolian court, and when the patriarchal seat was vacant in 1275, a strong party favoured his appointment to that position instead of Veccus.[2]

During the period of the Palaeologi the church frequently served as a mausoleum for members of the imperial family. Here in 1317 was buried Irene, the second wife of Andronicus II., a Spanish princess and daughter of the Marquis of Monferrat. She came to Constantinople in 1285, when only eleven years old, a beautiful girl, Yolande by name, distinguished for the elegance of her manners, and for a time was the idol of the court. But what with the desire which she developed to amass wealth, and to see her sons share in the government of the Empire, she ultimately proved the cause of much unhappiness to her husband.[3] She deserves to be remembered for bequeathing the funds which enabled Andronicus II. to build the buttresses supporting the walls of S. Sophia on the north and east.[4]

Here, in 1425, Manuel II. was laid to rest after his long

---

[1] Belin, *Histoire de la latinité de C.P.* pp. 22-23, quoting Canale, *Nuova Storia*, ii. p. 153; cf. Sauli, i. p. 55. According to Fanucci, the Venetians themselves removed their national emblems from the Pantokrator and tore down the monastery.—Belin, *ut supra*, pp. 88, 92.

[2] Pachym. i. p. 402.

[3] *Ibid.* ii. pp. 87-88; Niceph. Greg. i. p. 167.

[4] *Ibid.* i. pp. 273, 233-34.

and troubled reign.[1] Beside him were buried his wife
Irene (1450)[2] and his three sons, Andronicus (1429),[3]
Theodore (1448),[4] John VI. Palaeologus (1448).[5] Here
also was placed the tomb of the Empress Maria of the
house of Trebizond, the fourth wife of John VII.
Palaeologus ;[6] and not far off was the grave of Eugenia,
the wife of the despot Demetrius and daughter of
the Genoese Gatulazzo, who had helped to over-
throw John Cantacuzene and to recover the throne for
the Palaeologi.[7] As we follow to the grave this procession of personages so closely associated with the fall
of Constantinople, one seems to be watching the slow
ebbing away of the life-blood of the Empire which they
could not save.

In 1407 John Palaeologus, then heir-apparent, added
to the endowments of the church by giving it a share
in the revenues of the imperial domains at Cassandra.[8]
It would appear that the affairs of the monastery about
this time were not in a satisfactory state, for on
the advice of the historian Phrantzes they were put for
settlement into the hands of Macarius, a monk from Mt.
Athos.[9]

A protosyngellos and abbot of the Pantokrator was
one of the ambassadors sent by John VII. Palaeologus
to Pope Martin V. to negotiate the union of the
Churches.[10]

The most famous inmate of the Pantokrator was George
Scholarius, better known as Gennadius, the first patriarch
of Constantinople after the Turkish conquest. On account
of his learning and legal attainments he accompanied the
Emperor John VII. Palaeologus and the Patriarch Joseph
to the Council of Ferrara and Florence in 1438, to take part
in the negotiations for the union of Christendom. As
submission to the Papal demands was the only hope of

[1] Phrantzes, p. 121.   [2] *Ibid.* p. 210.
[3] *Ibid.* p. 134.   [4] *Ibid.* p. 203.
[5] *Ibid.* p. 203.   [6] *Ibid.* p. 191.
[7] *Ibid.* p. 191.   [8] Muralt, ad annum.
[9] Phrantzes, p. 156.   [10] *Ibid.* p. 156

obtaining the aid of the West for the Roman Empire in the East, the emperor, with most of the Greek clergy in attendance at the council, subscribed the decrees of that assembly, and on the 8th July 1438 the two Churches were officially reconciled and bound to common action. But it was a union without sufficient religious motive on the one side and without strong political interest on the other. Instead of improving the situation it made matters worse. But drowning men clutch even unsubstantial objects, and accordingly the Emperor Constantine Dragases, a few years later, implored again the assistance of the Pope, begging him to send a commission of Roman ecclesiastics to Constantinople to confer once more with Greek theologians with the hope of making the union more effective. In response to that request a Commission was appointed, having at its head Cardinal Isidore, a Greek ecclesiastic, who at the Council of Florence had cast in his lot with the Latins and been created cardinal and titular archbishop of Kiev. Isidore and his colleagues were welcomed with great demonstrations of joy, and after several meetings with representatives of the Eastern Church terms of union were once more devised. The event was celebrated by a religious service in S. Sophia, according to Roman rite, in the presence of the emperor, the senate, and a large body of ecclesiastics. In the order of the prayers offered that day in the cathedral of the East the name of the Pope was mentioned first. But these proceedings only exasperated the opponents of the union, who had the advantage in numbers and in passionate convictions. Seeking for a leader they flocked to the monastery of the Pantokrator to consult Gennadius. It was a critical moment. Gennadius retired to his cell. Then opening the door he affixed his answer in writing upon it, and again shut himself in. The oracle had spoken : 'Wretched Romans, whither have ye strayed, and gone far from hope in God to put your trust in the Franks? Your city and your religion will perish together. You abandon the faith of your fathers and embrace impiety. Woe unto you in the day of judgment.' The words spread like wildfire and enflamed the excited crowd within and around the monastery.   Anathemas, cursing all supporters of the union in the past, in the present, and in the future resounded on every hand.   The answer of Gennadius was carried through the city and found an echo among all classes of the population.   Men ran to the taverns to drink undiluted wine, in derision of the Roman practice of mixing water with the wine of the Holy Communion; they shouted themselves hoarse with maledictions on the unionists ; they drank to the honour of the Theotokos, invoking her aid as in the days of old, when she delivered the city out of the hands of the Persians, the Avars, and the Saracens.   Far and wide rose the cry, 'Away with the help and the worship of the Latin eaters of unleavened bread.'[1]   The two scenes witnessed, on the 12th December 1452, in S. Sophia and at the Pantokrator displayed a discord that hastened the downfall of New Rome.   That day the party with the watchword, 'Better the turban of the Turk than the tiara of the Pope,' gained the victory.

Upon the capture of the city, the Greek community, owing to the recent death of the Patriarch Athanasius, found itself without an ecclesiastical chief.   The conqueror, anxious to conciliate his Greek subjects, proclaimed complete religious toleration, and gave orders that they should forthwith proceed to the free election of a new patriarch.   Under the circumstances there could be no question as to the right man for the place.   Gennadius, who had opposed the unprofitable Latin alliance, and saved the national Church notwithstanding the ruin of the Empire, was unanimously chosen to be the first guide of his people along the strange and difficult path they were now to follow.   The choice being confirmed by the Sultan, Gennadius left the Pantokrator to do homage to the new master of the realm. Every mark of honour was paid to the prelate.   He was invited to the royal table and granted a long audience, at which, following the practice of Byzantine emperors, the Sultan presented him with a magnificent pastoral staff, and promised to respect all the ancient privileges of the patriarchal see.   When Gennadius took leave, the Sultan

---

[1] Ducas, pp. 252-60.

accompanied him to the foot of the stairs of the palace, saw him mounted on a fine and richly caparisoned horse, and ordered the notables of the court to escort him to the church of the Holy Apostles, which was to replace S. Sophia as the cathedral of the Greek Communion.[1] It was certainly fortunate for the Orthodox Church at that cruel moment in its history to find in one of the cells of the Pantokrator a man able to win the goodwill of the Empire's conqueror. When nothing could save the State, Gennadius saved the nation's Church, and with the Church many forms of national life. Muralt, looking at these transactions from another standpoint, says, ' C'est ainsi que les Grecs virent accompli leur vœu d'être délivrés de l'union avec les Latins.'[2]

It would appear that the Pantokrator was abandoned by its Christian owners very soon after the conquest. The great decrease of the Greek population that followed the downfall of the city left several quarters of Constantinople with few if any Christian inhabitants, and so brought to an end the native religious service in many churches of the capital. For some time thereafter the deserted building was used by fullers and workers in leather as a workshop and dwelling.[3] But the edifice was too grand to be allowed to suffer permanent degradation, and some twenty years later it was consecrated to Moslem worship by a certain Zeïrek Mehemed Effendi.[4] Its actual name, Zeïrek Kilissi Jamissi, recalls the double service the building has rendered, and the person who diverted it from its earlier to its later use.

Architectural Features

As it stands the Pantokrator is a combination of three churches, placed side by side, and communicating with one another through arched openings in their common walls. The three buildings are not of the same date, and opinions differ in regard to their relative age. On the whole, how-

---

[1] Phrantzes, pp. 304-7.
[2] *Essai de chronographie byzantine*, ii. p. 889.   [3] Ducas, p. 318.
[4] Chadekat, vol. i. p. 118, quoted by Paspates, p. 312.

ever, the northern church may be safely considered the earliest structure ; the central church is somewhat later ; the southern church is the latest.

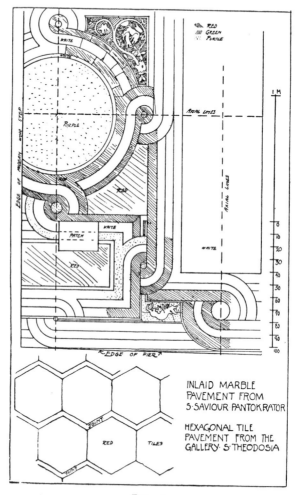

FIG. 76.

The Northern Church.—This is a simple and dignified building of the domed 'four column' type, with a gynaeceum above the narthex. The narthex is in four bays covered with cross-groined vaults on transverse arches. Its southern bay, however, is a later extension, running about half-way in front of the central church to give access to a door into that building. Only two bays of the original narthex have doors opening into the north church ; the third door which once existed in the northern bay has been partly built up. The narthex is very much out of repair, and the western wall threatens to fall outwards. The dome, pierced by eight windows, shows so many Turkish features that it may be pronounced as mostly, if not wholly, a Turkish construction. The four square piers which support it are manifestly Turkish. When Gyllius visited the church in the sixteenth century the dome arches rested on four columns of Theban granite, ' hemispherium sustentatur quatuor arcubus, quos fulciunt quatuor columnae marmoris Thebaici.'[1] Barrel vaults cover the arms of the cross, which, as usual in churches of this type, appears distinctly above the roof on the exterior. The southern arm extends to the central church and its vault is pierced by two windows, inserted, probably, to compensate for the loss of light occasioned by the erection of that building. These windows furnish one indication of the earlier date of the north church. The gynaeceum, like the narthex below it, is covered with cross-groined vaults and contains a small fireplace. The prothesis and diaconicon have barrel vaults and apses with three sides projecting slightly on the exterior. The main apse has a very lofty triple window, and shows five sides. All the apses are decorated with high shallow blind niches, a simple but effective ornament.[2]

The Central Church.—The central church is an oblong hall covered by two domes, and terminates in a large apse. It is extremely irregular in plan, and does not lie parallel to either of the churches between which it stands. The domes are separated by a transverse arch. The western dome, though flattened somewhat on the four sides, is

[1] *De top. C.P.* iv. c. 2.
[2] 'The breaking of wall surfaces by pilasters and blind niches is a custom immemorial in Oriental brickwork.'—*The Thousand and One Churches*, by Sir W. Ramsay and Miss Lothian Bell, p. 448.

approximately circular, and divided into sixteen shallow concave compartments, each pierced by a window. Some of these windows must have been always blocked by the roof of the north church. The eastern dome is a pronounced oval, notwithstanding the attempt to form a square base for it by building a subsidiary arch both on the south and on the north. It is divided into twenty-four concave compartments, twelve of which have windows. The drums of the domes adjoin each other above the transverse arch, so that the central west window of the eastern dome is pierced through to the western dome. The two windows on either side of that window are blind, and must always have been so. The floor in the archway leading into the south church is paved with inlaid marbles forming a beautiful design (Fig. 76). If the whole floor of the church was thus decorated the effect must have been extremely rich. On the exterior the apse shows seven sides, decorated with shallow blind niches. Like the church it is very irregularly set out. (Plate LXIX.)

The central church probably served as a mausoleum for the tombs of the imperial personages interred at the Pantokrator. In its form and in the arrangement of its domes, as well as in its position on the south of the church to which it strictly belongs, it resembles the parecclesion of S. Saviour in the Chora (p. 310).

The South Church.—The south church is of the same plan as the north church, but is larger and more richly decorated. It has two narthexes, which extend to both the north and south beyond the body of the building. The outer narthex, entered by a single door placed in the centre, is in five bays, covered with cross-groined vaults resting on pilasters. Its floor is paved with large slabs of Proconnesian marble surrounded by a border of red marble. Five doors lead to the esonarthex—the three central doors being framed in red marble, the other two in verd antique. On either side of the central door is a window also framed in verd antique, the jambs of the windows being cut from old columns, and retaining the circular form on their faces. Over the central door and the windows beside it is a large

arch between two smaller arches—all three, as well as their
bracket capitals, now partially built up.   There is a door
framed in verd antique in each end bay of the narthex.   Like
the outer narthex the esonarthex is in five bays, and was
paved with marble in a similar fashion.   But while its
other bays are covered with cross-groined vaults the central
bay is open to the gallery above, and is overhung by a
drum dome.   The gallery was thus divided into two parts
by the open central bay, and both gallery and narthex were
lighted by the dome.   The exterior of this dome is twelve-
sided, with flat angle pilasters and level moulded plaster
cornice.   It has evidently been repaired by the Turks.   The
inside, however, preserves the Byzantine work.   It is in
twenty-four concave apartments pierced by twelve windows,
of which those facing the west cross arm of the church are
blind.   As the original west window still shows from the inside, though built up, it would appear that the gynecaeum
dome was added after the completion of the main church.   At
present the open bay is ceiled by the woodwork that forms the
floor of the tribune occupied by the Sultan when he attends
worship in the mosque.[1]   A door in the northern wall of the
north bay communicates with the narthex of the north church,
while a door in the eastern wall of the bay gives access to
the central church.   Two doors in similar positions in the
bay at the south end of the narthex led to buildings which
have disappeared.   The three doors leading from the narthex
into the church are framed in red marble, the other doors
in white marble.   The main dome of the church is in sixteen compartments, and is pierced by as many windows.   Its
arches rest on four shafted columns, somewhat Gothic in character, and crowned with capitals distinctly Turkish.   These
columns have replaced the columns of porphyry, seven feet
in circumference, which Gyllius saw bearing the arches of
the dome when he visited the church : 'maximum (tectum)
sustentatur quatuor columnis pyrrhopoecilis, quarum perimeter habet septem pedes.'[2]   The southern wall is lighted
by a triple window in the gable and a row of three windows

---

[1] It is reached by an inclined plane built against the exterior of the south wall
of the church.   [2] *De top. C.P.* iv. c. 2.

below the string-course. The northern wall was treated on the same plan, but with the modifications rendered necessary by the union of the church with the earlier central church. The triple windows in the gable of that wall are therefore almost blocked by the roof of the central church against which it is built ; while the three windows below the string-course are blind and are cut short by the arch opening into the central church, as that arch rises higher than the string-course.

As explained, the gynaeceum above the inner narthex is divided by the open central bay of that narthex into two compartments, each consisting of two bays. The bays to the south are narrow, with transverse arches of decidedly elliptical form. A window divided by shafts in three lights, now built up, stood in the bay at the extreme south, and similar windows looked down into the open bay of the narthex from the bays on either hand. The northern compartment of the gynaeceum connects with the gynaeceum of the north church.

In the interior the apse retains a large portion of its revetment of variously coloured marbles, and gives some idea of the original splendour of the decoration. Fragments of fine carving have been built into the pulpit of the mosque, and over it is a Byzantine canopy supported on twin columns looped together, like the twin columns on the façade of S. Mark's at Venice.

The lateral apses are covered with cross-groined vaults, and project in three sides externally, while the central apse shows seven sides. All are lighted by triple windows, and decorated on the exterior with niches, like the other apses in this group of buildings, and those of S. Theodosia.

In the brickwork found in the fabric of the Pantokrator, as Mr. W. S. George has pointed out, two sizes of brick are employed, a larger and a smaller size laid in alternate courses. The larger bricks look like old material used again.

As already intimated, the monastery was autonomous,

(αὐτοδέσποτος, αὐτεξούσιος), and its abbot was elected by the brotherhood in the following manner :—On some suitable occasion the abbot for the time being placed secretly in a box the names of three members of the fraternity whom he considered fit to succeed him after his death, and having sealed the box deposited it in the sacristy of the church. Upon that abbot's death the box was opened in the presence of the whole fraternity, and the names recommended by the late chief were then put to the vote. If the votes were unanimous the person thus chosen became the new abbot without further delay. But in case of disagreement, a brother who could neither read nor write placed the same names upon the altar of the church ; there they remained for three days ; and then, after the celebration of a solemn service, another illiterate monk drew one name off the altar, and in doing so decided the question who should fill the vacant office. The church was served by eighty priests and fifty assistants, who were divided into two sets, officiating on alternate weeks.

In connection with the monastery there was a bath, capable of containing six persons, in which the monks were required to bathe twice a month, except during Lent, when the bath was used only in cases of illness.

The home for old men supported by the House accommodated twenty-four persons, providing them with bread, wine, oil, cheese, fuel, medical attendance, and small gifts of money.

The hospital had fifty beds for the poor. It was divided into five wards : a ward of ten beds for surgical cases ; another, of eight beds, for grave cases ; a third, of ten beds, for less serious complaints ; the fourth ward had twelve beds for women ; the fifth contained ten beds for what seemed light cases. Each ward was in charge of two physicians, three medical assistants, and four servitors. A lady physician, six lady medical assistants, and two female nurses, took charge of the female patients. The sick were visited daily by a house doctor, who inquired whether they were satisfied with their treatment, examined their diet, and saw to the cleanliness of the beds. The ordinary diet consisted of bread, beans, onions, oil, and wine.[1]   Throughout their history the monasteries of Constantinople remembered the poor. (See Plate III.)

[1] For these particulars we are indebted to MS. 85, formerly in the library of the theological seminary at Halki. According to the same authority, near the Pantokrator stood a church dedicated to the Theotokos Eleousa, and between the two buildings was the chapel of S. Michael that contained the tombs of the Emperor John Comnenus and the Empress Irene. But according to Cinnamus (pp. 14, 31), as we have seen (p. 221), those tombs were in the Pantokrator. Is it possible that of the three buildings commonly styled the church of the Pantokrator, one of the lateral churches was dedicated specially to the Theotokos Eleousa, and that the central building which served as a mausoleum was dedicated to the archangel Michael ? The parecclesion of the Chora where Tornikes was buried (p. 310) was associated, as the frescoes in its western dome prove, with the angelic host.

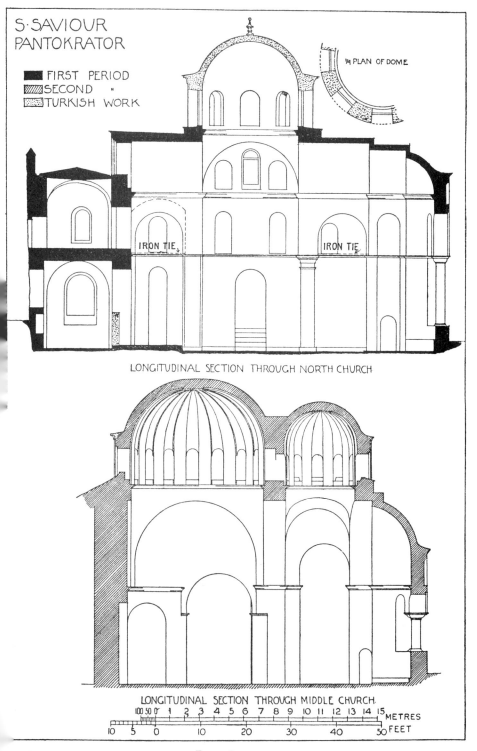

S·SAVIOUR
PANTOKRATOR

■ FIRST PERIOD
▨ SECOND "
▧ TURKISH WORK

¼ PLAN OF DOME

IRON TIE

IRON TIE

LONGITUDINAL SECTION THROUGH NORTH CHURCH

LONGITUDINAL SECTION THROUGH MIDDLE CHURCH.

100 50 0'   1   2   3   4   5   6   7   8   9   10 11 12 13 14 15 METRES
10   5   0   10   20   30   40   50 FEET

FIGS. 78 AND 79.   R

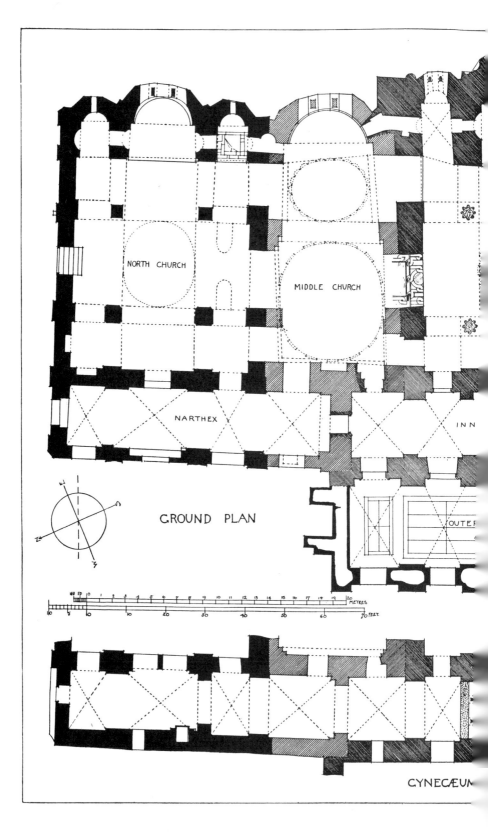

NORTH CHURCH

MIDDLE CHURCH

NARTHEX

INN

GROUND PLAN

OUTER

METRES

FEET

CYNECÆUM

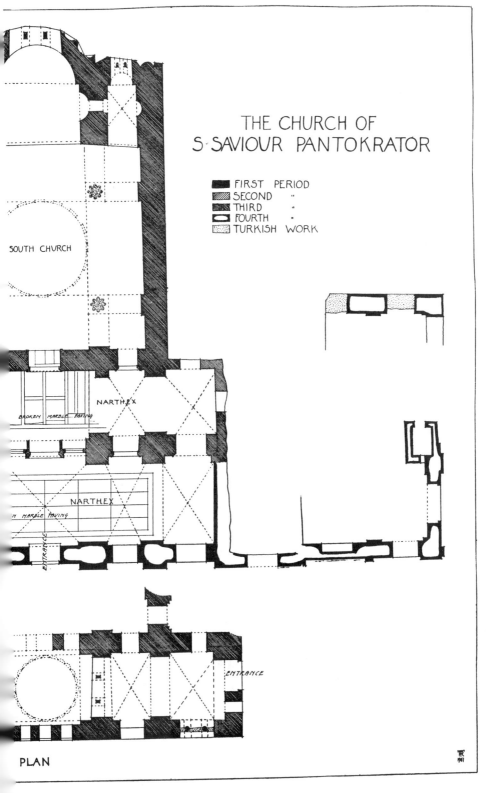

THE CHURCH OF
S·SAVIOUR PANTOKRATOR

- ▨ FIRST PERIOD
- ▨ SECOND "
- ▨ THIRD "
- ▢ FOURTH "
- ▨ TURKISH WORK

SOUTH CHURCH

NARTHEX

BROKEN MARBLE PAVING

NARTHEX

IN MARBLE PAVING

ENTRANCE

ENTRANCE

PLAN

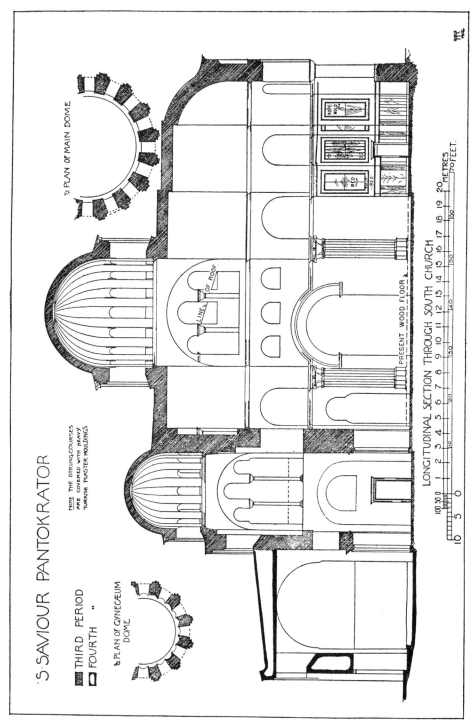

S. SAVIOUR PANTOKRATOR

NOTE: THE STRING COURSES ARE COVERED WITH HEAVY TURKISH PLASTER MOULDINGS

THIRD PERIOD
FOURTH "

½ PLAN OF GYNECÆUM DOME

½ PLAN OF MAIN DOME

LINE OF ROOF

PRESENT WOOD FLOOR

LONGITUDINAL SECTION THROUGH SOUTH CHURCH

FIG. 80.

CHAPTER XVI

THE CHURCH OF S. THEODORE, KILISSI MESJEDI

HIGH up the western slope of the Third Hill, in a quiet Turkish quarter reached by a narrow street leading off Vefa Meidan, stands a small but graceful Byzantine church, known since its use as a mosque by the style Kilissi Mesjedi. Authorities differ in regard to its dedication. Gyllius[1] was told that the church had been dedicated to S. Theodore. On the other hand, Le Noir, on the strength of information furnished by Greek friends, and after him Bayet, Fergusson, Salzenberg, claim it as the church of the Theotokos of Lips. But the church of that dedication was certainly elsewhere (p. 123). Mordtmann[2] suggests that we have here the church of S. Anastasia Pharmacolytria ($\tau\hat{\eta}s$ $\phi\alpha\rho\mu\alpha\kappa\sigma\lambda\upsilon\tau\rho\iota\alpha s$),[3] and supports his view by the following argument. In the first place the church of S. Theodore the Tiro was situated in the quarter of Sphorakius,[4] which was in the immediate vicinity of S. Sophia,[5] and therefore not near Vefa Meidan. Secondly, the indications given by Antony of Novgorod and by the Anonymus of the eleventh century respecting the position of S. Anastasia point to the site of Kilissi Mesjedi. The fact that the church was ever supposed to be dedicated to S. Theodore is, in Mordtmann's opinion, a mistake occasioned by the circumstance that both S. Theodore and S. Anastasia were credited with the power of exposing sorcery and frauds, so that a church associated with one of these saints might readily be transferred to the other,

---

[1] *De top. C.P.* iii. c. 6. [2] *Esq. top.* paragraphs 110, 114, 124, 125.
[3] Banduri, ii. p. 38. [4] *Ibid.* i. p. 10. [5] Const. Porphyr, *De cer.* p. 623.

especially in the confusion which followed the Turkish conquest.

In reply to this line of argument, it may be urged, first, that the presence of a church of S. Theodore in the district of Sphorakius does not prevent the existence of a church with a similar dedication in another part of the city. S. Theodore was a popular saint. There was a church named after him in the district of Claudius (τὰ Κλαυδίου) ; [1] another church built in his honour stood in the district Carbounaria (τὰ Καρβουνάρια) ; [2] the private chapel of the emperors in the Great Palace was dedicated to S. Theodore ; [3] and according to Phrantzes,[4] a church dedicated at once to S. Theodore the Tiro and S. Theodore the General, as at Athens, was erected in Constantinople in his day. As to the indications supposed to favour the view that the church of S. Anastasia stood at Kilissi Mesjedi, they are, to say the least, exceedingly vague and inconclusive. According to Antony of Novgorod[5] the shrine of S. Anastasia was found near the church of the Pantokrator, on the Fourth Hill, whereas Kilissi Mesjedi stands on the Third Hill. Furthermore, the order in which the Anonymus[6] refers to the church of S. Anastasia Pharmacolytria, immediately before the Leomacellum, which Mordtmann identifies with the Et Meidan, would allow us to place S. Anastasia in the valley of the Lycus. Under these circumstances it is wiser to accept the information given to Gyllius as correct ; for while the Greeks of his day were not infallible in their identification of the buildings of the city, there is no evidence that they were mistaken in this particular case.

Paspates[7] agrees so far with this view, but maintains, at the same time, that the building was the church of S. Theodore ' in the district of Sphorakius.' That identification is inadmissible, for beyond all dispute the district of Sphorakius stood close to S. Sophia and not at Vefa Meidan. Mühlmann[8] likewise regards Kilissi Mesjedi

---

[1] Banduri, iii. pp. 16, 48.   [2] Ibid. i. p. 17.
[3] Const. Porphyr, De cer. p. 640.   [4] P. 140.
[5] Itin. russes, pp. 105-6.   [6] Banduri, i. p. 16 ; ii. p. 38.   [7] P. 314.
[8] See his paper in the Mitteilungen des deutschen Excursions - Club, Konstantinopel, Erstes Heft, 1888.

as a church of S. Theodore, and identifies it with the church dedicated to that saint in the district of Carbounaria. This is possible, although the Anonymus [1] mentions the Carbounaria before the Anemodoulion and the forum of Taurus (the region of the Turkish War Office), and consequently suggests a position for the Carbounaria much farther to the east than Vefa Meidan. Still the order in which the Anony-

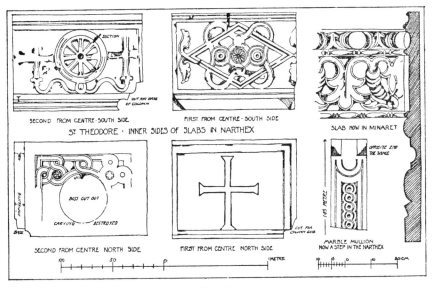

FIG. 81.
(For other details see Figs. 19, 54.)

mus mentions places and monuments cannot be confidently appealed to as coincident with their relative positions.

To which of the many saints named Theodore in the Greek Calendar this church was actually dedicated is a point open to discussion, but we cannot go far wrong in ascribing it to one of the two most prominent saints of that name, or, as sometimes was the case, to both of them, S. Theodore the Tiro and S. Theodore the General. The former was a young soldier in the Roman army who was tortured and put to death in 306 for not taking part in the persecution

[1] Banduri, i. p. 16.

of Christians under Maximian. The latter was a general in the army of Licinius, and won the martyr's crown for refusing to sacrifice to false gods, and for breaking their images in pieces. He was the titular saint of the great church in Venice before that honour was bestowed upon S. Mark the Evangelist. His relics were carried to Venice from Constantinople in 1260, and his figure still stands on one of the columns in the Piazzetta of S. Mark, with the attribute of a dragon or a crocodile, symbolic of the false gods he destroyed.[1]

Architectural Features

The church is a good example of the 'four column' type, with an outer and an inner narthex. The former is in five bays, and extends to the north and south, by one bay, beyond the inner narthex and the body of the church. The terminal bays, it would seem, led to cloisters built against the exterior of the northern and southern sides of the building. Le Noir and Salzenberg[2] show a cloister along the south side of the church, with four columns and an apse at its end. The central bay and the two terminal bays are covered with domes on high drums, without windows. The dome of the central bay has sixteen lobed bays, while its companions have each eight flat ribs. All traces of the mosaics which Salzenberg saw in the central dome have disappeared. On the exterior the three domes are octagonal, decorated with flat niches and angle shafts supporting an arched cornice. The exonarthex deserves special attention on account of its façade. It is a fine composition of two triple arcades, separated by a solid piece of masonry containing the door. On either side of the door, and on the piers at each end of the façade, are slender flat niches, similar to those which occur in S. Mark's, Venice. The finely carved capitals of the columns differ in type, the two northern being a variant of the 'melon type,' the pair to the south being Corinthian. They are probably old

---

[1] See *The Monastery of St. Luke of Stiris*, p. 61.
[2] *Altchristliche Baudenkmäler von K.P.* plates 34, 35.

capitals re-used.   Throughout the building are traces of stones from some older building recut or adapted to the present church.   Between the columns is a breastwork of carved marble slabs similar in style to those seen in S. Mark's and in S. Fosca, Torcello.[1]   The upper part of the façade does not correspond to the composition below it, but follows the divisions of the internal vaulting.   It is in five circular-arched bays, each containing an arched window. The infilling is of brick in various patterns.   The cornice looks Turkish.   While the masonry of the lower portion of the arcade is in alternate courses of one stone and two bricks, that of the upper portion has alternate courses of one stone and three bricks.   Moreover, while the design of the upper portion is determined by the vaulting of the narthex, the lower portion takes a more independent line.   These differences may indicate different periods of construction, but we find a similar type of design in other Byzantine buildings, as, for example, in the walls of the palace of the Porphyrogenitus, where the different stories are distinct in design, and do not closely correspond to one another.   The outer narthex of S. Theodore may have been built entirely at one time, or its upper story, vaults, and domes may have been added to an already existing lower story.   But in any case, notwithstanding all possible adverse criticism, the total effect produced by the façade is pleasing.   It presents a noteworthy and successful attempt to relieve the ordinary plainness and heaviness of a Byzantine church exterior, and to give that exterior some grace and beauty. The effect is the more impressive because the narthex is raised considerably above the level of the ground and reached by a flight of steps.   'Taking it altogether,' says Fergusson,[2] 'it is perhaps the most complete and elegant church of its class now known to exist in or near the capital, and many of its details are of great beauty and perfection.'

The esonarthex is in three bays covered with barrel vaults, and terminates at both ends in a shallow niche. The outer arches spring from square buttresses.   From

[1] Pulgher, *Les Anciennes Églises de C.P.* p. 23.
[2] *History of Architecture,* i. 458.

each bay a door conducts into the church, the central door being set in a marble frame and flanked by two Corinthian columns, which support a bold wall arcade.

The drum of the dome is a polygon of twelve sides, and was lighted by the same number of windows. It rests on four columns, which were originally square, but now have large champs at the angles, dying out at top and bottom. Barrel vaults cover the arms of the cross, and dome vaults surmount the chambers at its angles. As in the Pantokrator (p. 235), the eastern arm is pierced by two windows in the vaulting surface. The central apse is lighted by a triple window, having oblong shafts, circular on their inner and outer faces, and bearing capitals now badly injured. A niche indents the northern, eastern, and southern interior walls of the apsidal chapels. The windows in the northern and southern walls of the church have been built up almost to their full height, leaving only small openings for light at the top. There can be little doubt that they were triple windows with a parapet of carved marble slabs between the shafts. On the exterior the apse shows five sides, and is decorated by an arcade of five arches and an upper tier of five niches. The lateral apses do not project beyond the face of the eastern wall, but are slightly marked out by cutting back the sides and forming angular grooves. Bayet[1] assigns the church to the ninth or tenth century, the age of Leo the Wise and Constantine Porphyrogenitus. Fergusson[2] is of the same opinion so far as the earlier portions of the building are concerned. But that date is based on the mistaken view that the building is the church of the Theotokos erected by Constantine Lips. Diehl[3] assigns the church to the second half of the eleventh century.

In the library of the Royal Institute of British Architects, in London, are four volumes of Texier's sketches and drawings of buildings in or near Constantinople. In that collection is found a complete set of drawings of this church, showing a chapel on both the north and south sides of the building, and even giving measurements on the south

---

[1] *L'Art byzantin*, p. 126.   [2] *History of Architecture*, vol. i. p. 458.
[3] *Manuel d'art byzantin*, p. 414.

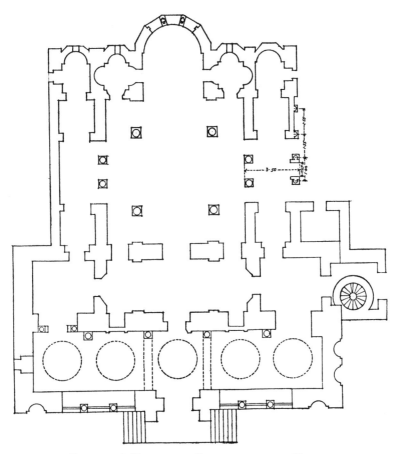

FIG. 82.—S. Theodore. Plan as given by Texier.

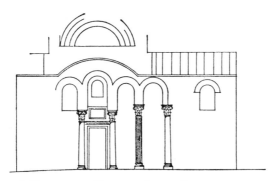

FIG. 83.—S. Theodore. Part of South Elevation showing the
Side Chapel as given by Texier.

side. Texier's drawings are unfortunately very inaccurate, so that little trust can be placed in any of them. In addition to the plan of the church an elevation is given, and two sketches covered with indications of elaborate decoration, but evidently quite imaginary. The chapel on the north side is noticed by no other writer, and was probably added by Texier for the sake of symmetry. That on the south side, as shown by him, differs in some respects from Salzenberg. The only thing certain is that a side chapel did exist here.

This church presents a good example of the greater interest taken during the later Byzantine period in the external appearance of a church. To the exterior of the walls and the apses some decoration is now applied. The dome is raised on a polygonal drum, with shafts at its angles, and an arched cornice over its windows ; the roof gains more diversity of form and elevation by the multiplication of domes, by the protrusion of the vaults of the cross arms and of the apses, thus making the outward garb, so to speak, of the building correspond more closely to the figure and proportions of its inner body. In all this we have not yet reached the animation and grace of a Gothic cathedral, nor the stateliness that crowns an imperial mosque ; but there is, at all events, a decided advance towards a fuller expression of artistic feeling.   (See Plates LXXIV., LXXV.)

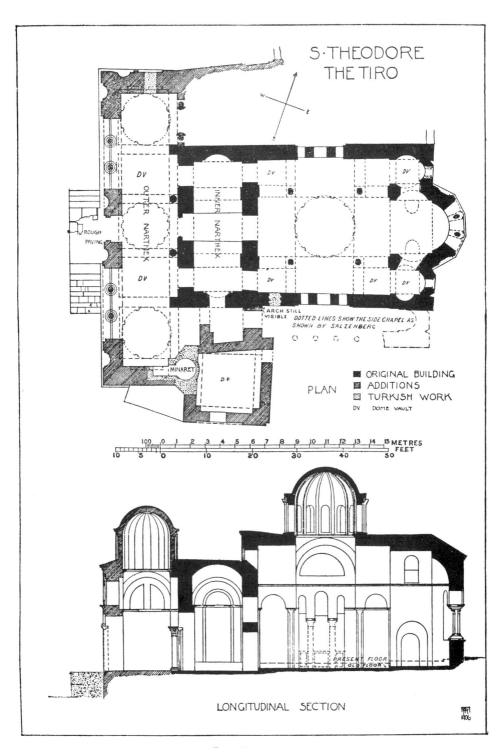

S·THEODORE
THE TIRO

W   E

DV   OUTER NARTHEX   INNER NARTHEX   DV   DV

ROUGH
PAVING

DV   DV   DV   DV

ARCH STILL
VISIBLE   DOTTED LINES SHOW THE SIDE CHAPEL AS
SHOWN BY SALZENBERG

MINARET   D.V.

PLAN

■ ORIGINAL BUILDING
▨ ADDITIONS
▩ TURKISH WORK
DV   DOME VAULT

100   0 1 2 3 4 5 6 7 8 9 10 11 12 13 14 15 METRES
FEET
10   5   0   10   20   30   40   50

PRESENT FLOOR
OLD FLOOR

LONGITUDINAL   SECTION

FIGS. 84 AND 85.   251

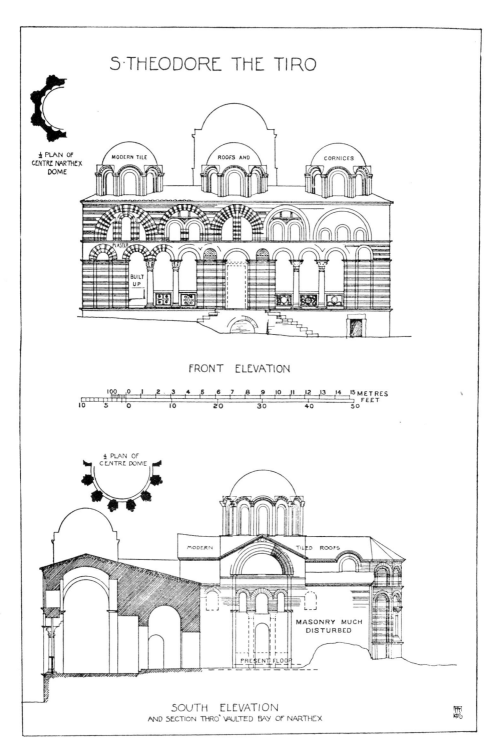

S·THEODORE THE TIRO

¼ PLAN OF
CENTRE NARTHEX
DOME

MODERN TILE

ROOFS AND

CORNICES

PLASTER

BUILT
UP

FRONT ELEVATION

| 100 | 0 | 1 | 2 | 3 | 4 | 5 | 6 | 7 | 8 | 9 | 10 | 11 | 12 | 13 | 14 | 15 METRES |

| 10 | | 5 | | 0 | | 10 | | 20 | | 30 | | 40 | | 50 | FEET |

¼ PLAN OF
CENTRE DOME

MODERN

TILED ROOFS

MASONRY MUCH
DISTURBED

PRESENT FLOOR

SOUTH ELEVATION
AND SECTION THRO' VAULTED BAY OF NARTHEX

FIGS. 86 AND 87.

CHAPTER XVII

THE MONASTERY OF MANUEL, KEFELÉ MESJEDI

THE mosque known as Kefelé Mesjedi, in the quarter of Salma Tomruk, is commonly supposed to represent the monastery founded by Manuel,[1] a distinguished general in the wars with the Saracens during the reign of Theophilus (823-842). This opinion is doubtless based upon the circumstance that the monastery in question stood in the vicinity of the cistern of Aspar,[2] σύνεγγυς τῇ κιστέρνῃ τοῦ Ἀσπαρος (the large open reservoir to the east of the Gate of Adrianople), near which Kefelé Mesjedi is also situated. But that circumstance alone cannot be regarded as sufficient ground for the identification of the two buildings. There are at least five other monasteries mentioned in Byzantine history, all distinguished by the mark of their proximity to the cistern of Aspar.[3] And at a short distance to the west of Kefelé Mesjedi, and nearer to the cistern of Aspar, we find the remains of an old church, now Odalar Mesjedi, which might with equal force claim to represent the monastery of Manuel. The commonly received identification may, however, be correct as a happy conjecture. Mr. Siderides,[4] indeed, considers the identification of the monastery of Manuel with Kefelé Mesjedi a mistake. According to him, that monastery was a reconstruction or enlargement of the ancient monastery of SS. Manuel, Sabel, and Ishmael, which stood on the heights above the Phanar, now crowned by the mosque of Sultan Selim. To the objection that

[1] Scarlatus Byzantius, p. 369 ; Patr. Constantius, p. 81 ; Paspates, p. 304.
[2] Leo Gramm. pp. 218, 222.
[3] Siderides, in *Proceedings of the Greek Syllogos of C.P.* vol. xxviii. p. 265.
[4] *Ibid.* p. 263.

there it would not be near the cistern of Aspar, Mr. Siderides replies by denying the correctness of the identification of that cistern with the open reservoir (Tchoukour Bostan) to the east of the gate of Adrianople, and in the vicinity of Kefelé Mesjedi. In Mr. Siderides' opinion the cistern of Aspar is the beautiful covered cistern, generally known as the cistern of Pulcheria, to the south-west of the mosque of Sultan Selim.[1] But the dimensions of the cistern ascribed to the famous sister of Theodosius II. do not accord with the size of the cistern of Aspar. The latter was 'a very large cistern,' $\tau\grave{\eta}\nu$ $\mu\epsilon\gamma\acute{\iota}\sigma\tau\eta\nu$ $\kappa\iota\nu\sigma\tau\acute{\epsilon}\rho\nu\alpha\nu$,[2] while the former is only m. 29.1 long by m. 18 wide, with a roof supported on four rows of seven columns[3]—not a large cistern as works of that class went in Constantinople. But if the cistern of Aspar was not situated in the district now marked by the mosque of Sultan Selim, neither could the monastery of Manuel have been there. Mr. Siderides,[4] moreover, identifies the monastery of Manuel with that of Manoueliou ($\tau o\hat{v}$ $\mathrm{M}\alpha\nu o\nu\eta\lambda\acute{\iota}o\nu$) which appears in the Proceedings of the Synod held at Constantinople in 536 under Justinian.[5] This, however, does not agree with the statement that the monastery of Manuel was originally the private residence of the well-known general of that name in the ninth century. Furthermore, it is always dangerous to assume that the same name could not belong to different buildings, especially when the name occurs at distant intervals in the history of the city. Many mistakes in the topography of Constantinople are due to this false method of identification. As a matter of fact, the monastery of Manuel near the cistern of Aspar was not the only House of that name in the capital of the East. Another monastery of Manuel stood beside the Golden Horn, in the Genoese quarter, between the gate of the Neorion (Bagtché Kapoussi) and the gate of Eugenius (Yali Kiosk Kapoussi). It had a pier, known as the pier of the venerable monastery of Manuel, $\sigma\kappa\acute{\alpha}\lambda\alpha$ $\tau\hat{\eta}s$ $\sigma\epsilon\beta\alpha\sigma\mu\acute{\iota}\alpha s$ $\mu o\nu\hat{\eta}s$ $\tau o\hat{v}$

---

[1] *Proceedings of the Greek Syllogos of C.P.*, ut supra, p. 258.

[2] *Pasch. Chron.* p. 593.

[3] *Die byzantinischen Wasserbehälter von Konstantinopel*, von Dr. Forscheimer und Dr. Strzygowski, pp. 62-63, 175-176.

[4] *Ut supra.*   [5] Mansi, viii. col. 990, col. 1054.

Μανουήλ).[1]   Paspates is consequently wrong in associating that pier with Kefelé Mesjedi.[2]

Mordtmann[3] accepts the identification of Kefelé Mesjedi with the monastery of Manuel as correct, but he identifies it also with the church and monastery which Gerlach found in this neighbourhood, and describes under the name of Aetius (τοῦ 'Αετίου).[4] When visited by Gerlach in 1573, the church had been converted into a mosque, and was a beautiful building in excellent preservation.   If all that remains of it is the bare structure of Kefelé Mesjedi, the city has to mourn a great loss.[5]   (Plate LXXVII.)

Manuel, the founder of the monastery, was the uncle of

[1] Miklosich et Müller, pp. 28, 50, 53, 54.

[2] P. 305.   On p. 163 he places the pier in its proper position.

[3] Esq. top. p. 76 ; Archaeological Supplement to vol. xviii. of the Proceedings of the Greek Syllogos of C.P. p. 9.

[4] Türkisches Tagebuch, pp. 455-56 ; cf. Crusius, Turcograecia p. 190.

[5] The question thus raised presents serious difficulties.   That some building * in the neighbourhood of Kefelé Mesjedi was known by the name of Aetius † is undoubted.   It was a cistern (Du Cange, i. p. 96), and formed one of the landmarks by which the church of S. John in Petra, situated in this quarter of the city, was distinguished (Du Cange, iv. p. 152 ἔγγιστα τοῦ 'Αετίου).   But while that is the case, Gyllius (De top. C.P. iv.), who explored this part of the city in 1550, does not mention any Byzantine church that answers at all to Gerlach's description of the church of Aetius, unless it be the Chora.   That Gyllius should have overlooked so beautiful a monument of Byzantine days as the church of Aetius, if different from the Chora, is certainly very strange.   But it is not less strange to find that Gerlach does not speak of the Chora.   Can the difficulty thus presented be removed by the supposition that Gerlach refers to the Chora under the name of Aetius ?   The position he assigns to the church of Aetius in relation to the church of S. John in Petra and to the palace of Constantine (Tekfour Serai) favours that view, for he places the church of Aetius between S. John and the palace, exactly where the Chora would stand in that series of buildings.   Looking towards the north-west from the windows of a house a little to the east of the Pammakaristos, Gerlach says ' Ad Occasum, Boream versus, Prodromi μονὴ est, olim πέτρα ; longius inde, Aetii μονὴ ; postea, Palatium Constantini' (Turcograecia, p. 190).   On the other hand, Gerlach's description of the church of Aetius differs in so many particulars from what holds true of the Chora, that it is difficult, if not impossible, to believe that in that description he had the latter church in mind.   Unless, then, we are prepared to admit grave mistakes in Gerlach's description, we must either assume an extraordinary failure on his part and on the part of Gyllius to notice a most interesting Byzantine monument, directly on the path of both explorers in this quarter of the city, or regret the disappearance of an ancient sanctuary that rivalled the Chora in splendour.

* It was probably the ruined cistern with twenty-four columns arranged in four rows of seven pillars each, near the mosque Kassim Aga, a short distance above Kefelé Mesjedi. Gerlach associates it with the church of Aetius.

† Tagebuch, pp. 455-56 ; cf. Crusius, Turcograecia, p. 190.   In the documents associated with the Synod of 536 in Constantinople the cistern of Aetius serves to identify the monastery of Mara (Mansi, viii. cols. 910, 930, 990). Cf. Banduri, iii. p. 49 ; v. p. 106.

the Empress Theodora, wife of the Emperor Theophilus, and proved a loyal and devoted servant of the imperial family. Twice at the peril of his own life he saved the emperor from capture, if not from death, during the wars with the Saracens. Nevertheless, being accused of treason he fled to the court of Baghdad and took service under the Caliph Mutasim, until assured that Constantinople would welcome him back.

He was one of the three counsellors appointed by Theophilus to assist Theodora during the minority of Michael III., and so highly was he esteemed, that he was acclaimed emperor by the populace in the Hippodrome, and might have worn the crown but for his fidelity to the little prince. Silencing the shouts raised in his favour, he exclaimed, 'You have an emperor; my duty and highest honour is to defend his infancy and to secure for him, even at the price of my blood, the heritage of his father.' In the iconoclastic controversy Manuel supported the policy of Theophilus, and therefore found himself in a difficult position when Theodora decided to restore the use of eikons. The story is, that while he lay dangerously ill at the time, monks of the Studion assured him that recovery was certain if he vowed to uphold the orthodox cause. The vow was taken, and upon his restoration to health Manuel favoured the measures of Theodora. Probably he felt that the current of public feeling on the subject was too strong for him to oppose. But the task of working in harmony with his colleagues in the regency, Theoctistus and Bardas, was soon found impossible, and rumours of a plot to blind him and remove him from the administration of affairs led him to retire to his house near the cistern of Aspar. For some time, indeed, he continued to appear occasionally at the palace, but at last he quitted for ever that scene of intrigue, and converted his residence into a monastery, where he might spend the closing days of his life in peace and finally be laid in a quiet grave.[1]

---

[1] There is some uncertainty a to the identity of Manuel. Some authorities distinguish Manuel the genera. from Manuel the uncle of Theodora, on the ground that the former is said to have died of wounds received in battle during

The building which Manuel bequeathed was reconstructed almost from the foundations, a large and beautiful edifice, by the celebrated Patriarch Photius.[1]   It
underwent extensive restoration again at the command of
the Emperor Romanus Lecapenus (919-945),[2] in token of
his friendship for Sergius, the abbot of the monastery,
a nephew of Photius, and eventually an occupant of the
patriarchal throne for twenty years (999-1019).   In it
the Emperor Romanus Argyrus (1028-1034) confined
Prussianus, a relative of the Bulgarian royal family, on a
charge of treason ;[3] and there Michael VII., nicknamed
Parapinakes (the peck-filcher), because he sold wheat at one-
fourth of its proper weight, and then at an exorbitant price,
ultimately retired after his deposition.[4]   The connection of
so many prominent persons with the monastery implies the
importance of the House.

Architectural Features

Kefelé Mesjedi is a large oblong hall, m. 22.6 long
by m. 7.22 wide, with walls constructed in alternate courses
of four bricks and four stones, and covered with a lofty
timber roof.   It terminates to the north in an arch and
a semicircular apse in brick.   Two niches, with a window
between them, indent the walls of the apse, and there
is a niche in each pier of the arch.   The building is
entered by a door situated in the middle of the western
wall.   Originally the eastern and western walls, which form
the long sides of the building, were lighted by two ranges
of round-headed windows, somewhat irregularly spaced.
The upper range is situated a little below the ceiling, and
forms a sort of clearstory of ten lights ; the lower range has
five windows, except in the western wall, where the place of

the reign of Theophilus (see Leo Gramm. p. 222).   But it would be strange for
different Manuels to reside near the cistern of Aspar, and to convert their resid-
ences into the monastery of Manuel in that vicinity.   For other reasons for the
identification see Bury, *Eastern Roman Empire*, Appendix viii. p. 476.

[1] Theodore Balsamon, vol. i. p. 1041 ; Canon VII. of the Synod of Constantinople held under Photius.

[2] Theoph. Cont. p. 433, μονὴ τοῦ Μανουῆλου.

[3] Cedrenus, ii. p. 487.   [4] Scylitzes, in Cedrenus, ii. p. 738.

one window is occupied by the entrance. The southern wall is also lighted by two ranges of windows, the lower windows being much larger than the higher. At some time buttresses were built against the eastern wall. Under the west side is a cistern, the roof of which rests on three columns. In view of all these features it is impossible to believe that the building was a church. Its orientation, the absence of lateral apses in a structure of such dimensions, the position of the entrance, are all incompatible with that character. We have here, undoubtedly, the refectory and not the sanctuary of the monastic establishment. It resembles the refectory of the Laura on Mt. Athos,[1] and that of Daphni near Athens. It recalls the 'long and lofty building,' adorned with pictures of saints, which formed the refectory of the Peribleptos at Psamathia.[2]

There is a tradition that the use of the building was granted at the conquest to the Armenian colony which was brought from Kaffa in 1475 to repeople the capital. Hence the Turkish name of the building.[3]

NOTE

As Gerlach's work is rare, the reader may wish to see his description of the church of Aetius in the original (*Tagebuch*, pp. 455-56) :—
Nicht weit hiervon [the church of S. John in Petra] ist eine sehr schöne Kirche, τῆς Ἀετίου, da vor Zeiten ein sehr gross und weites Closter gewesen seyn und viel Häuser der Lehrer und Lernenden in sich gehabt haben solle. Jetzt wird nichts mehr davon gesehen als das zerfallene Gemäuer einer herrlichen Pforten und eine trockene Ziternen, darinnen die Juden die Seiden spinnen, zwirnen und bereiten (*serica nectunt fila*). Vor der Kirchen ist ein weiter Hoff, rings aber umb denselbe herumb ein bedeckter Gang (*porticus*), welcher mit schönen auff vergüldten viereckichten gläsern Taffeln künstlich gemahlten Figuren auss dem Alten und Neuen Testament, und mit griechischen Überschrifften gezieret ist, aber alte Gesichter derselben ausgekratzet sind. Die Wände dieser Umbgänge sind mit Marmel von allerhand Farben bekleidet. Hat auch 3 oder 4 hohe Crepidines oder Absätze mit der Propheten, Apostel und Christi Bildnüssen von Gold. Der Hauss- oder vielmehr Bau- herr oder auch der Stiffter (ὁ κτήτωρ), und sein Weib, sind da auch gemahlet in einem

---

[1] H. Brockhaus, *Die Kunst in den Athos-Klöstern*, p. 34 ; G. Millet, *Le Monastère de Daphné*.   [2] Gerlach, *Tagebuch*, p. 337.   [3] Paspates, p. 395.

Habit, fast wie man heut zu Tage gehet, aber mit einer ganz frem-
den Hauptzierde (*capellitii genere*), dass man darauss abnehmen kan,
er sey einer aus den vornehmsten Käyserlich Bedienten gewesen,
dann diese Zierde siehet auss fast wie ein Hertzogs Bareht von Seiden
und Beltzwerck, der Bund oder das Umgewundene (*cinctura*) von
mancherley Farben, wie heut zu Tage die Juden und Armenier
weiss und blau durcheinander tragen.   Sein Weib hat einen Schleyer
(*peplum*) fast wie die Griechinnen.   Der bedecte Gang und die Kirche
sind ein Gebäu (*porticus muro etiam templi continetur*), und gehet
man durch zwey hohe Pforten hinein, welche 4 Theil in sich begreifft,
oder in 4 Theil abgetheilet ist.   1. der bedeckte (*Porticus*) Gang,
dessen Wände mit Marmelstein biss auff die Helffte bekleidet sind.
Der Obertheil, da die Schwibbögen (*Laquearia*) anheben, hat er wie
auch die Schwibbögen selber die Gemählde.   In diesem Gang oder
Halle (*porticu*) stehen die Weiber, und kommen nicht in die Kirchen
hinein, wie auch in andere Kirchen nicht, als wann sie zum Abend-
mahl gehen.   2. ist die Kirche für sich so mit Türckischen Dep-
pichen (*aoreis*) beleget und hat nur ein Thor.   Ist ein hohes Gewölb
(*laquearia*) und wie auch die überige 2 Gewölbe (*laquearia*) ganz ver-
güldet und übermahlet, und die Wände von unten an biss an die
Schwibbögen mit dem schönsten Marmelstein bekleidet.   Auss
diesem gehet man 3. durch einen niedern Crepidinem in dem dritten
Theil der Kirchen, da der Bauherr oder Stiffter mit andern sehr
schönen Bildnüssen mit Gold gemahlet stehen, mit einem etwas
niedern als der vorige Schwibbögen (*laquearia*).   Auss diesem gehet
man in den 4ten gewölbten auch gemahlten aber etwas finstern und
viel kleine Fenster in sich haltenden Ort.   Aussen an der Kirch-
mauren stehet diese Schrift.

Vor dem Vorhoff (*vestibulo*, προπιλίω) dieser Kirchen τῆς Ἀετίου
zeigte mir Theodosius den Ort, da der letzte Christliche Käyser Constantinus als er bey der Türckischen Eroberung der Stadt fliehen
wollen, von Pferde gestürtzet, und tod gefunden seyn solle.

'Not far from here is a very beautiful church where there is said
to have been in times past a very large monastery with many houses
for teachers and scholars within its walls.   Nothing of all that is to
be seen now except the ruins of a splendid gate and a dry cistern in
which the Jews spin, throw, and prepare silk.   In front of the church
there is a large court surrounded by a covered passage (*porticus*), which
is adorned with beautiful figures from the Old and New Testaments
painted on gilded quadrangular glass cubes with Greek inscriptions; but

the ancient faces of these (figures) are scratched out. The walls of this passage are covered with marble of different colours. It has also three or four high crepidines[1] or vaulted compartments (?) with the pictures of the prophets, of the apostles, and of Christ in gold. The master of the house, or rather the builder, or perhaps the founder, ὁ κτήτωρ, and his wife are also painted there in a costume very much the same as is worn to-day, but with a very strange head-ornament, from which we may conclude that he was one of the most distinguished of the imperial staff, for this ornament looks almost like a duke's biretta of silk and fur ; the belt (*cinctura*) is of different colours, such as nowadays the Jews or Armenians wear, white and blue mixed. His wife has a veil (*peplum*) almost like that which Greek women have. The covered passage and the church form one building (*porticus muro etiam templi continetur*), entered by two high gates, and comprising four parts, or divided into four parts. 1. The covered passage (*porticus*), the walls of which as far as half their height are covered with marble. On the upper part, where the arches begin, and on the arches themselves are the paintings. In this passage or hall stand the women, and do not enter the church as they do not enter other churches, unless they go to the Lord's supper. 2. Is the church, as such, covered with Turkish rugs, and has only one gate. It has a high dome, which, like the remaining two domes, is entirely gilded and painted, and the walls up to the arches are covered with the most beautiful marble. From this one enters 3. through a low vaulted compartment, with a somewhat lower arch than the foresaid arches, the third part of the church, where the founder with other very beautiful portraits (pictures) is painted in gold. From this one enters 4. a vaulted and also painted, but rather dark place, with many small windows. On the outside of the walls of the church there is this inscription [2]—

$$\begin{matrix} & \Theta & & \stackrel{|}{\wedge}_{_{0}} \\ \text{A}' & & \text{E} & \\ & \text{O} & & \stackrel{\curlyvee}{\underline{}} \end{matrix}$$

In front of the porch, vestibulo, προπιλίῳ of this church Theodosius showed me the place where the last Christian emperor Constantine, intending to flee at the Turkish conquest of the city, is said to have fallen from his horse and to have been found dead.'

---

[1] In Parker's *Glossary of Architecture*, p. 506, the term is defined 'quae vulgariter a volta dicitur' (Matt. Par. 1056). Du Cange defines the word 'caverna ubi viae conveniunt.'

[2] According to the Patriarch Constantius (*Ancient ana Modern Constantinople*, p. 76), the monogram—

$$\begin{matrix} & \Theta & \\ \text{O} & & \Delta \\ & \text{P} & \end{matrix}$$

was to be seen in his day on the exterior western wall of the Chora.

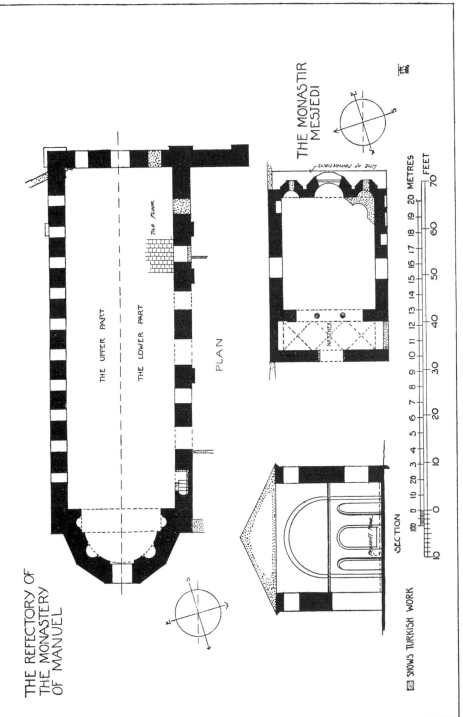

THE REFECTORY OF
THE MONASTERY
OF MANUEL

THE UPPER PART

THE LOWER PART

THE TILE FLOOR

PLAN

THE MONASTIR
MESJEDI

LINE OF FOUNDATIONS

NARTHEX

SECTION

PRESENT FLOOR

⬛ SHOWS TURKISH WORK

METRES

FEET

FIGS. 88 AND 89.

261

CHAPTER XVIII

MONASTIR MESJEDI

AT a short distance within Top Kapoussi (Gate of S. Romanus) that pierces the landward walls of the city, and a little to the south of the street leading to that entrance, in the quarter of Tash Mektep, Mustapha Tchaoush, stands a lonely Byzantine chapel which now goes by the name Monastir Mesjedi, the Chapel of the Monastery. Its present designation tells us all that is certain in regard to the history of the edifice ; it was originally a chapel attached to a Christian monastery, and after the Turkish conquest became a Moslem place of worshp. Paspates[1] is disposed to identify the building with the chapel of the Theotokos erected in this vicinity, in the thirteenth or fourteenth century, by Phocas Maroules[2] on the site of the ancient church dedicated to the three martyr sisters Menodora, Metrodora, and Nymphodora.[3] The chapel built by Maroules in fact belonged to a convent, and owing to its comparatively recent date might well be standing to this day. But the evidence in favour of the proposed identification is slight. In a city crowded with sanctuaries more than one small chapel could be situated near the gate of S. Romanus. An old font, turned upside down and made to serve as a well-head by having its bottom knocked out, lies on a vacant lot on the same side of the street as Monastir Mesjedi, but nearer the gate of

[1] P. 376.
[2] Miklosich et Müller, i. 221.
[3] For lives of these saints, see Synax., September 10 ; Symeon Metaphrastes, ii. p. 653.

S. Romanus, and seems to mark the site of another sanctuary. So likewise do the four columns crowned with
ancient capitals which form the porch of the mosque
Kurkju Jamissi, on the north side of the street.

Phocas Maroules was domestic of the imperial table
under Andronicus II. Palaeologus (1282-1328). He appears also as the commander of the guards on the city walls
that screened the palace of Blachernae, when Andronicus
III. Palaeologus, accompanied by John Cantacuzene, the
protostrator Synadenus, and an escort of thirty soldiers,
stood before the gate of Gyrolimné to parley with the elder
emperor. The domestic was the bearer of the messages
exchanged between the imperial relatives on that occasion.
It was a thankless task. But what troubled the mind of
Maroules most was how to avoid giving offence to both
sovereigns and succeed in serving two masters. To salute
the grandson as became his rank and pretensions would
incur the grandfather's displeasure ; to treat rudely the
young prince, who had come on a friendly errand, and
addressed the domestic in gracious terms, was an impropriety
which the reputation of Maroules as a paragon of politeness
would not allow him to commit. Furthermore, fortune
being fickle, he felt bound as a prudent man to consult her
caprices. Accordingly, allowing less discreet officials beside
him to insult the younger emperor as much as they pleased,
he himself refrained both from all taunts and from all
courteous speech. In response to the greetings of Andronicus
III. he said nothing, but at the same time made a respectful
bow, thus maintaining his good manners and yet guarding
his interests whatever turn the dispute between the two
emperors might take. John Cantacuzene, a kindred spirit,
extols the behaviour of Maroules in this dilemma as beyond
all praise.[1]

After the death of Maroules his widow and son attempted
to turn the convent into a monastery. But the patriarchal
court, before which the case came in 1341, decided in
favour of the claims of the nuns, on the principle that the
intention of the founder should in such matters be always

[1] Cantacuzene, i. p. 255 ; Niceph. Greg. ix. pp. 407, 409.

respected. Hence convents were not allowed to be changed into monasteries, nor monasteries into convents.[1]

Architectural Features

(For Plan see p. 261.)

The building is a small oblong hall roofed in wood, and terminates at its eastern end in three semicircular apses. It is divided into two unequal compartments by a triple arcade placed near the western end. The side apses are shallow recesses, scarcely separated from the central apse, and show three sides on the exterior. The central apse projects six sides, and is now lighted by a large Turkish window. The western compartment, forming the narthex, is in three bays covered with cross-groined vaults. The cushion capitals on the columns of the arcade are decorated, on the east and west, with a rudely cut leaf, and on the north and south with a cross in a circle. Along the exterior of the south wall are traces of a string-course, of a cloister, and of a door leading to the western compartment. On the same wall Paspates[2] saw, as late as 1877, eikons painted in fresco. The western entrance stands between two pilasters, and near it is an upright shaft, buried for the most part in the ground, probably the vestige of a narthex. In the drawing of the church given by Paspates,[3] three additional shafts are shown beside the building.

[1] Miklosich et Müller, i. p. 221.   [2] P. 376.   [3] Ut supra.

CHAPTER XIX

BALABAN AGA MESJEDI

A SMALL Byzantine building, now used for Moslem worship under the name of Balaban Aga Mesjedi, is situated in the quarter of Shahzadé, off the south side of the street leading to the mosque of Sultan Mehemed and the gate Edirné Kapoussi. Mordtmann[1] proposes to identify it with the church of the Theotokos in the district of the Curator (τοῦ Κουράτορος), the foundation of which is ascribed to Verina, the consort of Leo Macellus (457-474).[2] The only reason for this conjecture is that the church in question stood where Balaban Aga Mesjedi stands, in the neighbourhood of the forum of Taurus,[3] now represented by the open area beside the War Office and the mosque of Sultan Bajazet. But the plan of the building does not correspond to the description given of the Theotokos in the district of the Curator. The latter resembled the Holy Sepulchre at Jerusalem,[4] and was therefore circular, whereas Balaban Aga Mesjedi is a hexagon. Indeed, it may be questioned whether the building was ever a church, seeing it has no room for either a bema, or an apse, or an eikonostosis. It may have been the library of a monastic establishment.

Architectural Features

(For Plans see p. 267.)

Internally the building is an accurate hexagon, with a deeply arched recess in each side. Five recesses have a

[1] *Esq. top.* p. 70.   [2] Banduri, i. p. 18.
[3] Synax., July 22nd, December 7th.   [4] Banduri, *ut supra*.

window, while in the sixth recess, instead of a window, there is a door. The cornice and wooden ceiling are Turkish. Externally the edifice shows four sides, two circular and two flat projecting bays, arranged in alternate order. In each of the circular sides are two windows, while the fifth window and the entrance are respectively in the flat sides. A Turkish narthex fronts one-half of the building. (Plate LV.)

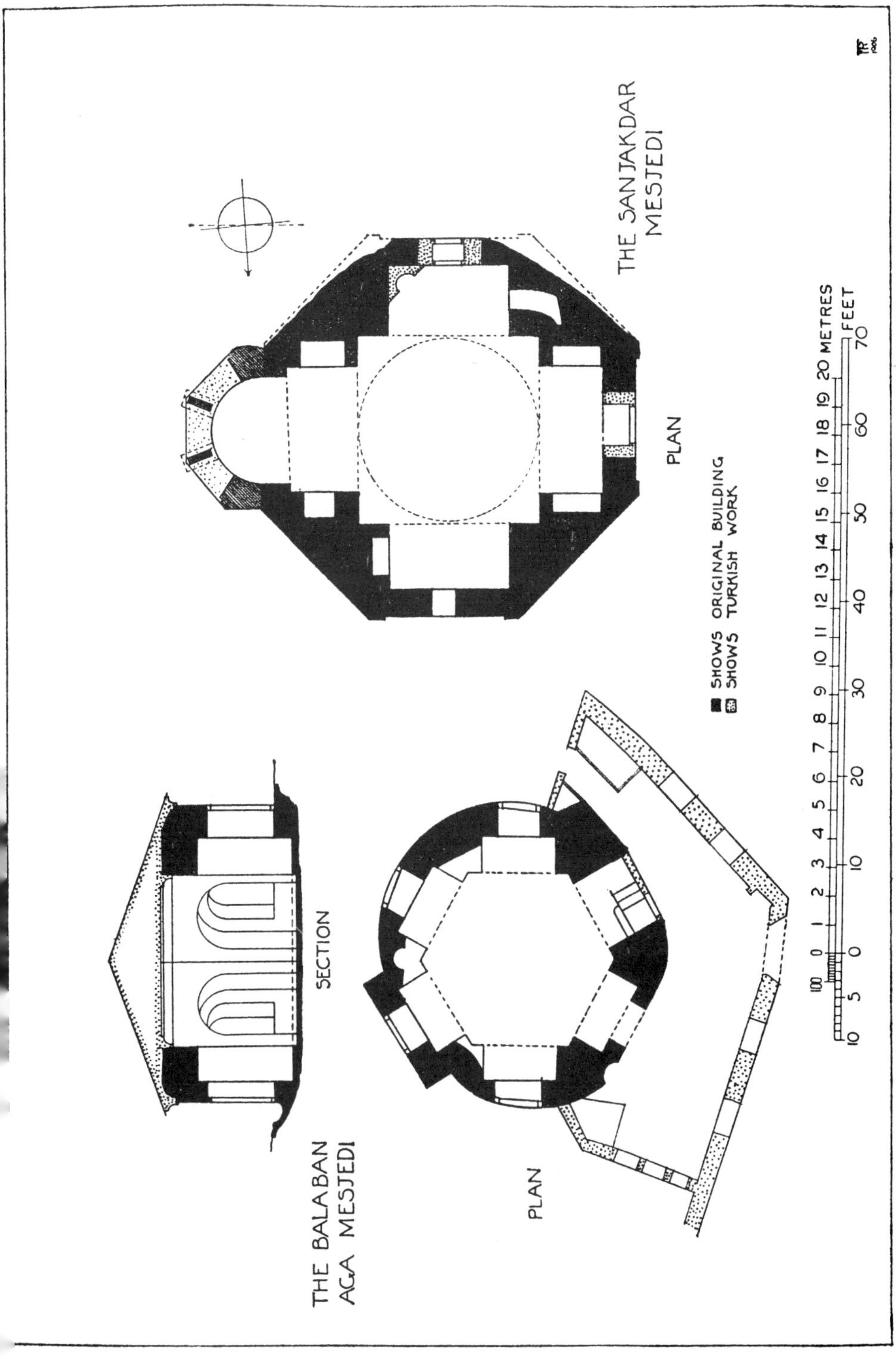

THE SANJAKDAR MESJEDI
PLAN
SHOWS ORIGINAL BUILDING
SHOWS TURKISH WORK
10 5 0 1 2 3 4 5 6 7 8 9 10 11 12 13 14 15 16 17 18 19 20 METRES
10 5 0 10 20 30 40 50 60 70 FEET
THE BALABAN AGA MESJEDI
SECTION
PLAN

FIGS. 90, 91, AND 92.

CHAPTER XX

THIS mosque is situated in the quarter of Psamathia, at a short distance to the north of the Armenian church of S. George (Soulou Monastir), which stands on the site of the Byzantine church of S. Mary Peribleptos. Paspates,[1] who first recognized the Byzantine character of the edifice, regards it as the chapel attached to the convent of the Gastria (Μονὴ τῶν Γαστρίων, τὰ Γάστρια, i.e. in the district of the Flower-pots). His reasons for that opinion are : first, the building is situated in the district of Psamathia, where the convent of the Gastria stood ; secondly, it is in the neighbourhood of the Studion, with which the convent of the Gastria was closely associated during the iconoclastic controversy ; thirdly, the copious and perennial stream of water that flows through the grounds below the mosque would favour the existence of a flower-garden in this part of the city, and thus give occasion for the bestowal of the name Gastria upon the locality. The argument is by no means conclusive. A more fanciful explanation of the name of the district is given by Byzantine etymologists after their wont. According to them the name was due to the circumstance that the Empress Helena, upon her return from Jerusalem with her great discovery of the Holy Cross, disembarked at Psamathia, and having founded a convent there, adorned its garden with the pots (τὰ γάστρια) of fragrant shrubs which accompanied the sacred tree on the voyage from Palestine.[2] More sober historians ascribe the foundation of the convent to

---

[1] P. 304.

[2] Banduri, iii. p. 54.

268

Euphrosyne, the step-mother of the Emperor Theophilus,[1] or to his mother-in-law Theoctista.[2] Both ladies, it is certain, were interested in the House, the former taking the veil there,[3] while the latter resided in the immediate neighbour-hood.[4] Probably the convent was indebted to both those pious women for benefactions, and it was unquestionably in their day that the monastery acquired its greatest fame as the centre of female influence in support of the cause of eikons. Theoctista was especially active in that cause, and through her connection with the court not only strengthened the opposition to the policy of her son-in-law, but also disturbed the domestic peace of the imperial family. Whenever the daughters of Theophilus visited her she took the opportunity to condemn their father's views, and would press her eikons on the girls' lips for adoration. One day, after such a visit, Pulcheria, the youngest princess, a mere child, in giving an account of what had transpired, innocently told her father that she had seen and kissed some very beautiful dolls at her grandmother's house. Whereupon Theophilus, suspecting the real facts, forbade his daughter to visit Theoctista again. On another occasion the court fool, Denderis, surprised the Empress Theodora in her private chamber kissing eikons and placing them over her eyes. 'What are these things?' he inquired. 'My beautiful dolls which I love,' she replied. Not long afterwards the jester was summoned to amuse Theophilus while sitting at table. 'What is the latest news?' asked the emperor. 'When I last visited "mamma" (the jester's familiar name for the empress) I saw most beautiful dolls in her room.' Instantly the emperor rose, beside himself with rage, and rushing to his wife's apartments violently denounced her as a heathen and idolater. 'Not at all,' answered Theodora, in her softest accents, 'that fool of yours saw me and my maidens looking into a mirror and mistook the faces reflected there for dolls.' The emperor did not press the case, but a few days later the servants of Theodora caught Denderis and gave him a sound thrashing for telling tales, dismissing

[1] Leo Gram. p. 214.   [2] Zonaras, iii. p. 358.
[3] Theoph. Cont. pp. 625, 628, 790.   [4] Ibid. p. 90.

him with the advice to let dolls alone in the future. In consequence of this experience, whenever the jester was afterwards asked whether he had seen his 'mamma's' dolls recently, he put one hand to his mouth and the other far down his back and whispered, 'Don't speak to me about dolls.'[1]   Such were the pleasantries that relieved the stern warfare against eikons.

On the occasion of the breach between Theodora and her son Michael III., on account of the murder of her friend and counsellor Theoctistos at Michael's order, she and her four daughters, Thekla, Anastasia, Anna, and Pulcheria, were confined in the Gastria, and there, with the exception of Anna, they were eventually buried.[2]   At the Gastria were shown also the tombs of Theoctista, her son Petronas, Irene the daughter of Bardas, and a small chest containing the lower jaw of Bardas[3] himself.   It is this connection with the family of Theophilus, in life and in death, that lends chief interest to the Gastria.

Architectural Features

(For Plan see p. 267.)

Although the building is now almost a complete ruin, it still preserves some architectural interest.   On the exterior it is an octagonal structure, with a large arch on each side rising to the cornice, and thus presents a strong likeness to the Byzantine building known as Sheik Suleiman Mesjedi, near the Pantokrator (p. 25).   The northern, southern, and western arches are pierced by windows. The entrance is in the western arch.   The interior presents the form of an equal-armed cross, the arms being deep recesses covered with semicircular vaults.   The dome over the central area has fallen in.   The apse, semicircular

[1] Theoph. Cont. pp. 91-92.

[2] *Ibid.* pp. 174, 658, 823 ; Codinus, p. 208.   The Anonymus (Banduri, iii. p. 52) and Codinus (*De aed.* p. 97) say that Theodora and her daughters were confined in the convent of Euphrosyne at the Libadia, τὰ Λιβάδια.   Their mistake is due to the fact that the convent at Gastria and the convent at Libadia were both connected with ladies named Euphrosyne.   Cf. Codinus, p. 207.

[3] Constant. Porphyr. p. 647.

within and showing five sides on the exterior, is attached
to the eastern arm. Its three central sides are occupied
by a triple-shafted window. Two shallow niches represent
the usual apsidal chambers. A similar niche is found
also on both sides of the entrance and on the eastern side
of the northern arm of the cross. In the wall to the west
of the southern arch is a small chamber. The joint
between the apse and the body of the building is
straight, with no bond in the masonry ; nor is the masonry
of the two parts of the same character. In the former it
is in alternate courses of brick and stone, while in the latter
we find many brick courses and only an occasional stone
band. Evidently the apse is a later addition. In view of
these facts, the probable conclusion is that the building was
originally not a church but a library, and that it was transformed into a church at some subsequent period in its
history to meet some special demand.

CHAPTER XXI

THE CHURCH OF S. MARY OF THE MONGOLS

THE church of S. Mary of the Mongols (τῶν Μογγολίων, τῶν Μουγουλίων, τοῦ Μουχλιοῦ, Μουχλιώτισσα), which stands on the heights above the quarter of Phanar, a short distance to the west of the Greek Communal School, was founded in the thirteenth century by Maria Palaeologina, a natural daughter of the Emperor Michael Palaeologus (1261-1282). As the church has been in Greek hands ever since its foundation its identity cannot be disputed. The epithet given to the Theotokos in association with this sanctuary alludes to the fact that Maria Palaeologina married a Khan of the Mongols,[1] and bore the title of Despoina of the Mongols (Δέσποινα τῶν Μουγουλίων).[2] The marriage was prompted by no romantic sentiment, but formed part of the policy by which her father hoped to secure the goodwill of the world for the newly restored Empire of Constantinople. While endeavouring to disarm the hostility of Western Europe by promoting the union of the Latin and Greek Churches, he sought to conciliate the people nearer his dominion by matrimonial alliances with their rulers. It was in this way that he courted, with greater or less success, the friendship of Servia, Bulgaria, the Duchy of Thebes, and the Empire of Trebizond. And by the same method he tried to win the friendship of the formidable Mongols settled in Russia and Persia. Accordingly he bestowed the hand of one natural daughter, Euphrosyne, upon Nogaya,[3] who had established a Mongolian principality

---

[1] Pachym. i. pp. 174-75.   [2] *Ibid.* ii. pp. 620-37.   [3] *Ibid.* i. p. 231.

272

near the Black Sea, while the hand of Maria was intended
for Holagu, famous in history as the destroyer in 1258 of
the caliphate of Baghdad. Maria left Constantinople for
her future home in 1265 with a great retinue, conducted
by Theodosius de Villehardouin, abbot of the monastery
of the Pantokrator, who was styled the 'Prince,' because

FIG. 93.—S. MARY OF THE MONGOLS. EXTERIOR.
(From a Photograph.)

related to the princes of Achaia and the Peloponnesus.
A rich trousseau accompanied the bride-elect, and a tent
of silk for a chapel, furnished with eikons of gold affixed
to crosses, and with costly vessels for the celebration of
the Holy Sacrifice. When the mission reached Caesarea
news came that Holagu was dead, but since reasons of state
inspired the proposed marriage, the bridal party continued

T

its journey to the Mongolian court, and there in due time Maria was wedded to Abaga, the son and successor of Holagu, after the bridegroom had received, it is said, Christian baptism.[1]

FIG. 94.—S. MARY OF THE MONGOLS. INTERIOR.

In 1281 Abaga was poisoned by his brother Achmed,[2] and Maria deemed it prudent, and doubtless welcome, after an absence of sixteen years, to return to Constantinople. She appears again in history during the reign of her brother

[1] Pachym. ii. pp. 174-75.
[2] Muralt, *Essai de chronographie byzantine*, vol. ii. ad annum.

Andronicus II. Palaeologus, when for the second time she was offered as a bride to the Mongolian prince, Charbanda, who then ruled in Persia,[1] the object of this new matrimonial alliance being to obtain the aid of the Mongols against the Turks, who under Othman had become a dangerous foe and were threatening Nicaea.   With this purpose in view Maria proceeded to that city, both to encourage the defence of an important strategic position and to press forward the negotiations with Charbanda.   The Despoina of the Mongols, however, did not comprehend the character of the enemy with whom she had to deal.   Her contemptuous demeanour towards Othman, and her threats to bring the Mongols against him, only roused the spirit of the Turkish chieftain, and before the Greeks could derive any advantage from the 30,000 Mongolian troops sent to their aid, Othman stormed the fortress of Tricocca, an outpost of Nicaea, and made it the base of his subsequent operations.[2]

The church was built for the use of a convent which the Despoina of the Mongols, like many other ladies in Byzantine times, erected as a haven of refuge for souls who had dedicated their lives to the service of God (λιμένα ψυχῶν κατὰ θεὸν προσθεμένων βιοῦν).   She also endowed it with property in the immediate neighbourhood (περὶ τὴν τοποθεσίαν τοῦ Φανάρι), as well as with other lands both within and beyond the city, and while Maria lived the nuns had no reason for complaint.   But after her death the property of the House passed into the hands of Isaac Palaeologus Asanes, the husband of a certain Theodora, whom Maria had treated as a daughter, and to whom she bequeathed a share in the convent's revenues.   He, as soon as Theodora died, appropriated the property for the benefit of his family, with the result that the sisterhood fell into debt and was threatened with extinction.   In their distress the nuns appealed to Andronicus III. Palaeologus for protection, and by the decision of the patriarchal court, to which the case was referred as the proper tribunal in such disputes, the convent in 1351 regained its rights.[3]

---

[1] Pachym. ii. pp. 620-21.   [2] Ibid. pp. 637-38.
[3] Miklosich et Müller, i. pp. 312, 317.

As already intimated, to this church belongs the interest of having always preserved its original character as a sanctuary of the Greek Orthodox Communion. This distinction it owes to the fact that the church was given to Christoboulos, the Greek architect of the mosque of Sultan Mehemed, as his private property, to mark the conqueror's satisfaction

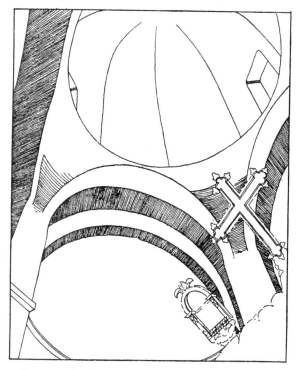

FIG. 95.—S. MARY OF THE MONGOLS. THE DOME.

with the builder's work. The grant was confirmed by Bajazet II. in recognition of the services of the nephew of Christoboulos in the construction of the mosque which bears that Sultan's name. Twice, indeed, attempts were subsequently made to deprive the Greek community of the church, once under Selim I. and again under Achmed III. But, like the law of the Medes and Persians, a Sultan's decree altereth not, and by presenting the hatti sheriff of

Sultan Mehemed the efforts to expropriate the building were frustrated.[1]

Among the Turks the building is known as Kan Kilisse, the church of Blood, and the adjoining street goes by the name Sanjakdar Youkousou, the ascent of the standard-bearer,[2] terms which refer to the desperate struggle between Greeks and Turks at this point on the morning of the capture of the city.[3]

Architectural Features

Although the building has always been in Christian hands it has suffered alterations almost more drastic than any undergone by churches converted into mosques. The interior has been stripped of its original decoration, and is so blocked by eikons, chandeliers, and other ornaments as to render a proper examination of the church extremely difficult. In plan the church is a domed quatrefoil building, the only example of that type found in Constantinople. The central dome rests on a cross formed by four semi-domes, which are further enlarged below the vaulting level by three large semicircular niches. It is placed on a drum of eight concave compartments pierced by windows to the outside circular and crowned with a flat cornice. Externally the semi-domes and apse are five-sided. From the interior face of the apse and on its northern wall projects a capital, adorned with acanthus leaves, which, as it could never have stood free in this position, probably formed part of an eikonostasis in stone. The narthex is in three bays, the central bay being covered by a barrel vault, while the lateral bays have low drumless domes on pendentives. The entrance is by a door in the central bay, and from that bay the church is entered through a passage cut in the central niche of the western semi-dome, and slightly wider than the niche. The end bays open, respectively, into the northern and southern semi-domes

---

[1] Patr. Constantius, pp. 84-86. The Greek community retains also other churches founded before the Turkish conquest, but they are wholly modern buildings. [2] *Ibid.* pp. 85-86. [3] N. Barbaro, p. 818.

by passages or aisles terminating in a diagonal arch. The arches between these aisles and the western semi-dome are pierced, and thus isolate the western dome piers. On the south the church has been greatly altered ; for the entire southern semi-dome and the southern bay of the narthex have been removed and replaced by three aisles of two bays each. These bays are equal in height, and are covered by cross-groined vaults with strong transverse pointed arches supported on square piers, the whole forming a large hall held up by two piers, and showing the distinct influence of Italian Gothic work. This part of the building is modern. On the eastern wall is a large picture of the Last Judgment.

The plan of this church may be compared with that of S. Nicholas Methana (Fig. 97).

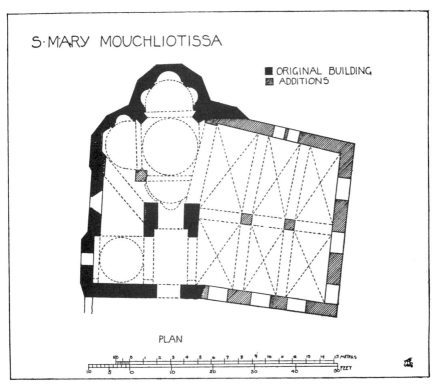

FIG. 96.

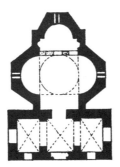

FIG. 97.
S. NICHOLAS METHANA (Lampakes).

279

CHAPTER XXII

BOGDAN SERAI

In a vacant lot of ground on the eastern declivity of the hill above the quarter of Balat, and at a short distance to the east of a mass of rock known as Kesmé Kaya, stands a Byzantine chapel to which the name Bogdan Serai clings. Although now degraded to the uses of a cow-house it retains considerable interest. Its name recalls the fact that the building once formed the private chapel attached to the residence of the envoys of the hospodars of Moldavia (in Turkish Bogdan) at the Sublime Porte ; just as the style Vlach Serai given to the church of the Virgin, lower down the hill and nearer the Golden Horn, is derived from the residence of the envoys of the Wallachian hospodars with which that church was connected. According to Hypselantes,[1] the Moldavian residence was erected early in the sixteenth century by Teutal Longophetes, the envoy who presented the submission of his country to Suleiman the Magnificent at Buda in 1516, when the Sultan was on his way to the siege of Vienna. Upon the return of Suleiman to Constantinople the hospodar of the principality came in person to the capital to pay tribute, and to be invested in his office with the insignia of two horse-tails, a fur coat, and the head-dress of a commander in the corps of janissaries. Gerlach[2] gives another account of the matter. According to his informants, the mansion belonged originally to a certain Raoul, who had emigrated to Russia in 1518, and after his death was purchased by Michael Cantacuzene as a

[1] Μετὰ τὴν ἅλωσιν, p. 61 ; cf. Paspates, p. 361.   [2] *Tagebuch*, p. 456.

home for the Moldavian envoys. It must have been an attractive house, surrounded by large grounds, and enjoying a superb view of the city and the Golden Horn. It was burnt[1] in the fire which devastated the district on the 25th June 1784, and since that catastrophe its grounds have been converted into market gardens or left waste, and its chapel has been a desecrated pile. But its proud name still haunts the site, calling to mind political relations which have long ceased to exist. The chapel stood at the north-western end of the residence and formed an integral part of the structure. For high up in the exterior side of the south-eastern wall are the mortises which held the beams supporting the floor of the upper story of the residence ; while lower down in the same wall is a doorway which communicated with the residence on that level. Some of the substructures of the residence are still visible. It is not impossible that the house, or at least some portion of it, was an old Byzantine mansion.   Mordtmann,[2] indeed, suggests that it was the palace to which Phrantzes refers under the name Trullus (ἐν τῷ Τρούλῳ).[3]   But that palace stood to the north of the church of the Pammakaristos (Fetiyeh Jamissi), and had disappeared when Phrantzes wrote. Gerlach,[4] moreover, following the opinion of his Greek friends, distinguishes between the Trullus and the Moldavian residence, and places the site of the former near the Byzantine chapel now converted into Achmed Pasha Mesjedi, to the south of the church of the Pammakaristos.[5]

Opinions differ in regard to the dedication of the chapel. Paspates,[6] following the view current among the gardeners who cultivated the market-gardens in the neighbourhood, maintained that the chapel was dedicated to S. Nicholas. Hence the late Canon Curtis, of the Crimean Memorial Church in Constantinople, believed that this was the church of SS. Nicholas and Augustine of Canterbury, founded by a Saxon noble who fled to Constantinople after the Norman

---

[1] Hypselantes, *ut supra*, p. 638.
[2] Archaeological Supplement to the *Proceedings of the Greek Syllogos of C.P.* vol. xviii. p. 8.
[3] Phrantzes, p. 307.
[4] *Tagebuch*, p. 456.
[5] See Chap. XII.
[6] P. 360.

conquest of England.   What is certain is that in the seventeenth century the chapel was dedicated to the Theotokos.   Du Cange mentions it under the name, Ecclesia Deiparae Serai Bogdaniae.[1]

Mordtmann has proved[2] that Bogdan Serai marks the site of the celebrated monastery and church of S. John the Baptist in Petra,—the title 'in Petra' being derived from the neighbouring mass of rock, which the Byzantines knew as Παλαιὰ Πέτρα, and which the Turks style Kesmé Kaya, the Chopped Rock.

According to a member of the monastery, who flourished in the eleventh century, the House was founded by a monk named Bara in the reign of Anastasius I. (491-518) near an old half-ruined chapel dedicated to S. John the Baptist, in what was then a lonely quarter of the city, between the Gate of S. Romanus (Top Kapoussi) and Blachernae.   The monastery becomes conspicuous in the narratives of the Russian pilgrims to the shrines of the city, under the designation, the monastery of S. John, Rich-in-God, because the institution was unendowed and dependent upon the freewill offerings of the faithful, which 'by the grace of God and the care and prayers of John' were generous. Thrice a year, on the festivals of the Baptist and at Easter, the public was admitted to the monastery and hospitably entertained.   It seems to have suffered during the Latin occupation, for it is described in the reign of Andronicus II. as standing abandoned in a vineyard.   But it was restored, and attracted visitors by the beauty of its mosaics and the sanctity of its relics.[3]

In 1381 a patriarchal decision conferred upon the abbot the titles of archimandrite and protosyngellos, and gave him the third place in the order of precedence among the chiefs of the monasteries of the city, 'that thus the outward honours of the house might reflect the virtue and

---

[1] Constant. Christ. iv. p. 162.

[2] See Archaeological Supplement to the *Proceedings of the Greek Syllogos of C.P.* vol. xviii. p. 8.

[3] Ruy Gonzalez de Clavijo in 1403, *Vida de Gran Tamorlan y itinerario*, p. 50 (Madrid, 1782): 'San Juan del a Piedra está cerca del palacio del Emperador' (*i.e.* near the palace of Blachernae).

piety which adorned its inner life.'[1]   Owing to the proximity
of the house to the landward walls, it was one of the first
shrines[2] to become the spoil of the Turks on the 29th of
May 1453, and was soon used as a quarry to furnish
materials for new buildings after the conquest.   Gyllius
visited the ruins, and mistaking the fabric for the church of
S. John the Baptist at the Hebdomon, gave rise to the
serious error of placing that suburb in this part of the city
instead of at Makrikeui beside the Sea of Marmora.[3]
Gerlach[4] describes the church as closed because near a
mosque.   Portions, however, of the monastic buildings and
of the strong wall around them still survived, and eikons of
celebrated saints still decorated the porch.   On an eikon of
Christ the title of the monastery, Petra, was inscribed.
Some of the old cells were then occupied by nuns, who were
maintained by the charitable gifts of wealthy members of the
Greek community.

Architectural Features

The building is in two stories, and may be described
as a chapel over a crypt.   It points north-east, a peculiar
orientation probably due to the adaptation of the chapel
to the position of the residence with which it was
associated.   The masonry is very fine and regular, built
in courses of squared stone alternating with four courses
of brick, all laid in thick mortar joints, and pierced
with numerous putlog holes running through the walls.
It presents a striking likeness to the masonry in the
fortifications of the city.   The lower story is an oblong
hall covered with a barrel vault, and terminates in an arch
and apse.   In the west side of one of the jambs of the
arch is a small niche.   The vault for one-third of its height
is formed by three courses of stone laid horizontally and
cut to the circle ; above this it is of brick with radiating
joints.   Here cows are kept.

The upper story is m. 3.75 above the present level

[1] Miklosich et Müller, i. ii. pp. 21-23.   [2] Ducas, p. 288.
[3] De top. C.P. iv. c. 4.   [4] Tagebuch, p. 455.

of the ground. It is a single hall m. 8.80 in length and m. 3.70 wide, terminating in a bema and a circular apse in brick. Over the bema is a barrel vault. A dome, without drum or windows, resting on two shallow flat arches in the lateral walls and two deep transverse arches strengthened by a second order of arches, covers the building. In the wall towards the north-west there is a window between two low niches ; and a similar arrangement is seen in the opposite wall, except that the door which communicated with the residence occupies the place of the window. The apsidal chambers, usual in a church, are here represented by two niches in the bema. Externally the apse shows five sides, and is decorated by a flat niche pierced by a single light in the central side, and a blind concave niche, with head of patterned brickwork, in the two adjacent sides. The dome, apse, vaults, and trans-verse arches are in brick, laid in true radiating courses. The absence of windows in the dome is an unusual feature, which occurs also in the angle domes of S. Theodosia. The pendentives are in horizontal courses, corbelled out to the centre, and at each angle of the pendentives is embedded an earthenware jar, either for the sake of light-ness, or to improve, as some think, the acoustics of the building. This story of the chapel is used as a hayloft.

A careful survey of the building shows clearly that the domical character of the chapel is not original, and that the structure when first erected was a simple hall covered with a wooden roof. Both the shallow wall arches and the deep transverse arches under the dome are insertions in the walls of an older fabric. They are not supported on pilasters, as is the practice elsewhere, but rest on corbels, and, in order to accommodate these corbels, the lateral niches, originally of the same height as the central window, have been reduced in height. A fragment of the original arch still remains, cut into by the wall arch of the dome. The flat secondary arches crossing the chapel at each end are similarly supported on corbels.

This view is confirmed by the examination of the plaster left upon the walls. That plaster has four distinct coats or layers, upon all of which eikons in tempera are painted.[1] The innermost coat is laid between the transverse dome arches and the walls against which they are built. Those arches, therefore, could not have formed parts of the building when the first coat of plaster was laid, but must be later additions.

In keeping with this fact, the second coat of painted plaster is found laid both on the arches and on those portions of the old work which the arches did not cover.

The secondary arches under the transverse arches at each end belong to a yet later period, for where they have separated from the arches above them, decorated plaster, which at one time formed part of the general ornamentation of the building, is exposed to view. At this stage in the history of the chapel the third coat of plaster was spread over the walls, thus giving three coats on the oldest parts where unaltered—two coats on the first alterations, and one coat on the second alterations. The fourth coat of plaster is still later, marking some less serious repair of the chapel.

The *voussoirs* of the lateral dome arches should be noticed. They do not radiate to the centre, but are laid flatter and radiate to a point above the centre. This form of construction, occurring frequently in Byzantine arches, is regarded by some authorities as a method of forming an arch without centering. But in the case of the lateral wall arches before us it occurs where centering could never have been required ; while the apse arch, where centering would have had structural value, is formed with true radiating *voussoirs*. The failure of the *voussoirs* to radiate to the centre therefore seems to be simply the result of using untapered *voussoirs* in which the arch form must be obtained by wedge-shaped joints. For if these joints are carelessly formed, the crown may very well be reached before the requisite amount of radiation has been obtained. On the other hand, if full centering had been used, we should expect to find marks of the centering boards on the mortar

---

[1] When Paspates (p. 360) visited the chapel, the eikons were more distinctly visible than at present, although they bore marks of deliberate injury by Moslem iconoclasts.

in the enormously thick joints. But neither here nor in
any instance where the jointing was visible have such marks
been found. Still, when we consider the large amount of
mortar employed in Byzantine work, it seems impossible
that greater distortions than we actually meet with in
Byzantine edifices would not have occurred, even during
the building, had no support whatever been given. It
seems, therefore, safe to assume the use of at any rate light
scaffolding and centering to all Byzantine arches.[1]

[1] See p. 23.

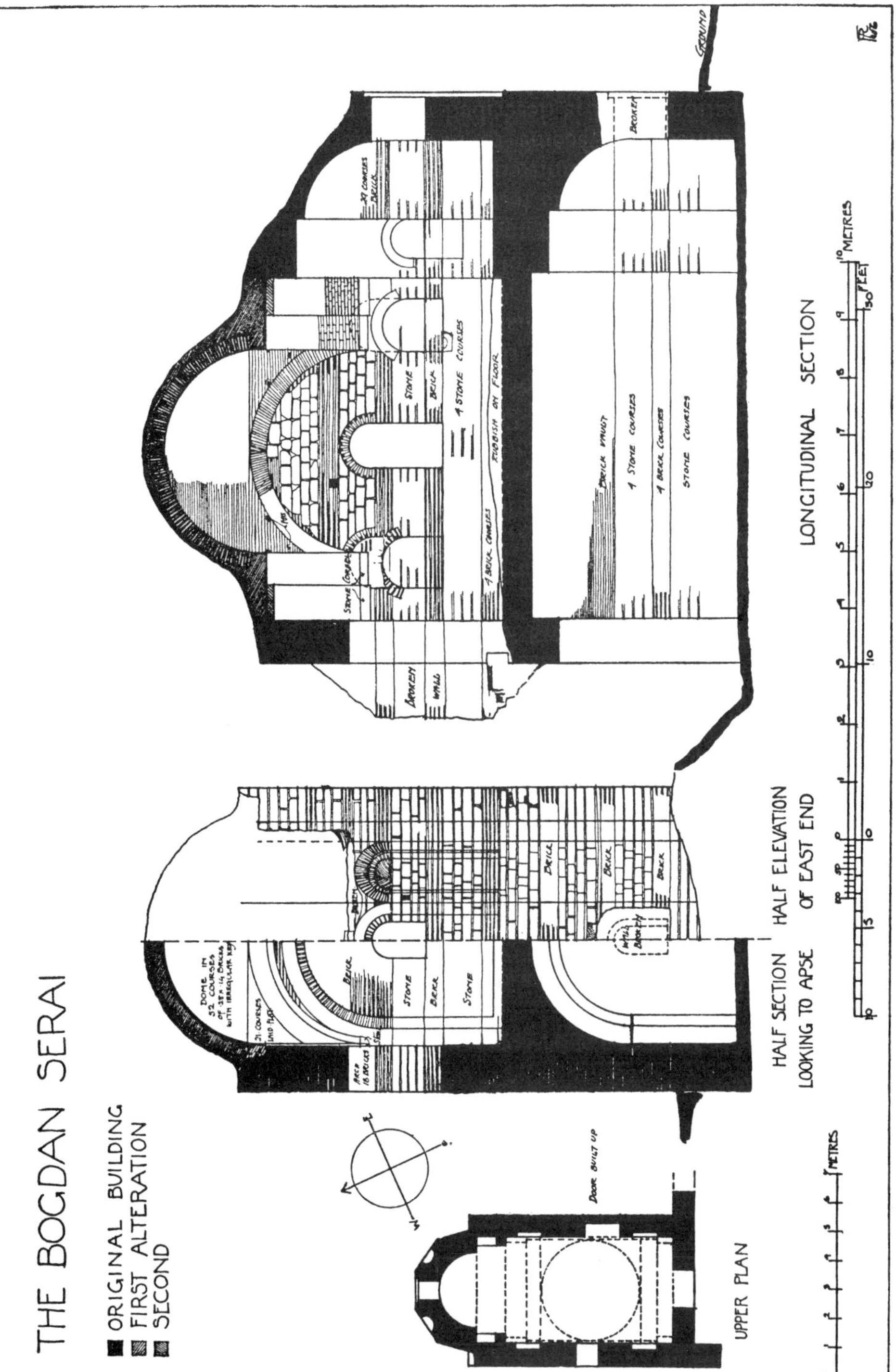
THE BOGDAN SERAI
ORIGINAL BUILDING
FIRST ALTERATION
SECOND
UPPER PLAN
DOOR BUILT UP
HALF SECTION
LOOKING TO APSE
HALF ELEVATION
OF EAST END
LONGITUDINAL SECTION
GROUND
STONE
BRICK
4 STONE COURSES
RUBBISH ON FLOOR
BRICK VAULT
STONE COURSES
METRES
FEET

FIG. 98.

CHAPTER XXIII

THE CHURCH OF S. SAVIOUR IN THE CHORA, KAHRIÉ JAMISSI

ACCORDING to the historian Nicephorus Gregoras,[1] who was long and closely connected with the church, the Chora was founded by Justinian the Great, and then presented the form of a basilica. But there is reason to believe that the edifice erected by that emperor was the reconstruction of an older shrine. The fame of a restorer often eclipsed the memory of the founder of a sanctuary, especially when the restorer was the superior in rank and reared a larger and more beautiful building.

According to Symeon Metaphrastes,[2] the site of the Chora was first consecrated by the interment of S. Babylas and his eighty-four disciples, who were martyred in 298 during the reign of Maximianus. The scene of their execution, indeed, was Nicomedia ; but friendly hands obtained possession of the bodies of the champions of the faith, and taking them to Constantinople, buried them outside the walls of the city, towards the north, in the place subsequently occupied by the monastery of the Chora. As will appear, the relics of S. Babylas and his disciples formed part of the treasures of the Chora in the ninth century.[3]

---

[1] Vol. i. p. 459.

[2] Synax., Sept. 4, πιστοὶ δέ τινες εὐσεβεῖς νυκτὸς ἐλθόντες καὶ τὰ λείψανα ἐν ἀκατίῳ ἐμβαλόντες εἰς τὸ Βυζάντιον διακομίζουσι καὶ ἐν τῷ βορείῳ μέρει ἔξω τειχέων ἐν τρισὶ λάρναξι καταθέντες, ἔνθα ἐστὶ μονὴ Χώρα ἐπονομαζομένη, δόξαν καὶ εὐχαριστίαν τῷ Θεῷ ἀνέπεμψαν.

[3] *Proceedings of the Greek Syllogos of C.P.* vol. xxiv., 1896, Supplement, p. 33.

The settlement of the approximate date of the foundation of the church depends, ultimately, upon the meaning to be attached to the term Chora (Χώρα). There are some writers who incline to the idea that in this connection that term was employed from the first in a mystical sense, to denote the attribute of Christ as the sphere of man's highest life ; and there can be no doubt that the word was used in that sense in the fourteenth century. That is unquestionably its meaning in the legends inscribed on mosaics which adorn the walls of the building.

$$\overline{\text{IC}}\ \overline{\text{XC}} \qquad\qquad \overline{\text{MHP}}\ \overline{\text{ΘY}}$$

$$\text{H XΩPA} \qquad\qquad \text{H XΩPA TOY}$$

$$\text{TΩN ZΩNTΩN} \qquad\qquad \text{AXΩPHTOY}$$

And it is in that sense that the term is employed by Cantacuzene[1] and Phrantzes.[2] On this view the description of the church as ' in the Chora' throws no light on the date of the church's foundation. Other authorities,[3] however, maintain that the term Chora was originally associated with the church in the obvious topographical signification of the word, to denote territory outside the city limits, and that its religious reference came into vogue only when changes in the boundaries of Constantinople made the literal meaning of Chora no longer applicable. According to this opinion the church was, therefore, founded while its site lay beyond the city walls, and consequently before the year 413, after which the site was included within the capital by the erection of the Theodosian wall.

Hence, the phrase ' in the Chora' had the same signification as the style ' in the fields' which is attached to the church of S. Martin in London, or the style *fuore le mura* which belongs to the basilica of S. Paul and other churches beyond the walls of Rome to this day.

It is certainly in this topographical sense that the term Chora is understood by the Byzantine writers in whose works it first appears. That is how the term is used by Simeon Metaphrastes[4] in his description of

---

[1] Vol. iii. p. 172.
[2] P. 36.
[3] Paspates, p. 326.
[4] Synax., Sept. 4.

U

the site of the monastery in his day, and that is how the Anonymus[1] of the eleventh century and his follower Codinus[2] understand the term ; for they take special care to explain how a building which lay within the city in their day could be styled 'Chora' ; because, say they, it once stood without the walls, on territory, therefore, called by the Byzantines, χωρίον, the country. The literal meaning of a word is earlier than its artificial and poetical signification. And one can easily conceive how, when the style Chora was no longer literally correct, men abandoned the sober ground of common-sense and history to invent recondite meanings inspired by imagination and sentiment.

This conclusion is confirmed by the history of the Chora given in the Life of S. Theodore,[3] an abbot of the monastery, which Mr. Gedeon discovered in the library of the Pantokrator on Mount Athos. According to that biography, S. Theodore was a relative of Theodora, the wife of Justinian the Great, and after serving with distinction in the Persian wars, and winning greater renown as a monk near Antioch, came to Constantinople about the year 530, at the invitation of his imperial relatives, to assist in the settlement of the theological controversies of the day. Once there he was induced to make the capital his permanent abode by permission to build a monastery, where he could follow his high calling as fully as in his Syrian retreat. For that purpose he selected a site on the property of a certain Charisius, situated, as the Chora is, on the slope of a hill, descending on the one hand steeply to the sea, and rising, on the other, to the highest point in the line of the Theodosian walls, the point marked by the gate named after Charisius (now Edirné Kapoussi). The site was already hallowed, says the biographer of S. Theodore, by the presence of a humble monastic retreat and a small chapel.

The edifice erected by S. Theodore was, however, soon overthrown by the severe earthquake which shook the city in 558, and all the hopes of the good man would also have

---

[1] Banduri, iii. p. 54, χωρίον ἦν ἐκεῖσε ἔξω τοῦ Βυζαντίου.

[2] *De aed.* p. 121, ἐκλήθη δὲ χώρα διότι τῶν Βυζαντίων χωρίον ἦν ἐκεῖ, καθὰ καὶ ἡ τοῦ Στουδίου μονή, ἔξω τῆς πόλεως ὑπῆρχεν.

[3] Written in the second quarter of the ninth century.

been dashed to the ground had the disaster not called forth the sympathy and aid of Justinian. In the room of the ruined buildings the emperor erected a magnificent establishment, with chapels dedicated to the Theotokos, the Archangel Michael, S. Anthimus of Nicomedia, and the Forty Martyrs of Sebaste. There also stood a hostel for the special accommodation of Syrian monks on a visit to Constantinople, and a hospital for diseases of the eye.[1]

In this account of the early history of the Chora, there may be, as Schmitt[2] thinks, many inaccuracies. It was easy, even for a member of the House who aspired to authorship, to confuse persons, to err in the matter of dates, and to overlook the changes which the buildings with which he was familiar had undergone before his day. But surely the biographer of S. Theodore can be trusted where his statements are supported by more reliable authorities, and we may therefore accept his testimony on the following points : that the original church of the Chora was earlier than the reign of Justinian ; that under Justinian the old sanctuary was replaced by a new and statelier building ; that the Chora maintained intimate relations with monasteries in Syria ; and that with it was associated a church dedicated to the Archangel Michael.

NOTE

The association of a church dedicated to S. Michael with the Chora, and the fact that the Chora stood on the property of Charisius, raise an interesting question. For among the subscriptions to the letter of the monks to Pope Hormisdas in 518, and the subscriptions to the Acts of the Synod held in Constantinople in 536, stands the name of the abbot of the monastery of the Archangel Michael of Charisius.[3] Was that monastery identical with the Chora? If it was, that fact would be additional evidence that the Chora was earlier than Justinian's time. On the other hand, it is always dangerous to identify buildings because they were situated in the same quarter of

---

[1] Supplement to vol. xxiv. of the *Proceedings of the Greek Syllogos of C.P.* p. 23. Cf. Schmitt, p. 28.

[2] In his great monograph on Kahrié Jamissi published by the Russian Institute of Constantinople, 1906.

[3] Mansi, *Sacrorum Conciliorum Collectio*, tomus viii. col. 906, col. 882, τοῦ ἁγίου Μιχαὴλ τῶν Χαρισίου : τῆς ἐπίκλην τῶν Χαρισίου.

the city and dedicated to the same saint.   The absence of all reference to the monastery of S. Michael of Charisius after the reign of Justinian, and yet the association of a church of S. Michael with the Chora after his reign, may be due either to the ruin of that monastery in the earthquake of 558, or to the subsequent union of the two establishments on account of their proximity.

The next important event in the history of the House was the confinement there of the celebrated general Priscus, Count of the Excubiti, at the command of the Emperor Heraclius (610-641).[1]   Priscus had taken a leading part in the revolution which overthrew his father-in-law, the infamous Phocas, and placed Heraclius upon the throne. But notwithstanding that service, the attitude of the general towards the new régime was not considered satisfactory, and with the cruel taunt, ' Wretch, thou didst not make a good son-in-law ; how canst thou be a true friend ? '   Heraclius relegated him to political nonentity by forcing him to become a monk at the Chora.   The new brother did not live long, but his wealth furnished the fraternity with the means for the erection of a large and beautiful church.

Schmitt, indeed, thinks that the biographer of S. Theodore, already cited, failed to recognise the identity of the person concerning whom he wrote, and assigned events which occurred in the time of Heraclius to the reign of Justinian.   According to Schmitt, S. Theodore is really Priscus under his name in religion, and to him, and not to Justinian, was the Chora indebted for its first great era of prosperity.   One thing is certain, the splendid church with which the biographer of S. Theodore was acquainted, and the wealth and beauty of which he extols in extravagant terms, was not the church erected by Justinian at the Chora. The latter was a basilica ;[2] while the church alluded to in the biography of S. Theodore was a domical building.[3] Probably the fame of Justinian veiled not only what others had done for the Chora before him, but also the services performed by others after his day.

---

[1] Banduri, iii. p. 54 ; Codinus. *De aed.* p. 121 ἡ χώρα πρῶτον μὲν εὐκτήριον ἦν, Πρίσκος ὁ ἔπαρχος καὶ γαμβρὸς τοῦ Φωκᾶ τοῦ τυράννου περιορισθεὶς ἐκεῖ παρὰ τοῦ ἰδίου ἔκτισε ταύτην μονὴν εἰς κάλλος καὶ μέγεθος, ἀποχαρισάμενος καὶ κτήματα πολλά.

[2] Niceph. Greg. iii. p. 459.   [3] Schmitt, p. 28

In 712 the Patriarch Kyros was confined in the Chora by the Emperor Philippicus for adherence to the tenets of the Sixth General Council (680),[1] which condemned the attribution of a single will to the person of Christ. The fidelity of the patriarch to orthodox opinion was commemorated annually in the services held at the Chora, as well as in S. Sophia, on the 8th of January.

The monastery was also honoured by the burial there, in 740, of the Patriarch Germanus (714-730), famous for his piety, his learning, and above all for his opposition to Leo the Isaurian, when that emperor commenced the crusade against eikons. The tomb of the patriarch was reputed to perform wonderful cures.[2] Another notable personage buried at the Chora was the patrician Bactagius, an associate of Artavasdos in the effort, made in 743, to drive Constantine Copronymus from the throne. Upon the failure of that attempt Bactagius was captured, beheaded in the Kynegion, and while his head was displayed to public view in the Milion for three days, his mutilated body was taken to the Chora. This might have seemed sufficient revenge. But the rebel's offence so rankled in the emperor's memory, that even after the lapse of some thirty years his resentment was not allayed. The widow of Bactagius was then forced to proceed to the Chora to disinter the bones of her husband from their resting-place in holy earth, and carry them in her cloak to the dreary burial-ground of Pelagion, where the corpses of persons who committed suicide were thrown.[3]

Like similar institutions the Chora suffered severely during the iconoclastic period. Because of its connection with the Patriarch Germanus it became the special object of the hatred of Constantine Copronymus for monks and was almost ruined. What he left of it was turned into a secular residence, and devoted to the confinement of Artavasdos and his family. There also that rebel, and his nine children and his wife, Constantine's sister, were eventually buried.[4]

---

[1] Theoph. pp. 554, 556 ; Synax. *ad diem* ; Cedrenus, i. p. 784.
[2] Theoph. pp. 626-680 ; Synax., May 12.
[3] Theoph. pp. 647-8.
[4] *Life of Michael Syncellus*, p. 31, in supplement to vol. xxiv. of the *Proceedings of the Greek Syllogos of C.P.* ; cf. Schmitt, p. 251.

With the triumph of the iconodules, in 842, under Michael III. and his mother the Empress Theodora, happier days dawned upon the Chora. It was then fortunate in the appointment of Michael Syncellus as its abbot, and under his rule it rapidly recovered from poverty and desolation. The new abbot was a Syrian monk distinguished for his ability, his sanctity, and his devotion to eikons. He came to Constantinople in 814, to remonstrate against the religious policy of Leo the Armenian, and, according to the custom of monks from Palestine on a visit to the capital, lodged at the Chora. But so far from succeeding in the object of his visit, Michael was imprisoned and then banished to one of the monasteries on Mount Olympus in Bithynia. Accordingly, when the cause for which he suffered proved victorious, no honour seemed too great to bestow upon the martyr. It was even proposed to create him patriarch, but he declined the office, and supported the appointment of his friend Methodius to that position. Methodius, in return, made Michael his syncellus and abbot of the Chora.[1] Under these circumstances it is not surprising that funds were secured for the restoration of the monastery, and that the brotherhood soon gained great influence in the religious circles of the capital. There is, however, no mention now of the church of the Archangel Michael or of the church dedicated to the Theotokos. Possibly the death of the abbot in 846 and lack of money prevented the reconstruction of those sanctuaries. The only churches attached to the Chora noticed in the biography of Michael Syncellus are the church of S. Anthimus, containing the relics of S. Babylas and his eighty-four disciples, the dependent chapel of S. Ignatius, and the church of the Forty Martyrs.[2] Let it also be noted that there is yet no mention of a church specially consecrated to the Saviour.

After its restoration in the 9th century the Chora does not appear again in history until the reign of Alexius I. Comnenus (1081-1118), when, owing to its great age, it

---

[1] *Life of Michael Syncellus, ut supra*, pp. 30, 31.
[2] See supplement to vol. xxiv. of the *Proceedings of the Greek Syllogos of Constantinople*, p. 33 ; cf. Schmitt, pp. 257-8.

was found in a state of almost complete ruin.[1] If for no other reason, the proximity of the church to the palace or Blachernae, which had become the favourite residence of the court, brought the dilapidated pile into notice, and its restoration was undertaken by the emperor's mother-in-law, Maria, the beautiful and talented granddaughter of Samuel, the famous king of Bulgaria, and niece of Aecatherina, the consort of Isaac I. Comnenus. Maria had married Andronicus Ducas, a son of Michael VII., and the marriage of her daughter Irene Ducaena to Alexius was designed to unite the rival pretensions of the families of the Comneni and the Ducas to the throne. It had been strenuously opposed by Anna Dalassena, the mother of Alexius, and its accomplishment in 1077, notwithstanding such formidable opposition, is no slight proof of the diplomatic skill and determination of the mother of the bride. Nor can it be doubted that Irene's mother acted a considerable part in persuading Alexius, when he mounted the throne, not to repudiate his young wife, as he was tempted to do in favour of a fairer face. Perhaps the restoration of the Chora was a token of gratitude for the triumph of her maternal devotion.

The church was rebuilt on the plan which it presents to-day, for in the account of the repairs made in the fourteenth century it is distinctly stated that they concerned chiefly the outer portion of the edifice.[2] To Alexius' mother-in-law, therefore, may be assigned the central part of the structure, a cruciform hall ; the dome, so far as it is not Turkish, the beautiful marble incrustation upon the walls, the mosaic eikons of the Saviour and of the Theotokos on the piers of the eastern dome-arch, and the exquisite marble carving above the latter eikon—all eloquent in praise of the taste and munificence that characterised the eleventh century in Constantinople. Probably the church was then dedicated to the Saviour, like the three other Comnenian churches in the city, the Pantepoptes, the Pantokrator, and S. Thekla.

The mother-in-law of Alexius I. was, however, not alone in her interest in the Chora. Her devotion to the monastery was shared also by her grandson the sebastocrator Isaac.

[1] Niceph. Greg. iii. p. 459.   [2] *Ibid.* i. p. 459.

Tall, handsome, brave, but ambitious and wayward, Isaac was gifted with the artistic temperament, as his splendid manuscript of the first eight books of the Old Testament, embellished with miniatures by his own hand, makes clear.[1] If the inscription on the mosaic representing the Deesis found in the inner narthex really refers to him, it proves that his influence was felt in the decoration of the building.[2] He certainly erected a magnificent mausoleum for himself in the church. Later in his life, indeed, he became interested in the restoration of the monastery of Theotokos Kosmosoteira at Viros, and ordered that mausoleum to be dismantled, and the marbles, bronze railing, and portraits of his parents which adorned it to be transported to Viros ; but he still allowed his own portrait ' made in the days of his youthful vanity ' to remain in the Chora.[3]

NOTE

Uspenski has identified Viros with Ferejik, a village situated 30 kilometres from Dedeagatch, and 20-25 kilometres from Enos, ' aux embouchures désertées et marécageuses de la Maritza.'

The church is now the mosque of the village. It has five domes and three apses. The central apse is pierced by a modern door. The exonarthex has disappeared and the old principal entrance is walled up. The plan of the church is almost identical with the plan of the Chora. While the architectural details are poor and indicate haste, the dimensions of the building imply considerable expense and the wealth of the restorer. There are traces of painting on the walls of the interior, especially in the domes (the Virgin) and in the two lateral apses. An epitaph of seven lines in the middle of the mosque contains the title ' despotes.' According to Uspenski, the

---

[1] The manuscript was discovered in the Seraglio Library by Professor T. Uspenski, and has been photographically reproduced by the Russian Institute of Constantinople.

[2] The inscription has been injured. It now reads :—

$$\dagger \ \dot{o} \ . \ . \ \dot{o}s \ \tau o\hat{v}$$
$$\psi \eta \lambda o \ . \ . \ \tau o \nu$$
$$. \ . \ . \ \sigma \iota \lambda \acute{\epsilon} \omega s \ . \ . \ .$$
$$. \ . \ . \ \xi \iota o \nu \ . \ . \ .$$
$$. \ . \ o\hat{v} \ . \ . \ .$$

See Schmitt, pp. 38-39, who restores the inscription thus :

$$\dot{o} \ \upsilon \dot{\iota} \grave{o} s \ \tau o\hat{v} \ \dot{\upsilon} \psi \eta \lambda o \tau \acute{a} \tau o \upsilon$$
$$\beta \alpha \sigma \acute{\iota} \lambda \epsilon \omega s \ ' A \lambda \epsilon \xi \acute{\iota} o \upsilon \ \tau o\hat{v}$$
$$K o \mu \nu \eta \nu o\hat{v}.$$

[3] See Schmitt, pp. 39-40.

sebastocrator died soon after 1182, the year during which he was engaged on the Typicon of the monastery at Viros.   The monastery was visited by the Emperor Andronicus Comnenus in 1185, by Isaac Angelus in 1195, and by Villehardouin in 1205.   Early in the fourteenth century it was converted into a fortress, and the country round it was ravaged in 1322 by the Bulgarians.   It was attacked in vain by John Cantucuzene, but was captured in 1355 by John VI. Palaeologus.

Another name associated with the Chora at this period is that of the Patriarch Cosmas, who was commemorated annually in the church on the 2nd of January.   He had occupied the patriarchal seat in days troubled by the intrigues and conflicts which drove first Michael VII. Ducas, and then Nicephorus Botoniates from the throne, and invested Alexius Comnenus with the purple.   They were not days most suitable to a man who, though highly esteemed for his virtues, was without education or experience in public affairs, and nearly ninety years old.   Still, to his honour be it said, it was at his earnest request that Botoniates finally agreed to forego a bloody contest with the Comneni, and to withdraw quietly to the monastery of the Peribleptos. Moreover, when it seemed uncertain whether the victorious Alexius would remain faithful to Irene Ducaena and raise her to the throne, Cosmas, notwithstanding all the efforts of Anna Dalassena (who was ill-disposed towards Irene) to persuade him to lay down his office, firmly refused to resign until he had placed the imperial crown upon the emperor's lawful wife.   Soon after that event, on the 7th of May 1081, the festival of S. John the Evangelist, Cosmas, having celebrated service in the church dedicated to that apostle at the Hebdomon (Makrikeui), turned to his deacon, saying, 'Take my Psalter and come with me ; we have nothing more to do here,' and retired to the monastery of Kallou. His strength for battle was spent.

After its restoration under the Comneni, the Chora again disappears from view until the reign of Michael Palaeologus (1261-1282).   In the interval the fortunes of the Empire had suffered serious reverses, what with domestic strifes and foreign wars.   Bulgaria had reasserted her independence

and established the capital of a new kingdom at Tirnovo,
while Constantinople itself had been captured by the forces
of the Fourth Crusade and made the seat of a Latin
kingdom.   Consequently, it is not surprising to find that
the Chora, like other churches of the ravaged city, was in
a deplorable condition at the close of those calamitous days.
Nothing seemed to have been done for the repair of the
church immediately upon the recovery of the capital in
1261.   The ruin which the Latin occupants of Constantinople left behind them was too great to be removed at once.
The first reference to the Chora at this period occurs some
fourteen years after the restoration of the Byzantine Empire,
when the monastery, owing to its proximity to the palace
of Blachernae, was assigned to the Patriarch Veccus
as the house in which to lodge on the occasion of his
audiences with Michael Palaeologus, on Tuesdays, to present
petitions for the exercise of imperial generosity or justice.
But the decay into which the establishment had fallen
could not be long ignored, and a wealthy, talented, and
influential citizen who resided in the neighbourhood,
Theodore Metochites,[1] decided to restore the edifice as a
monument of the artistic revival of his own day.

Theodore Metochites was one of the most remarkable
men of his day.   His tall, large, well-proportioned figure,
his bright countenance, commanded attention wherever he
appeared.   He was, moreover, a great student of ancient
Greek literature and of the literature of later times, and
although never a master of style, became an author and
attempted verse.   He was much interested in astronomy,
and one of his pupils, the historian Nicephorus Gregoras,
recognised the true length of the year and proposed the
reform of the calendar centuries before Pope Gregory.
Theodore's memory was so retentive that he could converse
on any topic with which he was familiar, as if reading from
a book, and there was scarcely a subject on which he was
not able to speak with the authority of an expert.   He
seemed a living library, 'a walking encyclopaedia.'   In fact,
he belonged to the class of brilliant Greek scholars who

[1] Niceph. Greg. i. p. 459.

might have regenerated the East had not the unfortunate political situation of their country driven them to Italy to herald and promote the Renaissance in Western Europe. Theodore Metochites was, moreover, a politician. He took an active part in the administration of affairs during the reign of Andronicus II., holding the office of Grand Logothetes of the Treasury ; and such was his devotion to politics, that when acting as a statesman it might be forgotten that he was a scholar. The unhappy strife between Andronicus II. and Andronicus III. caused Theodore Metochites the profoundest anxiety, and it was not his fault if the feud between the grandfather and the grandson refused to be healed. His efforts to bring that disgraceful and disastrous quarrel to an end involved great self-sacrifice and wrecked his career. For the counsels he addressed to Andronicus III. gave mortal offence, and when the young emperor entered the capital and took up his quarters in the palace of the Porphyrogenitus (Tekfour Serai), his troops sacked and demolished Theodore's mansion in that vicinity. The beautiful marbles which adorned the residence were sent as an imperial present to a Scythian prince, while the fallen statesman was banished to Didymotica for two years. Upon his return from exile Theodore found a shelter in the monastery which he had restored in his prosperous days. But there also, for some two years longer, the cup of sorrow was pressed to his lips. A malady from which he suffered caused him excruciating pain ; his sons were implicated in a political plot and thrown into prison ; Andronicus II., between whom and himself all communication had been forbidden, died ; and so the worn-out man assumed the habit of a monk, and lay down to die on the 13th of March 1331, a month after his imperial friend. His one consolation was the beautiful church he bequeathed to succeeding generations for the worship of God.

To the renovation of the church Theodore Metochites devoted himself heart and soul, and spent money for that object on a lavish scale. As the central portion of the building was comparatively well preserved,[1] it was to the

---

[1] Niceph. Greg. i. p. 459 οὗτος ἀβροτέρᾳ χρησάμενος δεξιᾷ, πλὴν τοῦ μεσαιτάτου νεῶ πάντα καλῶς ἐπεσκεύασε, cf. ii. p. 1045.

outer part of the edifice that he directed his chief attention —the two narthexes and the parecclesion. These were to a large extent rebuilt and decorated with the marbles and mosaics, which after six centuries, and notwithstanding the neglect and injuries they have suffered during the greater part of that period, still excite the admiration they awakened when fresh from the artist's hand.

The connection of Theodore Metochites with this splendid work is immortalised not only by historians of his day and by himself,[1] but also by the mosaic which surmounts the main entrance to the church from the inner narthex. There the restorer of the building, arrayed in his official robes, and on bended knees, holds a model of the church in his hands and offers it to the Saviour seated on a throne. Beside the kneeling figure is the legend, ὁ κτήτωρ λογοθέτης τοῦ γεννικοῦ Θεόδωρος ὁ Μετοχίτης, 'The builder, Logothetes of the Treasury, Theodore the Metochites' (Plate XCI.).

The restoration of the church must have been completed before the year 1321, for in that year Nicephorus Gregoras[2] describes it as then recently (ἄρτι) renovated, and in use for the celebration of divine service. How long before 1321 the work of repair precisely commenced cannot be determined, but it was in process as early as 1303, for that date is inscribed in Arabic numerals on the mosaic depicting the miracle at Cana, which stands to the right of the figure of Christ over the door leading from the outer to the inner narthex. But to have reached the stage at which mosaics could be applied the work of restoration must have been commenced sometime before 1303.

One of the most distinguished members of the Chora was the historian Nicephorus Gregoras, who learned to know the monastery through his friendship with Theodore Metochites. The two men met first when Nicephorus came from his native town Heraclea on the Black Sea to Constantinople, a youth eager to acquire the knowledge

---

[1] *Theodori Metochitae carmina*, ed. Treu. A 1004, *et passim*.
[2] Niceph. Greg. i. p. 303 ἄρτι τοῦ νεουργεῖν ἐπέπαυτο τὴν τῆς Χώρας μονήν, ὁπόσος ὁ ἔνδον ἐτύγχανε κόσμος.

that flourished in the capital. Being specially interested in the science of astronomy, the student placed himself under the instruction of Theodore, then the greatest authority on the subject, and won the esteem and confidence of his master to a degree that ripened into the warmest friendship and the most unreserved intellectual intercourse. In his turn, Nicephorus Gregoras became the instructor of the children of the grand logothetes, and was treated as a member of the family. He was also associated with the restoration of the Chora, attending particularly to the collection of the costly materials required for the embellishment of the church. Thus the monastery became his home from youth to old age, and after Theodore's death was entrusted to his care.[1] During the fierce controversy which raged around the question whether the light beheld at the Transfiguration formed part of the divine essence, and could be seen again after prolonged fasting and gazing upon one's navel, as the monks of Mount Athos and their supporters maintained, Nicephorus Gregoras, who rejected that idea, retired from public life to defend what he deemed the cause of truth more effectively. But to contend with a master of legions is ever an unequal struggle. The Emperor John Cantacuzene, taking the side of the monks, condemned their opponent to silence in the Chora, and there for some three years Nicephorus Gregoras discovered how scenes of happiness can be turned into a veritable hell by imperial disfavour and theological odium. Notwithstanding his age, his physical infirmities, his services to the monastery, his intellectual eminence, he was treated by the fraternity in a manner so inhuman that he would have preferred to be exposed on the mountains to wild beasts. He was obliged to fetch water for himself from the monastery well, and when, on one occasion, he was laid up for several days by an injury to his foot, none of the brothers ever thought of bringing him water. In winter he was allowed no fire, and he had often to wait till the frozen water in his cell was melted by the sun before he could wash or drink. The vision of the light

[1] Niceph. Greg. ii. pp. 1045-6.

of the Transfiguration did not transfigure the character of
its beholders.

During this trying period of his life one ray of comfort
wandered into the cell of the persecuted man. On the
13th December 1351, in the dead of night, while the
precincts of the monastery were crowded with worshippers
attending the vigil of the festival of the Conception of the
Theotokos, a strange figure climbed into the prisoner's
room through an open window. It proved to be an old
friend and former pupil named Agathangelus, who had
not been seen for ten years owing to his absence from
the city. Taking advantage of the darkness and of the
absorption of the monks in the services of the festival, he
had made this attempt to visit his revered master. Eagerly
and hurriedly, for the time at their command was short, the
two friends recounted the story of their lives while separated.
Rapidly Agathangelus sketched the course of affairs in State
and Church since the seclusion of Nicephorus Gregoras ;
and the brief visit ended and seemed a dream. But the
devoted disciple was not satisfied with a single interview.
Six months later he contrived to see his master again, and,
encouraged by success, saw him again three times, though
at long intervals, during the three years that Nicephorus
Gregoras was detained in the Chora. One great object of
these visits was to keep the prisoner informed of events
in the world beyond the walls of his cell, and on the basis
of the information thus supplied Nicephorus Gregoras wrote
part of his important history. When at length, in 1354,
John Cantucuzene was driven from the throne, and John
Palaeologus reigned in his stead, Nicephorus was liberated,[1]
and to the last defended the opinions for which he had
suffered.

Another name associated with the Chora at this time is
that of Michael Tornikes, Grand Constable in the reign of
Andronicus II. He was related, on his mother's side, to
the emperor, and stood in high favour at court not only
on account of that kinship, but because of the talents,
character, and administrative ability which he displayed.

[1] Niceph. Greg. iii. p. 243.

He was, moreover, a friend of Theodore Metochites, and his political supporter in the efforts made to end the strife between Andronicus II. and Andronicus III.[1] Upon his death, Tornikes was buried in the parecclesion of the Chora, and the epitaph composed in his honour has kept its place there to this day (Plate XCII.).

In 1342, Sabbas, a monk of the monastery of Vatopedi, who came to Constantinople as a member of a deputation from Mount Athos to reconcile the Regent Anna of Savoy with Cantacuzene, was confined in the Chora on the failure of that mission.[2]

In view of its proximity to the landward walls, the Chora acquired great importance during the fatal siege of 1453. For the inhabitants of the beleagured capital placed their hope for deliverance more upon the saints they worshipped than upon their own prowess ; the spiritual host enshrined in their churches was deemed mightier than the warriors who manned the towers of the fortifications. The sanctuaries beside the walls constituted the strongest bulwarks from which the 'God protected city' was to be defended, not with earthly, but with heavenly weapons. The eikon of the Theotokos Hodegetria was, therefore, taken to the Chora to guard the post of danger.

It represented the Theotokos as the Leader of God's people in war, and around it gathered memories of wonderful deliverances and glorious triumphs, making it seem the banner of wingless victory. When the Saracens besieged the city the eikon was carried round the fortifications, and the enemy had fled. It led Zimisces in his victorious campaign against the Russians ; it was borne round the fortifications when Branas assailed the capital in the reign of Isaac Angelus, and the foe disappeared ; and when Constantinople was recovered from the Latins, Michael Palaeologus only expressed the general sentiment in placing the eikon on a triumphal car, and causing it to enter the city before him, while he humbly followed on foot as far as the Studion. But the glory of the days of old had departed, and no sooner did the troops of Sultan

[1] Cantacuzene, i. p. 54.　　　　[2] Cantacuzene, ii. p. 209.

Mehemed force the Gate of Charisius (Edirné Kapoussi) than they made for the Chora, and cut the image to pieces. The church of S. Saviour in the Chora was the first Christian sanctuary to fall into the hands of the Moslem masters of Constantinople.

The building was converted into a mosque by Ali Atik Pasha, Grand Vizier, between 1495 and 1511, in the reign of Bajazet II. Gyllius visited the church in 1580, and expatiates upon the beauty of its marble revetment, but makes no reference to its mosaics and frescoes.[1] This, some authorities think, proves that these decorations were then concealed from view, because objectionable in a place consecrated to Moslem worship. But the silence of the traveller may be due to the brevity of his description of the church.

There is evidence that the building has suffered much since the Turkish conquest from earthquake and from fire, but the precise dates of these disasters cannot be accurately determined. The mosque disappeared from general view until 1860, when it was discovered by a Greek architect, the late Pelopidas D. Kouppas. Mr. Carlton Cumberbatch, then the British Consul at Constantinople, was informed of the fact and spread the news of the fortunate find.

The building was in a pitiful condition. The principal dome and the dome of the diaconicon had fallen in ; the walls and vaults were cracked in many places and black with smoke ; wind, and rain, and snow had long had free course to do what mischief they pleased. Happily there still remained too much beauty to be ignored, and the Government was persuaded to take the work of restoration in hand. The building now takes rank with the most

---

[1] *De top. C.P.* iv. c. 4 :—Inter palatium Constantini et portam urbis Adrianopolitanam extat ædes in septimo (?) colle, quæ etsi jam tot secula sit intra urbem tamen etiamnum χριστὸς χώρας appellatur, ex eo, quod olim esset extra urbem. Ex tribus partibus, ut mos est Græcorum ædium sacrarum, porticu cingitur. Parietes ejus intrinsecus vestiti crustis marmoris varii quadratis, ita inter se conjunctis ut distinguantur ab immo sursum versus modulis astragalorum, aliorum baccatorum, aliorum ter etiam sine baccis. Supra quadratas crustas discurrunt tres fasciæ et tres velut astragali, quorum duo teretes, supremus quadratus velut regula. Supra fasciam, denticuli ; supra denticulos, folia Corinthia. Denique marmor sic mensulis distinguitur ut in commissuris eluceat labor Corinthicus. Sed is plenior apparet in æde Sophiæ.

interesting sights of the capital, presenting one of the finest embodiments of the ideal which inspired Byzantine art.

Architectural Features

As the history of the church prepares us to expect, the building presents a very irregular plan. The central area is a short-armed Greek cross surmounted by a dome, and terminating to the east in a large apse flanked by side chapels

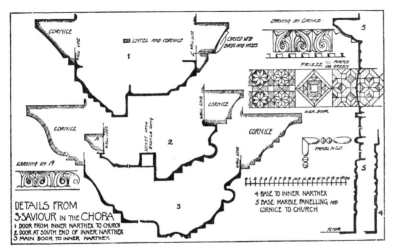

FIG. 99.

now disconnected from it. To the west are two narthexes, on the south a parecclesion, and on the north a gallery in two stories.

As the central part of the church is the oldest and of the greatest interest, the description will begin with the interior, and deal afterwards with the later exterior accretions.

Only two doors lead from the inner narthex to the church, one of them in the centre of the axis and the other to the north. The absence of the corresponding and customary third door, for which there is space on the south side, should be noticed, as it throws light on the original plan of the building. The doors are beautifully treated with marble

X

mouldings and panelled ingoes ; the door to the north recalls the sculptured door in the south gallery of S. Sophia, but, unfortunately, the carved work of the panels has been destroyed. Above the central door, on the interior, is a porphyry cornice carved with peacocks drinking at fountains (Plate LXXXVII.). Large portions of the beautiful marble revetment on the walls of the church happily remain intact, and nowhere else in Constantinople, except in S. Sophia, can this splendid method of colour decoration be studied to greater advantage. Slabs of various marbles have been split and placed on the walls so as to form patterns in the veining. The lower part is designed as a dado in Proconessian striped marble, with upright posts of dark red at the angles and at intervals on the longer stretches of wall, and rests on a moulded marble base. Above the dado are two bands, red and green, separated from the dado and from each other by white fillets. The upper part is filled in with large panels, especially fine slabs of brown, green, or purple having been selected to form the centre panels. The plainer slabs of the side panels are framed in red or green borders, and outlined with fillets of white marble either plain or carved with the ' bead and reel.' The arches have radiating voussoirs, and the arch spandrils and the frieze under the cornice are inlaid with scroll and geometrical designs in black, white, and coloured marbles. The cornice is of grey marble with a ' cyma recta' section, and is carved with an upright leaf.[1]

On the eastern walls of the north and south cross arms, and flanking the apse, eikon frames similar to those in the Diaconissa (p. 186) are inserted. The northern frame encloses a mosaic figure of Christ holding in His hands an open book, on which are the words, ' Come unto Me all ye who labour and are heavy laden.' [2] In the corresponding frame to the south is the figure of the Virgin, and, above it, an arch of overhanging acanthus leaves enclosed within a square frame with half figures of angels in the spandrils. The arch encloses a medallion bust, the head of which is defaced, but which represented the Saviour, as is proved by the indication

---

[1] Cf. description by Gyllius, *De top. C.P.* iv. c. 4.

[2] δεῦτε πρός με πάντες οἱ κοπιῶντες καὶ πεφορτισμένοι κἀγώ. . . .—Matt. xi. 28.

of a cross on the aureola. The spaces at the sides of the medallion are filled in with a pierced scroll showing a dark slab of porphyry behind it, making a very beautiful arrangement. These frames are distant from the eikonostasis, which stretched across the front of the bema arch, nearer to the apse. On the south side are two doors leading to the parecclesion, and on the north side above the cornice is a small window from the north gallery.

The dome rests on a ribbed drum of sixteen concave segments, and is pierced by eight windows corresponding to the octagonal form of the exterior. The original crown has fallen and been replaced by the present plain Turkish dome. The prothesis and the diaconicon are represented by chapels to north and south of the apse. As already stated, they do not now communicate with the bema, although the position of the old passages between them and the bema is marked by niches in the marble revetment. From the fact that the Byzantine marble work is continued across these passages it is evident that the chapels were cut off from the apse in Byzantine days. The north chapel is covered by a drum dome of eight concave sections, and is entered from the lower story of the gallery on the north side of the church. It should be noticed that the chapel is not placed axially to this gallery. The south chapel is covered by a plain drum dome, and is now entered from the parecclesion, evidently as the result of the alterations made when the parecclesion was added.

The exterior is very simply treated. The side apses show three sides of an octagon. The central apse has five sides of a very flat polygon, and is decorated with hollow niches on each side of a large triple window. It was at one time supported by a large double flying buttress, but the lower arch has fallen in. As the buttress does not bond with the wall it was evidently a later addition.

The inner narthex is entered from the outer narthex by a door to the west. It is with its resplendent marble revetment and brilliant mosaics a singularly perfect and beautiful piece of work, one of the finest gems of Byzantine art. It is divided into four bays, and is not symmetrically placed to the church. The door stands opposite to the large door of the church and is in the central axis of the building. The bay which it occupies and that immediately to the north are covered by dome vaults resting on strong transverse arches and shallow segmental wall arches.[1] The northern end bay is covered with a drum dome of sixteen hollow segments pierced by eight windows. The bay to the south of the door is considerably larger than the other bays, and is covered by a dome similar in character to that over the northern end bay but of greater diameter. At the south end of the narthex a small door leads to the return bay of the outer narthex in front of the parecclesion.

The double-storied annex or gallery on the north of the building is entered by a door in the north bay of the inner narthex. The lower story is covered by a barrel vault with strong transverse arches at intervals. Its door to the outside at the west end is now built up. At the east end a door, unsymmetrically placed, leads to the small chapel which was originally the prothesis. This story of the gallery seems never to have had windows. The upper story, reached by a stone stair at the west end in the thickness of the external wall, is paved in red tiles, covered with a barrel vault, and lighted by two small windows in the north wall and one at the east end. These windows still show grooves and bolt holes for casement windows or shutters opening inwards in two leaves (Figs. 19, 100). In the south wall is the little window overlooking the church.

The outer narthex has a single door to the exterior, placed on the central axial line, and is planned symmetrically. The central bay is larger than the others, and is covered by a dome vault resting on shallow wall arches. On each side are two bays covered by similar dome vaults, but as the bays are oblong, the wall arches are brought forward strongly so as to give a form more approaching the square as a base for the dome. The transverse arches are strongly pronounced and have wooden tie beams. At the south end two bays are returned to

---

[1] For the description of these vaults see p. 22.

form an entrance to the parecclesion. In these the transverse arches are even more strongly marked and rest on marble columns set against shallow pilasters. The cubical capitals are of white marble and very beautifully carved with figures of angels and acanthus wreaths. Any marble revetment which may once have covered the walls has disappeared,

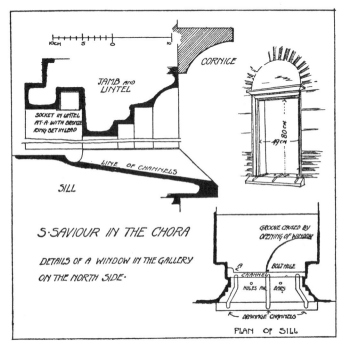

S·SAVIOUR IN THE CHORA

DETAILS OF A WINDOW IN THE GALLERY ON THE NORTH SIDE·

FIG. 100.

but mosaics depicting scenes in the Saviour's life still decorate the vaulting and the lunettes of the arches, whilst figures of saints appear upon the soffits. The mosaics are damaged and have lost some of their brilliancy ; the background is of gold, and the mosaic cubes are small, averaging about $\frac{1}{8}$ to $\frac{3}{16}$ of an inch.

The parecclesion is entered from the return bays of the outer narthex through a triple arcade, now partly built up. The capitals of the columns are Byzantine Corinthian, and retain sufficient traces of their former decoration in dark blue, gold, and red to give some idea of the effect of colour on marble in Byzantine churches.

The parecclesion is in two bays. The western bay is covered by a high twelve-sided drum dome, with windows in each side separated by flat ribs. In the compartments are figures of the archangels in tempera, with the legend, 'Holy Holy, Holy, is the Lord God.'

The eastern bay is covered by a dome vault, and terminates in an apse semicircular within and lighted by a triple window. It has neither prothesis nor diaconicon of its own, but communicates with the original diaconicon of the main church. The three transverse arches in the bay are tied with wooden tie beams carved with arabesques and retaining traces of gilding.

On the north and south walls of the western bay are large arches enclosed in square frames and with finely carved archivolts. Above the south arch is a slab inscribed with the epitaph to the memory of the celebrated general Tornikes. There are no indications of an entrance under the arch. It may have covered a niche, now built up, intended to receive a tomb, possibly the tomb of the sebastocrator Isaac.

The archivolt of the arch in the north wall is formed of acanthus leaves turned over at the points ; the spandrils are filled with the figures of the archangels Michael and Gabriel, bearing appropriate emblems, and above the crown of the arch is a small bust of Christ. In both arches the carved work is exactly like that of the eikon frame in the south-eastern pier of the church, and closely resembles the work on the lintel of the eikon frames in the church of the Diaconissa. Both archivolts were originally coloured, the background blue, the carved ornament gilt. The use of figures in the decoration of the church is remarkable. They are in bold relief and executed freely, but shown only from the waist up. The windows, like those in the outer narthex, have a central arch between two semi-circles (Fig. 63).

Two passages, which cut through the north wall, lead

from the parecclesion to the church. Off the passage to the west is a small chamber whose use is not apparent. It may be simply a space left over when the chapel was added. Higher up, in the thickness of the wall, about ten feet from the floor, and a little above the springing level of the vaulting in the parecclesion, is a long, narrow passage, lighted by a window at the east end, and covered by a small barrel vault, corbelled at the springing, on two courses of stone and three courses of brick laid horizontally, thus narrowing the space to a considerable degree. From this corbelling spring the vaulting courses, which are steeply inclined and run from both ends to the centre, where the resultant diamond-shaped opening is filled in with horizontal courses (Fig. 48). On the north side of the passage is a broad opening roughly built up, but which seems originally to have communicated with the south cross arm. The opening is almost central to the cross-arm, and is directly above the doors leading from the church to the parecclesion.

The exterior of the parecclesion and the outer narthex are treated with arcades in two orders of the usual type. On the piers of the arcades are semicircular shafts which in the parecclesion rise to the cornice, but on the west front stop at the springing course. Here they may have supported the wooden roof of a cloister or porch. The apse of the parecclesion has five sides with angle shafts and niches, alternately flat and concave in three stories. The north wall is a fine example of simple masonry in stripes of brick and stone, and with small archings and zigzag patterns in the spandrils of the arches.

Below the parecclesion are two long narrow cisterns having their entrance on the outside of the apse.[1]

The original plan of the church (Fig. 102). The greater part of the alterations made in the church date from Byzantine times, and the marble coverings then placed upon the walls

---

[1] Schmitt (*op. cit.* pp. 92-94) maintains that the parecclesion was originally the refectory of the monastery. But a refectory there would occupy a very unusual position. Nor do the frescoes on the walls of the parecclesion correspond to the decoration of the refectory with representations of flowers and of Christ's miracles, as described by Theodore Metochites : . . . κεκοσμήαται ἄνθεσι ποικίλοι ί τε πουλυχρούοισί τε βαφῶν . . . καί τε διαπερὲς ἀπηγέαται μυστήρια θωύματα Χριστοῦ.

have effectually covered up any traces which might have given a clue to the original form of the building. In consequence any attempt at restoration must be of a very tentative character.

It is evident that there has been a serious movement in the structure due to the weight of the dome and the thrust of the dome arches, for the walls below the dome are bent outwards in a very pronounced manner. It was in order to check this movement that the flying buttress was applied to the apse, and in all probability the enormous thickness of the walls surrounding the central cross is due to the same cause. Had the walls originally been as thick as at present it is hard to imagine that movement could have taken place.

The axial line from east to west, passing through the doors of both narthexes, divides the present building into two dissimilar parts. We know that the parecclesion is a later addition, and if it be removed and the plan of the north side repeated to the south the resulting plan bears a striking resemblance to S. Sophia at Salonica (Fig. 101). The position of the prothesis and diaconicon in particular is identical in the two churches.

Some proof that this was the original form of the building is given by the small chamber in the wall thickness between the church and the parecclesion. For it corresponds to the angle of the south 'aisle,' and on its west wall is a vertical break in the masonry which may be the jamb of the old door to the narthex.

This plan gives a narthex in five bays—the three centre ones low, the two outer covered by domes and leading to the 'aisles.' When the parecclesion was added, the south gallery and two bays of the inner narthex were swept away. The third door leading into the church was built up, and the present large domed bay added to the shortened narthex.

Traces of the older structure remain in the wall between the church and the parecclesion. The space already described, which originally opened from the passage at the higher level to the south cross-arm, corresponds in width both to the window above and to the space occupied by the doors below. At S. Sophia, Salonica, the side-arms are filled in with arcades in two stories forming an aisle and gallery. This is the normal domed basilica construction. Here, if we regard the floor of the upper passage (B on plan, p. 318) as the remains of the old gallery floor,—and no other view

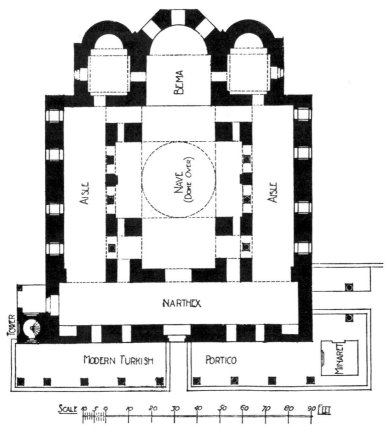

FIG. 101.—S. SOPHIA, SALONICA.

seems to account for its existence,—the internal elevation was in three stories, an aisle at the ground level, above it a gallery, and above that, in the arch tympanum, a triple window. Such an arrangement is, so far as we know, unique in a small church, but it is the arrangement used in S. Sophia, Constantinople, and may well have been derived

from that church.   The opening is only about one-half of
the space, leaving a broad pier at each side.   In this it
differs from S. Sophia, Salonica, but such side piers are
present in S. Sophia, Constantinople.   The diagrams show a
restoration of the plan and internal bay based on these
conclusions (Figs. 102, 103).

The gallery on the north side is an addition.   The

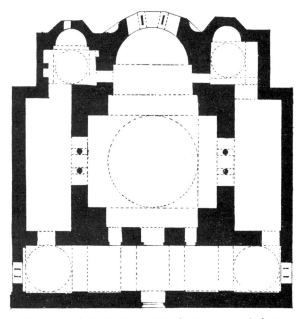

FIG. 102.—S. SAVIOUR IN THE CHORA (restored plan).

character of the brickwork and of the windows is later than
the central church, but the lack of windows on the ground
floor suggests that the 'aisle' was originally lighted from
the body of the church.   The vaulting gives no clue, nor
are there traces of an opening in the wall between the
'aisle' and the church.   The floor level is much higher
than that of the passage 'B' (p. 318) on the opposite side,
and seems to be a new level introduced when the addition
was made and the wall thickened.

If these conclusions are correct the church was originally

a domed basilica resembling S. Sophia, Salonica, in plan and S. Sophia, Constantinople, in elevation. The side dome arches had double arcades in two stories, and above them windows in the dome arches. There are at present no traces of a western gallery, but such may have existed below the present west windows. Later in the history of the church came alterations, which included the ribbed domes and the gallery on the north side. The side aisles still communicated with the church and the lateral chapels with the bema.

FIG. 103.—S. SAVIOUR IN THE CHORA (restored bay).

The filling up of the arcades, the thickening of the walls, the isolation of the lateral chapels, the removal of the southern aisle, the alteration of the narthex, the building of the parecclesion and outer narthex, and most of the decoration which forms the glory of the church, belong to the great work of restoration by Theodore Metochites early in the fourteenth century.

The representation of the church in the mosaic panel above the large door to the church shows a building with a central dome, a narthex terminating in domed bays, and a window in the west dome arch. It seems to represent the church as the artist was accustomed to see it previous to the additions (Fig. 115).

Plain cross plans, or cross plans with only one lateral gallery, are not unknown. The church of the Archangels, Sygé,[1] shows such a plan and is here reproduced for purposes of comparison.

[1] F. W. Hasluck. Bithynica, *B.S.A. Annual XIII.*, 1906-7.

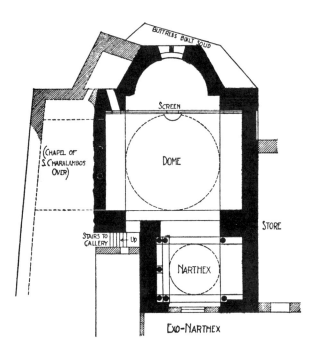

FIG. 104.—CHURCH OF THE ARCHANGELS AT SYGÉ.

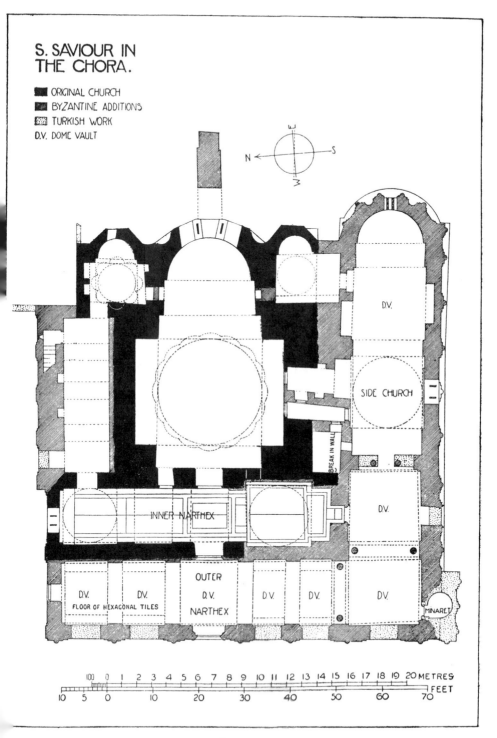

S. SAVIOUR IN
THE CHORA.

■ ORIGINAL CHURCH
▨ BYZANTINE ADDITIONS
▨ TURKISH WORK
D.V. DOME VAULT

N ← ⊕ → S
(E / W compass)

D.V.

SIDE CHURCH

BREAK IN WALL

D.V.

INNER NARTHEX

OUTER

D.V.   D.V.   D.V.   D.V.   D.V.   D.V.
FLOOR OF HEXAGONAL TILES   NARTHEX

MINARET

100 0 1 2 3 4 5 6 7 8 9 10 11 12 13 14 15 16 17 18 19 20 METRES
10   5 0   10   20   30   40   50   60   70 FEET

FIG. 105.

317

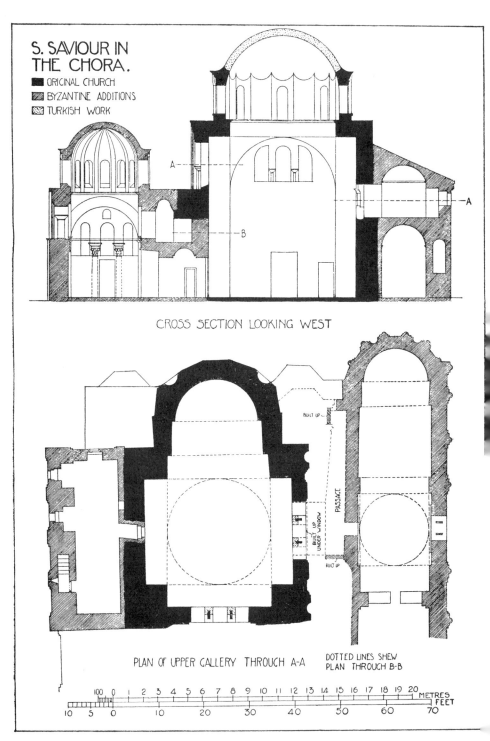

S. SAVIOUR IN THE CHORA.

■ ORIGINAL CHURCH
▨ BYZANTINE ADDITIONS
▧ TURKISH WORK

A

A

B

CROSS SECTION LOOKING WEST

BUILT UP

PASSAGE

BUILT UP
UNDER WINDOW

BUILT UP

PLAN OF UPPER GALLERY THROUGH A-A

DOTTED LINES SHEW
PLAN THROUGH B-B

100 0 1 2 3 4 5 6 7 8 9 10 11 12 13 14 15 16 17 18 19 20 METRES
                                                                              FEET
10 5 0   10   20   30   40   50   60   70

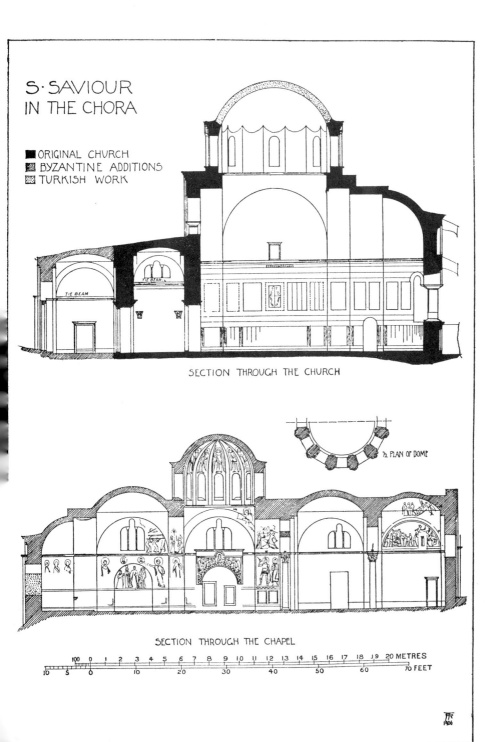

S·SAVIOUR
IN THE CHORA

■ ORIGINAL CHVRCH
▨ BYZANTINE ADDITIONS
▨ TVRKISH WORK

TIE BEAM

TIE BEAM

SECTION THROUGH THE CHURCH

½ PLAN OF DOME

SECTION THROUGH THE CHAPEL

FIGS. 108 AND 109.

319

S·SAVIOUR IN THE CHORA

PLAN OF DOME

■ ORIGINAL CHURCH
▨ BYZANTINE ADDITIONS

PLASTER

PLASTER

SECTION THROUGH INNER NARTHEX

LINE OF APSE OVER

GABLE OVER

CHURCH   SIDE CHAPEL

BUILT UP

PLAN OF GALLERY
BETWEEN CHURCH AND CHAPEL

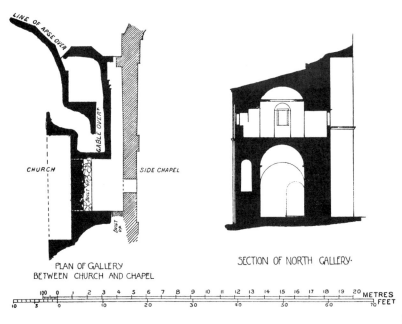

SECTION OF NORTH GALLERY·

100 0   1   2   3   4   5   6   7   8   9   10 11 12 13 14 15 16 17 18 19 20 METRES
10   5   0   10   20   30   40   50   60   70 FEET

CHAPTER XXIV

THE MOSAICS IN S. SAVIOUR IN THE CHORA

As stated already, the mosaics on the vaults and lunettes of the arches in the outer narthex of the church portray scenes from the life of Christ, as recorded in the canonical

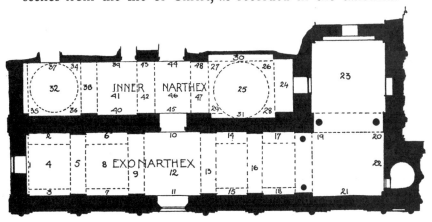

FIG. 114.—PLAN OF THE NARTHEXES OF THE CHURCH, INDICATING POSITION OF THEIR MOSAICS.

and the apocryphal Gospels, while on the faces and soffits of the arches are depicted the figures of saints 'who desired to look into these things.' Scenes from the Saviour's life are also portrayed in the two bays to the west of the parecclesion, and in the domes and southern bay of the inner narthex. Inscriptions on the mosaics explain the subjects depicted. The scenes will be described according to the groups they form in the compartments of the narthex.

Outer Narthex

First Bay (at the north end).

1. In the northern lunette.—The angel announcing to Joseph, in a
   dream, the birth of Jesus.   To the right, journey of Joseph
   and Mary from Nazareth to Bethlehem.   Simon the son of
   Joseph walks ahead, carrying a bundle.   In the background,
   meeting of Mary and Elizabeth.

2. In the eastern lunette.—The registration of Joseph and Mary at
   Bethlehem before Cyrenius.   (Said to be unique in the East.[1])
   On the arch over the eastern lunette.—Busts (in medallions)
   of SS. Mardarius, Auxentius (only one letter of the name remains), SS. Eustratius, Orestes.

3. On the western lunette.—The Holy Family on the way to the
   first passover of Jesus at Jerusalem.
   On the arch over the western lunette.—The busts (in medallions)
   of SS. Anempodistus, Elpidephorus, Akindynus, Aphthonius,
   Pegasius.

4. In the vault.—The scene has disappeared.   Possibly it represented
   Jesus among the doctors in the temple.

5. On the soffit of the transverse arch, between the first and second
   bays.—To the east, S. Andronicus ; to the west, S. Tarachus.

Second Bay

6. In the eastern lunette.—The birth of Jesus.   In the background,
   to left, the angel appearing to the shepherds ; to right, the
   magi beholding the star shining over the manger in which lies
   the Holy Child, while an ox and an ass feed in it.   In the
   centre, Mary on a couch.   In the foreground, to left, two
   women bathing the Holy Child ; to the right, Joseph seated
   on the ground and gazing at the Holy Child.
   On the arch above the eastern lunette.—The busts (in medallions)
   of SS. Philemon, Leukius, Kallinikus, Thyrsus, Apollonius.

7. In the western lunette.—Return of the Holy Family from Egypt
   to Nazareth.
   In the arch above the western lunette.—The busts (in medallions)
   of SS. Engraphus (?), Menas, Hermogenes, Laurus, Florus,
   Menas, Victor, Vikentius.

8. In the vault.—The baptism of Jesus ; the scenes in the tempta-
   tion of Jesus.

9. On the second transverse arch.—To the east, S. George ; to
   the west, S. Demetrius.

---

[1] Diehl, *Études byzantines : Les mosaïques de Kahrié Djami.*

The Third or Central Bay

10. In the eastern lunette, over the door leading to the inner narthex.—Christ in the act of benediction.
11. In the western lunette.—The Theotokos, in the attitude of prayer, with the Holy Child, in a nimbus, on her breast ; the legend
$$\overline{\text{MP}} \qquad \overline{\Theta\Upsilon}$$
H ΧΩΡΑ ΤΟΥ ΑΧΩΡΗΤΟΥ (the country of the Infinite) ; on the right and left, an angel.
12. In the vault.—In the north-eastern corner, the miracle of water turned into wine.   The date 1303, in Arabic numerals, is on this mosaic.   In the south-eastern corner, the miracle of the loaves.
    These mosaics, placed on either side of the figure of Christ, are emblems of His character as the Giver of Life.
    In the north-western corner.—The sacrifice of a white bullock.
    In the south-eastern corner.—The second miracle of the loaves.
13. On the third transverse arch.—Two saints, not named.

The Fourth Bay

14. In the eastern lunette.—To the left, the magi, on horseback, guided by a star, on their way to Jerusalem ; to the right, the magi before Herod.
    On the arch above.—The busts (in medallions) of SS. Abibus, Ghourias, Samonas.
15. In the western lunette.—Elizabeth fleeing with her child John from a soldier who pursues her with a drawn sword in his hand.
    The scenes in the vault have disappeared.
16. On the fourth transverse arch.—Two saints, not named.

The Fifth Bay

17. In the eastern lunette.—Herod inquiring of the priests where the Christ should be born.
    The busts of three saints on the arch above have disappeared.
18. In the western lunette.—Mothers at Bethlehem seated on the ground, and mourning the death of their infant children.
    The mosaics in other parts of this bay have disappeared.

The Outer Bay fronting the parecclesion

In the eastern pendentive.—To the left (19) the healing of a paralytic ; to the right (20) the healing of the man sick of the dropsy.
21. In the western pendentive.—To the left, the healing of another paralytic ; to the right, Christ with the Samaritan woman at

the well of Sychar ; in the lunette, the massacre of the Innocents at Bethlehem.

22. In the southern lunette.—To the left, Herod orders the massacre of the Innocents at Bethlehem ; to the right, the massacre of the Innocents.

　　The other mosaics in this bay have disappeared.

The Inner Bay fronting the parecclesion

23. In the vault.—In the south-western corner. Uncertain. Possibly, the fall of the idols in Egypt at the presence of the Holy Child ; to the south of that scene, Zacchaeus on the sycamore tree.

INNER NARTHEX

First Bay (at the south end of the narthex)

24. On the soffit of the first transverse arch.—To the east, the healing of the man with a withered arm ; to the west, the healing of a leper.

South Dome

25. In the crown.—Christ the Pantokrator.

　　In the flutings, thirty-nine figures, arranged in two tiers, representing the ancestors of Christ from Adam to Esrom, Japhet, and the eleven sons of Jacob not in the line of ancestry.

26. On the south-eastern pendentive.—The healing of the woman with a bloody issue.

27. On the north-eastern pendentive.—The healing of Peter's mother-in-law.

28. On the south-western pendentive.—The healing of a deaf and dumb man.

29. On the north-western pendentive.—The healing of two blind men at Jericho.

30. On the eastern wall below the dome, colossal figures of Mary and Christ, technically named the Deësis.

31. On the opposite wall.—Christ healing divers diseases.

　　The mosaics in the three other bays of this narthex depict scenes in the life of Mary as described in the apocryphal Protoevangelium of S. James and other apocryphal Gospels.[1]

First Bay (at northern end).—The North Dome

32. In the centre.—The Theotokos ; in the flutings, twenty-seven figures arranged in two tiers representing sixteen royal

---

[1] An English translation of the Protoevangelium is found in the Ante-Nicene Christian Library, vol. xvi.

ancestors of Christ, from David to Salathiel, and Melchisedec, Ananias, Azarias, Misael, Daniel, Joshua, Moses, Aaron, Ur, Samuel, Job.

33. In the north-eastern pendentive.—The scene has disappeared.

34. In the south-eastern pendentive.—S. Joachim (Mary's father) with his sheep in the desert, praying and mourning that his offerings have been rejected because he was childless.

35. In the north-western pendentive.—The High Priest judging Mary.

36. In the south-western pendentive.—The Annunciation to Mary.

37. In the eastern lunette below the dome.—The Annunciation to S. Anna, the mother of Mary.

38. On the soffit of the transverse arch between the first and second bays.—To the east, the meeting of S. Anna and S. Joachim ; to the west, Joseph taking leave of Mary before his home, and proceeding to his work in another part of the country, accompanied by a servant.

Second Bay

39. In the eastern lunette.—The birth of Mary.

40. In the western lunette.—Joseph receiving the rod which marks him the successful suitor for Mary's hand, and taking her as his bride-elect.

41. In the vault.—To the east, Mary held in the arms of S. Joachim, receiving the blessing of three priests seated at a banquet ; to the west, the child Mary caressed by her parents. This scene shows much feeling.

42. On the soffit of the transverse arch.—To the east, Mary taking her first seven steps ἡ ἑπταβηματίζουσα ; to the west, the high priest praying before the rods, one of which, by blossoming, will designate the future husband of Mary.

43. On the eastern wall, to the north of the main entrance into the church.—The Apostle Peter with the keys in his hand.

The Third Bay

44. In the lunette over the main entrance to the church.—Theodore Metochites on his knees offering the church to Christ seated on a throne. The legend ὁ κτήτωρ λογοθέτης τοῦ γεννικοῦ Θεόδωρος ὁ Μετοχίτης.[1]

---

[1] The remarkable head-dress he wears was given him as a special distinction by the Emperor Andronicus II. Palaeologus. The poet Philes (ode 41 in the appendix to vol. ii. of his works, lines 117-19) says φοροῦντα χρυσῆν ἐρυθρὰν τὴν καλύπτραν ἣν δῶρον αὐτῷ συνανέχοντι κράτος Ἄναξ ὁ λαμπρὸς Ἀνδρόνικος παρέσχε.

45. In the western lunette.—Mary receiving purple and scarlet wool to weave in the veil of the temple.

46. In the vault.— On the east, Mary admitted to the Holy of Holies when three years of age, lest she should go back to the world ; on the west, the procession of maidens escorting Mary to the temple.

47. The third transverse arch.—To the east, Mary in the temple receiving bread from the archangel Gabriel ; to the west, Mary in the temple receiving instruction.

48. On the eastern wall, to the south side of the main entrance to the church. —The Apostle Paul.

FIG. 115.—MODEL OF THE CHURCH OF S. SAVIOUR IN THE CHORA.

The scenes represented on these mosaics are not peculiar to this church, but are a selection from cycles of subjects which from the eleventh century became favourite themes for pictorial treatment on the walls of important churches in the Byzantine world. Several of these scenes are found portrayed also at Daphni, Mistra, S. Sophia at Kiev, in the churches of Mt. Athos, on diptychs and manuscripts,[1] as well as in the chapel of the arena at Padua. The cycle of subjects taken from the life of Mary was developed mainly in Syria, and Schmitt[2] goes so far as to maintain that the mosaics of the Chora are copies of Syrian mosaics executed by a Syrian artist, when the church was restored in the ninth century by Michael Syncellus, who, it will be remembered, came from Syria.

Kondakoff assigns most of the mosaics to the Comnenian restoration of the church by Maria Ducaena in the eleventh or twelfth century. One of them at least, the Deësis, has survived ; and there may be others of that period, for, as that mosaic proves, the narthex of the church was decorated when

---

[1] A work reproducing, under the Pope's authority, the eighty-two miniatures illustrating the *Life of the Madonna*, which was composed by a monk James in the twelfth century (*Cod. Vatic. Gr.* 1162), is announced (Danesi, Editore, Roma, 1911), with a preface and descriptions of the miniatures by Cosimo Stornajolo. The miniatures are said to rival those of the Greek Codex 1028 in the National Library in Paris.   [2] *Op. cit.* pp. 134-41.

the church was restored by that benefactress of the Chora. But the testimony of Nicephorus Gregoras,[1] of Theodore Metochites,[2] and the date marked on the scene representing the miracle of the wine at Cana, on the right of the figure of Christ over the door leading from the outer to the inner narthex, prove these mosaics to be as a whole the production of the fourteenth century. And this conclusion is confirmed by their unlikeness to mosaic work in the twelfth century, and by their affinity to other work of the same character done in the fourteenth century.[3]

In fact, the mosaics in the Chora represent a remarkable revival in the history of Byzantine art. They are characterised by a comparative freedom from tradition, by closer approximation to reality and nature, by a charm and a sympathetic quality, and by a scheme of colour that indicate the coming of a new age and spirit. Curiously enough, they are contemporary with the frescoes of Giotto at Padua (1303-1306). But whatever points of similarity may be detected between them and the work of the Italian artist, or between them and the Italian school before Giotto, should be explained as due to a common stock of traditions and to the simultaneous awakening of a new intellectual and artistic life in the East and the West, rather than to any direct influence of one school of art upon another. The mosaics of the Chora are thoroughly Byzantine.[4]

The Frescoes in the Parecclesion :—

1. Round the apse : Six Fathers of the Church (only one figure remains, and that badly damaged. No names are inscribed).
2. In the vault of the apse : a full-length figure of Christ in a vesica dotted with stars. On either side are groups of figures.
3. In the crown of the apse-arch : an angel in a medallion.

---

[1] i. p. 303.   [2] *Carmina* (ed. Treu), A. 1004, 1039-1042 ; B. 322-334.
[3] Diehl, *Études byzantines : Les mosaïques de Kahrié Djami.*
[4] See on the whole subject, C. Diehl, in the *Gazette des Beaux-Arts*, troisième période, tome 33, and in his *Manuel d'art byzantin*, pp. 732-41 ; Schmitt in his monograph on the Chora ; Mühlmann, *Archiv für christliche Kunst*, 1886-87.

4. In the northern wall, next the apse : Christ with two
   attendants ; in the background a walled city.

   The Eastern Bay.

On the northern wall :

5. Above the arched recess : two medallion heads of SS. Sergius
   and Bacchus.

6. Portions of the figure of a warrior.

7. In the arch above Nos. 5 and 6 : the Gate of Paradise.

8. In the centre, one of the cherubims on a pillar. On the
   left hand, a multitude, painted on black background
   outside Paradise ; on the right, Paradise, a garden full of
   trees on a white background. Here also are John the
   Baptist and a figure, probably the Virgin and Child, on
   a throne, attended by two angels.

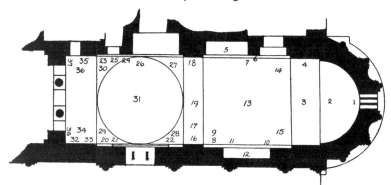

FIG. 116.—PLAN OF THE PARECCLESION, INDICATING POSITIONS OF ITS
FRESCOES.

On the southern wall :

8. A portion of the figure of an armed angel.

   Above No. 8 and at the side of the window :

9. Two men carrying a bier or platform. In front of them
   a third person giving directions.

10. In the arched recess : full-length figures of Andronicus II.
    and his family. In the soffit of the arch, the head of
    Christ in a medallion, with rays issuing from behind the
    aureola.

11. and 12. In the spandrils above the recess : two heads in
    medallions.

13. In the dome vault : the Last Judgment. Christ in
    judgment fills the centre ; behind Him are the twenty-
    four elders seated on a long throne ; farther back is
    gathered the heavenly host.

14. On the north-eastern pendentive : the Virgin and Child in a Paradise, with trees on a white background.
15. On the south-eastern pendentive : the Mouth of Hell.
16. On the south pilaster of the dome : an armed angel.
17. Above that angel, on the arch : a man bearing the Seven-Branched Candlestick, and beside him another man bearing with both hands some object above his head, perhaps the Table of Shew Bread.
18. On the northern pilaster : a warrior.
19. In the centre of the arch: the Head of Christ in a medallion.
   The Western Bay.
20. At the south-western corner where the wall is much damaged, a saint.
21. Above No. 20, to the west of the window : Christ appearing to His disciples.
22. To the east of the window, an indistinct scene, perhaps the Entombment.
23. At the north-western corner : S. Samona.
24. A saint, not named.
25. Over the door two saints, one of whom holds a cross.
26. The northern archway : In the centre is the door to the narrow passage between the parecclesion and the church. To the left, Jacob's Ladder ; to the right, Moses at the Burning Bush. In the bush is a medallion of the Virgin and Child, and from the bush an angel addresses Moses, who holds his veil in his hand.
27, 28, 29, 30. In the pendentives of the dome : the Four Evangelists sitting at desks.
31. The dome is divided into twelve segments by ribs, and is pierced by twelve windows. Above each window is an angel holding a spear, and below him is the legend ' Holy.' In the crown are the Virgin and Child in a medallion.
32. A saint holding a small cross ; below, in the south wall, the archivolt with the epitaph to Tornikes above it.
33. A warrior saint with his sword and shield.
34. Above Nos. 32 and 33 on the arch, a figure, clad in a white mantle and blue robe with a scroll in his hand, points to an angel, who holds his drawn sword in the right hand and the scabbard in the left hand, and seems to be attacking several persons in the right-hand corner. Behind him is a walled and fortified city, probably Jericho.
35. On the north wall : S. Eutadius.
36. The Adoration by the magi.
37, 38. On the west wall : the figures of two saints, not named.

Epitaph in honour of Tornikes :—

ὅσους ἂν ἀθροίζοι τις ἐνθάδε κρότους
νεκροὺς ὁ ταφεὶς ἐξελέγξει Τορνίκης,
ὁ τρὶς ἀριστεὺς ἢ κονσταῦλος μέγας,
ὥσπερ μίμους, βέλτιστε, πιθήκους λέων.
5 ὅς, βασιλικῶν ἀποτεχθεὶς αἱμάτων,
παρέσχεν αὐτοῖς προσφυῆ καὶ τὸν τρόπον.
ποῖον γὰρ οὐκ ἦν ἀρετῆς εἶδος φέρων,
ὡς ὁ πρέπων ἕκαστον ἐζήτει χρόνος;
βουληφόρος δ' οὖν, καὶ πρὸ τῆς ἡλικίας
10 καὶ δημαγωγός, καὶ κριτὴς ἦν ἀγχίνους.
καὶ πρὸς μὲν ἐχθροὺς τακτικὴν ἔπνει φλόγα,
κεραυνὸς ὢν ἄφυκτος αὐτοῖς ἀθρόοις,
τῇ δὲ στρατιᾷ πατρικῶς ἐπεστάτει,
φρουρῶν τὰ κοινά, μὴ κλαπῇ τὸ συμφέρον.
15 κήδους δὲ τυχὼν εὐγενοῦς καὶ κοσμίου
καὶ βασιλικὸν προσλαβὼν αὖθις γένος
καὶ λαμπρὸν ὑπόδειγμα παρεὶς τὸν βίον,
κεῖται μοναστὴς εὐτελὴς ἐν ὀστέοις.
ἥλιε καὶ γῆ καὶ τελευταῖοι κρότοι.
20 πενθεῖ δὲ μικροῦ πᾶν τὸ Ῥωμαίων γένος,
ὅσον περ αὐτὸν ἀγνοοῦν οὐ τυγχάνει.
ἀλλ' ὦ μόνε, ζῶν καὶ μεθιστῶν τὰς φύσεις,
εἴ πού τι καὶ πέπραχεν αὐτῷ μὴ πρέπον
λύσιν παρασχὼν τὴν Ἐδὲν κλῆρον δίδου.

In line 7 the inscription reads φϲρωΝ instead of φέρων ; in line 23 ΙΙρϲπΟΝ for πρέπον.

Good Friend !   However many dead applauses (celebrities)
One may collect here,
The entombed Tornikes, who was thrice a foremost man or Grand
   Constable,
Will put them to shame as a lion will put to shame mimicking apes.
He who was by birth of royal blood,
Presented also a manner of life conformed to that descent.
For what form of virtue did he not possess
Such as the fitting occasion demanded each ?
Therefore he was a councillor before the usual age,
And a popular leader and an acute judge,
And upon enemies he breathed a strategic flame (such as military
   rules required),
And was an irresistible thunderbolt upon their serried ranks.

He presided over the army like a father,
Guarding the commonweal lest any advantage to it should be stolen.
Contracting a highly-born and seemly marriage connection,
And securing thus again royal affinity,[1]
And leaving his life as a splendid example,
He lies a poor monk among bones !
O sun, O earth, O final applauses !
Well-nigh the whole Roman race laments him,
As much of it as is not ignorant of him.
But O only living One and transformer of natures,
If perchance he did aught that was not fitting for him,
Granting him pardon, give him Eden as his inheritance.[2]

---

[1] Alludes to his marriage with a relative of the imperial family.

[2] In the translation I have been assisted by Sir W. M. Ramsay, Professor Bury, and Mr. E. M. Antoniadi. The meaning of τελευταῖοι κρότοι is not clear. Various interpretations have been suggested ; to read βροτοί, mortals, instead of κρότοι, and to construe τελευταῖοι adverbially, 'finally, O mortals !' ; to understand a reference to the judgment day, 'O applauses given at the final judgment' ; to take the phrase as equivalent to, 'O celebrities at (or to) the very end of time' ; to understand it as signifying the eulogies actually given to the deceased by the poet. Professor Tendès, of Athens, whom I thank for his courtesy in this connection, suggests that the meaning is similar to that of the phrase τὰ τελευταιά in the modern Greek form of eulogy, ἔκαμε πολλά, ἀλλὰ τὰ τελευταιά του. . . . 'He did many things, but his last performances !' (surpassed all his previous deeds). Here the meaning would therefore be, 'O grandest achievements that men praise !'

CHAPTER XXV

THE dating of the Constantinople churches is a problem of great difficulty, and, in the absence of documentary evidence, we must often be contented with very indefinite suggestions. Many churches are known to have been founded at dates which are evidently earlier than the existing buildings, and have apparently been rebuilt at some later date of which the record has been lost. Other churches are known to have been 'repaired,' and here the question of how far 'repair' means 'rebuilding' is sometimes insoluble. Repair may mean simply a fresh coat of paint.

The architectural characteristics afford a certain clue, and the following chronological scheme has been drawn up by their guidance :—

The pre-Justinian period is characterised by simple construction and detail of a late Roman type. Of this we have one example—the basilica of S. John of the Studion, founded about 463. The existing building appears to be original.

The Justinian period commences with the beginning of the sixth century. It is characterised by the development of the drumless dome on pendentives. The plan is complicated, and the buildings are large in comparison with those of later date. To this period belong SS. Sergius and Bacchus (527 A.D.), the baptistery of S. Sophia, and 'the Great Church' of S. Sophia itself. S. Andrew in Krisei and S. Saviour in the Chora probably date from this period. The carved detail of the former closely resembles that of

332

SS. Sergius and Bacchus, and the plan of the latter connects it with S. Sophia, Salonica (sixth century).

The Justinian period roughly includes the seventh century, and is followed by a long decline, marked by the great iconoclastic controversy which lasted almost until the middle of the ninth century. To this period belongs S. Irene (740 A.D.). In plan it is a double-domed cross church. In the arrangement of the dome - arches and galleries it resembles S. Theodosia, whilst in the presence of a western gallery over the narthex and in the number of columns in the ' nave arcade ' it is like S. Sophia.

The accession of Basil the Macedonian (867 A.D.) marks the beginning of the second great period—the ' Basilian Renaissance.' We know that this was a period of great religious activity, and though we have, unfortunately, no known dates to guide us, the development of plan leads us to place a group of churches in the ninth, tenth, and eleventh centuries. These are S. Mary Pammakaristos, S. Mary Panachrantos, S. Theodosia, S. Mary Diaconissa, and SS. Peter and Mark.

They are all churches of considerable size ; S. Mary Diaconissa and S. Theodosia being indeed large. They are characterised by the use of the ambulatory and domed cross plans. The carving is coarse and the capitals are of the clumsy Byzantine Corinthian type. The dome is raised on a high drum in S. Mary Pammakaristos and S. Mary Panachrantos, though this may be a later addition. The domes of the other three churches seem to be Turkish. S. Mary Pammakaristos and the south church in S. Mary Panachrantos are identical in plan with S. Andrew in Krisei, and it would be possible to date them earlier had we any evidence whatsoever. Unfortunately both have been very much altered.

S. Theodosia, S. Mary Diaconissa, and SS. Peter and Mark, taken in this order, form a series showing the gradual disappearance of the galleries and the evolution of the domed cross church into the ' four columned ' church of the next period.

The Myrelaion (919-945), if the present church is of

that date, is an unusually early example of this four-columned type. It is generally considered that this plan type dates at the earliest from the eleventh century. There is, however, no reason to believe that the church was rebuilt later ; it is a perfectly normal example of its class, and nowhere is an early example more probable than in Constantinople. The Myrelaion may accordingly be taken as marking the commencement of the late Byzantine period in Constantinople.

The churches are now smaller ; the gynecaeum, where present, is placed over the narthex ; the use of patterning in the brickwork of the exterior, which occurs in some of the Basilian churches (*e.g.* the cornice of S. Theodosia), now becomes important, and alternate coursing in brick and stone is used with great effect. From this time onwards narthexes were frequently added to the existing churches.

S. Saviour Pantokrator (1118-1143 A.D.) is the largest late church in Constantinople, and is an unusually large church of its type. S. Saviour Pantepoptes (1081-1118), S. Theodore, and S. John in Trullo, belong to the same class. The last, with its circular dome and apse, is probably the latest of the three. S. Thekla (1057-1059) and Bogdan Serai are examples of hall churches of the same period.

The monastery of Manuel was founded in 829-842 A.D., but the building believed to be the refectory is probably much later. As part of the monastery it might, of course, have been built at any date subsequent to the foundation of the House.

The architecture of the Sanjakdar does not correspond to the date of the foundation of the monastery of the Gastria in the ninth century. The building is certainly of late date, subsequent to the eleventh century. Of the Balaban Mesjedi it is impossible to say anything. It is the remnant of some Byzantine structure.

From 1204 to 1261, during the Latin Empire, we need not look for much building in the Greek Church. Soon after the fall of that empire comes the erection of S. Mary of the Mongols (1261-1282) and Monastir Jamissi (1282-1328). In both cases the architectural character is what we should expect. Following on this we have, in the fourteenth century, the alterations made in S. Saviour in the Chora (*c.* 1300), and the parecclesion of the Pammakaristos (*c.* 1315).

This was the last effort of pure Byzantine architecture in Constantinople. During the hundred years preceding the Turkish conquest in 1453 the gradually increasing pressure from the East put a stop to all architectural schemes ; the craftsmen and artists fled to Italy, and there took their part in the great revival known as 'The Renaissance.'

SUGGESTED CHRONOLOGICAL TABLE

Century.
- V.   S. John of the Studion, 463.
- VI.   SS. Sergius and Bacchus, 527-36.
  - S. Sophia, 532-37.
  - S. Saviour in the Chora (the Justinian foundation).
  - S. Andrew in Krisei.
- VIII.   S. Irene, 740.
  - S. Mary Panachrantos (South Church); possibly earlier.
  - S. Mary Pammakaristos ; possibly earlier.
- IX.   S. Theodosia.
  - S. Mary Diaconissa.
  - SS. Peter and Mark.
- X.   The Myrelaion.
  - S. Mary Panachrantos (South Church).
- XI.   S. Thekla.
  - S. Saviour in the Chora (restoration in the reign of Alexius I. Comnenus).
  - S. Saviour Pantepoptes.
  - S. Saviour Pantokrator.
- XII.   S. Theodore.
  - S. John in Trullo.
  - Refectory of the monastery of Manuel ?
  - Bogdan Serai ?
- XIII.   S. Mary of the Mongols.
  - Monastir Jamissi.
- XIV.   S. Saviour in the Chora, 1306.   Final restoration by Theodore Metochites.
  - Parecclesion of the church of S. Mary Pammakaristos, *c.* 1315.
  - Sanjakdar Mesjedi (Gastria) ?
  - Balaban Mesjedi ?

Classification of the Churches according to their Type

Basilica.—S. John of the Studion.

Octagon.—SS. Sergius and Bacchus.

Domed Basilica.—S. Saviour in the Chora.

Ambulatory.—S. Andrew in Krisei; S. Mary Panachrantos (South Church); S. Mary Pammakaristos.

Domed Cross Church.—S. Irene; S. Theodosia; S. Mary Diaconissa; SS. Peter and Mark.

Four Column Church.—Myrelaion; S. Saviour Pantepoptes; S. Saviour Pantokrator; S. John in Trullo; S. Mary Panachrantos (North Church); Parecclesion of S. Mary Pammakaristos.

Foiled Plan.—S. Mary of the Mongols.

Halls.—Bogdan Serai; Central Church of the Pantokrator; Monastir Mesjedi; Refectory of the monastery of Manuel; Parecclesion of S. Saviour in the Chora; S. Thekla.

Irregular.—Sanjakdar Mesjedi; Balaban Mesjedi.

BOOKS CONSULTED IN THE PREPARATION
OF THIS WORK

Ante-Nicene Christian Library.
Anthologia Graeca epigrammatum, Stadt-Mueller, 1894.
ANTONIADI, E. M. Ἔκφρασις τῆς Ἁγίας Σοφίας.
BANDURI, ANSELMI. Imperium Orientale, sive Antiquitates Constantinopolitanae. Paris, 1711.
BARONIUS. Annales ecclesiastici. Luccae, 1741.
BELIN, M. A. Histoire de la Latinité de Constantinople. 2me édition.
BELL, Miss LOTHIAN. Notes on a Journey through Cilicia and Lycaonia.
BONDELMONTIUS. Librum insularum Archipelagi.
BROCKHAUS. Die Kunst in den Athosklöstern. Leipzig, 1891.
BREÜNING, HANS JACOB. Orientalische Reyss, 1579-80.
BRUNN, PH. Constantinople, ses sanctuaires et ses réliques au commencement du XV siècle. Odessa, 1883.
BUTLER. Architecture and other Arts, II. Syria. New York, 1903.
CHEVALIER, J. B. Voyage de la Propontide et du Pont-Euxin. Paris, 1800.
CHOISY. L'Art de bâtir chez les Byzantins. Paris, 1883.
CHOISEUL-GOUFFIER. Voyage pittoresque en Grèce.
CLAVIJO, RUY GONZALEZ DE. Vida de Gran Tamorlan y itinerario. Madrid, 1782.
CONSTANTIUS, Patriarch. Κωνσταντινιὰς Παλαιὰ τε καὶ Νεωτέρα, Ancient and Modern Constantinople, Translation by J. P. Brown. London, 1868 ; Συγγραφαὶ αἱ Ἐλάσσονες. Κωνσταντινούπολις, 1866.
Corpus Scriptorum Historiae Byzantinae. Bonn.
CRUSIUS, M. Turcograecia.
DEHIO und BEZOLD. Die kirchliche Baukunst des Abendlandes.
DETHIER, PH. A. Siège de Constantinople.
DIDRON. Christian Iconography (Translation from the French). London, 1910.
DIEHL, C. Manuel d'art byzantin ; Figures byzantines.
DU CANGE, C. Historia Byzantina, Pars II. Constantinopolis Christiana. Paris, 1680.
DÜRM. Handbuch.
Eastern Palestine Memoirs.
EBERSOLT. Le Grand Palais de Constantinople.
FERGUSSON, JAMES. History of Ancient and Mediaeval Architecture.
FINLAY, G. History of the Byzantine Empire.
FRESHFIELD, EDWIN. Archaeologia.
GARDNER, MISS ALICE. Theodore of Studium.

GERLACH. Tagebuch der Gesandtshaft an die Ottomanische Pforte durch David Ungnad, 1573-78.

GOODYEAR, W. H. Catalogue of an Exhibition of Architectural Refinements. Edinburgh, 1905.

GYLLIUS, P. De Constantinopoleos Topographia. Elzevir ed. 1632.

„ De Bosporo Thracio. Elzevir ed. 1632.

HASLUCK, F. W. Bithynica.

HENDERSON, A. E. Builder, January 1906.

KANITZ. Serbiens byzantinische Monumente.

KHITROVO, Madame de. Itinéraires russes (Translation from Russian).

LABARTE, JULES. Le Palais impérial de Constantinople.

LAMPAKIS, Professor. Les Antiquités chrétiennes de la Grèce. Athens, 1902.

LENOIR. Architecture monastique au moyen âge.

LETHABY. Mediaeval Art.

LETHABY and SWAINSON. Sancta Sophia.

LEUNCLAVIUS. Pandectes historiae Turcicae. (Migne, vol. clix.)

MANSI. Sacrorum Conciliorum collectio.

MARIN, Abbé. Les Moines de Constantinople.

MIGNE. Patrologia Graeca.

MIKLOSICH et MÜLLER. Acta et diplomata Graeca. Vienna, 1865.

MILLINGEN, A. VAN. Byzantine Constantinople.

MORDTMANN. Esquisse topographique de Constantinople.

MÜHLMANN. Archiv für christliche Kunst, 1886-87.

MURALT, ÉDOUARD DE. Essai de chronographie byzantine. Geneva, 1873.

Notitia Dignitatum. Ed. Seeck.

PARGOIRE, Père J. Les Mamas de Constantinople.

PARKER. Glossary of Architecture.

PASPATES, A. Μελέται Βυζαντιναί.

„ The Great Palace. Translation from the Greek by Mr. Metcalfe

PHILES. Carmina.

PULGHER, D. Les Églises byzantines de Constantinople. Vienna, 1878.

RAMSAY, Sir WILLIAM, and Miss LOTHIAN BELL. The Thousand and One Churches.

RIANT, Conte de. Exuviae sacrae.

RIVOIRA, T. G. Lombardic Architecture. (Translation from Italian.) London, 1910.

ROTT, H. Kleinasiatische Denkmäler. Leipzig, 1908.

SALZENBERG. Altchristliche Baudenkmäler Constantinopels.

SCARLATUS BYZANTIUS. Ἡ Κωνσταντινούπολις. Athens, 1862.

SCHLUMBERGER, G. L'Épopée byzantine à la fin du sixième siècle.

SCHMITT, F. G. Kahrié Djamissi.

SCHULTZ and BARNSLEY. The Monastery of S. Luke of Stiris. London, 1901.

SCHWEIGGER, SOLOMON. Ein neue Reyssbeschreibung auss Deutschland nach Constantinopel, 1581.

SIDERIDES. Articles in the *Proceedings of the Greek Syllogos of Constantinople*.

SOCRATES. Ecclesiastical History.

STRZYGOWSKI, J. Orient oder Rom. Leipzig, 1901.

„ Kleinasien, Die byzantinischen Wasserbehälter von. Dr. P. Forcheimer und Dr. J. Strzygowski.

TEXIER. Four volumes of Sketches in the Library of the Royal Institute of British Architects. London.

TEXIER and PULLAN. Byzantine Architecture.

USPENSKI, T. Articles in the *Journal of the Russian Institute at Constantinople*.

VILLEHARDOUIN. La Conquête de Constantinople.

VOGÜÉ, DE. La Syrie centrale.

WULFF, O. Die Koimisiskirche in Nikaia. Strasburg, 1903.

PERIODICALS

Atti della R. Accademia di archeologia, lettere, e belle arte, vol. xx. Napoli,
  1900.
Revue Archéologique.
Byzantinische Zeitschrift.
Bulletin de correspondance hellénique.
Annual of the British School at Athens.
Proceedings of the Greek Syllogos of Constantinople.
Mitteilungen des Deutschen Excursions-Club, Konstantinopel.
English Historical Review.

LIST OF EMPERORS

Constantine I. the Great .	306-337	
Constantius II. . . .	337-361	
Julian . . .	361-363	
Jovian . . .	363-364	
Valens	364-378	
Theodosius I. the Great .	378-395	
Arcadius	395-408	
Theodosius II. . .	408-450	
Marcian . . .	450-457	
Leo I.	457-474	
Leo II. . . .	474-474	
Zeno	474-491	
Anastasius I. . .	491-518	
Justin I. . . .	518-527	
Justinian I. the Great .	527-565	
Justin II. . . .	565-578	
Tiberius	578-582	
Maurice . . .	582-602	
Phocas . . .	602-610	
Heraclius . . .	610-641	
Heraclius Constantine III.		
and Heracleonas .	641-642	
Constans II. . . .	642-668	
Constantine IV. .	668-685	
Justinian II. . .	685-695	
Leontius . . .	695-697	
Tiberius III. . .	697-705	
Justinian II. (restored) .	705-711	
Philippicus . .	711-713	
Anastasius II. . .	713-715	
Theodosius III. .	715-717	
Leo III. the Isaurian .	717-740	
Constantine V. Copronymus	740-775	
Leo IV.	775-779	
Constantine VI. .	779-797	
Irene	797-802	
Nicephorus I. . .	802-811	
Stauracius . . .	811	
Michael I. Rhangabe .	811-813	
Leo V. the Armenian .	813-820	
Michael II. the Amorian .	820-829	

Theophilus . . .	829-842	
Michael III. . . .	842-867	
Basil I.	867-886	
Leo VI. the Wise . .	886-912	
Constantine VII. Porphyro-		
genitus . . .	912-958	
Co-Emperors		
Alexander . . .	912-913	
Romanus I. Lecapenus	919-945	
Constantine VIII. and		
Stephanus, sons of		
Romanus I. reigned		
five weeks in . .	944	
Romanus II. . . .	958-963	
Basil II. Bulgaroktonos	963-1025	
Co-Emperors		
Nicephorus II. Phocas	965-969	
John I. Zimisces .	969-976	
Constantine IX. .	976-1025	
Constantine IX. (sole		
Emperor) . .	1025-1028	
Romanus III. Argyrus .	1028-1034	
Michael IV. . . .	1034-1042	
Michael V. . . .	1042	
Zoe and Theodora . .	1042	
Constantine X. Mono-		
machus . . .	1042-1054	
Theodora (restored) .	1054-1056	
Michael VI. Stratioticus .	1056-1057	
Isaac I. Comnenus .	1057-1059	
Constantine XI. Ducas .	1059-1067	
Michael VII. Ducas .	1067-1078	
Co-Emperor		
Romanus IV. Diogenes	1067-1078	
Nicephorus III. Botoniates	1078-1081	
Alexius I. Comnenus .	1081-1118	
John II. Comnenus . .	1118-1143	
Manuel I. Comnenus .	1143-1180	
Alexius II. Comnenus .	1180-1183	
Andronicus I. Comnenus .	1183-1185	
Isaac II. Angelus . .	1185-1195	

Alexius III. Angelus	1195-1203
Isaac II. Angelus (restored),	
Alexius IV. Angelus	1203-1204
Nicolas Canabus . .	1204
Alexius V. Ducas Murt-	
zuphlus . . .	1204

LATIN EMPERORS OF CONSTANTINOPLE

Baldwin I. . . .	1204-1205
Henry	1205-1216
Peter	1217-1219
Robert	1219-1228
John of Brienne .	1228-1237
Baldwin II. . .	1227-1361

BYZANTINE EMPERORS AT NICAEA

Theodore I. Lascaris	1204-1222
John III. Ducas .	1222-1254
Theodore II. Ducas .	1254-1259
John IV. Ducas .	1259-1260

UNDER THE RESTORED BYZANTINE EMPIRE

Michael VIII. Palaeologus	1260-1282
Andronicus II. Palaeologus	1282-1328
Co-Emperor Michael IX.	1295-1320
Andronicus III. Palaeo-	
logus . .	1328-1341
John V. Palaeologus .	1341-1391
Co-Emperor	
John VI. Cantacuzene	1341-1355
Manuel II. Palaeologus .	1391-1425
John VII. Palaeologus .	1425-1448
Constantine XII. Palaeo-	
logus . . .	1448-1453

INDEX

Lovitz, 210
S. Luke, 227
Lycus, 122, 126, 244

Macarius, 230
Macedonius, Patriarch, 86, 87
Mahomet, 208
Maimas, 199
Makrikeui, 283, 297
S. Mamas, suburb of. *See* Church
Manuel, General, 253, 254, 255, 256, 257
Maria, wife of Constantine VI., 38
Maria, wife of John VII. Palaeologus, 230
Maria Despoina of the Mongols, 229, 272, 273, 274, 275
Maria Ducaena, 295, 326
Maria Palaeologina, wife of Michael Ducas Glabas Tarchaniotes, 140
Maria, daughter of Isaac I. Comnenus, 197
Maritza, 296
S. Mark, Evangelist, 246
Marmora, Island of, 73
Marmora, Sea of, 36, 48, 62, 138, 146, 196, 224, 283
Maroulas, Phocas, 262, 263
Martin V., Pope, 230
Martin, Abbot, 224, 225, 226
Mecca, 113
Mehemed I., Sultan, 145
Mehemed the Conqueror, Sultan, 158, 175, 214, 232, 276, 277, 304
Menodora, 262
Methodius, Patriarch, 294
Metrodora, 262
Michael Glabas Tarchaniotes, 139, 140, 141, 155, 156, 157, 158
Michael Palaeologus Tarchaniotes, 140
Michael, Syncellus, 294, 326
Milan, 78, 118
Milion, 293
Minerva Medica, Temple, 1
Mistra, 326
Modius, 199
Moldavia, 203, 280, 281
Monemvasia, 16
Monferrat, Marquis of, 229
Mongols, Mongolian, 272, 274, 275, 334, 335
Moses, 68
Mosque, Achmed Pasha Mesjedi. *See* S. John in Trullo
Aivas Effendi, 209

Mosque, Atik Mustapha Pasha Jamissi. *See* S. Andrew in Krisei
Atik Mustapha Pasha. *See* Church of SS. Peter and Mark
Balaban Aga Mesjedi. *See* Church
Boudrom Jamissi. *See* Myrelaion
Demirjilar Mesjedi, 122
Emir Ahor Jamissi. *See* Studion
Eski Imaret Jamissi. *See* Church of the Pantepoptes
Eski Jumah, Salonica, 53
Eyoub, 208
Fetiyeh. *See* Church of the Pammakaristos
Gul Jamissi. *See* Church of S. Theodosia
Hassan Pasha Mesjedi. *See* Church of S. Theodosia
Hoja Mustapha Pasha Mesjedi. *See* Church of S. Andrew in Krisei
Kalender Haneh Jamissi. *See* S. Mary Diaconissa
Kahriyeh Jamissi. *See* Church of S. Saviour in the Chora
Kassim Aga Mesjedi, 255
Kefelé Mesjedi. *See* Monastery of Manuel
Kurku Jamissi, 263
Kutchuk Aya Sofia. *See* Church of SS. Sergius and Bacchus
Laleli Jamissi, 173
Monastir Mesjedi. *See* Church
Odalar Mesjedi, 253
Pheneré Isa Mesjedi. *See* S. Mary Panachrantos
Rustem Pasha Jamissi, 27
Sanjakdar Mesjedi. *See* Gastria
Shahzadé Jamissi, 27, 183, 184, 199, 265
Sultan Bajazid, 27, 116, 117, 265
Sultan Mehemed the Conqueror, 122, 125, 265
Sultan Selim I., 27, 253, 254
Sultan Suleiman, 27
Sheik Suleiman Aga Mesjedi, 25, 270
Toklou Dedè. *See* Church of S. Thekla
Zeirek Kilissi Jamissi. *See* Church of the Pantokrator
Mousikos, 44
Murad II., Sultan, 146
Murad III., Sultan, 148
Musmiyeh, 2
Mustapha Pasha, 113

THE END

PLATES

PLATE II.

THE MYRELAION (SINCE IT WAS BURNED), FROM THE NORTH-WEST.

THE MYRELAION (SINCE IT WAS BURNED), FROM THE SOUTH-EAST.

(By kind permission of H. M. Dwight, Esq.)

To face page 20.

PLATE III.

SULEIMAN AGA MESJEDI, BESIDE S. SAVIOUR PANTOKRATOR.

To face page 24.

THE MYRELAION (SINCE IT WAS BURNT).
INTERIOR, LOOKING EAST.

(By kind permission of H. M. Dwight, Esq.)

PLATE IV.

S. SAVIOUR IN THE CHORA.
BRACKET IN THE INNER NARTHEX.

S. THEODORE.
SCULPTURED MARBLE SLAB BUILT INTO
THE MINARET OF THE MOSQUE.

S. MARY DIACONISSA.
HEADS OF WINDOWS IN SOUTH ARM.

S. MARY DIACONISSA.
SCULPTURED SLAB ON THE WEST WALL.

To face p

PLATE V.

S. JOHN OF THE STUDION.
RUINED INTERIOR, SEEN FROM THE MINARET OF THE MOSQUE.

S. JOHN OF THE STUDION, FROM THE WEST.

To face page 36.

PLATE VI.

S. JOHN OF THE STUDION.
THE RUINED INTERIOR : WEST END OF THE NORTH SIDE.

S. JOHN OF THE STUDION.
FAÇADE OF THE NARTHEX.

PLATE VII.

S. John of the Studion.
Entablature and Anta Capital in the Narthex.

S. John of the Studion.
Cornice in the Narthex, looking up.

To face page 44.

PLATE VIII.

S. JOHN OF THE STUDION, FROM THE SOUTH-EAST.

To face page 48.

PLATE IX.

E. M. Antoniadi.

S. JOHN OF THE STUDION.
EAST END.

S. JOHN OF THE STUDION.
NORTH SIDE, EAST END.

To face page 52.

PLATE X.

S. JOHN OF THE STUDION.
CISTERN.

To face page 54.

PLATE XI.

SS. Sergius and Bacchus.
Interior, looking north-west.

To face page 62.

PLATE XII.

SS. SERGIUS AND BACCHUS.
CAPITAL.

S. JOHN OF THE STUDION.
CAPITAL IN THE NARTHEX.

To face page 66.

PLATE XIII.

SS. Sergius and Bacchus, from the south-east.

SS. Sergius and Bacchus.
In the Gallery over the Narthex.

PLATE XIV.

SS. Sergius and Bacchus.
Portion of the Entablature.

To face page 74.

SS. Sergius and Bacchus.
The Interior, looking north-east.

PLATE XV.

The Baptistery, S. Sophia.
The Interior, Looking West.

To face page 76.

The Baptistery, S. Sophia, from the East.

PLATE XVI.

S. IRENE, FROM THE SOUTH-EAST.

To face page 84.

PLATE XVII.

S. Irene, South Side.

S. Irene, North Side. In the distance, S. Sophia.

To face page 86.

PLATE XVIII.

S. IRENE.

THE INTERIOR, LOOKING EAST.

(From a photograph by Sebah and Joaillier, Constantinople. Berlin, E. Wasmuth.)

PLATE XIX.

S. Irene.

The Northern Arch of the Main Dome,
seen from the South Gallery.

To face page 92.

S. Irene.

Vaulting at the north-west Corner of
the Atrium.

PLATE XX.

S. IRENE.
MOSAIC ON SOFFIT OF AN ARCH BETWEEN THE NARTHEX AND THE ATRIUM.

S. IRENE.
PORTION OF THE MOSAIC INSCRIPTION ON THE OUTER ARCH OF THE APSE.

To face page 96.

PLATE XXI.

S. IRENE.

DOOR AT THE EAST END OF THE NORTH AISLE.

To face page 98.

S. IRENE.

INTERIOR, LOOKING NORTH-WEST.

PLATE XXII.

S. IRENE.
VAULTING OVER THE SOUTH AISLE.

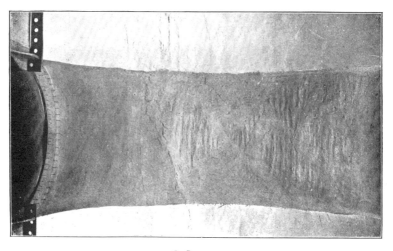

S. IRENE.
A COMPARTMENT OF SOUTH AISLE VAULTING
(LOOKING DIRECTLY UPWARD).

To face page 100.

PLATE XXIII.

S. IRENE.
CAPITAL IN SOUTH ARCADE, SEEN FROM
THE SOUTH AISLE.

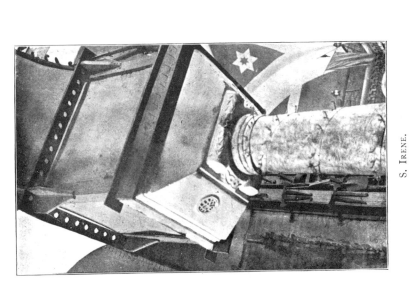

S. IRENE.
BASE OF COLUMN IN THE SOUTH AISLE,
SEEN FROM THE SOUTH AISLE.

To face page 102.

PLATE XXIV.

S. Andrew in Krisei.
East End.

(From a Photograph by A. E. Henderson, Esq.)

PLATE XXV.

S. Andrew in Krisei, from the south-west.

S. Andrew in Krisei.
The Interior, looking south.

To face page 108.

PLATE XXVI.

S. Andrew in Krisei.
Capital in the Inner Narthex.

S. Andrew in Krisei.
Capital in the Arcade under the West Dome Arch.

PLATE XXVII.

S. ANDREW IN KRISEI.

CAPITAL IN THE OUTER NARTHEX.

(From a Photograph by A. E. Henderson., Esq.)

To face page 112.

S. ANDREW IN KRISEI.

CAPITAL IN THE OUTER NARTHEX.

PLATE XXVIII.

S. Andrew in Krisei.
Outer Narthex.

S. Andrew in Krisei.
Inner Narthex, looking south.

To face page 114.

PLATE XXIX.

S. ANDREW IN KRISEI.

THE CHAIN ON THE WITHERED TREE IN THE COURT
ON THE WEST OF THE CHURCH.

To face page 116.

S. ANDREW IN KRISEI.

IN THE CLOISTER ON THE SOUTH SIDE
OF THE CHURCH, LOOKING EAST.

PLATE XXX.

S. ANDREW IN KRISEI.
THE DECORATED DOORWAY IN THE CLOISTER.

PLATE XXXI.

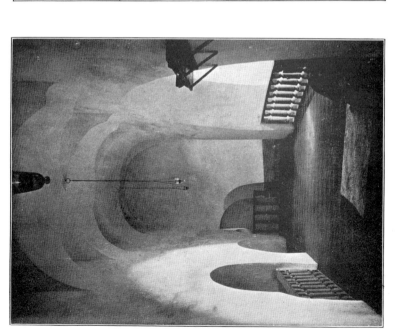

S. MARY PANACHRANTOS.

VAULT OF THE AMBULATORY PASSAGE ON THE WEST OF THE
DOME IN THE SOUTH CHURCH, LOOKING NORTH.

S. MARY PANACHRANTOS.

THE INTERIOR OF THE NORTH CHURCH, LOOKING NORTH.

To face page 122.

PLATE XXXII.

S. Mary Panachrantos.
The North Church, looking east.

S. Mary Panachrantos.
The North Church, looking west.

To face page 126.

PLATE XXXIII.

S. MARY PANACHRANTOS.

THE ARCH UNDER WEST SIDE OF THE CENTRAL DOME
IN THE SOUTH CHURCH.

To face page 128.

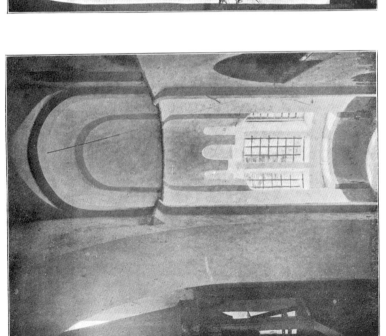

S. MARY PANACHRANTOS.

THE DIACONICON, LOOKING EAST.

PLATE XXXIV.

S. MARY PANACHRANTOS.
EAST WINDOW OF THE SOUTH CHURCH.

S. MARY PANACHRANTOS.
THE OUTER NARTHEX, LOOKING SOUTH.

PLATE XXXV.

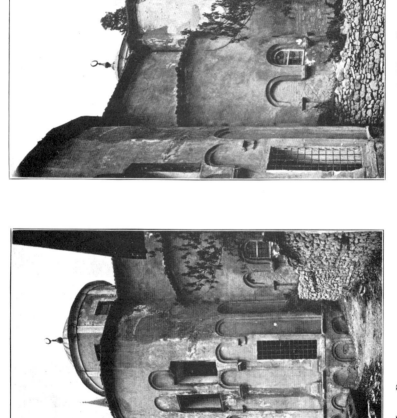

S. MARY PANACHRANTOS.
EAST END OF THE SOUTH CHURCH.

S. MARY PANACHRANTOS.
EAST END OF THE NORTH CHURCH.

To face page 132.

PLATE XXXVI.

S. MARY PAMMAKARISTOS, FROM THE SOUTH-EAST.

S. MARY PAMMAKARISTOS, FROM THE WEST.

To face page 138.

PLATE XXXVII.

S. MARY PAMMAKARISTOS.
INNER NARTHEX, LOOKING SOUTH.

S. MARY PAMMAKARISTOS.
THE DOME, LOOKING WEST.

To face page 142.

PLATE XXXVIII.

S. MARY PAMMAKARISTOS.
THE PARECCLESION FROM THE SOUTH-EAST.

To face page 144.

PLATE XXXIX.

To face page 148.

S. MARY PAMMAKARISTOS.
THE WEST COLUMN IN THE PARECCLESION.

S. MARY PAMMAKARISTOS.
EAST END OF THE PARECCLESION.

PLATE XL.

S. MARY PAMMAKARISTOS.
THE WEST COLUMN IN THE PARECCLESION.

To face page 150.

S. MARY PAMMAKARISTOS.
COLUMN FLANKING THE EAST WINDOW OF
THE APSE OF THE PARECCLESION.

S. MARY PAMMAKARISTOS.
THE EAST COLUMN IN THE PARECCLESION.

PLATE XLI.

To face page 154.

S. MARY PAMMAKARISTOS.

MOSAIC IN THE DOME OF THE PARECCLESION.

S. MARY PAMMAKARISTOS.

INTERIOR VIEW OF THE DOME OF THE PARECCLESION.

PLATE XLII.

S. Mary Pammakaristos.
South Side of the Parecclesion.

To face page 156.

PLATE XLIII.

S. THEODOSIA.
THE EAST END.

(*E. M. Antoniadi.*)

S. THEODOSIA, FROM THE SOUTH-EAST.

PLATE XLIV.

S. THEODOSIA.
THE EASTERN DOME ARCH.

S. THEODOSIA.
INTERIOR, LOOKING NORTH-EAST.

PLATE XLV.

S. THEODOSIA.
DOME OVER THE STAIRCASE TO THE GALLERIES.

S. THEODOSIA.
THE NARTHEX, LOOKING NORTH.

To face page 172.

PLATE XLVI.

S. Mary Diaconissa.
VIEW OF THE NORTH-WEST SIDE, TAKEN FROM THE AQUEDUCT OF VALENS.

S. Mary Diaconissa.
THE NORTH ARM, LOOKING EAST.

PLATE XLVII.

S. MARY DIACONISSA.

THE INTERIOR, LOOKING SOUTH-EAST.

To face page 184.

S. MARY DIACONISSA.

THE INTERIOR, LOOKING NORTH-EAST.

PLATE XLVIII.

S. MARY DIACONISSA.

EAST END, NORTH SIDE (UPPER PART).

To face page 186.

S. MARY DIACONISSA.

EAST END, NORTH SIDE (LOWER PART).

PLATE XLIX.

S. Mary Diaconissa.
South Eikon Frame.

S. Mary Diaconissa.
Detail in the South Eikon Frame.

PLATE L.

S. Mary Diaconissa, looking west.

S. Mary Diaconissa.
Capital on Column at the Entrance to the Church.

PLATE LI.

SS. Peter and Mark, from the South-East.

SS. Peter and Mark.
Font outside the Church.

To face page 192.

PLATE LII.

To face page 194.

SS. PETER AND MARK.

LOOKING ACROSS THE DOME FROM THE SOUTH-WEST.

SS. PETER AND MARK.

INTERIOR OF THE DOME, LOOKING NORTH.

PLATE LIII.

MYRELAION.
THE SOUTH SIDE.

MYRELAION.
THE NARTHEX, LOOKING NORTH.

PLATE LIV.

To face page 198.

MYRELAION.
THE SOUTH-WEST CROSS ANGLE.

MYRELAION.
THE INTERIOR, LOOKING EAST.

PLATE LV.

S. John in Trullo, from the south-west.

Balaban Mesjedi (page 265).
Interior View.

To face page 202.

PLATE LVI.

To face page 208.

S. THEKLA.
EAST END.

S. THEKLA.
NORTH SIDE, FROM THE NORTH-WEST.

PLATE LVII.

S. Saviour Panteptes.
The Dome, looking west.

To face page 212.

S. Saviour Panteptes.
Door leading from the Outer to the Inner Narthex.
View looking north.

PLATE LVIII.

S. Saviour Pantepoptes.
Exterior Decoration in Brick, on South Side.

S. Mary Pammakaristos.
Bracket at the South-east Angle of the Exterior
Wall of the Parecclesion.

PLATE LIX.

S. SAVIOUR PANTOKRATOR, FROM THE WEST.

To face page 220.

PLATE LX.

S. Saviour Pantokrator, from the North-West.

S. Saviour Pantokrator.
Fragments of Sculptured Marbles in the Church.

To face page 222.

PLATE LXI.

S. Saviour Pantokrator.

The Southern Arm of the South Church.

To face page 224.

S. Saviour Pantokrator.

Interior of the South Church, looking east.

PLATE LXII.

S. SAVIOUR PANTOKRATOR.

ENTRANCE FROM THE NARTHEX TO THE SOUTH CHURCH.

S. SAVIOUR PANTOKRATOR.

THE INTERIOR, LOOKING FROM THE SOUTH CHURCH THROUGH
INTO THE NORTH CHURCH.

To face page 226.

PLATE LXIII.

S. SAVIOUR PANTOKRATOR.

THE INTERIOR OF THE NORTH CHURCH, LOOKING EAST.

To face page 228.

S. SAVIOUR PANTOKRATOR.

GALLERY OF THE NORTH CHURCH, LOOKING SOUTH.

PLATE LXIV.

S. SAVIOUR PANTOKRATOR.

ARCH IN THE NORTH WALL OF THE SOUTH CHURCH,
SEEN FROM THE CENTRAL CHURCH, LOOKING SOUTHWARDS.

To face page 230.

S. SAVIOUR PANTOKRATOR.

ARCH IN THE NORTH WALL OF THE SOUTH CHURCH,
SEEN FROM THE SOUTH CHURCH, LOOKING NORTHWARDS.

PLATE LXV.

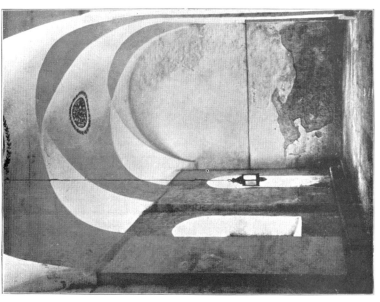

S. Saviour Pantokrator.

Outer Narthex of the South Church, looking north.

To face page 232.

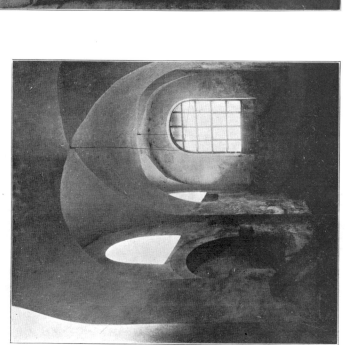

S. Saviour Pantokrator.

Narthex of the North Church, looking north.

PLATE LXVI.

To face page 234.

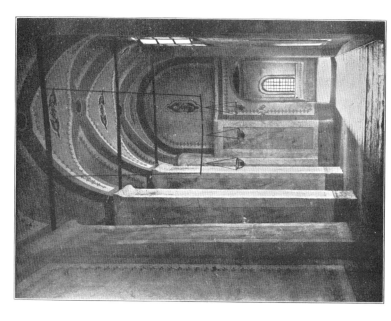

S. SAVIOUR PANTOKRATOR.

IN THE NORTH CHURCH, LOOKING SOUTH.

S. SAVIOUR PANTOKRATOR.

SOUTH BAY IN THE GALLERY OF THE SOUTH CHURCH.

PLATE LXVII.

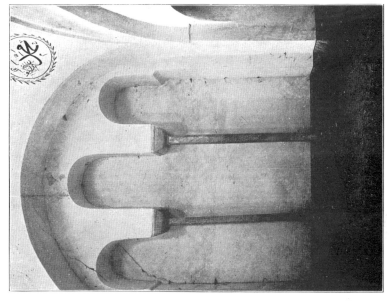

S. SAVIOUR PANTOKRATOR.

WEST SIDE OF THE CENTRAL BAY IN THE
GALLERY OF THE SOUTH CHURCH.

To face page 236.

S. SAVIOUR PANTOKRATOR.

THE PULPIT IN THE SOUTH CHURCH.

PLATE LXVIII.

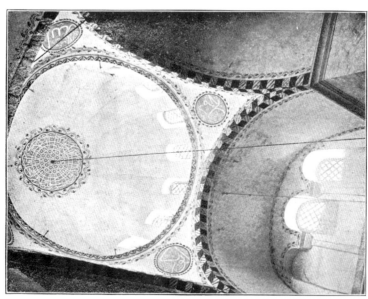

S. Saviour Pantokrator.

Interior of the Dome in the South Church,
looking north.

To face page 238.

S. Saviour Pantokrator.

Interior of the East Dome in the Central Church.

PLATE LXIX.

S. Saviour Pantokrator.
The East End, from the south.

S. Saviour Pantokrator.
The East Window of the Central
Church.

S. Saviour Pantokrator.
The East End, from the north.

PLATE LXX.

S. THEODORE.

THE CHURCH, FROM THE NORTH-WEST.

S. THEODORE.

NORTH END OF THE WESTERN FAÇADE.

PLATE LXXI.

S. Theodore.
The Central Dome, from the south.

S. Theodore.
The Western Façade, from the south.

To face page 246.

PLATE LXXII.

To face page 248.

S. THEODORE.

THE EAST END, FROM THE SOUTH.

S. THEODORE.

SOUTH CROSS ARM (EXTERIOR), FROM THE SOUTH-EAST.

PLATE LXXIII.

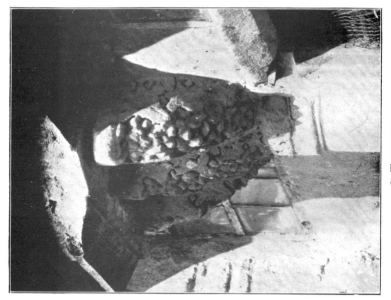

S. THEODORE.

CAPITAL IN THE FAÇADE OF THE NARTHEX.

To face page 250.

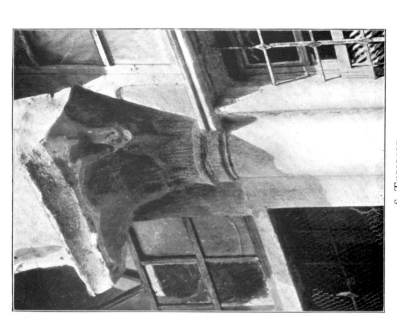

S. THEODORE.

CAPITAL ON THE SOUTHERNMOST COLUMN IN THE FAÇADE.

PLATE LXXIV.

To face page 254.

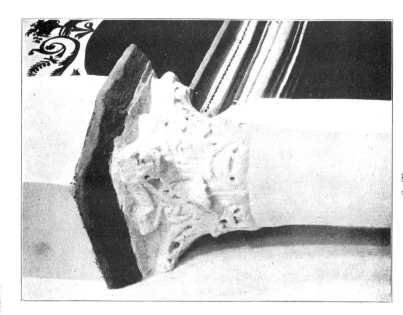

S. THEODORE.

CAPITAL TO THE NORTH OF THE DOOR LEADING FROM THE OUTER TO THE INNER NARTHEX.

S. THEODORE.

THE OUTER NARTHEX, LOOKING NORTH.

PLATE LXXV.

To face page 256.

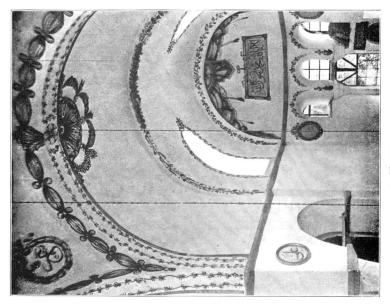

S. THEODORE.

THE INTERIOR, LOOKING EAST (UPPER PART).

S. THEODORE.

THE INTERIOR, LOOKING EAST.

PLATE LXXVI.

THE REFECTORY OF THE MONASTERY OF MANUEL,
FROM THE WEST.

THE REFECTORY OF THE MONASTERY OF MANUEL,
FROM THE SOUTH-EAST.

To face page 258.

PLATE LXXVII.

THE CISTERN OF AETIUS.

With the kind permission of Sir Benjamin Stone.

To face page 262.

PLATE LXXVIII.

GASTRIA (SANJAKDAR MESJEDI).
EAST END.

GASTRIA (SANJAKDAR MESJEDI).
THE ENTRANCE.

PLATE LXXIX.

GASTRIA (SANJAKDAR).
FROM THE WEST.

GASTRIA (SANJAKDAR).
THE INTERIOR.

To face page 270.

PLATE LXXX.

BOGDAN SERAI.
APSE OF THE UPPER CHAPEL.

BOGDAN SERAI.
A PENDENTIVE OF THE DOME.

BOGDAN SERAI.
THE CHAPEL FROM THE NORTH-WEST.

To face page 280.

PLATE LXXXI.

S. Saviour in the Chora, from the west.

S. Saviour in the Chora, from the south-east.

To face page 288.

PLATE LXXXII.

S. Saviour in the Chora, from the north-east.

S. Saviour in the Chora.
The North Side.

To face page 292.

PLATE LXXXIII.

S. SAVIOUR IN THE CHORA.

THE INNER NARTHEX, LOOKING SOUTH.

To face page 296.

S. SAVIOUR IN THE CHORA.

THE INNER NARTHEX, LOOKING SOUTH.

PLATE LXXXIV.

To face page 300.

S. SAVIOUR IN THE CHORA.
CAPITAL IN THE OUTER NARTHEX.

S. SAVIOUR IN THE CHORA.
CAPITAL IN THE OUTER NARTHEX.

PLATE LXXXV.

S. Saviour in the Chora.
The Outer Narthex, looking south.

To face page 304.

S. Saviour in the Chora.
The Interior, looking north-west.

PLATE LXXXVI.

S. Saviour in the Chora.
Eikon Frame on the south-eastern Pier.

S. Saviour in the Chora.
The Interior, looking east.

To face page 308.

PLATE LXXXVII.

S. SAVIOUR IN THE CHORA.
INTERIOR CORNICE OVER MAIN DOOR OF THE CHURCH.

S. SAVIOUR IN THE CHORA.
ARCHIVOLT ON THE NORTH SIDE OF THE PARECCLESION.

S. SAVIOUR IN THE CHORA.
WINDOW HEADS IN THE CENTRAL APSE.

To face page 310.

PLATE LXXXVIII.

S. Saviour in the Chora.
East End of the Parecclesion.

S. Saviour in the Chora.
Capital at the Entrance to the Parecclesion.

PLATE LXXXIX.

S. Saviour in the Chora.
The Parecclesion, looking south-east.

S. Saviour in the Chora.
The Parecclesion, looking west.

To face page 316.

PLATE XC.

Sebah and Joaillier.

S. SAVIOUR IN THE CHORA.

MOSAIC REPRESENTING THE CARESSING OF MARY BY HER
PARENTS, AND THE BLESSING OF MARY BY PRIESTS AT
A BANQUET.

To face page 322.

Sebah and Joaillier.

S. SAVIOUR IN THE CHORA.

MOSAIC REPRESENTING THE MIRACLE OF WATER TURNED
INTO WINE. THE DATE 6811 (A.D. 1303), IN ARABIC
NUMERALS, IS ABOVE THE LAST FIGURE ON THE RIGHT.

PLATE XCI.

S. SAVIOUR IN THE CHORA.
MOSAIC REPRESENTING THE REGISTRATION OF JOSEPH AND MARY AT BETHLEHEM.

S. SAVIOUR IN THE CHORA.
MOSAIC REPRESENTING THEODORE METOCHITES OFFERING THE CHURCH TO CHRIST.

To face page 326.

PLATE XCII.

S. SAVIOUR IN THE CHORA.

ARCHIVOLT ON THE SOUTH WALL OF THE PARECCLESION, WITH THE EPITAPH IN HONOUR OF TORNIKES.

To face page 330.

Reprinted in Great Britain by
Kingprint Limited, Richmond, Surrey